I0795438

EXIT OF A HERO

AFRICAN PERSPECTIVES

Kelly Askew, Laura Fair, and Pamila Gupta
Series Editors

Exit of a Hero: Photography and the Visual Culture of Commemoration in Southern Nigeria
Okechukwu Nwafor

The Post-Global City: Theorizing Technology Cultures in Urban Africa
Katrien Pype, Omolade Adunbi, and Michael M. J. Fischer, Editors

The Institutionalization of Islam in Southern Senegal: Intermarriage, Qur'anic Education, and Jihād
Aly Dramé

The Education Alibi: Tracing Education's Entanglements Across Contemporary Africa
Elizabeth Cooper, Erdmute Alber, and Wandia Njoya, Editors

The Homeowner Ideology: Economic (F)Utility of Real Property Rights in Four African Cities
Singumbe Muyeba

Typologies of Humor in African Literatures
Adwoa A. Opoku-Agyemang

Between HIV Prevention and LGBTI Rights: The Political Economy of Queer Activism in Ghana
Ellie Gore

Protest Arts, Gender, and Social Change: Fiction, Popular Songs, and the Media in Hausa Society across Borders
Ousseina D. Alidou

The Imaginative Vision of Abdilatif Abdalla's Voice of Agony
Abdilatif Abdalla, edited by Annmarie Drury

Congo Style: From Belgian Art Nouveau to African Independence
Ruth Sacks

A complete list of titles in the series can be found at www.press.umich.edu

Exit of a Hero

Photography and the Visual Culture of Commemoration in Southern Nigeria

Okechukwu Nwafor

University of Michigan Press
Ann Arbor

Copyright © 2026 by Okechukwu Nwafor
Some rights reserved

CC BY-NC

This work is licensed under a Creative Commons Attribution-NonCommercial 4.0 International License. *Note to users*: A Creative Commons license is only valid when it is applied by the person or entity that holds rights to the licensed work. Works may contain components (e.g., photographs, illustrations, or quotations) to which the rightsholder in the work cannot apply the license. It is ultimately your responsibility to independently evaluate the copyright status of any work or component part of a work you use, in light of your intended use. To view a copy of this license, visit http://creativecommons.org/licenses/by-nc/4.0/

For questions or permissions, please contact um.press.perms@umich.edu

Published in the United States of America by the
University of Michigan Press
First published May 2026

A CIP catalog record for this book is available from the British Library.

Library of Congress Cataloging-in-Publication Data

Names: Nwafor, Okechukwu author | Michigan Publishing (University of Michigan) publisher
Title: Exit of a hero : photography and the visual culture of commemoration in Southern Nigeria / Okechukwu Nwafor.
Other titles: African perspectives (University of Michigan, Press)
Description: Ann Arbor : University of Michigan Press, 2026. | Series: African Perspectives | Includes bibliographical references (pages 225–259) and index.
Identifiers: LCCN 2025046984 (print) | LCCN 2025046985 (ebook) | ISBN 9780472078066 hardcover | ISBN 9780472058068 paperback | ISBN 9780472905829 ebook other
Subjects: LCSH: Igbo (African people)—Funeral customs and rites—History | Igbo (African people)—Obituaries—History | Igbo (African people)—Social life and customs | Postmortem photography—Nigeria, Southern—History | Death—Anthropological aspects—Nigeria, Southern | Memorialization—Nigeria, Southern—History | Memorial rites and ceremonies—Nigeria, Southern—History
Classification: LCC DT515.45.I33 N844 2026 (print) | LCC DT515.45.I33 (ebook)
LC record available at https://lccn.loc.gov/2025046984
LC ebook record available at https://lccn.loc.gov/2025046985

DOI: https://doi.org/10.3998/mpub.14426701

The University of Michigan Press's broader open access publishing program is made possible thanks to additional funding from the University of Michigan Office of the Provost and the generous support of contributing libraries.

Cover image: Memorial photograph of the late Nwankwo Nwafor (Okachamma). Photograph taken by Sammy Sparkle, circa 1950 in Ndiukwuenu, Orumba North, Anambra State, Nigeria.

The authorized representative in the EU for product safety and compliance is Access System Europe, Mustamäe tee 50, 10621 Tallinn, Estonia, gpsr.requests@easproject.com

Obiora Nwafor, with a giant stride, you stepped into the world and offered your best
In the embrace of destiny, you found rest
You exited as a Hero

Onyeka Nwafor, you ran the race of life courageously
At the appointed destination where your "chi" decreed, you fell graciously
You exited as a Hero

Adieu! My two lovely brothers

CONTENTS

Digital materials related to this title can be found on the Fulcrum platform via the following citable URL: https://doi.org/10.3998/mpub.14426701

FIGURES

ACKNOWLEDGMENTS

This book owes its existence to the support and encouragement of many. I am deeply grateful to the University of Michigan's African Presidential Scholars Program (UMAPS), which first awarded me a fellowship to work on this book in 2018, even though I ended up using the time to complete my first book. The second leg of the UMAPS fellowship took me to the University of the Witwatersrand's Wits Institute for Social and Economic Research (WISER), where I had the privilege of working with Professor Pamila Gupta. Scholars at Wits, including Achille Mbembe, Sara Nuttall, and Hlonipha Mokoena, were generous during my stay and made valuable contributions during my presentations at WISER.

While I was at Wits, the Centre for Humanities Research at the University of the Western Cape invited me to present a part of this book. I received some of the most insightful feedback from scholars there. I am grateful to Patricia Hayes, who has always encouraged my scholarship, as well as Ciraj Rassool, Leslie Witz, Premesh Lalu, Heidi Grunebaum, Maurits van Bever Donker, Paolo Israel, and others.

My heartfelt thanks go to Wesleyan University, where I teach, for providing the financial support that enabled me to copyedit the manuscript. Most importantly, at a significant moment upon my arrival at Wesleyan, my colleagues in the Faculty of Arts and Humanities, as well as the Art and Art History Department, provided crucial support. I extend my warmest appreciation to Michael Roth, the president, Nicole Stanton, the provost, Roger Mathew Grant, the current dean of arts and humanities at Wesleyan University; Mark Hovey, associate provost for budget and personnel; Tula Telfair, my former department chair at Wesleyan; and Katherine Kuenzli, my current department chair, and her husband Michael Printy for their unwavering support in every possible way.

Katherine Kuenzli and Joe Siry generously read the first draft of this manuscript and offered invaluable feedback. I remain deeply grateful for their boundless kindness. My other colleagues in the department have also been exceptionally supportive: Nadja Aksamija, Joe Ackley, Talia Andrei, Phil Wagoner and his wife, Rieko, Elijah Huge, Jason Di Resta, Charlie Coffey, Julia Randall, Tammy Vo Nguyen, Keiji Shinohara, Sasha Rudensky, Kate TenEyck, Christian Hart Nakarado, Ilana Yacine Harris-Babou, Yu Nong Khew, Benjamin Chaffee, and Jennifer Tucker have all been exceptionally warm and encouraging. I also thank Peter Mark, whom I replaced at Wesleyan, for his willingness to assist me whenever I call on him.

To my colleagues at African Material Culture at Wesleyan Initiative, Laura Ann Twagira, Iddrisu Saaka, Wendi Field Murray, and Lily Saint, I remain grateful for the opportunity to think together.

The African History and Anthropology Workshop (AHAW) at the University of Michigan invited me to present an aspect of this book and provided invaluable suggestions that positively impacted several chapters. I am most grateful to the facilitator Derek Peterson as well as other supportive members of AHAW, especially Anne Pitcher, Tamanda Comfort Mthetwa, Sauda Nabukenyi, Jessie Bakitunda, and others.

Special thanks to these friends and senior colleagues for their encouragement and advice in numerous and varied ways over the years: Ray Silverman, Peter Probst, Christine Feak, Omolade Adunbi, Kelly Askew, Corrine Kratz, Noëleen Murray, and Sylvester Okwunodu Ogbechie. When I doubted my confidence in pursuing this line of thought, Moses Ochonu and Ugochukwu Smooth-Nzewi encouraged me and assured me of the pioneering potential of commemorative photography.

I extend my heartfelt thanks to those who allowed me to use their photographs for this research and for patiently answering my numerous questions. They are too numerous to mention here, but I am especially grateful to Chinedu Eliyas, Okey Charles Ogu, Ejike Okaphor, Ugo Martins Ekweozor (Eselu Obizi), Ezimma Nnabuife, Eva Anyaeze, Ifeanyi Michael Nrialike, Chijioke Onuora, Ogochukwu Okafor, and Anthony Okoye.

I am deeply grateful to the astute reviewers of the manuscript for their insightful and meticulously constructive feedback. My deepest thanks also go to the University of Michigan Press and its consistently supportive staff. Managing the book's production, Marcella Landri, Kianna Delly, Mary Hashman, Richard Isomaki, exhibited the strategic expertise of seasoned planners. They remain the best.

I was fortunate to receive the expert editorial guidance of Elizabeth Tucker, whose direction has been exceptionally wise, shrewdly constructive, and perceptive in both major and minor details. Insofar as this book fulfills its objectives, it stands as a testament to her early productive editorial intervention.

Special thanks to family and friends who have tolerated my scholarly obsession and did not discourage me from pursuing it: most especially my wife, Nkiruka Jane Uju, and my children, Ijeoma, Chinua, Chioma, and Chisom, for tolerating my years of itinerant scholarship. I will always remember and appreciate the unwavering support of my in-laws, Dr. Godfrey Uju and Dr. Reke Uju, over the years.

At last, my parents, Chief Michael Nwafor and Maria Nwafor, have lived long enough to witness the significant progress their son has made as an author of books.

I wish, finally, to acknowledge the families of the late Ozo Chief Elias Patricius Oyeoka Offodile, the late Professor Nonso Nnabuife, the late Chief Herbert Kingsley Nnaedozie Ezisi, the families of the late Michael Nwankwo Nwafor (Okachamma), the late Chief George Nwoshi Nwobu, the late John Iliemenam Nwabude, the late Ajie Cletus Onwuha Ochije, the late Mazi Chinwendu David Okoro, Chidimma Okoro, the late Professor Tina Okoye, the late Florence Ukamaka Nwudi, the late Chief Innocent Ezeanyaku Ofor, the late Chief George Nwabueze Onwuegbune, the late Okon-Obiorah, Chuks Obiweluozo, Ogochukwu Okafor, Jude Ilozumba, the late Nwosisi's family, the late Mrs. Christiana Nkechi Okaphor, and the late Okpuo's family.

CHAPTER 1

Introduction

A HISTORY OF THE COMMEMORATIVE IMAGE IN PRECOLONIAL AFRICAN ART

On November 13, 2017, a tragedy struck at the residence of Chief Richard Ikediugwu in Enugu, southeastern Nigeria. Richard had just passed away at the age of ninety-three. The household was engulfed in loud, distressing screams, which drew the immediate attention of nearby residents. Many individuals who learned of his passing hurried to Richard's house to console the grieving family. Villagers returning from the market paused to join the growing assembly of people who had gathered to offer their condolences to the devastated family. Ike, the eldest son of Chief Richard Ikediugwu, called their aunt residing in Lagos to convey the sorrowful news.

By the evening, Onyi, one of Richard's daughters, had posted a message on her Facebook wall with her father's photograph, announcing their father's passing. The message quickly garnered significant attention and numerous condolence messages. Some individuals expressed their sorrow through written messages on the Facebook photo, while others used emojis. The following day, the Ikediugwu family sent official notifications to their in-laws and convened a meeting of all family stakeholders to discuss the burial and funeral arrangements. When the appointed date came, all invited stakeholders attended, and the meeting proceeded smoothly. Among the many topics discussed were the modalities for the burial and funeral. One of Richard's family members, who happened to be my cousin, informed me of every activity they undertook to ensure a successful burial and funeral. During the planning, I was consulted to assist in arranging for a photographer to document the occasion. My involvement stemmed from their knowledge of my extensive interactions, during my research, with individuals who organized burials and funerals. I reached out to one of the many photographers I had previously collaborated with, and we negotiated and agreed upon a price.

At the end of the funeral, Onyi's social media pages were subsequently adorned with numerous photographs of the burial and funeral events. Similarly, Onyi's other siblings shared many photographs and videos of the successful funeral on their own social media. Their late father was eulogized and celebrated as a hero in the public sphere of social media. The funeral was extensively photographed, and the photographs were widely distributed through funeral booklets, fliers, posters, pinups, and social media, among other formats.

The above reveals what transpires at the interval between death and funeral: a quick glimpse of an elaborate system of visual spectacles and rituals that cannot be summarily captured in just one singular narrative. Thus, this book is a comprehensive articulation of a historical and contemporary exploration of this visual spectacle that attends commemoration in southern Nigeria. An important component is Onyi's immediate actions following their father's death: the posting of their late father's photograph on Facebook and the arrangement of a photographer to document the funeral ritual. This book is particularly interested in the immediate and extended visual commemoration of the dead, such as that of Onyi's late father, examining how, for example, Onyi's family utilized the tools of photography to reimagine their father's public image and status as a hero. In tracking history, I start by asking how precolonial Africans commemorated their dead and how the idea of a heroic image was publicly visualized.

Africans have commemorated the dead in different ways. Sculptural images have been carved in wood and other media in the form of portraits, masks, full figures, or installed funerary shrine objects. Examples of these artistic forms abound in many African cultures, such as in Bwa, Dogon, Ibibio, Baule, Yoruba, Kuba (Mack 2018; Salmons 1980; Vogel 1977; Borgatti 1976, 1990; 1976; Abiodun 1976; Vansina 1972). Indeed, the list is inexhaustible. In recognizing the sociocultural contexts under which commemorative sculptures and art have been made in Africa, one needs to understand the inherent relationship between Africans and their ancestors. In many African traditions, ancestors are regarded as members of human society who only went on a journey to intercede spiritually for the sake of the living. Thus, commemorative portraiture as a genre reveals the wider realities of personal and community values and aspirations. African scholars like Rowland Abiodun and Babatunde Lawal have examined the nature of representation and the meanings of the portrait image in Yoruban commemorative practice and have identified the concepts of honor and heroism as fundamental to the Ako funeral ritual of the Yoruba (Abiodun 2013). While the formal features of Ako funerary figures express the fullness of individual accomplishment, we know that, ultimately, African memorial traditions aim to attract and fix a spiritual and cosmological force rather than to strive for verisimilitude (Abiodun 2013; Borgatti 1990, 36; Lawal 1977). Through iconic imagery, the commemorative object immortalizes the heroic attributes of the deceased. It is particularly instructive that African portraits have been deployed in the homes of ordinary individuals as well as royal institutions to commemorate common people along with kings and queens (Mack 2018). The dead have always exerted a significant influence on the living, and I have introduced this book with the above examples to explore the connections and continuities between visual images and commemorative practices across historical and cultural settings.

This book explores the cultural, political, and socioeconomic implications of photography in commemorative practices in southern Nigeria. In this context, the commemorative ritual is incomplete without a photograph, compelling families to invest heavily in visual images of remembrance. Specifically, I examine to what extent photographs reenact the historical role of funeral masks in these practices. For example, in a recent case, a funeral dance incorporating photographs evoked the performative and symbolic experiences of a traditional Igbo funerary masquerade dance. I also explore other innovative modes of visual culture that have commemorated the deceased in southern Nigeria since the 1880s.

A NOTE ON ETHNOGRAPHY

This book is set in southern Nigeria, with a focus on Lagos on the one terminus and southeastern Nigeria on the other. The choice of Lagos, a city in western Nigeria, is deliberate for several reasons. First, Lagos was one of the initial points of contact between Nigerians and European colonizers. Second, existing literature on colonial Lagos often overlooks its pan-Nigerian demographics. For this reason, in chapters 2 and 3, I lay the archival groundwork of this book in colonial Lagos before transitioning to the Igbo states of southeastern Nigeria. This approach reflects Nigeria's cultural demographics after the arrival of European colonizers. For example, Nnamdi Azikiwe, a prominent journalist and the first president of Nigeria, who was an Igbo from

Onitsha in southeastern Nigeria, achieved significant success in his career in colonial Lagos, where he became an important advocate for the photographic portraiture of Nigerians in the press. His influence extended beyond Lagos as he expanded his journalistic endeavors to Port Harcourt and eastern Nigeria. Chapter 4 of this book briefly touches on Azikiwe's contributions and legacy in this regard. Highlighting Azikiwe's ethnicity as an Igbo politician who impacted the Lagos political landscape in the early twentieth century makes a significant intervention in bridging the demographic marginality of ethnic groups other than the Yoruba, and especially the Igbo, in colonial Lagos.

Beyond the contributions of Nnamdi Azikiwe, the demographic narratives of colonial Lagos have often excluded other ethnic groups and perpetuated the misconception that Lagos was solely occupied by the Yoruba, even into the 1930s and 1940s. This book challenges this prevailing notion. Lagos is presented as a cosmopolitan hub that defines urban modernity, subsequently influencing practices across southern Nigeria. By establishing the historical framework in which colonial commemorative modernity flourished, this book demonstrates how Igbo local practices integrated with and enriched this evolving visual culture.

Chapters 4, 5, 6, and 7 are based on my extensive travels, in the company of funeral photographers, to various towns in Anambra, Imo, Enugu, and Abia States. These arduous journeys were undertaken as a curious participant observer and visual historian aiming to understand the use of photography in Igbo commemorations. My observations revealed a consistent pattern in the use of photography across the various Igbo communities I visited. However, the objective of this book is not to conduct an ethnography of funerals or burials per se but to examine the role of photography, specifically, in commemoration.

The predominantly Christian Igbo communities have been significantly influenced by Christian models of commemoration in recent times. My research aimed to explore how photography has transformed commemorative practices and how Christian commemoration and funerals have deployed photography to create a new visual culture. Essentially, while I track these transformations from the mid-nineteenth century, I also offer a comparative analysis of sculptural traditions, such as the Igbo Ikenga sculpture, which I contend has influenced contemporary commemorative photographic portraiture.

To gain insights into the use of photography, I conducted interviews with the bereaved, mourners, photographers, and individual camera phone users, among others. Given the sensitive nature of funerals, it was often challenging to interview those deeply immersed in grief. Consequently, many interviews were conducted either before the funeral or several months or years afterward. Some individuals who were initially unwilling to speak with me scheduled appointments many months after the burial and funeral.

As a participant observer, I engaged in the drafting of biographies and facilitated the recruitment of photographers for funerals, just like that of the late Richard Ikediugwu. I played a crucial role in negotiating prices, acting as an intermediary between the bereaved families and the photographers to reach mutually agreeable terms. My involvement extended to attending funerals and burials, either as an observer or as someone personally affected by the loss of a relative or friend. During these events, I took photographs and participated in selfies and group photos. Additionally, I scavenged family photo archives with the bereaved, scouted for funeral booklets and posters, and visited computer technicians who edited photographs of the deceased, observing and interviewing them to understand their processes. Immersing myself in these everyday practices, I gained profound insights into how digital photography is utilized in popular culture. This immersion revealed the transformative impact of photography on daily life, highlighting the urgent need to explore new discourses on the everyday uses of digital photography in Africa. This development prompted new interpretations of digital photography, which, as Richard Vokes (2019a, 217) articulates, merely extends a trend that dates back to the inception of the first studios on the continent, thereby reinforcing existing cosmopolitan imaginaries. This book advances Vokes's thesis by exploring how digital photography serves to perpetuate traditional cultural practices of ancestral veneration.

This exploration led to my second form of ethnography, known as netnography, discussed in chapter 6. Hence, I weave a practical and experiential account of my ethnographic research into most of the chapters. I chronicle my participation in several funerals, where I encountered emerging everyday commemorative photographic practices that enabled me to develop new theoretical frameworks. Chapter 6 integrates a dual approach of ethnography and netnography. Over several years, I observed and documented various commemorative photographic trends on social media platforms. This extensive research revealed that commemorative photography has evolved beyond its traditional applications to assume more creative and innovative roles that have reshaped the landscape of mourning. My findings indicate that commemorative photography on social media is more dynamic and pervasive than in physical contexts, underscoring the necessity to redirect scholarly energies to the digital realm.

One of the primary challenges in conducting netnography is navigating the ethical considerations and privacy concerns associated with the safe use of online photographs. While social media images are uncontainable and can traverse time and space freely online, they assume a distinct constrictive ethical dimension when incorporated into printed texts arising from academic research. An ethical tension arises as photographs transition between their physical, textual, and social media worlds, as well as between netnographic and ethnographic methodological frameworks. In media platformization, images enjoy considerable mobility with minimal constraints, whereas they are subject to stringent regulations when transitioning from the digital realm to physical spaces. This dilemma of two fractious, irreconcilable social worlds of social media photographs and their analog lives presented a methodological challenge to this project. The major question is how online photographs' radical mobility feeds algorithmic and platform capitalism on the one hand and impedes its physical movement when it navigates outside social media spaces. Here the limits of the ethical economy are stretched beyond their cultural and political contexts. While acknowledging these limitations, I posit that the photograph, whether in analog or digital form, assumes a heroic life within a certain cultural milieu. It is crucial to understand how this heroism has been historically constituted within the African context.

HEROIC FIGURES

It is important to compare the meanings of heroism in African memorial sculptures with the meaning of heroism in contemporary commemorative photography. First, let us explore the meanings of heroism in a commemorative sculpture such as that of Queen Idia. The commemoration of Queen Idia through the sculptural pendant mask of "Queen Mother" by her son, Oba Esigie, one of Benin's most important kings during the sixteenth century, recognizes his mother's heroic attributes. Queen Idia helped her son claim the throne and provided him wise counsel during his reign. Queen Idia's sculptural pendant serves multiple purposes: first, as a commemorative or memorial object of Benin; second, as a prestigious and heroic symbol of Benin royalty; third, as a symbol of modernity and cross-cultural encounter for the Benis; and fourth, as a spiritual embodiment of Benin's cosmological universe and ancestral connectedness.

In one of my contemporary case studies, cited in the beginning, in which the children of the late Richard Ikediugwu commissioned many life-size portrait photographs of their late father, the portrait can be seen to serve each of these purposes as well, on behalf of the smaller cultural unit of Ikediugwu's family. After the funeral, the portrait, which the children captioned "exit of a hero," was hung on the wall of their family house for many years. Each year, during their father's memorial service, the portrait was brought out, decorated, and positioned in a frontal pose during the family's group photograph. Such photos are decorated by computer technicians and posted on Facebook and other social media platforms. The exhibiting of photographs on Facebook opens a new and technologically significant chapter in the commemorative practice of contemporary Igbo society. Again, Ikediugwu's image, like the mask of Queen Idia, serves as a commemorative or memorial object for Ikediugwu's family, as a prestigious and heroic symbol of the family, as a symbol of their modernity and cross-cultural encounter, and as a spiritual embodiment of their ancestral connectedness. I will elaborate on each of these functions.

With respect to cross-cultural encounter, on the top edges of the Queen Mother pendant we find the incorporation of miniature Portuguese faces to reference trade between Benin and the Portuguese and the wealth that such mercantile modernity brought to the Benin royal family. By comparison, we find that in his portrait, Ikediugwu is dressed in his traditional Igbo Ozo title attire and holds an elephant tusk, a symbol of accomplishment in Igbo society. Cross-cultural encounter enters when such Igbo concepts of accomplishment are launched through the modern, Western technological medium of photography.

On the spiritual function of both images, one finds mudfish attached along the crown of the Benin Queen Mother mask. By living on the land and the sea, mudfish represent the duality of the Oba's humanness and divinity. This attribute gave the mask the power to protect its wearer from evil spirits. In the case of the Ikediugwu, the constant use of photographs during the yearly memorial service and the sense of immortality and immediacy enabled by Ikediugwu's memorial photos as they are posted on social media recall the Igbo belief in the continual invocation of ancestral memory and the omnipresence of the ancestral spirit.

This book's argument is premised on a radical logic of the artistic evolution of the commemorative image. Whereas the sixteenth-century Oba of

Benin had court artists who documented and memorialized events through sculpture, the contemporary Oba has photographers who document events of the royal institution. In society at large, each family observes a similar visual commemorative ritual. This book aims to illuminate this overlooked aspect of African visual culture and to demonstrate how the indigenous practice of sculptural commemoration has been supplanted by photographic memorialization (see Bredenbröker 2024; Parker 2021, 317–318). In the manner that ancestral sculptures embody family memories of progeny, power, and success, contemporary commemorative photography documents similar attributes of a family's history. In this way, similar heroic attributes of ancient commemorative sculptures such as Ikenga are visually replicated in contemporary Igbo commemorative photographs through funeral posters, billboards, funeral booklets, and obituary photos in newspaper publications, among other locations. McCaskie (2006, 349) argues that advertising death was an aspirational modernity that "built upon a legacy of customary oral practice," while Bredenbröker (2024) focuses on the materiality and use of these "image-objects" to unpack the intertwined relationship between Ghanaian funeral banners as sculptural but flexible representations of the dead and the image-like but inflexible qualities of dead bodies. This book examines how the precolonial African commemorative image transformed into a contemporary photographic device and has been deployed to forge individual subjectivity and chart collective aspiration.

In tracking this transformation, we see how, during the sixteenth century, Queen Idia's sculptural portrait personalizes the memory of the king's motherly affections and simultaneously embodies a distinctive and superior emblem of royal authority. Similarly, in the twenty-first century, Ikediugwu's photograph perpetuates the memory of the late father through the modern photographic device. Thus, in this book, I argue that the visual commemoration of the dead in West Africa from the 1880s evolved in tandem with a modernity that came with photography and the reconstitution of the public sphere. New meanings of the heroic persona became intertwined with new attitudes associated with the fashioning of power, prestige, and individual subjectivity. Likewise, in the present, the advent of visual software such as Photoshop and CorelDRAW has offered alternative means of reimagining individual and family wealth and memory outside the traditional sculptural forms.

ON EVOLVING ARTISTIC PRACTICES IN AFRICA

This book argues that African commemorative arts have evolved from sculptural figures into photographic objects. Sidney Kasfir has suggested that the determination of cultural authenticity around notions of "African traditional society" is essentially an ideologically driven Western agenda (1992, 41). She suggests that what is called "traditional society" is a legacy of the Victorian past and owes as much to nineteenth-century Romanticism and the social-evolutionary notion of disappearing cultures as to any reality found in Africa itself. In African studies, this term still persists as a more polite way of referring to the outdated concept of "primitive society" (Kuper 1988). Before colonialism, the West imagined Africa as a space of isolated and harmonious societies. This myth was so influential and ingrained that it continues to inform and drive scholarly concerns, even though it is far from the truth (Kasfir 1992, 41).

To challenge the rigid anthropological or art historical categories established by Western epistemes, I call for a review of what is "authentically African art." I join Sidney Kasfir (1992, 41) in "[talking] about authenticity" by first "unpacking the meanings assumed for 'traditional society,' and by extension, 'traditional art.'" Strother (1995), echoing Kasfir, has also challenged the notion that African art is a static and conservative expression of tradition and that it is only valuable when it conforms to the expectations and classifications of Western collectors and scholars. To support Strother and Kasfir in proposing a new understanding of African art, I suggest that the earliest form of commemorative photography was styled in the form of, for example, Ikenga ancestor sculptures. In other words, Africans did not see the use of photography to commemorate their dead as an entirely new visual culture but an act that was taken up when a new generation gained access to modern visual technologies. Jennifer Bajorek (2023, 36) traces this dynamic by contending that the portraiture of some African photographers illustrates how ancient and ancestral practices continue to serve as essential tributaries of contemporary photographic expression—existing in dialogue with emerging technologies, cosmological frameworks, and ecological imaginaries.

FROM THE 1880S

As of the 1880s, the name *Nigeria* was not in existence. Lagos and other parts of what is today known as Nigeria were part of the administrative enclave of West African colonialism. In nineteenth-century Lagos, commemorative photographs were entangled in the colonial discourses of power, prestige, and class. Commemorating the dead extended beyond the discourses of memorialization to foreground the institutionalization of colonial policies in the imperial outposts. The newspapers often solicited subscriptions to support photographs commemorating important citizens. Photographs were often printed and enlarged in London and eventually mounted in memorial halls, of which Glover Memorial Hall was the only outstanding example in colonial Lagos. The caption "unveiling the photograph" was constantly published in newspapers. These unveilings were usually marked by elaborate and prestigious ceremonies performed by the governor or deputy governor of the colony. A few such newspaper captions include "Unveiling of Bishop Johnson's Photograph," published in *Lagos Standard* on November 27, 1918; "The unveiling of a photograph of the late Mrs. C. A. Sapara Williams at the Glover Memorial Hall," published on December 10, 1904, in the *Lagos Weekly Record*; "Unveiling of a portrait of the late Lady Denton at the Glover Memorial Hall," on February 9, 1901, in the *Lagos Weekly Record*; and "Unveiling of Blyden's portrait memorial" on November 27, 1918, in the *Lagos Standard*, to mention a few. The newspapers emphasized how subscriptions by the public enabled these unveilings to be realized. In this book, I argue that the two actions of subscription and unveiling enunciated a unique visual culture in colonial Lagos, where public viewership of, and journalistic reports on, obituary photographs were socially significant for the colonial public sphere.

Nnamdi Azikiwe (Zik) introduced the style of photographic self-fashioning in his *West African Pilot* newspaper in 1937. By the 1940s, more Africans established newspapers as an ideological means of confronting colonial power,[1] although the function of newspapers extended beyond this (Barber 2007, 137–150; Newell 2011, 26–42) to include the promotion of subaltern agency in lifestyle and the constitution of the African political subject. Portrait photography emerged as one of the compelling anti-colonial forms of visual culture in colonial newspapers owned by nationalists. In a particularly outstanding example, newspapers published in the 1940s in colonial Lagos were dotted with portraits of politicians in enchanting poses often geared toward promoting party manifestoes (Kunstmann 2014, 518). At that time as well, the first obituary photographs of Africans appeared in these newspapers. Portraits of Nigerian elites replaced initial images of domination and empire promoted by colonial authorities. Although some of these images adopted colonial stylistic forms of self-presentation and poses to suggest the internalization of colonial stereotypes, they nonetheless align with Ariella Azoulay's (2014) concept of the "civil contract of photography," according to which the portrait photographs "function as sites of resistance to the hegemonic views prescribed by the state" (Kunstmann 2014, 519; Thomas and Green 2014, 3). These sites of resistance were apparent in photographs of Nigerian elites that replaced colonial images in anticipation of the emerging democratic nation (Duyile 1987, 141; Coker 1968, 34–44; Omu 1978, 87). In Zik's newspapers, for example, photographs accompanied obituaries as more Africans gained access to the public sphere. In 1960, Nigeria gained independence from Britain, and a new postcolonial citizenry emerged that imbibed an Afrocentric ideal. Representing the dead in print took a different turn as many Africans aspired toward the celebrity prototype of Zik and other nationalists. The appearance of a deceased's photo in print was seen as a remarkable means to forge agency and achieve prominence in the competitive public space convened by the postcolonial print culture. Obituary visibility in colonial newspapers became a subtle means of asserting the cultural identity of selfhood and ancestral veneration (Sprague 2003). Thus, as many photographs accompanied obituaries from the 1940s through the 1960s, the visualization of personhood expanded to symbolic gestures of power and class, aided by advancements in newspaper print technology.

By the 1970s and 1980s, when Nigeria's oil market boomed, the rise of the middle class ensured that many individuals gained greater access to the financial means required to achieve public visibility. By this time, photographs were incorporated into televised death announcements (see Gore 2001, 330). Eventually, the still photograph was replaced by a video of the deceased attending important social events with background music and a narrative voice characterized by insinuations of family prestige, progeny, honor, and importance (Nwoye 1993; Sprague 1978, 54; Gore 2002, 330). This was not just peculiar to Nigeria but was the norm throughout West Africa. By the late 2000s, the invention of new digital devices and printing technologies enabled photographs in family photo albums and snapshots to be repurposed to serve new funerary and commemorative needs. Analog photographs were digitized and transferred to different social media platforms to fill the unbearable voids of loss. The public sphere was reconfigured in that social media enabled underperforming families to envision heroism from the ubiquitous online presence of their deceased.

As time passed, commemorative photography migrated from professional, commercial photographers' studios to amateur photographers' laptop screens and smart phones. Social media spaces were populated with photographs of the dead in a new form of subjectivity. In this new norm, a community of virtual mourners and well-wishers who shared the experience of grieving and the display of memory and history produced a new photographic subject who enjoyed acclaim in a global public sphere. Here, the new meaning of the deceased's photograph as a fetishized hero of the social media public who maintains a permanent presence in the lives of the living is underscored by the viral impetus activated by social media. It can even be said that social media have emerged as highly influential modernist frames of immortality: they enable the commemoration of the deceased in the public sphere and the construction of their digital afterlives (Recuber 2023).

IMAGES OF THE DEAD

Earlier scholarly research on funeral photography was shaped by Stanley Burns's (1990) *Sleeping Beauty: Memorial Photography in America*, among other books. Burns amassed the world's largest private collection of early medical and postmortem photography, with more than one million historic photographs. *Sleeping Beauty* contains eighty images from Burns's collection and a chronology of attitudes toward death and mourning in America. Jay Ruby's *Secure the Shadow: Death and Photography in America* (1995) explores the social conventions of American postmortem memorial photographs from 1840 to 1995. Portraying the dead as if they were alive was a somewhat common practice in the nineteenth century.[2] Ruby showed how photographers borrowed from the long-established artistic tradition of mourning and posthumous painting to develop various styles in postmortem memorial photography.[3] Ruby, for example, notes photographing the deceased immediately after death, before the decomposition of the corpse, allowing a naturalistic impression analogous to sleep. The same visual analogy of sleep was a subject of study in *Photography and Death* by Audrey Linkman (2011). In this book, Linkman provides a compelling account of nineteenth-century practices of photography and death with a major concentration on the Western world, starting immediately after the invention of photography in 1839. She recognized the impact of high child mortality rates in the imagined proximity between sleep and death in mid-nineteenth-century photographs. Her descriptive investigation into photographing the dead as though they were asleep as well as her analysis of the sitting practices and production processes added a new dimension to earlier literature on postmortem photography. These photographs eventually found their way into regular family albums. While Burns and Ruby did not explore the theoretical aspects of postmortem and funeral photography, Linkman expanded the narratives by briefly touching on the relationship between death and the internet and how memorial websites have emerged to change mourning and commemorative practices. I am indebted to Linkman's brief theoretical reflection on death, photography, and the internet in undertaking a theoretical exploration of how the internet has come to produce a heroic persona of the deceased, extend their life, and expose their hidden body in the public sphere.

In his much-celebrated book *Camera Lucida*, Roland Barthes ([1980] 1985) argues that in every photograph of living individuals, their future death is visible. For Barthes, photography "must be discussed in terms of death, a witness of something that is no more, a photographed moment that is gone." Barthes recognizes the trauma of loss that accompanies this moment: "This is an enormous trauma for humanity, a trauma endlessly renewed. Each reading of a photo and there are billions worldwide in a day, each perception and reading of a photo is implicitly, in a repressed manner, a contract with what has ceased to exist, a contract with death" (356). When critically analyzed, Barthes's ideas enable us to see how photography plays a key role in commemorative practices across different parts of the world. According to Barthes, the "punctum" is what makes the photograph transcend time and space. It reveals a hidden tragedy that was already destined to occur even when the photo was captured. In Nwankwo Nwafor (Okachamma)'s commemorative photograph discussed in chapter 7 of this book, fourteen members of the family seen flanking the corpse are now dead and marked with the inscription "RIP." The photograph, when taken in 1986, thus concealed "its embodied catastrophe" (Barthes 1981, 96), which the inscriptions now reveal. Barthes's intimate perspective on photographs lies at the core of his argument—for him as well, photographs awakened his memory and connected him to the people in the snapshots. He suggested that our affinity with photographs is invariably a subjective one, as the advent of photography coincided with the intrusion of the private into the public domain and, consequently, the disclosure of privacy. Immersed in the excessive stimulation of the media, Barthes intentionally selected images that provoked agony in him, for they preserved his individual recollections (Barthes 1980, 148). Hans Belting contends that in the photograph captured during the existence of the departed, life has already become embalmed. In Okachamma's photograph, many lives were already embalmed. If "death has no place in such pictures, then this is also true of life" (Belting 2017, 159).

This book is not about ancient African commemorative sculptures, but it is necessary to review a few pieces of literature to suggest how contemporary commemorative photography could have emerged from that previous tradition. John Mack's book *The Artfulness of Death in Africa* examines how African commemorative arts capture and convey the essence of the deceased, but also how they are visually embedded in the larger context of mortuary and funeral practices. Mack discusses photography as an ancillary but significant element of the commemoration process. In his argument, there is a tendency to invoke the tropes of the Western anthropological episteme, as argued by Kasfir. Hence, he relates that photography was relegated to an otherworldly, detached experience by Ghanaians: "In Ghana, photographs are referred to by the Akan/Asante word *saman*, 'ghosts of the dead.' Negatives are especially troubling. They turn black skin into white, the color of the dead, and then the process is reversed, and the image is duplicated in the form of a print" (Mack 2019, 109). While Mack regards photography as an alienating and fetishistic practice in the Ghanaian context, I examine the ways in which African commemorative photography constitutes an embodied, performative, heroic, and experiential mode of agency that warrants greater scholarly attention, especially since it has been practiced for more than a century. Mack, likewise briefly, attends to the modern application of photographs in commemoration:

> The application are numerous: they very often announce a death in local and/or national media, as they do elsewhere, but often filling many newspaper pages on a weekly basis, including photographs republished on the anniversary of someone's demise, sometimes twenty or more years later; they may be displayed outside the house of someone who has died; they are used on funeral invitations, associated brochures and receipts for those making a donation to funeral expenses; they may be reproduced on T-shirts, handkerchiefs and memorial cloth, or pinned on the clothing of mourners; they have been reproduced on stickers, buttons, bottle openers, and key rings; the image of the deceased may be printed on plates and posters associated with funerary processes; they may be carried in front of a wrapped corpse at a

> second burial ceremony and be displayed on graves, memorials, and shrines. (2019, 109)

By listing the many ways photography has spread in commemorative practice, Mack shows how it has become not only a social and cultural mortuary practice but an enduring means of commemorative art. Mack argues, "In adopting such photographic conventions, it is clearly the social standing and the role the individual may hold that is commemorated rather than the individual in him or herself" (Mack 2019, 110). African commemorative sculptures as well celebrate the accomplishments of the deceased rather than aiming for verisimilitude. A royal sculptural portrait commemorates the prestige, dignity, and personality of its subject while enhancing the spiritual and aesthetic value of its office. For example, in southwestern Nigeria, the thirteenth-century Ife commemorative portrait sculpture is distinguished by prestigious sartorial paraphernalia such as beads, anklets, decorative crowns, and bangles, among other decorations. The Ife's sense of the fashionable found greater sophistication in the body of their king, in accentuating the king's dignity, which he must flaunt in public. The fashion ensembles seen on the king's body should not be found on the bodies of ordinary persons.

Similarly, in Akan of present-day Ghana, a Scottish merchant who visited the Fante in the nineteenth century described the commemorative ensemble made in honor of the Fante elite: "Upon the death of a great man, they make representations of him sitting in state with his wives and attendants seated around him. These act as monuments to the memory like the statues of the great men in the Western world" (La Gamma 2011, 77). The Congo *ndop* commemorative figure embodies the majestic aesthetics of Kuba royal ancestry. Its formal features reflect the power, influence, and royal paraphernalia of the office of the late king. For example, in the *ndop* commemorating the early seventeenth-century dynastic founder King Shyaam the Great of the Kuba kingdom, the Shyaam's identity "as a hero and Woot complement is denoted by the inclusion of three rows of cowrie shells in his belt and by the incorporation of an open square pattern known as 'Woot' on the upper surface of the royal cap" (Blier 1998, 233). Not the visual likeness of the king, but what the royal institution would remember as the emblem of the king's authority, was emphasized. Likewise, the Akuaba funeral figures from Ghana downplay verisimilitude to emphasize important elements that heroize the Queen Mother, such as the segmented neck showing fat rolls, a symbol of prosperity, the coiffures, "coiled tendrils of hair arranged in arced bands," or "elaborate conical mounds of coiled hair" that suggest the majestical and magisterial elegance associated with royal femininity (La Gamma 2011, 85). Similarly, among the Okpella in Edo of midwestern Nigeria, a typical commemorative mask of a dead mother is a wooden helmet mask that epitomizes a woman of status and affluence who has taken a title in the Olimi celebration. The mask has a sculpted superstructure that mirrors the predilections and accomplishments of the woman being memorialized (Borgatti 1979). In the same way as these traditional figures emphasized the heroic attributes of the deceased through recognizable vignettes, recent commemorative photographs reinvent such attributes. Acting as heroic monuments of the dead, such photographs can be found in funeral albums, posters, booklets, newspaper obituaries, videos, and social media photographs, among other places. These photographs serve a similar function to historic African commemorative sculptures, although the photographs emphasize both the physiognomy and heroic attributes of the deceased, whereas the ancient sculptures downplayed resemblance for civic status.

Some recent research has examined the complex roles visual images are beginning to play in Nigerian funerals and commemorative practices (see, for example, Ikwuemesi and Onwuegbuna 2018; Smith 2018). Ikwuemesi and Onwuegbuna (2018, 197) discuss the use of photography, videography, and graphic production in funerals, but they omit family photographs from their investigations. Other studies have also overlooked how a photographic-conscious public could reinvent the commemorative ritual found in traditional African sculptures. For example, among the Igbo of southeastern Nigeria, there is an emphasis on individual achievement that renders the funeral arena a highly visual and spectacular space for the validation of success. A new trend among the Igbo is the circulation, at burials and funerals, of printed pamphlets and books containing photographic depiction of the deceased's accomplishments. For the bereaved, returning from the city or diaspora locations to bury the dead entails the huge financial and social responsibility of conspicuous consumption and conspicuous redistribution (Basden 1983, 118; Smith 2004, 2018, 73; Uchendu 1965; Onyibor 2012, 2019). Such acts of conspicuous consumption should be understood in terms not only of providing food items or other goods during funerals but also of the production of photographic materials that deploy multiple visual devices to commemorate the dead. The manipulation of the photograph of the deceased in commemorative posters and booklets to convey visual signs of achievement is an essential method to glorify the dead and transcend visual disgrace and social invisibility. Individuals desire funerals that are conspicuous, not only through attendance by large crowds of mourners but also through explosive visual image campaigns, including photos published in elite magazines and funeral booklets or posted on social media. Smith (2004) offers a compelling metaphor illustrating how funerals manifest the conversion of wealth into social prestige and political power. He argues that "spending money to secure social and political honor and prestige is perhaps more crucial than ever" (Smith 2024, 9). Smith follows Guyer's (1995) "wealth in people" to validate a similar assertion by Lentz, regarding the Dagara of Ghana, that "funeral celebrations have to be lavish in order to demonstrate the deceased's exceptional social and political standing" (2009, 191). This book also shows how wealth is transformed into prestige through images of glamour in newspapers, posters, booklets, magazines, and social media. These avenues act as a public sphere where the status of the deceased and their families are heroized and monumentalized.

Marleen de Witte (2011) has investigated the role of photographs and changing technologies of remembrance in the Asante funeral culture of Ghana, in one of the most relevant research projects dealing with the visual culture of African funeral rituals. She investigates how images are produced in Asante funerals, how such images circulate, and how they invoke concepts of wellness, remembrance, materiality, and spirituality. De Witte, again, analyzed how media such as newspapers, radio, television, video, and photography have expanded the sociocultural discourses of funerals, further revealing how the dead body necessitates the mass reproduction and public dissemination of images of the living body in the public space. Her study analyzes such elaborate displays of luxury and wealth focused on the dead body and the mass reproduction of pictures of the deceased as part of the changing modes of creating personhood, ancestorship, and remembrance (see also Adu-Gyamfi 2010). She argues: "At death, *imaginations* of good life are turned into *images* of good life, represented by the body of the deceased—images in flesh and in photographs, but also in cloth, paint, plaster, and cement." De Witte, like other scholars, recognizes a growing need to investigate and interpret the multiple appeals to the visual in African funerals, although she as well pays little attention to the use of family photos. Other relevant studies include Elizabeth Hallam and Jenny Hockey (2001), *Death, Memory and Material Culture*, Michael Arnold et al. (2018), *Death and Social Media*, and Antonius C. G. M. Robben's *Death and Anthropology*. The above books, in one way or another, touch on the subject of death and photography but do not specifically unravel how colonial relations shaped the commemorative photograph. I look more deeply at the complex meanings that emerged when photography featured as a visual culture of colonial modernity, with the result that, ultimately, memorialization has been reconstituted as a new type of photographic event capable of reconfiguring the meaning of public space.

This book demonstrates how interdisciplinarity can address the challenging and specific scholarly concerns in African studies by blending different disciplines in a unique way. My goal is to explore the intersections of visual culture, the public sphere, print culture, and art history and how they shape scholarly inquiries around commemoration. Patricia Hayes and Gary Minkley (2019, 2) have suggested that "not only does photography feature in the history of different disciplines and in relation to almost any subject or thing, it also has been a catalyst for different clusters of interdisciplinarity." However, despite its unimaginable ubiquity, photography is often received with ambivalence, especially with respect to its "indeterminacies, subsidiaries, desires, prefigurations and postfigurations; and its metaphors, emptiness, shadows, and silhouettes" (3). Thinking about ambivalence may help frame the complex interdisciplinary networks I explore in this book, ranging from the place of photography in visual culture and art history to the public sphere and print culture.

WHAT IS A MEMORIAL OR COMMEMORATIVE PHOTOGRAPH?

There are two major categories of photographs I discuss in this book. First, there is the memorial or commemorative photograph, which I define as a photograph that is taken while the individual is still alive and then "framed" or decontextualized after death so as to indicate that the sitter is now deceased. Second, there is the postmortem or mortuary photograph, which is taken after death, although it can equally be deployed for memorialization purposes. Both types may be used in the context of funerals, and the social uses of both types are fundamental to memory and history. The introduction of digital photography and social media has created an additional function for memorial and postmortem photographs: ultimately, to fill a gap created by loss (Meese, Nansen, et al. 2015). I examine the connection both types of photographs have had with death, funeral, and commemoration in Nigeria since the nineteenth century. I recognize that every culture experiences this connection in different ways in different historical epochs. For example, in her work on postmortem photography of the Victorian era, Nancy Martha West (2000) argues that photography's association with death and loss varies across historical periods, reflecting shifting cultural, technological, and aesthetic concerns. West's study indicates that during the early to mid-twentieth century, photography was overtly linked to the discourse of mortality, a notion that has recently been supplanted by a more abstract reflectivity (Murray 2008, 154). In terms of the history of photography in Nigeria, some of these funeral photographs occupy a pivotal moment in time, during a period of transformation from slow, painstaking labor in studio portraiture to the swift and casual click of the snapshot. Both studio photography and amateur snapshots are constituted as part of the visual economy that gave impetus to commemorative photography.

THE PLACE OF PHOTOGRAPHY IN MORTUARY CYCLES

The centrality of the photograph in mortuary cycles has gained increasing recognition not just by scholars but by a growing number of mourners who now deploy photographs throughout the funeral and, especially, in the funeral procession, where they constitute an obligatory part of the funeral dance (see Jindra and Noret 2011). In difficult circumstances of disappearance, dead bodies have been replaced with photos, while decorations of the funeral parlor have been possible using family photographs (Jindra and Noret 2011). Family photos transferred into obituary booklets can afford us the opportunity of sustained engagement with the role of photographs in funerals and commemoration, especially since these albums are beginning to construct an agentive process that inhabits multiple spaces of the social as well as the ritual world. Again, their gradual incursion into the funerary rites of southeastern Nigerians could echo the attendant temporality and symbolic materialization of life through the appurtenances of visual technologies.

In Nigeria, obituary booklets are printed pamphlets that accompany burial and funeral rites. In the past twenty years, these pamphlets have contained relatively few (about five) pages announcing the order of funeral activities. The pamphlets have been produced through lithographic printing or photocopied and bound together. Recently, these pamphlets have transformed into, in some cases, one-hundred- to three-hundred-page full-color books, reflecting the wealth of each family. Such publications now boast a section in the middle referred to variously as "photo speak," "photo gallery," or "photo album," among other terms. Even less affluent families endeavor to include a few photos in the most modest form. One of the reasons for this trend seems to be the exuberant sociality that came with elite accumulation and class reinvention during the economic decline of the 1980s and 1990s. Another reason is the late capitalist expansion in printing technology during the late 1990s, when the Nigerian economy opened to large-scale business exchanges with China. I explore the notion of the "global family photo album" specifically by interrogating the apparent rise to prominence of previously concealed family photographs, which have surfaced through channels such as funeral posters, booklets, and social media platforms. Notably, existing scholarly literature on family photo albums in Africa has predominantly focused on the complex social meanings associated with their collective dissemination during significant life events, including weddings and other communal gatherings (Buckley 2000–2001; Mustafa 2002, 2005–2006; Buggenhagen 2014).

THE PUBLIC SPHERE OF SOCIAL MEDIA

Little has been written on how social media have enabled ordinary citizens to compete with the rich in discourses of commemoration. "In Memoriam" newspaper advertisements of earlier periods in southern Nigeria offered only the rich the opportunity to publicly heroize their deceased. For example, in the *Daily Times* newspaper of January 19, 1966, on page 13, "Mrs Beatrice Taiwo Smith (Nee Johnstone)" was commemorated as one "who crossed the veil 21 years ago" (Fig. 1).

The subscription for this announcement was paid by her daughter Beatrice Taiwo (Jr.) and her husband, Akin Smith. In comparison, Ifeanyi Nrialike posted a photograph of his late father, who died forty years before, on his Facebook page in 2020. Juxtaposing these commemorations is important for understanding the transformation of the commemorative public space and the nature of access afforded to ordinary citizens. In 1966 Lagos, those who were able to see Beatrice's mother's "In Memoriam" twenty-one years after her death were only those who could buy the newspaper in Lagos while the issue was available, whereas Ifeanyi's Facebook friends around the world gained access to his late father's photograph. The advantage of Ifeanyi's Facebook resides in its immediacy. While Beatrice would have been required to go through the onerous processes of getting a photo, sending it through surface mail to the publisher, and waiting for many weeks for the publish-

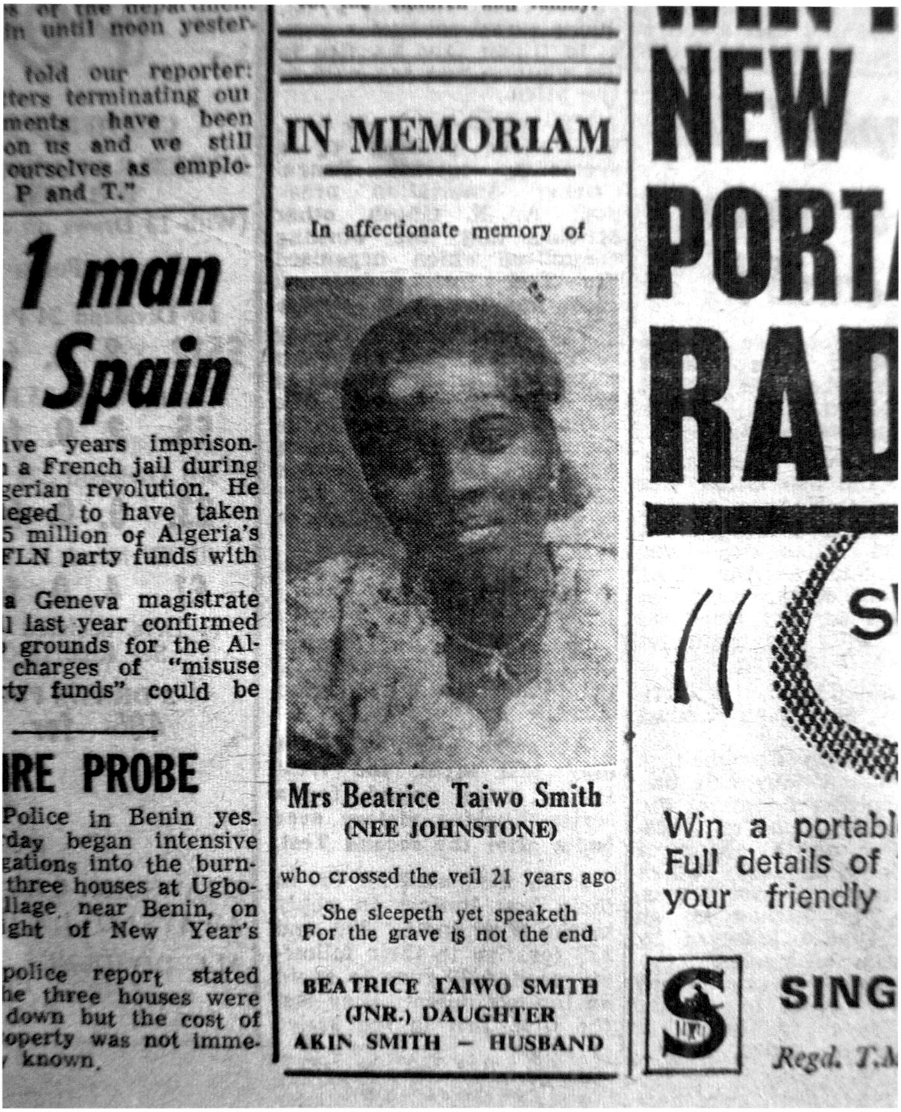

in until noon yester-

told our reporter:
ters terminating our
ments have been
on us and we still
ourselves as emplo-
P and T."

1 man
Spain

ive years imprison-
a French jail during
gerian revolution. He
leged to have taken
5 million of Algeria's
FLN party funds with

a Geneva magistrate
l last year confirmed
grounds for the Al-
charges of "misuse
ty funds" could be

IRE PROBE

Police in Benin yes-
day began intensive
gations into the burn-
three houses at Ugbo-
llage, near Benin, on
ight of New Year's

police report stated
he three houses were
down but the cost of
operty was not imme-
known.

IN MEMORIAM

In affectionate memory of

Mrs Beatrice Taiwo Smith
(NEE JOHNSTONE)

who crossed the veil 21 years ago

She sleepeth yet speaketh
For the grave is not the end

BEATRICE TAIWO SMITH
(JNR.) DAUGHTER
AKIN SMITH – HUSBAND

NEW
PORT
RAD

Win a portabl
Full details of
your friendly

SING
Regd. T.M

Fig. 1. A photograph of the late Mrs. Beatrice Taiwo Smith (née Johnstone) was published in the *Daily Times of Nigeria*, January 19, 1966

ers to make a decision and publish the photo in the newspaper, Ifeanyi just requires internet access to launch his late father's photograph on his Facebook page in seconds. Instead of requiring the tedious bureaucratic paperwork of human officials, public tribute is now a swift and seamless process powered by technology.

While Beatrice's friends were required to travel to the newspaper stand to purchase a copy of the newspaper to view her late mother's commemoration, Ifeanyi's friends needed only internet access and a click to view his late father's commemorative photograph. Whereas Beatrice's photograph and commemoration did not afford an interactive space for sorrowful compliments from friends, Ifeanyi got immediate complimentary condolences on his Facebook wall and would continue to do so as long as the photo remained on his Facebook page. Thus, social media comes with a new promise of immortality and reshapes how we think about the social, challenging and transforming the public sphere. As this book shows, as the public sphere opens up to more voices, a historic gap is bridged.

In recent times, social media pages of family members have been filled with commemorative photos from the pre-internet era (see Nwafor 2024). Thus, I have written about how the Nigeria Nostalgia Project (NNP) Facebook page acts as a public monument where commemorative photographs of Nigerian nationalists are "emotionally and politically charged to assume new status as heroic traces of Nigerian political leadership that have become obscured by the unfortunate and infamous escapades of today's political class." (Nwafor 2024, 81). These photos act as public monuments that allow future generations to remember and bond with their ancestors. Social media become a memorial monument, an ancestral screen, just like the ancestral sculptures that act as commemorative monuments of the dead.

Many texts and online platforms have explored how digital media have transformed the ways people mourn, memorialize, and interact with the dead online (Brubaker et al. 2013; Wright 2014; Degroot 2012; Arnold et al. 2018; Kasket 2012; Meese, Gibbs, et al. 2015; Stokes 2012). For example, through the circulation of commemorative analog photographs that have been digitized and posted on the NNP, we find a new discourse and intersection of visual history, art history, print media, and social media. Here I suggest that this is a new commemorative practice that raises critical debates about photographic temporalities, postcolonial historiography, and the new media. What is unique about the NNP is that individuals scan their analog photographs of their deceased, which were taken before the advent of digital photography, and post them online, raising the need to explore a provocative theory of "scanning commemorative history into the present." In addition to evaluating many texts that discuss online photo practice in terms of the experiential immediacy of the digital mode deployed on Facebook, Instagram, and the mobile social networking platforms (Hajek 2012; Fiefer 2013; Gibbs, Carter, et al. 2014; Dilmaç 2018; Haroche 2011; Henaff 2011), I examine the transformation of commemorative analog photos to digital photos and what it means for the expression of personal subjectivity online. Through commemorative photos online, individuals make and remake connections between the local, the national, and the global, between the mundane and the extraordinary. Going beyond some texts on photographic practices on Facebook (Miller and Sinanan 2017; Hand 2012; Agbo 2018, 2019), which deal scantily with Africa and national identity, this book discusses commemorative photographs posted online as "archives in motion" (Røssaak 2010), an archival materiality (Mbembe 2002) that articulates power and agency (Derrida 1995). Other recent studies have reinforced Africans' agency in colonial photographic discourses and explored postcolonial subjectivities, identities, personhood, and fantasies through photography (Paoletti 2024; Vokes and Newbury 2018; Bajorek 2012; Haney 2010a; Abiodun 2013; Peffer and Cameron 2013; Buckley 2000, 2006; Werner 2001). Some of the most recent texts on African photography, (Paoletti 2024; Bajorek 2020; and Hayes and Minkley 2019) have charted a more radical course by highlighting previously underappreciated photographic practices in Africa, including the digital turn. Giulia Paoletti (2024) and Bajorek (2020) raise one of the major theoretical ideas that I explored in this book: intermediality. Paoletti, following Bajorek, for example, emphasizes the need to rethink photography as a form of intermedial transaction in the African context. She argues that Senegalese photography deviates from Western notions of mimesis, objectivity, and indexicality, terms that have historically informed Western theoretical frameworks of the medium.

Bajorek examined the role photography played in forging new decolonial identities and "reconfiguring new media networks" as Africa emerged from the twilight of colonial rule (2020, 14), while Hayes and Minkley's text problematizes the "methodological implications of photographs and photography in their African setting" (2019, 3). In this book, I make an argument similar to Bajorek's and extend the above literature on photography to show how southern Nigerians have produced and reinvented themselves and imagined a new community of heroes through commemorative photographs. A generational transfer of memories is enabled through these photographs. Many young relatives of Nrialike's father who did not know him but heard about him were able to see his photo for the first time and commented in that regard. Just as on the NNP, discourses of Nrialike's bereavement and mourning eventually shifted from shared grief to narratives of glamour, sociocultural and political connectedness, and family gossip. In this way, social media acts as a resurrection space where the dead and the living eventually re-commune.

Hajek (2012, 375) has asked the question, "What happens when photo albums go digital, and private snapshots become available to all?" This is a question that is at the core of this book: What happens to private family photo albums of the deceased when they are made available to all, in the public sphere, through newspapers, magazines, funeral posters, funeral booklets, and social media? The answer to this is provided through my exploration of the impact of digital media and social media networks on collective and individual identities. As Van Dijck (2008, 60) observes, "We use photographs of family and friends not just to fix memory and yearn for the lost times that this memory evokes," but "to constantly reassess our past lives and reflect on what has been as well as what is and what will be." In southern Nigeria, there is a shift such that visual spectacles are now yardsticks for measuring a successful funeral. This explains why each funeral is surrounded by videographers and photographers, two agents who serve each family's desire to see and be seen. Through ubiquitous photographs of the funeral, "Each family constructs a portrait of itself—a portable kit of images that bear witness to its connectedness of individuals considered as members of families" (Sontag 1977, 5). In this book, I illustrate how families construct their histories and perhaps the history of their communities through the family photo published in the funeral booklets and on social media. Further scholarly works on obituary posters in Ghana and Nigeria have shown different levels of contestations around history, kinship, and sociopolitical relations (Adotey 2018) or how obituary posters can serve as a source of biographical information (Omoruyi 1988; Adjah 2007). Behrend (2000, 70), citing Miller (1995), has observed how an innovation by Likoni studio photographers of Kenya produced a posteriori experience out of the local consumption of global elements. Behrend further notes how "the scenarios Likoni photographers create give presence to, and praise, above all, the foreign and the global—a richer, cosmopolitan world that appears to be at the subject's disposal." My book draws on this concept of the "global" to investigate and extend Behrend's argument beyond the analog discourses to show how southern Nigerians are deploying the tool of global technology to transform their local commemorative experience into a cosmopolitan, globalized experience. In this context, "being global" is theorized as a continuous search for social belonging through the apparatus of social media technology. Appadurai (1986a, 1990, 296) has described this uniquely modern situation as "the global cultural economy."[4]

METHODOLOGY

In the material cultures of death, the interplay between the tangible and the intangible, the visible and the invisible, influences memorialization and remembering (Hockey and Hallam 2001, 106). The visual materials that I analyze throughout this book, such as sculptures, posters, photography, and video, which provide multiple means of documenting and retrieving experiences of death in southeastern Nigeria, are products of different, historically contingent technologies. Visual-historical and anthropological perspectives have therefore proved most effective in approaching them. Relationships between texts, visual images, and material objects have been analyzed through ethnographic fieldwork, archival research, and scholarly writing. I draw upon rich photographic archives of obituary photos of private individuals in analog and social media, most of which have not been explored. Comments and texts that follow these photos, which weave uncommon political narratives of grave national and international concern around the digital remains of the deceased, suggest that something deeper is happening. For example, specific photos of dead Nigerians have been repurposed to champion the cause of domestic abuse and gender subordination, political victimization, or the country's failed security apparatus and failed medical system, among others. This development gives commemorative photography the force and cause of sociocultural revolution.

However, a prevailing paradigm in research that borders on African commemorative practices is the concentration by authors on recovering texts and objects that deal with social history and public memory, with minimal insight into mundane objects and private lives. I have shifted my attention in this book to private family photo albums (see Rose 2016), private burials, and funeral arrangements through my attendance at more than one hundred burial and funeral ceremonies in southeastern Nigeria. I personally observed, studied, and analyzed more banal visual cultural practices such as photographing funerals—which is regarded as, and in fact remains, the most unstudied ritual aspect of the funeral by scholars in Nigeria and West Africa.

A NOTE ON CLASS

At this moment in history, photography has become affordable and ubiquitous—in other words, it transcends the strict categorization of class. More generally, I align with Karin Barber's approach to class categories in Africa. According to Barber,

> Everywhere in Africa, social mobility, aspirational self-positioning and the uncertainty and fragility of economic and occupational status all mean that neither the elite nor the non-elite are ever boundaried, empirically enumerable categories. Members of an elite group almost always have poor relatives; the most disadvantaged often have pathways to the better-off though clientship or communal solidarity. Subjectively as well as objectively, the boundaries of social strata are fluctuating and indeterminate. Neither elites nor non-elites are a monolithic group; rather, they are often unstable congeries of social groupings, between which there are many fault lines as well as shared interests. (2018, 11)

She recognizes the constant movement and exchange between favored and relegated cultural forms, as well as the shifting power relations and shared assimilation that seem to characterize the class category as a site of struggle (to rephrase Hall 1981). Therefore, the penchant to strictly identify a category as "rich" or "poor" in Africa must be resisted. Barber continues that "the temptation to identify certain genres, themes or styles as inherently and permanently 'popular' is one which Africanist scholarship, also, needs to be wary of" (2018, 11). Here I would turn to the example of Jude, a computer technician I interviewed, who used editing software to rework photographs of all classes of individuals who contracted him, including those perceived as the not-so-rich. Sometimes, a clear class distinction would be achieved through the number of colored photographs and specific editing techniques Jude deployed in the photos of the rich, which may not be so painstakingly applied in photos of the not-so-rich. This enabled me to differentiate the two classes of individuals. In another type of example, the insinuation of wealth exhibited through the immense size of the photographs on funeral billboards immediately reveals the class of the deceased. However, there are instances where the not-so-rich would go out of their way to mobilize funds to achieve photographic acclaim rivaling that of some rich individuals. It was also difficult to establish a class distinction in images that embody symbolic aspirations of power and success. For example, computer technicians retouched images of the deceased with the sartorial markers of the rich, such as *akwa isi agu* (lion's head dress), *mkpo* (staff), *okpu mmee* (titled red hat), *ugbene ugo* (the eagle's feather), among others. With this costuming through photographic retouching, underachievers transformed into heroes and climbed the elevated ladders of the rich. It is important to note that in funeral ceremonies, enormous funds are expended in such a manner that even the poor sometimes appear rich. In any case, whether symbolic or practical, wealth remains critical to my analysis, also when thinking about visual technologies that deploy images of symbolic wealth to rupture the distinction between classes.

THEORETICAL ORIENTATION

This book is grounded in the theory of the public sphere (Habermas 1974), the social life of photographs (Pinney 1997; Peffer and Cameron 2013, 15–19), and photographic materialities (Edwards 2009). Traditional frameworks of photographic history in Africa have largely ignored how its technical development and artistic accomplishments influence the wider social and cultural perspectives (see Ryan 1997, 18). As Allan Sekula (1982, 86) has pointed out, "If we accept the fundamental premise that information is the outcome of a culturally determined relationship, then we can no longer ascribe an intrinsic or universal meaning to the photographic image." Equally John Tagg has challenged a uniform history of photography: "Photography as such has no identity. Its status as technology varies with the power relations which invest it. Its nature as a practice depends on the agents and institutions which set it to work . . . and its products are legible and meaningful only within the particular currencies they have" (Tagg 1988, 23). Photography embodies a form of discursive authority that shows how visual perception is both historically and culturally constructed. Representation is a multifaceted cultural phenomenon, and, hence, photographs need to be interpreted as instances in wider dialogues of "ways of seeing," which demand historical contextualization (Ryan 1997). Ryan suggests that the photographic image acquires its indexical power not merely from its ontological relation to a prior reality but from the technical and cultural processes and discursive structures by which it is rendered significant (Ryan 1997, 19; see also Edwards 2009). In this book, I emphasize an approach to photography as a culturally constructed way of seeing that is tied to the intertextuality of photographic discourse. I want to join Ryan in arguing that photographs, in their transcendent capacity, extend beyond mere visual representation. The ostensibly explicit boundaries defining various modes of semiotic expression—such as text, photography, cartography, and artistic forms—are essentially linked to the historical contexts in which they emerge (Ryan 1997, 26, 19; Edwards 2009). The commemorative photographs I examine demonstrate a convergence of the linguistic and the visual, employing framing strategies, symbolic representations, and ways of seeing that facilitate the interpretation of photographs in diverse, intricate interactions with semiotic systems. This book is informed by a contextual approach that situates the images within their broader historical and cultural milieu and argues that commemorative photographs—constructed, disseminated, circulated, and consumed within a specific social network in southern Nigeria—disclose the creative imaginaries of colonial and postcolonial culture as much as they do the material spaces or individuals captured in their frame.

Strother (2013) has shown how Africans embraced photography to represent their cosmopolitan aspirations while colonial ethnographers "misrepresented them by recycling them as postcards and ethnographic illustrations for consumption overseas as exotic or unflattering ethnic types" (Peffer 2013, 16). In other words, certain Africans' private photographs were popularized through their distribution in the global economy of images.[5] One objective of this book is to return to the objectives of African self-representation in its own sphere. But here as well, photographs live multiple social lives: They are not just transient material things but material things that add tangible value to the status of the deceased and the bereaved family. For example, a photograph, originally diminutive in size and meaning, is suddenly overblown and extravagantly transformed into a giant and prominent obituary billboard; a photo previously tucked away inside a family album is ubiquitously advertised in newspapers, social media, obituary posters, and funeral booklets. A silently forgotten photo is excavated and publicly exhibited online. In the theory of the social life of photographs, the status of a hero or accomplished individual in a society can never be socially consummating except when publicly visualized in the above-mentioned multiple visual contexts. Nuances of heroism and visibility are, therefore, intertwined.

One important theoretical idea that has emerged through my studies is the concept of personhood. This concept enables me to explore how individuals participate actively in the game of social life, especially how "dead persons continue to interact meaningfully with living persons and continue to play a part in the lives of their living intimates and their community" (Arnold et al. 2018, 7). The social life of the dead is sustained virtually via "pre-recorded social media interventions" (Arnold et al. 2018, 8). This book examines how this process extends the temporal frame of the deceased. Locally, heroes are understood as having transcended the challenging predicament to live a fulfilled life in Nigeria. They are also interpreted as having impacted the lives of surviving relatives so positively that they "touch our hearts, fill us with admiration, and make us reconsider our view of the world" (Cherry, 2023). A deeper philosophical exploration of the hero image draws on important literature that reimagined heroism as a concept that lacked a universal template for judgment (Fiske and Taylor 2008). Igbo individuals have addressed their deceased as heroes in photographs, on social media, and in other visual culture forms for being altruistic, self-sacrificing, inspiring, helpful, unblemished, and beautiful.

CHAPTERIZATION

Chapter 1 introduces the premise of this book and touches on the significant theoretical concerns, methodologies, and overriding scholarly arguments surrounding commemorative photography.

Chapter 2 dwells on the meanings of the obituary and commemorative notices in the newspapers of nineteenth-century Lagos before the introduction of obituary photography. Using Jürgen Habermas's notion of the public sphere, I show how obituary notices in nineteenth-century newspapers of colonial Lagos did more than just capture death; they equally introduced gossipy anecdotes and sensationalism to define the colonial public sphere as one that is characterized by insinuations of social and economic class with occasional interjections of anti-racial and anti-colonial sentiments. In this public sphere, the dead were heroized as important members of ancestral progeny.

Chapter 3 shows how memorial photographs became entangled in the politics of the colonial public sphere in nineteenth-century Lagos through what was then known as subscription and unveiling. Memorial photographs were brought into public through their printing on multiple surfaces, including in magazines, almanacs, earthenware, and pamphlets, among other placements. On the other hand, citizens heeded calls for subscriptions for memorial photographs in colonial newspapers and contributed moneys used to print, enlarge, frame, and mount the photographs on the walls of Glover Memorial

Hall. I show how the above activities engendered a robust visual and verbal culture that was not just critical for the discourses of the colonial public sphere but significant in perpetuating the deceased in the public memory of colonial Lagos. Subscription and unveiling of the photograph with grand ceremonial fanfare performed by important colonial officials, such as the governor or deputy governor of the colony inside Glover Memorial Hall, marked part of the cult of attention essential in commemorating colonial citizens. The materiality of the photograph, its tangible thingness, was subsumed into the colonial status symbol and invested with multiple significations of power and multiple subjectivities, in spite of the surface where the photo was printed.

In chapter 4, I use funeral posters to investigate how wealth is conceptualized as an imaginary and symbolic display of fame and power. In funeral posters, individuals have attempted to visually announce the exit of their loved ones by decorating the dead with various insignia of prestige. In doing this, families satisfy their yearning for accomplishment in their own eyes. I examine how meanings are constructed through these posters and their captions by examining the implications of a heroic figure in traditional Igbo society. The complex decorations and performativity of photos of the deceased, in light of the general proliferation of funeral posters across the length and breadth of many town and city intersections, amount to a visual spectacle that is significant in the discourse of the public sphere. The public exhibition of these funeral posters at the village intersection and the accompanying public spectatorship underscores the funeral photograph's situatedness in everyday life.

In chapter 5, I show how European colonists exported what is known as a funeral booklets, a print practice of documenting the dead, to the Lagos colony in the wake of the colonial encounter. I argue that these funeral booklets constituted a new form of the public sphere in which to announce one's presence and seek visibility. I employ the concept of intermediality to enable an understanding of how the hitherto hidden family photos reappear in funeral booklets in Nigeria. Scholarly texts on family photo albums in Africa have centered on the social meanings surrounding their collective and individual circulation in weddings or other social functions (Buckley 2000–2001; Mustafa 2002, 2005–6; Buggenhagen 2014). No known book has examined the rising practice of including family photo albums in funeral booklets and how this, in different ways, exemplifies a different photographic consumption that relies on intermediality. I show how this trend reflects a new social life of the photograph, one that advocates and emphasizes its mediatized affordances and power of affect (Spyer and Steedly 2013). I argue that in migrating from family albums into funeral booklets, photographs assume a new public life, defining meanings and shaping identities (cf. Schneider 2013) across families, communities, and national and international networks. Funeral booklets thus forge new subjectivities; they become socially itinerant actors engendering further questions around family status, aspiration, and morality (cf. Werbner 2002). Photographs printed in funeral booklets allow each family's photo album to cross the border, actively constituting the family as part of the social milieu that is sine quo non in the photographic proliferation. Thus, "The practices involved in creating personal photographic albums disrupt emergent notions of individualism" (Vokes 2012, 15) and shape family subjectivities.

In chapter 6, I provide the first substantial review of how cultural understandings of commemoration in Nigeria have been expanded through photographs and videos on social media. While the community produced the individual as an ordinary citizen whose presence is obscured in the public sphere, I argue that social media reinvented the commemorative photograph of the deceased as a hero of the internet public sphere. This realm destabilized notions of nationhood by creating an imagined community of citizens who countered the linear official narratives of nation-states. The chapter shows how the monopoly of visibility achieved by the rich in the 1990s through elite magazines such as *Ovation* was transcended by the poor through social media. In addition, I show how the Igbo culture of extravagance in funerals has been reproduced on social media. In other words, it is in the moment of sharing hitherto hidden family photos of the deceased on social media that the family exhibits its imagined prestige, influence, and venerability.

In chapter 7, I reflect on my ethnography and chronicle the methodological approach to this research by telling the stories of funeral photographers. Through storytelling, I developed a unique visual anthropology of burial and advanced theories of the funeral altar and funeral dance.

CHAPTER 2

The Public Sphere of Obituary and Commemoration in Colonial Lagos

In the 1880s, a shift in the colonial administrative policy occasioned the creation of the northern and southern "protectorates," specifically in 1882, over an area known as Nigeria today. This was an effort by the British colonial government to counter the competitiveness sparked by French colonial powers in Africa. The Berlin Conference of 1884–1885 had already defined the strict rights of European powers as to their "spheres of influence" in Africa. The northern and southern protectorates of the area known as Nigeria today were joined in 1914 by the General Frederick Lord Lugard–led colonial government to establish the Colony and Protectorate of Nigeria. But before Nigeria was created, between the 1880s and 1920s, colonial newspapers in Nigeria became a space where Africans could perform selfhood, build political alignments, and hold constituted authorities accountable. Colonial newspapers were not purely products of unequal power relations between the colonialists and Africans but a space where power was negotiated and where different groups debated colonial policies.[1]

Some of these literary practices shaped the culture of obituary publications in colonial Lagos newspapers (Peterson and Hunter 2016; Krautwald 2021, 5–28). In this chapter, I explore the significance of obituary and commemorative notices in the newspapers of nineteenth and early twentieth-century Lagos, prior to the advent of obituary photography. Employing Jürgen Habermas's concept of the public sphere, I demonstrate that obituary notices in the colonial Lagos newspapers of the nineteenth and early twentieth centuries transcended mere documentation of death. These notices also infused gossipy narratives and sensationalism, thereby shaping the colonial public sphere. This sphere was marked by insinuations of social and economic class distinctions, interspersed with occasional expressions of anti-racial and anti-colonial sentiments. I show that the colonial newspaper was a public sphere where the dead were heroized as important members of an ancestral progeniture.

A BRIEF NOTE ON COLONIAL LAGOS NEWSPAPERS

Stephanie Newell (2013) notes that newspapers are a significant source to investigate the nature of political agency and sociocultural relations in Africa. Researching obituaries in colonial newspapers advances the investigation of social histories of death in Africa. While many studies examined how death could be used to understand the changing urban, class, gender, religious, national, and ethnic identities in Africa, others focused on the multiple ways in which the dead body is produced through the print culture.[2] While Newell suggests that new forms of subjectivity were produced in colonial newspapers through anonymous writing, I argue that obituary publications allowed Africans to reassert their presence in the colonial public sphere. From the late nineteenth to the early twentieth century, African and colonial elites in Lagos used obituaries to convey their adherence to Christianity, warn of the purported dangers of the African climate to frail European bodies, and confer social value on the deceased's life. Obituaries took a variety of forms, ranging from brief announcements to elegiac poems and extensive biographical portraits that enhanced the prestige of both the departed and their living next of kin. Through these diverse print genres, Lagos's educated political and social elite asserted its prestige and status against lower-class Africans as well as European colonizers.

Colonial newspapers often depended on the patronage and approval of the imperial authorities or the missionary groups. Those who dared to challenge the censorship regime faced the risk of being shut down or silenced. Only the loyalist voices could survive and thrive in such a hostile environment (Hunter and James 2020). I studied the archives of some of these newspapers, including the *Lagos Weekly Record* (1891–1930), *Lagos Standard* (1894–1920), *Lagos Observer* (1882–1884), *Lagos Times and Gold Coast Colony Advertiser* (1880–1883), *The Mirror* (1887–1888), *The Times of Nigeria* (1914–1924), and *Nigerian Chronicle* (1908–1915).[3] The above-mentioned newspapers were under the proprietorship and editorship of educated African elites and appeared biweekly or weekly in Lagos from 1880 to 1920. The *Lagos Weekly Record* was a pioneering and influential newspaper that championed the causes of anticolonialism and African nationalism in Nigeria. It was founded and edited by John Payne Jackson, an Americo-Liberian journalist who migrated from Liberia to Lagos and became a prominent voice of the African elite. The *Lagos Standard* was established by George Alfred Williams in 1894, while the *Lagos Observer* was launched by Blackall Benjamin in 1882 with the help of Dr. Nathaniel T. King and Robert Campbell. The *Lagos Times and Gold Coast Colony Advertiser*—also known as the *Lagos Times*—was founded by Richard Blaize and edited by Andrew Thomas and Mojola Agbebi. It was one of the pioneer newspapers in Nigerian journalism, being the third newspaper in the country, following *Anglo African Newspapers* and *Iwe Iroyin. The Mirror* was a weekly paper that belonged to and was edited by P. Marke, while James Bright Davies (1848–1920) owned and edited *The Times of Nigeria*, a weekly publication that only maintained its frequency for six months. The *Nigerian Chronicle* was the first newspaper to use the word "Nigeria" in its name (Sawada 2016, 48). The publication was initiated by two siblings, Christopher and Emmanuel Johnson, who were educated in Britain and occupied prominent positions in Lagos society. The newspaper was issued weekly at their Kumola House office on Shitta Street, which also housed a high-class school. The *Nigerian Chronicle* had a distribution of four hundred to six hundred copies, each priced at three pence. The readership of these newspapers cut across the African elites and expatriates, but it is important to note that obituary advertisements were mainly from African elites, while the death of European expatriates seemed to be reported by their editors as news items due to their close relationships with them. Many of the newspapers benefited from the patronage of the colonial government and did not openly oppose the anti-African policies of the colonial administration. Whereas some newspapers such as the *Lagos Weekly Record*, the *Lagos Standard*, and the *Times of Nigeria* at times exhibited a relatively oppositional stance toward the government, all Lagos presses aligned with the British and endorsed the Allies during World War I. With the exception of the *Nigerian Chronicle*, which maintained its style and even intensified its cultural orientation and predilection for philosophical topics, the Lagos press assumed a significant role as a disseminator of British propaganda (Sawada 2016, 291).

Of course, announcing an obituary has a cultural history in precolonial West Africa. In the Igbo region of Nigeria, for example, it was usually accompanied by a loud cry in the deceased's household, a cry that was intended to draw public attention to a tragedy. Depending on the status of the deceased, it was sometimes announced through the town criers. In announcing the death of Ezeudu in Umuofia, for example, Chinua Achebe narrates how the sound of a drum and a cannon announced the death of Ezeudu, an important man in the village (Achebe 1958, 121). In a similar vein, it was reported that one night the town crier rang the *ogene*, or gong, and requested all the clansmen to gather in the market in the morning. At the gathering, Ogbuefi Ezeugo, a noted orator, announces that someone from the village of Mbaino murdered the wife of an Umuofia tribesman while she was in their market (Achebe 1958, 11). The drum brought the news of Ezeudu's death while the town crier announced the murder of the wife of an Umuofia tribesman. Thus, using the drum and the town crier to announce death exemplifies the synergistic relationship between the public and obituary announcements in precolonial Africa. Here the public was embodied in the town crier's and the drum's capacity for extensive information coverage across the communities. As a public address system through which death was announced, the town crier and the drum constituted one template for the connection between the public sphere and obituaries in precolonial Africa.[4] Local practices verbalized obituaries through many means, such as the town crier, oral praise poetry, dirges, eulogies, and other oral genres (Newell 2016, 390). McCaskie thus argues that the emergence of advertisements of death in newspapers and other printed formats and their incorporation into the local funeral rite is a ritualistic and aspirational modernity that builds upon a legacy of customary oral practice (2006, 349). Although colonial newspapers claimed to serve the public, they often became exclusive spaces for educated elites (Newell 2020). I look at the ways in which elite African newspaper editors, authors, and readers transformed obituary announcements from a public oral announcement in the village public sphere to the public sphere of print publications in colonial Lagos. Some authors have studied the printed publications that accompanied death and funerals in Africa to show how these publications transcribe oral mourning tributes, praises, and poetry into a new materialized chapter in the deceased's life (Gibbs 2005, 5; Adjah 2007, 33–44). In Lagos, obituary publication in colonial newspapers was one way through which Africans imbued death with social prestige and significance associated with the colonial modernity of the print.

In their study of newspaper obituaries in Nigeria, Rouven Kunstmann and Cassandra Mark-Thiesen have shown how the social identities and cultural conventions of the deceased and their families were maintained and affirmed in the public sphere (Kunstmann and Mark-Thiesen 2022). Death notices and obituaries disseminated social identities to a wide audience. Newell has shown how many Africans utilized the new political possibilities offered by anonymous newspaper writings in colonial Africa to assert their subjectivities, especially during the late nineteenth and early twentieth centuries. Although anonymity gave African authors certain freedoms to articulate their views, it also deprived them of the opportunity to imprint their names and announce their presence in the colonial public sphere. Obituary publications could be a means through which Africans wrote themselves back into colonial text, announced their presence in the colonial public sphere, and thereby reclaimed their subjectivity. Colonial Lagos newspapers allowed readers to participate in "debates about moral, cultural, economic, aesthetic, historical, and political issues" and helped engender a West African reading culture almost unprecedented in any other colonial setting (Newell 2013, 16). Although Lagos newspapers did not challenge colonial control, the insistence on naming the deceased and enumerating their accomplishments was an indirect riposte to colonial racism, which posited that Africans led meaningless lives that did not contribute to the development of their societies; every obituary was thus not only a monument to the deceased and their family but a beacon that signified the ingenuity, adaptability, and drive of Lagosians.

THE PUBLIC SPHERE

Jürgen Habermas has argued that a bourgeois space emerged in the eighteenth century to "mediate[] between society and state, in which the public organizes itself as the bearer or [*sic*, of] public opinion" (1974, 49). This "public sphere," according to Habermas, is a nonhierarchical setting convened within the spaces of coffee shops, salons, social clubs, and printed materials such as novels, periodicals, and pamphlets. Within these spaces, compromise and unanimous decisions are reached by means of unfettered, logical, and critical deliberation among bourgeois citizens freed from the feudal hierarchies of early modern Europe (Habermas 1991). However, this vibrant public sphere waned after the nineteenth century because of the intrusive meddlesomeness of the state and private corporations (Habermas 1991, 142). Habermas's public space differed from colonial space in fundamental ways: While one is constituted by equal, rational individuals, European colonialists defined colonial space as an environment of purportedly irrational and subhuman colonial subjects. Bart Cammaerts separates "Habermas's exemplary citizens" from colonial subjects and argues that while Habermas's citizens were "stripped of status" and "the strength of their rational arguments [was] more important than their position in society or personal wealth," African subjects of the colonial era were widely perceived by their rulers as lacking in rational capacity or civilized conduct, in need of intervention and tutelage from agents of modernity and enlightenment (Cammaerts 2008, 25–27, cited in Newell 2013, 37). Cammaerts's dichotomy allows one to see how the colonial newspaper's definition of the public could not conceive of the idea of a colonial citizen across racial boundaries.[5] Habermas used the public sphere to explore the emergence of the bourgeoisie and nation-states in the eighteenth century, a model that deviates significantly from the public discourses in precolonial and colonial societies (Bhattacharya 2005, 132). While Newell suggests that "newsprint introduced an anonymizing function" whereby "members of educated elites, school-leavers, clerks, men, women, and youth could participate in the formation of public opinion," thereby "masking the markers of social identity" (Newell 2013, 15), I contend that the newspaper obituary transcended anonymity through self-naming and the cultivation of celebrity to exclude certain classes of Africans from, while enlisting others into, the hierarchical colonial public sphere. In other words, obituary publications were one of the means through which Africans staked a claim to prestige and status in the public sphere engendered by both African- and European-owned newspapers.

Lagosians' assertion of their upper-class status through newspaper obituaries reflected both the persistence of local traditions in the public honoring of the dead as well as the wider global rise of privileged middle classes, even under colonial conditions. For example, Emma Hunter shows how the new African elite who emerged during the height of colonialism in East Africa used print media as a platform to express and spread their political visions. Hunter contends that the advent of modernity, the development of nationalism, and the global dissemination of Pan-Africanism and anti-colonial movements gave impetus to the formation of these ideas. Hunter (2018) argues that the print media produced the public sphere not just as a site of communication but also as a site of struggle and contestation over the meaning and practice of democracy, citizenship, and freedom in colonial East Africa.[6]

Further, Emma Hunter and Leslie James (2020) offer a useful model for understanding these processes as a space produced through a combination of multiple diverse forces. They argue that the colonial public sphere is constituted through the infrastructure for communication, the addressivity of cosmopolitan and local public spaces, the performativity inherent in the colonial text, and the periodicity of the printed material (Hunter and James 2020). Thus, the public sphere can become a powerful arena of social change, where diverse groups can challenge the validity of existing norms or serve the rationalization of political domination and the agency of instrumental governmentality.[7] Mrinalini Sinha (2001) has provided a counternarrative to Habermas by defining the colonial public sphere as one that produced visible differences of race and whiteness deployed to engender social inclusion, social ineligibility, or subalternity. Drawing on Sinha's work, I argue that the newspaper obituary served as a central space where the social statuses of colonial elites were further reinforced and advertised and where different educated African elites sought visibility for their families.

HEROES IN OBITUARY REPORTS

One dimension, among others, in which Lagosians asserted their presence in the colonial sphere was through Christian obituaries in the newspapers. The Lagos Christian community dealt with the exigency of death through their belief that death was simply a pathway to heaven rather than an everlasting parting from loved ones. The notion of salvation made accepting death as a peaceful end easier. Publicly advertised obituaries, such as newspaper obituaries, helped reinforce the notion of religious camaraderie necessary for the eternal salvation of the departed. In this manner, many obituaries were deemed to elicit greater interest from the Christian community than the adherents of African religions and thus were preoccupied with Christian sentiments. Reporting the obituary of Chief Okenla, the *Lagos Observer* of September 14, 1882, wrote, "The Christians of Abeokuta and ourselves have sustained an irreparable loss in the death of their hero, Chief Okenla."[8] Here the Christians of Abeokuta were mentioned as the first bearers of the irreparable loss of Chief Okenla. In this way, the newspaper suggests that Christians were first positioned to suffer the crushing pains of loss and were privileged in the hierarchy of public emotions in obituary reports in Lagos.

Likewise, reporting the obituary of Miss Elfrida Esther Thomas, the *Lagos Observer* of September 13, 1883, carefully analyzed how Thomas discharged her duties: "It is well known that in the performance of her duties as a Sunday School Teacher, before her departure for Europe and after her return, she acted always with energy, self-denial, and devotion." The introduction of

"Sunday school," "self-denial," and "devotion" may underline the preponderance of Christian rhetoric and its attendant sympathy in most obituaries of these periods. Even while narrating the roles played by the deceased in traditional institutions, languages that subtly implied Christian virtues were introduced. Efforts to evangelize and convert the locals were part of the colonializing missions and were often seen to interject most colonial correspondences not just in obituary reports but in other endeavors of life. The *Lagos Observer* wrote: "John Owolotan, or Okenla as he is called, was made a Chief Warrior of all the Abeokuta Christians in 1960." The use of "Chief Warrior" seems to mimic the prevailing description of individuals notable for leading wars quite prevalent in Yorubaland during the nineteenth and early twentieth centuries. It was fashionable to describe specific individuals as "heroes," "great," or "chief warriors" to capture their outstanding roles in these Yoruba wars.[9]

The importing of war slogans into obituaries was to foreground the impactful Christian life of the deceased and emphasize why it is more significant than any other narrative. Reporting the death of Chief Okenla, the *Lagos Observer* wrote, "From all accounts he died of heart disease, not as is being circulated by the superstitious and ignorant, that his death is traceable to the diabolical machinations which they suppose resulted from his bold defiance of the heathen Chief Ogudipe, in his late attempt to persecute the Christians."[10] From this report, it was evident that the *Lagos Observer* was opposed to the purported "heathenism" of local religious beliefs. The tensions seen in such clashes between Christianity and traditional beliefs were even disseminated through obituaries. It is possible to conclude that newspaper obituaries were vehicles of evangelism deployed by the elite converts to oppose local thoughts they often perceived as rooted in "idolatrous" practices, "paganistic" backwardness, and superstition.

OBITUARIES AND NUANCES OF CLASS AND STATUS IN THE PUBLIC SPHERE

The vibrant intellectual atmosphere ignited in the Lagos colony by these newspapers came with a new definition of the public sphere. This was a commodified form of the public sphere, dependent on payment, that constructed a certain class status in the editorial pages of most of the newspapers. For example, a select public for obituaries was included under the strict terminology of "Advertisement." On page 3 of the *Lagos Times*, February 23, 1920, there was a rubric titled "Advertisement" where the price of subscription for various advertisements was published. It reads, "Twelve lines and under, 5s. Every additional line 6d, In Memoriam 4s, Birth 5s, Thanks for Sympathy 4s, One single column 25s, one-half column 15s, One-quarter column 10s, One-eight column 5s."[11] On another edition of the *Times* in 1915, a different subscription rate was provided for advertisements: "Advertisers scale—Five lines and under 2s. 6d., and 6d per line afterward for one insertion. Births, Marriages. Deaths, Thanks for Sympathy, for one insertion, 2s. 6d. rates for Contract Advertisement which can be arranged for."[12] 6d was a day's salary of a carpenter, a low-income government employee, or a blacksmith (Sawada 2016, 81). The newspaper itself sold for three pence. It was assumed, therefore, that publishing five lines of an obituary cost two shillings in 1915, while twelve lines cost five shillings in 1920.[13]

What this means is that anyone publishing more than five lines in 1915 would have paid an additional fee of six pence. The newspapers thus created a prestigious and class-exclusive public space for the dead. One way newspapers constructed this space was through longer poems to remember the dead. Longer poems were also published in the "In Memoriam" columns to remember the dead. While these poems were sometimes too long, and their subscription considered unaffordable due to their exorbitant subscription fees, they were thought to be published at the discretion of the editors who had a personal acquaintanceship with the deceased. The reading public was furnished with citations of poetry about death and loss from verses and lines from hymns such as "Brief Life Is Here Our Portion," "The Saints of God, Their Wanderings Done," and "For the Soul[s] Thou Holdest Dearest, Let Prayers Arise" (Sawada 2016, 169; Newell 2022, 401). A close study of the newspapers suggests that the length of the obituaries strictly adhered to the newspaper's subscription rates. Thus, it was thought that only the wealthy could afford such prices to either publish or be published in the "In Memoriam" section. Because of this overly constraining financial factor, the less affluent restricted their obituaries to only a few lines. Even though many obituaries were defined by textual brevity because of financial constraints, within these few lines, the essential elements of the dead's social class were highlighted. For example, the *Times of Nigeria* reported these obituaries: "Dissu Martins: Prosperous merchant of Martins Street, died at his farm, Yaba Road, Wednesday, 11th Instant. Member of the Ansaru-un-Deen, famous Muslim Society of Lagos. Aged, about 60 years."[14] The *Times of Nigeria* would employ similar prestigious wording in narrating the obituary of the late Rowland

Cole, the Sierra Leonean who was the former postmaster general of the Gold Coast. It described Cole as "a successful man of business" whose wife assisted in "conducting a very prosperous trade while he was in the public service."[15]

An analysis of these lines indicates that while the obituary announcement of the late Martins is just five lines, it captured his most prestigious attribute and framed his social capital with such phrases as "prosperous merchant" and "famous Muslim Society of Lagos." These words of admiration immediately identified Martins's social worth. On the same page of the newspaper, the obituary of James Alfred Agbaje, which is just seven lines, identified him as "a prominent citizen of Lagos" and father of "Dr. Savage and Mr. Spencer Savage" who "retired after a long and flourishing business career."[16] While the space is constraining to allow for an expanded narrative of Agbaje's social worth, the insertion of his educated son, Dr. Savage, ascribes that flair of class and social importance to his persona. He would immediately be associated with a class of what is known as *baba dokita* in the Yoruba language, meaning "doctor's father." In the African context, the social worth of parents is often measured by the success of their children, while children are often considered wealth in certain local parlance. Yoruba popular thoughts have reinforced "the superiority of children over wealth," such that "success or wealth, without children among the Yoruba, is either incomplete or devalued" (Omobowale et al. 2019, 22).

Among the Igbo, the local idiom *nze bu na nwa* means "The child exudes chiefly authority," while *Nwakaego* translates as "The child is worth more than money." The importance of wealth and power in colonial Lagos is evidenced by the omission of the poor and powerless who are not connected with the newspaper publishers and editors from the public sphere convened by obituary pages in most newspapers of the eras under study. Where the obituary publication of an individual exceeded certain prescribed subscription lines, it was assumed that the individual was wealthy or might have a certain familial relationship with the editor or publisher. However, some obituaries were obviously published out of the discretion of the publisher or editors, perhaps because of the position the individual occupied among the elite circles. This editorial preference for some obituary publications, according to Sawada, is sometimes informed by the African custom of paying homage to deceased heroes and "great men." Editors deployed poetry and sensationalism to define their subjective meanings of heroism in the obituary, while moderate-income Lagosians seized the opportunity offered by the cheaper, short-verse subscriptions in the "In Memoriam" section to inscribe their late wives, parents, spouses, and Western-educated Africans into the public sphere. Authors drew on poetry printed in hymnbooks, religious pamphlets, or other academic texts to memorialize loved ones and family members who were not public figures (Sawada 2016, 164–169).

Lay writers used the medium of newspaper print to memorialize loved ones and insert them into the public sphere convened by these newspapers. Obituaries were either presented in the form of short announcements, poems, or lengthy biographical writing where names of surviving relatives were mentioned to give social worth to the deceased's life. On Saturday, December 24, 1887, *The Mirror* reported the death of Mr. Martins, the keeper of the Jubilee Restaurant, under the "News Item" section. The report mentioned Mr. Martins as only the keeper of the Jubilee Restaurant, without mentioning his family; nor did it mention his father, mother, or siblings or any other information that would identify and accord him that social recognition. The report only stated that "he had been assisting in serving out refreshments to those who attended the conventions at Phoenix Hall up to within a few minutes of his death."[17] The obituary did not provide any significant family information that would elevate his social standing. This obituary was published under the "News Item" section of the newspaper rather than the "Advertisement" section, where most obituaries were subscribed with money. This suggests that it might have been published at the discretion of the editor and did not emanate from Mr. Martin's relatives—a logical reason why no name of any of his family members was included. The "News Item" section contains short news deemed less weighty than items to be given sustained attention by the newspaper editors. There are other short news pieces contained in this section. The brevity of Mr. Martins' obituary announcement may not constitute the condescending tenor of the obituary as reported by the editor but rather the omission of his social accomplishment. The style of reportage, therefore, seemed consistent with his social class (he was a bartender in the Phoenix restaurant). Its terseness did not capture salient aspects that were given attention in the shorter obituaries subscribed in the "Advertisement" sections, such as his children, parents, or a brief sensational remark on the cause of a person's death and his life's accomplishments. Perhaps he was not married and had no children, but the omission of his parents' names may be interpreted as a sign of social anonymity in the African context, while the absence of his obituary in the "Advertisement" section indicated that it was not subscribed. The meaning of subscription here suggests that families used money to negotiate for presence in the public sphere.

At the same time, some Africans invoked prestigious pedigrees to posthumously make up for marginalization in the colonial public sphere. In the obituary of Africans, there seems to be a tendency to mention the highly placed children, parents, or relatives of the deceased to pronounce their social worth. For example, the *Nigerian Times* of April 5, 1910, reported the death of Charles Randall Cole on March 28 and identified him as a native of Yorubaland along with his wife Berky, as well as his parents, who were also noted as "natives of Yorubaland." The *Nigerian Times* mentioned Cole's siblings and noted that his parents were enslaved in Sierra Leone but returned to Lagos in the 1860s. The newspaper reported that all six members of the family had died, leaving only an elder daughter of Charles Randall Cole "who survives them all and who is mourning the irreparable loss of members of her kindred."[18] The obituary took a historic leap into Cole's life's journey, how he was ill for four months and eventually "succumbed to his illness."[19]

The need to capture the family genealogy was in line with the tendency of Africans to launder the family's history in eulogies. Naming all deceased relatives allows Africans to reexamine and reconnect with ancestral genealogy and advertise the family's long-forgotten glories and credentials. Marleen de Witte sees the listing of surviving family members as an indication of social success, for the names reveal a network of dependents and influence (2011, 184). Sometimes it serves to recall the gift of longevity. While the manner and narrative of the obituary reportage of the less affluent Lagosians may convey an idea of unfortunate brevity, certain elements were introduced to poignantly foreground their social class. The *Lagos Weekly Record* of June 18–25, 1921, reports, "Not lost but gone before. The Home call came to Miss Caroline Adenike Fashanu at 1.30 PM on Tuesday the 21st instant, daughter of Mr. J. A. FASHANU, of 30 Martins Street, Lagos."[20] J. A. Fashanu was an important member of the Lagos colony who was also an active member of the Lagos Branch of the National Congress of British West Africa and a committee member of the West African National Conference (Olusanya 1968, 325). By mentioning the late Adenike father's name, the family placed emphasis on the humanizing attribute of Adenike's obituary and strongly articulated it through her father's name. One assumes that a mention of late Adenike's other family members would have been possible if space were sufficient. For example, in the *Lagos Standard* of February 20, 1895, the publication of the death of "Madam Martha Meroke on Wednesday the 13th instant" mentioned that she was the grandmother of Mrs. Mojola Agbebi of Bamboo House, Race Course, and great-grandmother of Rev. E. M. Lijadu, Agent of the C. M. S., at Ode, Ondo.[21] Meroke's longevity marked a salient component in the public memory of her death, as seen from the conscious attempt to canonize her centenarian status. To underscore Meroke's longevity, the newspaper deemed it necessary to notify the public that her daughter, Grace, passed on at seventy, before Meroke. The mention of Meroke's daughter, granddaughter, and great-granddaughter seemed a deliberate editorial choice to emphasize the nature of social status that progeny can bestow upon the deceased. In this instance, the three-generational progeny foreground not just Meroke's age and social worth but suggest how her children value progeniture.

Even while reporting obituaries in a very short, single-line sentence, the periodicals squeezed in the social worth of human life. For example, on page 3 of the *Nigerian Chronicle* of December 2, 1910, even though the obituary of Hon. J. Mensah Sarbah B. L. C. M. G. was reported in just a single line, the social worth of his life was captured by mentioning that he was "an unofficial member of the Gold Coast Legislature." To underline the importance of class and to prove that mention of the legislature was not in itself satisfactorily socially elevating for Sarbah's social class, on December 9, 1910, the *Nigerian Chronicle* singled out J. Mensah Sarbah's death, among the three reported in the previous edition, for a detailed, lengthy elucidation. Titled, "The Late Hon J. Mensah Sarbah," the article notes,

> The news of the death of the Hon'ble J. Mensah Sarbah C. M. G. Senior unofficial member of the Legislative Council of the Gold Coast Colony which reached us as we go to press last week created a very deep feeling. It was only a few months ago that we were congratulating the Sister Colony on the recognition bestowed upon her by the conferring of a Companionship of the Order of St. Michael and St. George upon her illustrious son Mensah Sarbah. In congratulating the Colony then, we felt that we are doing honour to our own selves as men of the stamp of Mr. Sarbah are not the property of one Colony but the common property of West Africans. By these achievements the outside world has been able to see to what intellectual and moral heights the West African can rise. His writings have enriched English literature as far as a native can contribute to it. His "Fanti Customary Laws" is now the acknowledged authority in Legal circle on Gold Coast customs and laws. Mr. Sarbah had lived a strenuous life and lived for his country. His sudden removal is to us a national calamity which we all mourn.[22]

The above indicated that the *Nigerian Chronicle* had initially treated Sarbah's obituary scantily, alongside others, "last week" because the news arrived belatedly as the newspaper was "about to go to press." However, in the subsequent edition, the death was extracted from the seemingly less newsworthy obituaries and given sustained attention. Of course, not all obituaries were published in colonial newspapers. It is assumed that those obituaries that made it to the newspapers were deemed important and recognized. In another example, the *Nigerian Chronicle* of December 2, 1910, articulated the social worth of Mrs. Sarah Abraham's obituary through a mention of her son, Mr. I. E. Abraham of Broad Street.[23] This suggests that the son may have placed the obituary advert. The above two obituaries seem to underscore either their subjects' class, wealth, status, or affiliation with an important institution in the Lagos colony.

ACCOMPANYING THE DEAD TO THE OBITUARY PUBLIC SPHERE

I have attempted to identify instances where the elite public sphere was constituted by individuals who possessed the financial means to "advertise" their deceased in colonial newspapers. In her study of Yoruba print culture in the early twentieth century, Karin Barber has demonstrated how Yoruba newspapers in the 1920s Lagos convened a progressive citizenry, equal in status on the printed page (Barber 2006, 29; 2007). In contrast, I argue that Lagosians displayed wealth and social status through references to progeny and social connections. Similarly, de Witte (2011) has employed the concept of "wealth in people" to illustrate how the numerous names of people displayed on funeral posters could be used as a mark of achievement. Dependents are powerful criteria to measure social responsibility and clout in Africa. The dependents of the big man and other recipients of his benefaction, more often than not, constituted the followers of the big man, and listing them in newspaper obituary seems a subtle strategy for announcing one's social accomplishments. Therefore, the newspaper obituary unveils a fruitful interplay between the social conspicuousness of the wealthy and the surrounding gaze of eulogizing adherents (Nwafor 2021, 85). The bereaved see the public sphere of the newspaper as a space that can bestow prestige upon the deceased and their families, while the narrative style and length of the obituary serve as a means through which this prestige could be exhibited and articulated.

Thus, colonial newspaper obituaries highlight the versatility of African societies in adapting to the colonial modernity of the print while safeguarding and continuing their most cherished cultural institutions. Despite the adoption of a seemingly new medium (the newspaper), African/Yoruba practices of wealth in people remained largely unchanged. The concept of wealth in people may provide ample room for further critical interrogation of the concept of the crowd and wealth in Yoruba cosmology. Jane Guyer deploys the concept of "wealth in people" to encapsulate the nature of studies of wealth in precolonial African societies. Some studies on wealth in precolonial Africa have touched on "the techniques by which pre-colonial war-lords built up, motivated and remunerated their followings," especially given the fact that the concept of followership is broad enough to apply to, for example, "wives, children, clients, political followers, religious acolytes, titled associates, occupational apprentices and so on" (Guyer 1995, 89). Whether living or dead, the Yoruba concept of the big man is measured by the number and rank of the individuals who associate with the big man and particularly who accompany him wherever he goes (Bascom 1951). The names of surviving relatives who accompany the deceased in the obituary publication reflect the cultural and social completeness sought in the public sphere of the newspaper obituary. In this way, obituaries in the media would surpass the mere act of chronicling facts. Rather, they might disseminate a particular ideology to their mass audiences. In Yoruba cosmology, the prestige of the elite is measured by the size of the dependent crowd (Cole 1975).

Patrick Cole noted that "emphasis was placed not only on how much an individual had but also on how much of it he was ready to redistribute as largesse among his followers and others around him" (Cole 1975, 199). Thus, when certain individuals die, they are immediately perceived in the light of a dignifying, transcendental, and heroic persona. Like an ancestor who is spiritually ubiquitous, such deceased individuals must also make a ubiquitous presence through many spectacular public avenues. Newspaper obituaries thus may become one of those avenues seen in this context as an extension of the Yoruba cultural belief in the physical and spiritual transcendence, expansion, and heroization of the dead.[24]

The above narratives are quite expository of new understandings of visibility, especially through the rituals of newspaper obituaries. These obituaries were strategically conditioned to participate in the political discourses of the public sphere. In Yorubaland, part of the political discourses of the public sphere revolves around procreation, wealth, and the heroic attributes of the advertised persona. Heroic tendencies are underscored by their association with the capacity of the families to prove that their deceased was a hero. Newspaper obituaries became a means of achieving this.

CONCLUSION

While the public anonymity of print allowed correspondents and columnists to achieve equality, as argued by Newell, obituaries enabled them to define class hierarchies and race. Key to the emergence of a new class of elite society through the high rate of subscription, the newspaper obituary advertisements thus excluded the poor from this public sphere. A class hierarchy was introduced, one that seemed to deviate from the Habermasian public sphere. The newspaper obituaries defied the model of the Habermasian bourgeoisie public and charted a different notion of the public characterized by a rhetoric of class, progeny, and wealth. The newspaper became a signboard for the public advertisement of family credentials by the editors and the surviving relatives.

The politics of visibility and conspicuousness constitute salient features of obituary announcements. Newspaper obituaries during the colonial period took death into the public sphere. Causes of death would do more than just chronicle medical facts; they also offered glimpses into colonial attitudes about the African environment and colonial policies as well as revealed sentiments toward the colonial mission of enlightenment and Christianization. Thus, obituaries examined in this study were analyzed in terms of their relationship to the public sphere. In conclusion, it would be apt to suggest that the colonial style of obituary announcement recognized the kinship network in the African context and, as such, included the surviving children and relatives of the deceased in the announcement. Perhaps the European lifestyle of individualism determined the pattern of an obituary notice of Europeans where mention was not made of their deceased relatives. In bringing the obituary into the newspaper public sphere, death was returned to its precolonial African context as collective grief and participatory mourning.

While this chapter examined newspaper obituary announcements as a means through which Lagos residents of the late nineteenth and early twentieth centuries negotiated visibility in the public sphere, reaffirming a commemorative tradition invested in cultural notions of heroism, chapter 3 will explore similar attitudes in memorial photographs. It will evaluate the roles of memorial photography in the pursuit of heroism while tracking the cosmopolitan politics that attended the negotiation of the public sphere in colonial Lagos. Within this politics, I will explore how Elizabeth Edwards's concept of materiality serves as an appropriate theoretical framework that is at the core of sartorial and socioaesthetic practices of early photography in colonial Lagos.

CHAPTER 3

A Cult of Attention

Memorial Photography in Nineteenth and Early Twentieth-Century Lagos

In nineteenth and early twentieth-century Lagos, commemorative photographs were entangled in the colonial discourses of power, prestige, and class. A death or anniversary of death became one of the most reported events that also constituted part of the existential infrastructures of colonial governmentality. Commemoration extended beyond the discourses of remembrance to foreground the institutionalization of colonial policies on the imperial outposts. Colonial newspapers frequently called for subscriptions to enable the printing, framing, enlargement, and mounting of commemorative photographs in Glover Memorial Hall which was one of the first memorial halls in colonial Lagos, Nigeria. Sometimes commemorative photographs were printed in almanacs or other surfaces and presented to the public for sale. Commemorative photographs were usually unveiled with grand ceremonial fanfare performed by important colonial officials, such as the governor or deputy governor, inside Glover Memorial Hall. This chapter begins by tracing the deployment of memorial photographs within quotidian events and other modes of visuality practiced by colonized subjects. It explores how such photographs were circulated on the parlor walls of the colonized as gifts that are invested with the moral significance of religious piety, virtue, and memory. The discussion then reviews the broader dissemination of these commemorative photographs across everyday surfaces such as almanacs, earthenware, pamphlets, and magazines. This visual proliferation, I argue, played a crucial role in shaping discourses of public attention and in reconfiguring the commemorative public sphere. The chapter further examines the intensification of journalistic engagement with this phenomenon in colonial Lagos newspapers—a rhetorical strategy that ultimately contributed to the symbolic reconstitution of Glover Memorial Hall. Within this practice, the concept of the public sphere gained deepened interpretive valence, culminating in what I conceptualize as a 'cult of attention.' Finally, I ask: How do the activities of subscription and unveiling contribute to our understanding of the colonial public sphere? What social and political messages emerge when the unveiling of the commemorative photograph is presented as a spectacular and performative public event?

THE COLONIAL CITIZEN'S PHOTO GIFT

Colonized people began to exchange photos through different channels to either inaugurate a prominent citizen into the public domain or to commemorate a significant deceased figure. For instance, portraits of church ministers who passed away were produced through a subscription by members and sold among members. While this was a way to ensure the spread of evangelism and the entrenchment of moral principles that attended Christian ministration, it also occasioned a new kind of visual culture in the colonies, in which memorial photographs became part of the "things that matter" in mourning and the memorial process.

Photos of church ministers were sold to Christian devotees. In most Christian homes, the parlor walls were described as befitting surfaces for these photos of church ministers and expected to form part of the emotional economies of religious devotion, conviviality, and familial relationships. As noted by Brody (1974), similar practices were found elsewhere in the Western world, where parlor walls were used for advertising success achieved through international family networks. The colonial parlor wall became a powerful surface where family lives were curated and significant memories were reconstituted. On the parlor wall, as a visual cemetery, portraits of deceased church ministers and family members coexisted. The presentation of deceased relatives was also common on nineteenth-century American parlor walls, as described by Ruby (1995).

The fields of visual history and material anthropology are intertwined with the mutual construction of social relations and cultural values. Thus, to truly grasp the social dynamics and historical significance around commemorative photography, one must also comprehend the complexity of material culture, for it is a constituent factor of sociohistorical relations (Miller and Tilley 1996,

6). Following Elizabeth Edwards's concept of photographic materialities, one observes an increasing "analytical interest in the socio-material practices of photography" and "the agency of objects in human relations" (2009, 135).[1] Here things such as photographs emerge as powerful and active players, extending or replacing embodied experiences and connecting with spiritual ones, such as, in the present case, a unique kind of memory embedded on the material surfaces of things. Pierre Bourdieu established the foundational premise of the sociomaterial practices of photography in the 1960s, enabling a more recent reformulation by photography theorists interested in material cultures and the anthropology of photography.[2] The dialogue between the photograph and everyday tangible surfaces such as parlor walls, almanacs, earthenware, and other materials has yet to be thoroughly examined by scholars. Daniel Miller suggests that our contemplation should transcend the mere symbolism of objects, which he believes favors a more rational engagement. Instead, he insists we should ponder the concepts of historical longing, "how things matter," and the "things that matter." He proposes that the concept of "mattering" carries a broader, more emotive connotation, one that more readily guides us to the lived experiences of the subjects, thereby creating room for personal perspectives (Miller 1998, 3, 11).

DISSEMINATING SURFACES FOR MEMORIAL PHOTOGRAPHS

By dwelling upon the more mundane sensory and material surfaces of banal objects such as almanacs, walls, earthenware, pamphlets, or magazines, we can untangle their more subtle connections with commemorative photography. How these surfaces are culturally, religiously, and socially objectified and animated through their material connections with the photograph needs to be further disentangled (Miller 1998, 9). More analytical insights could be gained from how mundane materials accumulate meaning over time, especially as they emerge from a deep intersection of value and materiality. Edwards (2009, 136) argues that "thinking about photographs in this way reveals them to be not merely symbols of the past, a generic form of pastness, but material forms that arise out of the intersection of experiences and imaginings of the past." My aim here is to demonstrate what Edwards describes as "active materiality," and to expand on the significance of active materiality in the colonial and postcolonial contexts. Debates surrounding their accuracy, verisimilitude, truthfulness, and authority were mired in the technical complexity of their production. In this chapter, I am interested in returning the material back to the center of historical discourse and elucidation, for according to Edwards (2009, 136), "It is the material that shapes existences and experiences."[3] Hence, the camera, photo chemicals, colors, and the printing processes were all entangled in the meaning of commemorative photographs. And while the parlor walls embodied deeper sociocultural histories of the colonial state and family units, many other surfaces acted as important channels that transported the memorial photograph's unique aura across time and space. Ultimately, these surfaces constituted the public spheres where the visual politics of prestige and cosmopolitan selfhood played out.

In Walter Benjamin's "The Work of Art in the Age of Mechanical Reproduction" ([1968] 1985d) aura is lost when the original image is mass produced, but in this chapter, we see how memorial photographs imprinted on banal surfaces in the early twentieth-century Lagos retained their aura (Richard 2011, 123). Howells (2011, 123) has challenged Benjamin's auratic theorization of the copied image by suggesting that "he failed to delve deeply enough into the ontology of the photographic image. For, while a painting or an engraving might be a work of total imagination or invention, the photograph is linked umbilically (no matter how distantly) to its subject matter; a subject matter which existed in time and space and upon whose physical existence at the moment of inception the photograph is inevitably dependent." For this reason, Howells (2011, 123) concludes that "the photograph's analogous relationship to the third-class holy relic in its religious sense is a source of its power, and not weakness." Howell's position enables us to understand how the materiality of the memorial photograph, its tangible thingness, was invested with multiple significations of power and subjectivities.

The surface upon which a commemorative photograph was imprinted did not appear to diminish the profound sense of reverence and awe elicited by the image. For example, an article in Sierra Leonean *Weekly News* of March 7, 1896, states: "We have received two samples earthenware plates beautifully made, on one of which is printed the picture of the late Sir John Pope Hennessy, K.C.M.G., and the words underneath it, 'The poor Man's Friend,' as a memento of the relief granted to the poorer inhabitants of the Colony in 1872." The newspaper further states, "Those who did not know Sir John in person will now have the pleasure of seeing his picture." There is a suggestive comparison between Sir John's physical presence and "his picture" such that "seeing his picture" would compensate for the lack of acquaintanceship with him during his lifetime. Photographs serve as a tangible connection to the departed, capturing their essence and acting as a direct representation. This quality of evoking presence in absence underscores their role as meaningful artifacts. The earthenware embodies the new familiarity offered by Pope Hennessy's image and becomes a vessel for family memories, attaining value beyond its function.

Upon the death of Reverend T. Truscott in Sierra Leone, a small-format photograph was sent to friends and reprinted in a brochure containing a eulogy. Both the photograph and the brochure were then also announced as available for sale in newspapers. The *Weekly News* of April 20, 1889, reports:

> A beautiful and true likeness of the late Rev. T. Truscott, was sent to us during the week. It is a *carte de visite* vignette likeness under which are the words "In Memoriam." The numerous friends and admirers of this beloved minister, who will like to have something to look at of "him whom they love"' will be pleased, no doubt, to know that a few copies of this excellent photograph can be obtained at a shilling a copy from the Rev. W. Vivian, Acting General Superintendent of the U.M.F.C.[4]

The *Lagos Weekly Record* (LWR) of November 4, 1893, in an article titled "In Memoriam address of the late Rev T. Truscott," states, "We have received from the author, Rev. William Vivian, a copy of an In Memoriam address bearing the above title and delivered at the unveiling of the Truscott Memorial Tablet in Centenary Tabernacle Church, Sierra Leone." According to the newspaper, the brochure contains on its opening page a beautiful vignette picture of the Rev T. Truscott, and the last page displays an illustration of the Memorial Tablet "erected by the Native Christians among whom he labored." The newspaper stated that in Sierra Leone and neighboring places, "Truscott can never die." While eulogizing his memorable efforts at raising the Christian congregation in the colony, the LWR, just like its *Weekly News* counterpart, urged the Christian community to imprint Truscott's memory on the sands of time by purchasing "the Memorial Address at 3d a copy from the Methodist Book Room, Broad Street, and at Mr. S. A Cole's, opposite Tanimehin House." In these articles it is evident that photographs, their circulation and viewing—also at cost—were strongly intertwined with narratives of memorialization and notions of immortality.

Such a practice of purchasing a popular figure's *carte de visite* had been prevalent in Western Europe during the nineteenth century and was now being introduced in the colonies. As the imperial capitalist system expanded, its technologies were spread. The death of the minister, thus, became an occasion to possess his "excellent" photograph in admiration of his fond memories.

In another interesting example, the LWR of November 16, 1901, reported that the people of Lagos proposed the distribution of copies of the *West Africa Magazine* of September 14, 1901, at their town hall meeting because it contained the photographs of Sir Alfred Jones. According to the article, the photos in the magazine afforded those present at the meeting the opportunity to appreciate Sir Jones's much-applauded goodness. The LWR remarked that "the picture of Sir Alfred Jones will be carefully preserved by many" and that even the white cap chiefs, the Lemomu, and others also showed delight and testified their appreciation of this photograph in the magazine. In corroboration of my claim that the material specificity of the medium did not compromise the photograph's potential to provoke a response among viewers, it is clear that Sir Alfred's photo was the only reason for the magazine's purchase and distribution among members. The statement that "the picture of Sir Alfred Jones will be carefully preserved by many" seems to suggest that the memorial photograph incited the citizens' desire to preserve history and that the insignificant and transient status of the magazine had been elevated and bestowed with significance due to its photographic content.

OBITUARY PHOTOS IN ALMANACS

Announcing the publication of the Nigerian almanac of 1911, *The Times of Nigeria* of December 1910 noted that "the almanac came with the usual quota of reproduction of photographs of local subjects," and that it "deserves to occupy a place on the wall of every household throughout the country."[5] The almanac was a genre of the British Atlantic world. By the mid-nineteenth century, Europeans and Americans had begun circulating promotional pictorial calendars to advertise their products (Aronson 2017, 310). Colonial printers inherited the form of the text from an established British model and imitated popular British authors and titles. Colonial readers shared much with British readers as well. They could all read a complicated calendar table, would recognize many of the same titles, and probably shared a similar understanding of astronomy. By consuming titles and authors that mimicked British models and sharing the same historical calendar that formed the foundation for British identity, colonial citizens of Lagos reimagined and reinvented themselves as part of a broader British Atlantic reading community. Calendars and almanacs were eventually reinvented in the colonies to serve commemorative purposes.

The *Lagos Standard* of May 26, 1906, reported: "The thanks of the editors go to the great African firm of Adeshigbin Sons & Co of Lagos, West Africa, who are the sole agents on the West Coast of a well-known Singer Sewing Machine Company, in this country, for a handsome calendar containing a beautiful picture of the African Prince Eleko and his white cap chiefs, and to our old and valued friend Dr. Mojola Agbebi, M.A. PHD for an illustrated copy of the Southern Nigerian Almanac." The *Lagos Standard* extolled his "fertile brain, and a most valuable contribution to African literature." Often, compliments directed toward almanac publishers were essentially linked to the almanac containing either a commemorative photograph or an image of a notable figure. For example, in announcing the publication of the *Southern Nigerian Almanac* of 1909, the LWR mentioned that it contains the "pictures of Alake of Abeokuta, Prince Eleko and the white cap chiefs, late chief Kuka of Ijebu Ode, Late chief Dada, Bale of Ibadan, the Oba of Ilesha Chief Ogedengbe the famous war chief and members of the Ijesha Council, among others."[6] A single copy of the almanac was sold for six pence. Likewise, the *Lagos Standard* of June 2, 1909, while acknowledging the 1909 almanac from the firm of Gustav H. Griesbauer, a firm represented in Lagos by J. L. Euba, Esq., commented that "the Alamance will make an attractive wall."[7] In the *Lagos Standard* of January 13, 1914, the same Adeshigbin Sons of Lagos was eulogized for printing a calendar "presenting . . . the faithful picture of the late Rev. M. L. Stone."[8] Similarly, the *Lagos Standard* of Wednesday, September 23, 1909, specifically has a title, "Almanack for 1909," and a very short accompanying text: "at Tawakaliatu Rabi Store on Martins Street opposite the entrance to Raymond House, Almanacks containing the Picture of the late King Tofa of Porto Novo for 1909."[9] In the brief texts of the 1909 and 1914 newspapers, there appears to be a deliberate effort to underscore the photos of "the late Rev. M. L. Stone" and "the late King Tofa of Porto Novo for 1909" as the ultimate reasons for announcing the publication of the almanacs. This emphasis suggests a strategic prioritization of these individuals' commemorative photos to enhance the almanac's public appeal. From the above, it was evident that commemorative photographs were a significant factor in the public consumption and popularity of almanacs. Discerning critics, in fact, condemned almanacs that lacked high-quality commemorative images. A good example can be seen in a letter to the editor of the *Lagos Observer* of March 2, 1882, by one Paulinus, titled "Mr. Bright's Almanac." Paulinus complained extensively about how he felt on receiving a copy of Mr. Bright's Almanac for that year, which contained a lithograph of "the ever-to-be-lamented Rev. T. B. Macauley." Paulinus complained of the ingratitude shown to the late minister by his former pupils for not "paying tribute to the memory of one who, whether taken as a minister of the Gospel or as the instructor of youths, has ever been faithful and just." He particularly mentioned how some individuals took to "criticizing the picture, feature by feature, and have discovered possibilities of improvement." These critics, however, were ignorant of the very distinct processes, "different from photography [which] the picture was made from." During this time, the technological processes involved in printing a photograph in a newspaper often left a hazy black-and-white impression that made it difficult to differentiate a hand-drawn print from a photograph. He remarked that while "photography is but the shadow of the object impressed by the agency of the sun," making its features more faithfully reproduced, the lithographic process was liable to deviations because it was the result of manual labor. In spite of the picture's shortcomings, the almanac quickly sold out. Paulinus saw this public demand for the almanac as a sign of public appreciation to Mr. Bright for presenting them with the "memento of a good and pious countryman as well as for undertaking singlehanded and unaided to accomplish what should have been done by a less grateful public." Throughout the article, Paulinus refers constantly to "the public" as the sphere in which memorialization ought to take place and in which, in this case, a laudable effort has been made that nonetheless falls short. It is crucial to consider the rationale behind Paulinus's detailed explanation of the distinction between lithographs and photographs. In the early twentieth century, the intersection of human agency and materiality in photography constituted a crucial discursive parameter in newspaper advertisements of photographic studios. For example, in the advertisement in the *Lagos Standard* of Wednesday, June 11, 1913, there is a comparison between photo enlargements and oil painting.

> The most beautiful ornament in your home is the Artistic Enlargement of a picture of some one who is dear to you—Send us your picture and Cash as under and we will send you immediately Entirely Free one of our most artistic enlargement which is equal to any Oil Painting. Send us your picture today. Right Now while you think of it. G.T. Koerner Nachif., Asstd., Hamburg Photo Studios, Hamburg 36.[10]

Between 1900 and 1940, Europe experienced what is frequently termed the "golden era" of hand-colored photography. During this period, hand-colored photographs emerged as cherished wedding gifts and favored souvenirs for other events. By simply submitting a photograph, individuals could receive a life-size colored print in return (Burns 1995). One would have understood the reason why the advert in *Lagos Standard* was specific in emphasizing, "Send us your picture and Cash . . . and we will send you immediately Entirely Free one of our most artistic enlargement which is equal to any Oil Painting." Initially, these life-size portraits were produced using large cameras; however, the advent of the solar enlarger in 1857 significantly improved the quality of these images (Henisch 1996). Moreover, studios like Hamburg employed advanced printing techniques, such as platinum or palladium printing, which endowed photographs with a broader tonal range and a painterly quality. These prints, renowned for their rich, subtle tones and exceptional durability, were highly valued for artistic purposes, enabling photo studios such as Hamburg to offer a harmonious blend of photography and fine art, resulting in images that were aesthetically contemporaneous (Glaser 2017).

From the above, it is obvious that photo studios frequently provided artistic enlargements of photographs that emulated the aesthetic of oil paintings. This process involved various techniques designed to augment the photographic image, imbuing it with a painterly quality. The newspaper advertorial clearly showed that by 1913, Hamburg was a bustling port city with a lively cultural scene where photo studios, such as the Hamburg Photo Studio, were among the numerous establishments that catered to the increasing demand for portrait photography.

Thus, it was clear that human agency impacted materiality in both a lithograph and a photograph, blurring the distinction sometimes. Other forms of commemoration had previously been suggested. Earlier, the *Lagos Observer* of March 2, 1883, had reported that "a number of spirited young men, formerly pupils of T.B. Macaulay, have organized a committee for the purpose of raising funds for a memorial to his memory."[11] The newspaper said they would approve the memorial insofar as "the committee aims at giving a practical and attainable form to the memorial." By implication, the form intended by the committee, "a full-length bronze statue, which is to cost 200 pounds being the sum they are hoping to raise," was neither practical nor attainable, since, according to the newspaper, "Such a work is likely to cost, not 200 but 2000 pounds." The authors suggested other "less pretentious forms which the memorial can assume," without offering further specifications. Presumably, the almanac described above by Paulinus, with its mediocre lithograph, was conceived as a "less pretentious form."

In both of these cases, the articles' authors conceive their role to be acknowledging the importance of commemoration as a public activity and exhorting their readers as "members of the public" to participate actively by giving money as well as by exercising their critical faculties to evaluate possible outcomes.

JOURNALISTIC DEBATE SURROUNDING COMMEMORATION

It is evident from these quotations that obituary publications in colonial newspapers of Lagos served not only to inform about an individual's death but also to inculcate readers with the moral principles and religious norms promoted by Christian devotees. Such publications also served to perpetuate imperial memory in the colonies.

Another public commemorative form was the portrait gallery. Photographs of notable citizens were inaugurated into portrait galleries in memorial halls; the inauguration served as a commemorative event. The newspapers solicited donations to support portraits of the deceased and devoted pages to debating how certain important individuals were commemorated. The complex process of making and transporting these photographic portraits from Europe to the colonies was not only representative of imperial capitalist sensibility but also indicated the kind of politics that attended photography's expansion in the early days of its invention, and specifically, the key role played by Europe in its spread. With photography constituting a key component of the commemoration, campaigns started appearing in many Lagos newspapers to defray the cost of commemorative photographs after the launch of the African press in Lagos in 1880. Following this were many reports in Lagos newspapers of the unveiling of these memorial photographs during the late nineteenth and early twentieth centuries.

The expense of enlarging and hanging such photographs was significant. An advertisement in the LWR of September 10, 1904, announced that "the proprietor of Lagos Weekly Record has concluded arrangements with a well known firm of Great Britain which will enable him to offer to any of his readers, a 3-Guinea Crayon Oval Portrait for 10/6."[12] It went further to announce that "The Weekly Record Crayon Oval Portraits are life-like pictures 15 × 12 oval mounted on a Superb Plate, with oval Indian-tinted centre, outside measurements 20 × 16 inches. Being the latest most artistic and highest class of work, ever presented to the public for the low sum of 10s 6d each."[13] In this advertisement, there is an explicit emphasis on the public in the statement, "Being the latest most artistic and highest class of work, ever presented to the public." Here it is assumed that portrait photography's ultimate destination is the public sphere, where the monetary investment in creating and disseminating it is justified by its ability to shape public perception and discourse. Furthermore, the intersection of art and photography is also revealed in the advertorial's further elucidation:

> The Oval Portraits are copied from any photograph (no matter how faded) sent them by "Weekly Record" whether Cabinet, Carte-de-visite or any other size or sort. They are worked on and finished by expert artists who use only pencil, brush crayon, and therefore the minute detail of the most elaborate photograph is finely produced.[14]

It concluded that "the enlarged Portrait will be sent to the address given together with the original photograph CARRIAGE PAID as soon as completed."[15] In the early twentieth century, a three-guinea crayon oval portrait is a type of portrait created using a combination of photography and crayon, often enhanced with other media like charcoal or pastels. The process involved enlarging a photograph onto drawing paper with a weak photographic emulsion to produce a faint image, which the artist then drew over to create a hand-drawn effect. This is the premise upon which the Lagos public expressed sentiments about a low-quality photographic enlargement. The advertisement underscores the complex relationship between the colonial margin and the imperial center, epitomized by the capitalist enterprise in photography. The repeated reference to "Great Britain" as the production hub, coupled with the phrase "Carriage Paid," highlights the financial transactions facilitating the transfer of goods from the colony to the metropole. This language reflects the extractive nature of capitalism, which has historically leveraged photographic technology to reinforce and perpetuate economic and cultural dominance. This is the suggestive problem voiced by many Lagos newspapers when they complain that Lagos citizens were unable to defray the cost of photographic enlargement of certain deceased individuals, while those who sponsored such subscriptions were hailed in overly laudatory terms. For example, an article in the *Lagos Standard* of February 14, 1912, praises a memorial photograph of Dr. R.Z. Bailey, noting that "the expense and trouble of getting the commemorative photograph, and obtaining permission from the Committee for hanging it in the Hall, was the work of a single person, the Genial and enterprising Dr. Adeshigbin Esq, senior partner of the firm Messrs. Adeshigbin & Sons (the well-known Sewing Machine importers)."[16] This outstanding feat leads the author to remember another occasion—the commemoration of "Mr. G. Josephus Cole, the late postmaster of Lagos"—when "a subscription list was opened and some money collected to defray the expenses of an enlargement of the photograph in Europe. The Enlargement was ordered and, in fact, did arrive in the Colony, but I understood that there were some incidental expenses to be met before the photograph could be available for hanging, and for meeting which expenses there were no longer funds on hand."[17] On the one hand, Cole's failed commemoration stands in the context of the replacement of native officials with white British colonial officers, as will be discussed below. For the time being, however, this statement serves to demonstrate the substantial costs associated with the production and mounting of commemorative photographs. In these transactions, Britain staged itself as the provider of technological advancements and the collector of associated revenue, underscoring the earliest capitalist bearing of commemoration in print technology.

At the same time as commemoration occasioned the importation of new technology, it also offered colonial citizens an opportunity for self-representation. In the newspapers, the nature of this representation was again a subject of heated debate. For example, the *Lagos Standard* of November 27, 1918, reported:

> Unveiling of Bishop Johnson's Photograph On Tuesday afternoon last. This function took place at the Glover Memorial Hall. When Henry Carr Esq. M. A. B. C Chancellor of the Diocese delivered a very telling address on the work of the dead Prelate after which his Excellency the Acting Governor A. G. Boyle unveiled the picture of the late Prince of the Church in his episcopal robes.[18]

The LWR reported the same unveiling of Johnson's memorial photo and offered a critique by first citing a quotation by Oliver Cromwell, "Paint me as I am." Writing further, the LWR reported that "the enlarged photo of the late Rt. Revd. Bishop Johnson in episcopal robes subscribed by the Christian Women of Lagos has been hung in the Glover Memorial Hall; to our mind the color of the picture is disappointing in that it represents the sainted bishop a BROWN man, rather than a BLACK man: trust this defect will be remedied at no distant date. The above quotation on the authority of Lord Macaulay is, we believe, apropos of the subject."[19] This quotation highlights the mode of analytical consciousness sparked by a memorial photograph among Lagos citizens. Again, I wish to emphasize that the quotation, "Paint me as I am" by the LWR seems essentially linked to the awareness of the experimental interplay between oil painting and photography by studios such as Hamburg, as discussed above. In other words, the newspaper's assertion that "this defect will be remedied" might be an acknowledgment of the artists' expertise in retouching photographs to restore the original color of the black skin. In her study of nineteenth and early twentieth-century Ghanaian photographs of the Wulff family, Haney (2010b) has observed how similar practice of retouching photographs redefined the meaning of the photographic material. According to Haney (2010b, 123), the photographs "record layers of creative interventions: faces outlined with charcoal, hair darkened with ink, some images left in tatters and others taped together, others overlaid with pencils that cover now invisible printed traces." This multimedia creative intervention prompts a reconsideration of the ontology of the photograph itself. The images, along with their iterative reproductions across and within archival assemblages, imply that the photographic medium is inherently polycentric—simultaneously layered, temporally cumulative, materially susceptible to decay, inscribed with intermedial traces, and continually reshaped by a constellation of practices that extend beyond the camera's mechanical operation (Haney 2010, 123). I want to argue that materiality seems to drive the cult of public attention and public appreciation of the commemorative photograph. Thus, color has been an obsessional preference in the aesthetic enhancement of photography by Africans. For example, Buckley, in his study of historical photographs from Gambia, describes a preoccupation with the aesthetic and visually engaging aspect of the photograph rather than what made the photographs historical (2006, 61). According to him, the lightening of skin colors redefined Gambians' political agency in performing visible selfhood and amounted to what the Gambian government saw as "an undesired expression of modernity" (Buckley 2006, 293). In the case of the late Rev. Bishop Johnson, the LWR's critique of his memorial photograph's skin color became a new way of seeking and asserting the racial identity that came with a new imagination of the public self. The appearance in the public sphere of the newspaper and the walls of Glover Memorial Hall amounts to a public presentation of race exemplified through what, in the author's opinion, should appear decidedly as black skin. Thus, while memorial portrait photos allegedly served the uncontroversial roles of perpetuation of memory and assertion of Christian values, they simultaneously came to assert the modernity of blackness.

REMEMBERING HEROES IN GLOVER MEMORIAL HALL

One of the earliest attempts to conceptualize memorial halls in colonial Lagos commenced with the death of Sir John Hawley Glover. Upon the death of Sir Glover in 1885, a meeting was held on November 17, 1885, at the Breadfruit School Room "for the purpose of considering the feasibility of raising a fund to enable the inhabitants of Lagos to perpetuate the name of the late Sir John Hawley Glover. Those present in the meeting were: viz, Messrs. J. A. Payne, who was elected Chairman, I. H. Willoughby, R. B. Blaize, W. Shitta, D. C. Taiwo, J. S. Bucknor, W. T. G. Lawson, Rev. J. Johnson, Rev. J. B. Thomas, and W. E. Cole, who acted as the Secretary of the committee by general consent."[20] In the meeting members of the committee "eulogized the deceased and rehearsed his laudable acts, his generosity, liberality and large-heartedness, and closed by urging each other to take up the matter as a duty."[21] The committee resolved to hold a "Representative meeting at the Court Hall, Tinubu Square"[22] to resolve the matter regarding the fund to immortalize the name of Glover.

Glover's personality as the former governor of the Lagos colony propelled the success of the Glover Memorial Fund, which attracted generous donations from Europeans, natives, and the colonial government.[23] A subscription list was opened in many Lagos newspapers for the purposes of the memorial fund. Contributors' names were published with the amounts they donated. Sometimes the names of the contributors were accompanied by messages that memorialized their own family members, such as "In memory of his late father" or "In memory of his late Grand Mother, Elizabeth Brown."[24]

In June 1887, during Queen Victoria's fiftieth anniversary on the throne, the total subscription by Lagosians for the construction of Glover Memorial Hall had reached the sum of £1,500. The foundation stone for the Hall was laid during the Queen's Golden Jubilee celebration at the old Customs' Warehouse with the land adjacent to it, which was approved by the colonial government of Lagos. The hall was completed in 1899, fourteen years after Glover's death. Lagos newspapers paid glowing tributes to Glover in sufficiently dignifying terms as an exceptional governor whose style of administration attracted official and unofficial commendations from natives and expatriates alike. For example, the *Lagos Observer* described the town hall meeting convened to discuss the Glover memorial as "densely crowded by all classes of natives . . . many standing outside, filling every available space in the windows and in the vestibule."[25] The emphasis on "all classes of natives" accorded with similar reverential acknowledgments, in many Lagos newspapers, of Glover's towering influence among those he governed. Through many letters to the editors, Glover was lauded in different ways and variously addressed by his local nicknames, "Oba Goloba" or "Baba Goloba," *oba* and *baba* being traditional Yoruba titles meaning "elder."[26] Some attributed his success to his profound empathy with the native condition and his predisposition to always reckon with the natives in policies that affected their welfare. Such achievements set a high standard for subsequent governors who were expected to follow in his footsteps.[27]

In spite of Glover's purported popularity with the native population of Lagos Colony, he was removed as governor of Lagos in June 1872 "because of his policy towards the Egba and accusations of extravagance" (Brown 1964, 139). It was reported that Glover had problems with local newspapers during the 1860s. One such newspaper was the *African Times*. It was reported that in 1866, Glover had an edition of the *African Times* confiscated by the postal authorities and subsequently arranged for slow deliveries whenever this was to his advantage (Brown 1964, 215).[28] Yet the editorial on the death of Glover referred to him as "an Englishman in whom was the embodiment of the qualities and virtues which make up the true gentlemen." The editorial claimed, "Never was a governor known to have had such particular concern for Africa and the Africans, no not before, nor after him."[29] Surely such effusive praise was inconsistent with Glover's dismissal as governor and his apparent intolerance of the local newspapers. I want to argue that the reportage of memorial projects in colonial Lagos newspapers may not present the readers with an objective assessment of colonial power relations. In spite of Glover's reputed victimization of the African press, the newspaper report of his memorial project eulogized his sympathy for the plight of the natives and credited him with many achievements, including "solely raising the Houssa Force from raw and hardy men of that tribe, disciplined them to an Armed Police, and reformed them into their new name of Gold Coast Constabulary," claiming that this alone was enough to perpetuate his name, especially since the achievements were at "no expense to the Imperial coffer."[30] The dialectic of memorial projects overall can be read from this apparent contradiction between Glover's record and the glowing tributes that attended his memorialization. A desperate search for the ideal upon death occasions the production of the deceased, through images and text, as an unimpeachable persona. This explains why the photograph of the deceased was decorated with impeccable design elements to conceal any imperfections and personal blemishes, as will be discussed in the next chapters.

Other achievements attributed to Glover's name include the establishment of a brick factory at Ebute Metta where natives were empowered through informal education in the skill of brickmaking and missionary work. The newspaper claimed that it would not relent until a fitting memorial was mounted in Glover's name for his effort at uplifting Lagos to an enviable and respectable standard in the colonial hinterlands.[31] Glover Memorial Hall eventually came to materialize as a memorialization space that seemed to transcend ethnic, religious, and political differences. Its role extended beyond memorialization to serve as a space for social events such as town hall meetings, weddings, entertainments, and political gatherings.

One distinguishing marker of Glover Memorial Hall was how it gave portrait photographs the desired prominence as material objects of value by allowing memorial portraits of eminent Africans to be permanently hung on the walls. One typical example was the memorial photograph of Edward Wilmot Blyden (1832–1912).

It is important to mention that walls have historically constituted themselves as barriers. In the case of Glover Memorial Hall, the walls could be described as constituting racial and class barriers, especially when the politics of representation is interrogated. Walls have also been presented as political spaces where portrait photographs have lived complicated public lives. In government offices, for example, walls are decorated with official portrait photographs of incumbent leaders. These portraits are replaced as soon as power shifts. For example, in the event of the "Rhodes Must Fall" protest initiated by the students at the University of Cape Town, which took down the statue of Cecil Rhodes, marking the long contestations surrounding decolonization in the Global South and north, photographs of white academics hung on walls of UCT were taken down and burned by the students (Nimis and Goni 2018).

In many family homes, walls are utilized to demonstrate relationships through framed family photographs. In estranged relationships, photographs that once suggested intimacy are removed. In the twentieth century, parlor walls in Africa were spaces deployed to disseminate subtle messages of power and influence through family photographs. These typical situations help in assessing the walls of Glover Memorial Hall in colonial Lagos, as embodied spaces where the politics of class and race were negotiated.

HANGING AND UNVEILING MEMORIAL PORTRAIT PHOTOGRAPHS ON THE WALLS OF GLOVER MEMORIAL HALL

The walls of Glover Memorial Hall became a space for mounting memorial portrait photographs of important colonial citizens. For example, while the process of making and mounting Edward Wilmot Blyden's portrait on the wall commenced in 1912, its completion took place on February 28, 1914. Blyden (1832–1912), described by some nineteenth-century Lagos newspapers as "one of Africa's greatest sons,"[32] was born in St. Thomas, Virgin Islands (the West Indies), and relocated to Liberia in 1851, where he had an outstanding career as a writer, educator, and statesman. During his one-year stint in Lagos as a government agent for native affairs, he was influential in enacting a developmental policy that espoused cultural nationalism based on racial equality. His personal convictions that the African race was a major player in the racial discourse of progress were well established and enabled dispelling contentions of racial differences between different groups in the colony (Blyden 1887, 126–127, 316–317). He equally suppressed the increasing discord occasioned by religious differences such that the questions of superiority or inferiority between races, religions, and ethnicities were extremely restrained. In Blyden's view, an essentialist view of Africa's progress was possible and could be appropriated for Africa's racial peculiarities. This view was widely embraced by the African elites in British West Africa (Zachernuk 1991). Examples of Blyden's influences were recorded in the "Weekly Notes" column of the LWR in 1904, where Africans were charged to rise above European modernity and chart a course of "a healthy development of the physical and mental" well-being, which would command the respect of others.[33]

An inaugural meeting was held at the Glover Memorial Hall on August 3, 1912, six months after Blyden's death, to discuss the nature of the memorial that would be instituted in his memory.[34] Among other suggestions, a big portrait photo of the deceased patriot was proposed to be mounted at a strategic location in Lagos. Another suggestion was a "Blyden Scholarship" and a "Blyden Memorial School" intended to be of great benefit to indigent African youths of whatever tribe, creed, country, or nation.[35] Eventually, a life-size memorial portrait photograph was decided. This unanimous preference for the portrait photograph was in line with the growing popularity of commemorative photographs in the colonies.

The undue delay that characterized previous memorial projects was witnessed in Blyden's memorial, which materialized in 1914, two years after the inaugural memorial meeting. Notice of the unveiling was placed in many newspapers, such as the LWR of February 27, 1914, which notes: "His Excellency, the Governor General, Sir F. J. D. Lugard, G. CM.G., C.B. D.SO., &c. &c., having kindly consented to unveil the Blyden Memorial picture, this function will D.V. take place at 5:30 pm at the Glover Memorial Hall Marine, on Saturday next the 28th February." Amid the euphoria that greeted this unveiling, a robust conversation regarding the African origins of memorialization was activated in Lagos newspapers. Among other interesting topics, debates over the capacity of the "negroes" to honor their ancestors were elaborated in the dichotomous characterization of "the hybrid Negro" and "the aboriginal Negro" with some believing that the latter has a long tradition of honoring ancestors through "hero-worshipping," in the form of "the stories of Sango, Oya, and other African deities."[36] This is a problematic yet interesting perspective that was inspired and sustained by Blyden's ancestry as an African and suggests once more that the African conceptualization of memorial was tied to mythic stories of heroism and visual culture. Indeed, African memorialization was tied to "hero-worshipping," as recognized by the newspaper, given the overwhelming attention Blyden's memorialization attracted. Even before the unveiling of Blyden's memorial portrait photograph, a portrait bust of Blyden was unveiled on June 19, 1913, in front of Wilberforce Memorial in Sierra Leone. The Sierra Leonean bust was described by the *Lagos Times* as the first memorial monument set up in Africa to "a negro, erected by both the black and white races."[37] And this seemed to have spurred the Lagos angle of Blyden's portrait memorial. Of course, the choice of a bust or a portrait to officially memorialize an African during the colonial period in Lagos resonated with the controversial meanings attached to these forms by different racial groups. While in the Europeans' perception, having a portrait made was an honorific pastime for the bourgeoisie, the Africans considered portraits and busts a visual materialization of an ancestral figure with cultural and religious significance. The politicization of the portrait memorial became a recurring factor in the subsequent memorial projects in colonial Lagos. Blyden's memorial was praised in many Lagos newspapers as an archetype of true African nationalism that would benefit posterity. Specifically, as the *Nigerian Chronicle* newspaper of March 6, 1914, stated, "If we Africans are to play an important role in this world's [*sic*] stage we must not place ourselves in a position uncongenial to our environments or inimical to our interest, but that we must go back to the standpoint of manhood of our fathers and not cut loose from our ancestral mooring which unfortunately many of us have done."[38]

In other words, Africa's capacity to transcend its apparent setbacks and become a key player in the global cultural dialogue could be enhanced through reconnection with ancestral links. The outcome was unfortunate for those who cut ties with their ancestors. Here, a conceptual parallel is demonstrated with ancestral sculptural figures through which Africans envisioned formal conceptualization of an aesthetic and artistic worldview.[39] These memorial sculptural forms are being redefined in photographic memorials in recent times.

THE CULT OF PUBLIC ATTENTION AND A ROBUST VISUAL CULTURE

As previously discussed, the walls of Glover Memorial Hall also initiated a robust conversation around a visual culture in which citizens were able to critically assess the material worth and aesthetic merits of each photograph. This new visual culture is what I describe as the cult of attention to commemorative portrait photographs.

Commentators did not hesitate to make critical comparisons between photographs. For example, the *Lagos Standard* contrasted the late Bishop Johnson's photograph with that of the late Dr. Blyden, the two of which had been hung next to each other. In the author's assessment, "One who did not know the bishop would take him for a Mulato from the colour of his face and hands; it was hoped that the defect would be remedied." This is a critical observation that pays due diligence to photographic appreciation while subtly problematizing its material production.[40] This same reference to the color of the black skin earlier mentioned in the late Bishop Johnson's memorial photo seemed a recurring point of critical concern. Especially for black Africans, the color of the black skin is a crucial component of this cult of attention, whereby a dark-skinned viewing public attends to the presence of images of like-colored figures on the walls of power. As mentioned earlier, the material manipulation of the photographs was aimed at a verisimilitude akin to oil painting, and the public was conscious of this human mediation. This consciousness elicited some public comments demanding a remedy for the photographic defects.

Again, it is possible to argue that the process of developing these photographs in the darkroom of early twentieth-century Europe was not just a technical task but also a site of ideological production. The choices made in the darkroom—such as how to frame a subject, what to emphasize or obscure, and how to manipulate the image—could significantly influence the narrative conveyed by the photograph. Moreover, the materiality of the darkroom process, including the use of chemicals and the physical manipulation of photographs, played a key role in shaping the representation of African subjects. These images often reflected the biases and intentions of the colonial photographers rather than the realities of the subjects themselves.

These unveilings were equally performative and drew official attention from colonial officials. For example, "The unveiling of a portrait of the late Mrs. C. A. Sapara Williams at the Glover Memorial Hall" was announced on December 10, 1904, in the LWR. This unveiling was a ceremonial one, and the portrait was realized through subscriptions by the members of the Ladies Recreation Club, of which the late Mrs. Sapara was president. The unveiling ceremony was performed by the deputy governor of the colony on Wednesday, December 7, 1904, in the presence of a sizable number of people. The portrait was given to the governor for unveiling by Bishop Oluwole on behalf of members of the club. The bishop paid a glowing tribute to the late Sapara in an opening remark that was published in detail in the newspaper. Among other things, the bishop particularly remarked how Sapara's "picture will have a place in this Memorial Hall," to enshrine her legacies as president of the Ladies Recreation Club. He referred to the portrait photograph as "the art that can immortalize," a "faithful picture," and a "true index of her mind and heart," demonstrating that the photograph's indexicality in the early twentieth century was tied to the deceased's physical and spiritual being.

The unveiling was an elaborate occasion that attracted the most influential personalities of the Lagos colony. The deputy governor unveiled the portrait photograph with a speech about how the late Mrs. Sapara endeared herself to members of the club and the community through her selfless philanthropy. Mr. H. Carr, assistant colonial secretary, remarked that "the portrait which has been subscribed for by the Ladies Recreation Club and which has just been unveiled to our view is a striking likeness and a fine work of art, suggesting both the refinement of character and the kindliness of nature of the lady whom we are met together to honour." The interesting phrase "unveiled to our view" suggests that the moment of unveiling served to constitute the viewing public as such.

While many other unveilings were reported in colonial newspapers, women were rarely commemorated. However, in another such example, the "unveiling of a portrait of the late Lady Denton at the Glover Memorial Hall" was reported by the LWR on February 9, 1901. Lady Denton was an influential woman who impacted many lives through her philanthropy and charity. She trained orphaned children and empowered them with opportunities in different crafts. In turn, the children she empowered contributed the subscription that enabled the realization of her portrait. The unveiling ceremony was performed by the governor of the colony, with many important colonial officials in attendance, such as the Honorable J. A. Otunba Payne, the registrar of colonial Lagos, who spoke on behalf of the unveiling committee.

The LWR of September 3, 1892, reported, after the meeting of the committee of subscribers for the Willoughby Memorial Fund, that it was "decided that the sum of 8 pounds will be expended in procuring from England an enlarged portrait of the deceased bearing a superscription rehearsing the circumstances through which he came to death; and the portrait to be hung in the Glover Memorial Hall."[41] In a related instance, during a meeting of the subscribers of the Lovell Memorial Fund, where the secretary of the fund, the Honorable E. A. Speed, was present, a resolution was reached that one-third of the sum of 75.86 pounds realized from the memorial fund would be "devoted towards obtaining from England, a portrait of the late gentleman to be hung in the Glover Memorial Hall, with the permission of the Trustees."[42] Similarly, on February 10, 1917, an extensive report titled "Report of the Unveiling of the Photograph of Lieut. H. A. Child C.M.G. R.N. Late Director, Marine, Nigeria" was published in the LWR.[43] This comprehensive report was accompanied by funeral eulogies and encomiums covering the entire newspaper and extolling Child's memorable virtues. The opening sentences started with "the imposing ceremony of the unveiling of the photograph of the late Capt. Child has crowned with success the efforts of the Native Staff to bring to light their esteem and affection for their noble leader." It went ahead to state that,

> immediately upon the receipt of the news of Child's death, a committee was formed to consider ways and means for perpetuating the devotion of the staff to their deceased Head of Department. It was intimated that the director lieut.

> J. Percival, N. N. R. Successor to Capt. Child would give the Native staff a free hand in whatever they wished to do to preserve the memory of Capt. Child. Many plans were considered and rejected, but at last, it was happily suggested that a large Mounted Photograph of the late Director should be purchased and hung in a conspicuous place in every Marine Divisional Office and that each subscriber should also be given a smaller one for his own personal possession. This plan was unanimously agreed to and was instantly set in motion.

This statement suggests that the memorial photograph's reproducibility is informed by the degree of importance or relevance attributed to the deceased. In Child's case, the deliberate duplication and dissemination of his memorial photo ensured that each subscriber possessed a personal copy, supplementing those displayed in the various Divisional Offices. This is a way to extend the commemorative photograph's significance across institutional and personal archives. It is important to mention that a memorial was also mounted for Child in England. The memorial was specifically listed as a memorial to those who died in World War I. The circumstances surrounding Child's death as a naval commander in battle in Africa warrant significant emphasis due to their broader historical and cultural implications. This event exemplifies the photographic commemoration of a white British representative of the colonial government, whose heroism was celebrated to an extraordinary degree. The outpouring of praise for Child was so immense that it occupied an entire newspaper edition, reflecting the colonial society's prioritization of such figures. The text that accompanied his memorial in the UK, reads

> AT THE OUTBREAK OF THE GREAT WAR ON THE EVE OF HIS RETIREMENT / HE ANSWERED THE CALL OF DUTY / AND WHILE SERVING WITH THE CAMEROON EXPEDITIONARY FORCE / LOST HIS LIFE BY DROWNING ON THE BAR OF THE NYONG RIVER. / ON OCTOBER 21ST 1914 IN THE 45TH YEAR OF HIS AGE. / HONOURING HIS LIFE AND WORK / THIS TABLET IS ERECTED BY HIS / BROTHER OFFICERS AND COMRADES.

Reflecting on the situation of World War I and its impact on colonial politics is essential to understanding the broader implications of Child's death within the context of military commemoration. World War I significantly altered the geopolitical landscape, intensifying debates on imperial authority and the role of colonial subjects in the war effort. The mobilization of colonial troops and resources during the war highlighted the complexities of colonial relationships and the shifting power dynamics between Africans and Europeans.

Child's military heroism, as a naval commander who died in battle in Africa, stands out from other forms of heroism within the colonial government. His death and subsequent commemoration in both Nigeria and the UK serve as a poignant example of how colonial powers used military heroism to reinforce racial hierarchy as well as justify and strengthen their rule. While most African fighters who fought in World War I were not commemorated in a similar reverential manner, Child was elevated to heroic status. This exceptionalism by colonial authorities sought to create a narrative that emphasized the nobility and righteousness of their cause and exacerbated the prevailing inequality that attended colonial relations. It also helped to legitimize and consolidate their presence and actions in the colonies, portraying them as protectors and civilizers rather than oppressors. This contrasts the more modest commemoration of other colonial figures and subjects, such as Glover or Nathaniel King, underlining the selective nature and differential treatment of individuals based on the colonial prescription of heroism and perceived importance within the colonial framework.

SUBSCRIPTION AND UNVEILING IN MEMORIAL PHOTOGRAPHY

As portrait photographs gained prestige in memorialization during the colonial period in Lagos, some individuals were deemed less worthy of a memorial portrait photograph due mainly to the politics of race and colonial bureaucracy. For example, the colonial government did not approve a portrait memorial for the late Dr. Nathaniel King, a Yoruba medical doctor trained in London, Edinburgh, and Aberdeen. Instead, King was given a memorial window, a form that had become relatively less prestigious.

To unveil is to unmask, to make public. It is within this word that I want to address the concept of the public sphere and its relationship to memorial photographs of the late nineteenth-and early twentieth-century Lagos. The unveiling of the memorial photograph was only made possible through public subscription. In a case where the public failed to raise enough money, the unveiling was never realized. A typical example was that of the late Postmaster Cole (cited above), who was not only a victim of a racist colonial policy that ousted black men from their positions as heads of department[44] but also a victim of a failed subscription for a commemorative photograph. Mr. Joseph Chamberlain, the European colonial minister, relieved black Africans of their positions as heads of departments and replaced them with less qualified Europeans. The *Times of Nigeria* described this as "immoral in principle"[45] and criticized Chamberlain for suppressing the black race and stifling their aspirations.[46] Cole was relieved of his duty as postmaster general. When he died, his obituary in the *Times of Nigeria* attracted condemnation of Chamberlain's racial maltreatment.[47] Despite calls for a subscription for Cole's commemorative photograph, enough money was never realized to offset the bills of production. Thus, the photograph did not see the light of the day.

Subscription emerges as one of the processes that bring the photograph into being. Money and materials are two components of a capitalist endeavor on which the commemorative photograph relied to become fully manifest in public. Money, in other words, is an inevitable constituent of the photograph's visibility. While the photograph was deemed less important while its subject was alive, upon his death, its value became elevated and attracted a public cause that was not only financially but verbally and performatively committed to. Photographs have a direct impact on our psyche, bypassing rational thought and provoking the politics of photographic appreciation. In this politics, public photographs embody different meanings for different viewers. This is because, according to Altheide (2019, 98), the significance of viewing one's own photo album is not confined to the album page but includes placing the photograph in a familial context: "The item simply calls forth these memories and background understandings." Unveiling a memorial photograph expands the scope of appreciation by suggesting that a less important photograph's entry into the visual economy of the public space elevates that photograph as recognizable and viewable material. As commemorative photographs negotiate the liminal spaces of the public realm, each unveiled memorial photograph acquires a social visibility that affirms the deceased's visual subjectivity. While the nature of visual subjectivity requires the double sensation of seeing and being seen (Vigliotti 2016), unveiling practices of nineteenth-century Lagos establish this "double-sighted" construction of the deceased subject as the means to produce a public space, an inherently heterotopic space. We can conceive the walls of Glover Memorial Hall as a modern heterotopic museum where individuals enter the archives of public visual memory via unveiling.

Beyond their function as memorial things of value, photographs were woven into the memorial services of important citizens. Funeral processions were marked by photographic displays of the deceased. In a prominent example, during the memorial service in connection with the funeral of the late King Edward VII held in St. Stephen's West African Episcopal Church on Friday, May 20, 1910, the *Lagos Standard* of June 1, 1910, reported, the choir sang a special hymn accompanied by a solemn procession of the Congregation of Lay Preachers and Readers "bearing pictures of the late King draped with black silk Ribbons and passing through Anikantamo, Idumagbo and Moloney bridge streets, singing the Hymn 'Hush blessed are the dead.'"[48] Here, beyond its function as a politicized artifact entangled within the discourse of print capitalism, the commemorative photograph also served as an object deployed in performance.

CONCLUSION

During the late nineteenth and early twentieth centuries, commemorative photographs garnered significant attention in West African colonies, especially Lagos and its environs. These photographs served as a nuanced channel through which elite consumption practices were disseminated. Within the Lagos community, subscribing to a commemorative photograph was perceived as a significant financial responsibility essential for achieving visibility and remembering the deceased and their kin. The subscription, unveiling, and public critique of memorial photographs reconfigured the public sphere and engendered an astute public well versed in visual appreciation. The next chapter tracks ways in which commemorative photographs published in funeral posters and billboards articulate a unique manifestation of cosmopolitan aesthetics and the public sphere. I show how discourses of heroism in precolonial Igbo society are reinvented in line with the technological advances that came with funeral posters.

CHAPTER 4

"Exit of an Icon"

Heroism in Obituary Posters from Southern Nigeria

This chapter argues that obituary posters and billboards in southern Nigeria function as cultural artifacts that symbolize heroism and prestige, showcasing the wealth, status, and public achievements of the deceased while engaging with the public sphere. Given the ubiquity of funeral posters and billboards across numerous town and city intersections, the photos of the deceased with their complex decorations and performative elements constitute a visual spectacle that holds significant relevance in the discourse of the Igbo public sphere.

PORTRAIT MODERNITY AND ANTI-COLONIAL NATIONALISM

Political activities in Nigeria after the 1930s concentrated primarily on how to end British rule. The Nigerian Youth Movement, a national political party, was formed in 1934, with members winning major elective positions in the Legislative Council. After 1940, political activities became more inclusive, and in 1944, Herbert Macaulay and Nnamdi Azikiwe mobilized more than forty different groups to establish the National Council of Nigeria and the Cameroons.[1] The British were experiencing increased tension from independent agitators as well as soldiers who had fought on the British side during World War II. Among the strategies deployed by the colonialists was the use of photographs to garner mass support for political parties. Thus, in the 1940s, portrait photography emerged as one of the compelling anti-colonial forms of visual culture in colonial newspapers owned by Nigerian nationalists. Portraits of politicians in enchanting poses were published and used to promote party manifestos. Nnamdi Azikiwe (known as Zik) introduced this style of self-fashioning using portrait photographs in the *West African Pilot* newspaper in 1937. Likewise, portrait photographs were also included in the layout of the *Daily Service* newspaper in the 1940s (Kunstmann 2014, 518). By portraying the local elites, the newspapers challenged and subverted the colonizers' narratives of power and supremacy. The photographs depicted how the subjects internalized Western sartorial styles and poses, but they also revealed something else: their participation in what Ariella Azoulay (2014) describes as the "civil contract of photography," in which photographs "function as sites of resistance to the hegemonic views prescribed by the state" (Kunstmann 2014, 519; Thomas and Green 2014, 3). As they envisioned the dawn of independence, Zik and other nationalists launched their aspirations in compelling photographs that challenged the colonial gaze and asserted their own identity.

In 1937, after introducing a new pictorial journalism using photographs, *West African Pilot* increased its readership to thirty thousand copies daily (Duyile 1987, 141). Its success sparked other newspapers, such as the *Nigerian Daily Times*, which adopted a similar pictorial style (Coker 1968, 34–44; Omu 1978, 87). In Zik's newspapers, photographs accompanied obituaries, and more Africans could access the public spheres of newspaper obituaries. In the 1940s, the first set of obituary photographs started appearing in colonial newspapers in Nigeria (Kunstmann 2014). At this time, the public sphere was becoming more visually attentive to the concerns of Africans, as manifest in the shift from the predominantly textual narratives of obituaries witnessed in nineteenth-century newspapers to the inclusion of photographs.

In 1960, when Nigeria gained its independence from Britain, new postcolonial citizens who imbibed an Afrocentric ideology ensured that representing the dead in print emulated a celebrity prototype established by Zik and other nationalists. The appearance of one's photo in print was seen as a remarkable means to forge agency and achieve prominence in the competitive public sphere of the postcolonial print culture. Photographic visibility was also a means of asserting the cultural identity of personhood. Many photographs thus accompanied obituaries from the 1960s. In the January 21, 1967, edition of the *Daily Times*, two obituary photographs were published on page 14 with captions, "In Memoriam." One of the photos, showing Jide Sode, captured his radiant smile and his elegant Western suit and tie, and came with a textual inscription that revealed his name and background: "Jide Sode, Chartered Accountant, 'Former Secretary of Nigerian Union of Great Britain Ireland,' who died January 21, 1965, at the age of 29, following a car crash. I will always remember him and his promises. Rest in Peace: his wife, Kumbi" (Fig. 2).

Another obituary titled "In Memoriam" reads:

> In evergreen and affectionate memory of our dearly beloved mother, Late Madam Durowade Ode (Omo Oseni Aderibigbe, Agbado Railway Station—Alias Mama Bajaih) (fig. 3) of No 50. Aitken Road Sabon-Gari Kano, who slept in the Lord on January 21, 1966, when none of your fruits was ripe for you to have a taste. You are a mother too dear to lose and too good to be forgotten. Your life was a pattern to follow. Your death was a painful grief. Mother, rest in perfect peace. Always remembered by: Madam Adetokunboh Sijuwade, Alhadji S. A. Ola Adesina, Messrs. Olusoji Abiodun, Gbolahan Bisola Adeniyi and Yinka.

Accompanying this narrative is a full-size photograph of their mother dressed in an ostentatious headscarf, necklace, earrings, and a decorative long skirt and a long-sleeved blouse widened at the edge. The photograph shows her seated with legs crossed, sporting a wristwatch and rings, gazing frontally at the camera. Atop this obituary photograph is another "In Memoriam" of Salmon Beckley Folami with only a textual inscription and devoid of photographs. Almost all obituary photographs published in the 1967 edition of the *Daily Times* were all "In Memoriam" of those who died years back, including that of Jacob Taiwo Oshodi, who died ten years previously on January 12, 1957, and "Mrs. Beatrice Taiwo Smith (Nee Johnstone) who crossed the veil 21 years ago." Therefore, advertising "In Memoriam" in West Africa from the 1960s was coterminous with the evolving modernity that came with the new powers of photographic technology and the fashioning of family power, wealth, and prestige. A new kind of public sphere was emerging, in which photography was beginning to make a compelling intervention in the articulation of racial, ethnic, and class identities of postcolonial citizens.

By the 1970s, full-page newspaper obituaries with accompanying photographs were already popular (McCaskie 2006, 349). A good example is the *Renaissance Newspaper* of April 28, 1973, which dedicated an entire page to the obituary of Dr. Reuben Chukwudinma Nzeribe (Fig. 4). Whereas in the first part of the twentieth century, newspaper obituaries were relegated to inconspicuous addenda within the "advertisement" pages, obituary publications of the 1970s began to occupy entire pages. This trend coincided with the economic prosperity of the 1970s oil boom, which enabled many to climb the

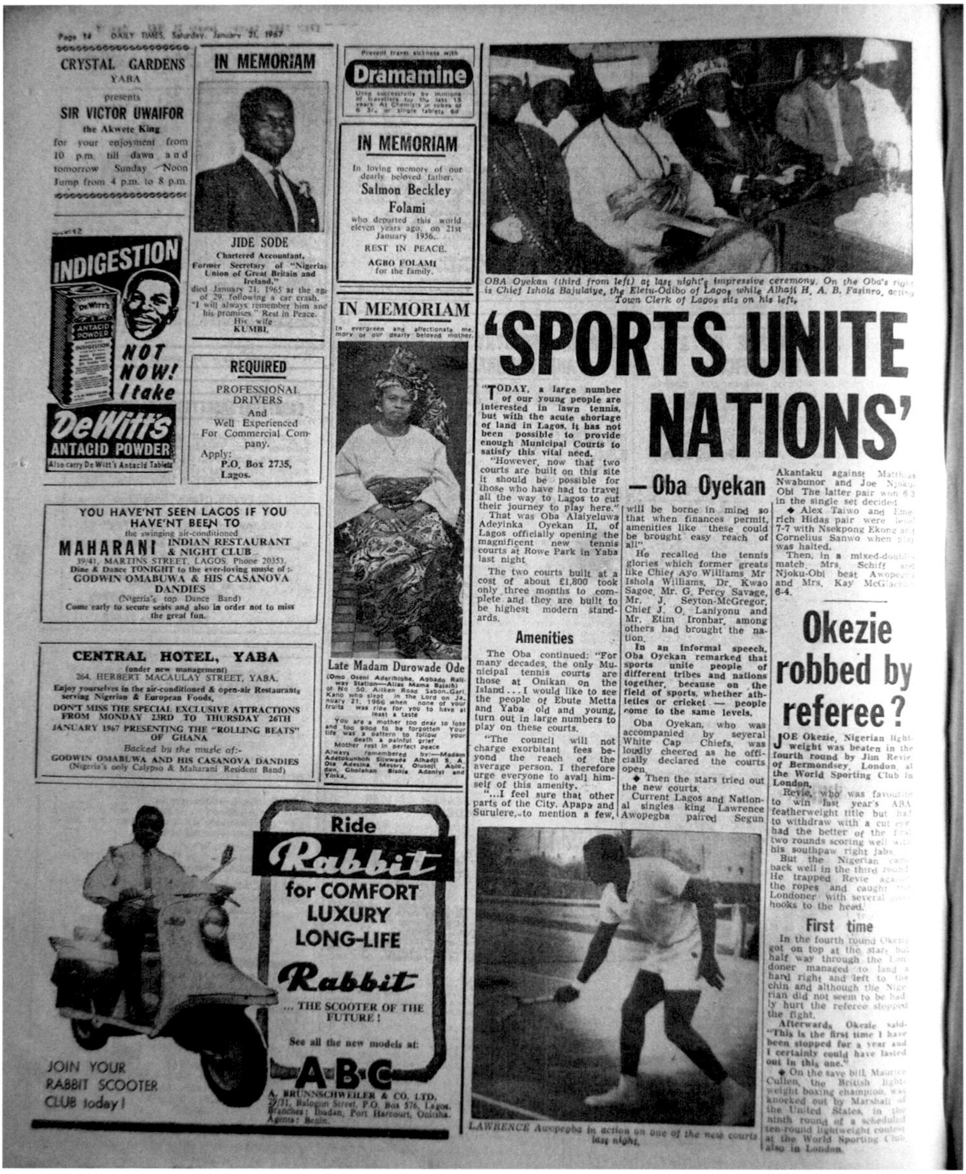

Page 14 DAILY TIMES, Saturday, January 21, 1967

CRYSTAL GARDENS
YABA
presents
SIR VICTOR UWAIFOR
the Akwete King
for your enjoyment from 10 p.m. till dawn and tomorrow Sunday Noon Jump from 4 p.m. to 8 p.m.

IN MEMORIAM

JIDE SODE
Chartered Accountant,
Former Secretary of "Nigerian Union of Great Britain and Ireland,"
died January 21, 1965 at the age of 29, following a car crash.
"I will always remember him and his promises." Rest in Peace.
His wife
KUMBI.

Prevent travel sickness with
Dramamine
Used successfully by millions of travellers for the last 15 years. At Chemists in tubes of 6 3/- or single tablets 6d

IN MEMORIAM
In loving memory of our dearly beloved father,
Salmon Beckley Folami
who departed this world eleven years ago, on 21st January 1956.
REST IN PEACE.
AGBO FOLAMI
for the family.

INDIGESTION
NOT NOW! I take
DeWitt's
ANTACID POWDER
Also carry De Witt's Antacid Tablets

REQUIRED
PROFESSIONAL DRIVERS
And
Well Experienced
For Commercial Company.
Apply:
P.O. Box 2735,
Lagos.

IN MEMORIAM
In evergreen and affectionate memory of our dearly beloved mother.

Late Madam Durowade Ode
(Omo Oseni Aderibigbe, Agbado Railway Station—Alias Mama Balaib) of No 50, Aitken Road Sabon-Gari, Kano who slept in the Lord on January 21, 1966 when none of your fruits was ripe for you to have at least a taste
You are a mother too dear to lose and too good to be forgotten. Your life was a pattern to follow your death a painful grief
Mother rest in perfect peace
Always remembered by:—Madam Adetokunboh Sijuwade Alhadji S. A. Ola Adesina, Messrs Olusoji Abiodun, Gbolahan Bisola Adeniyi and Yinka.

YOU HAVE'NT SEEN LAGOS IF YOU HAVE'NT BEEN TO
the swinging air-conditioned
MAHARANI INDIAN RESTAURANT & NIGHT CLUB
39/41, MARTINS STREET, LAGOS. Phone 20353.
Dine & Dance TONIGHT to the ever-loving music of :-
GODWIN OMABUWA & HIS CASANOVA DANDIES
(Nigeria's top Dance Band)
Come early to secure seats and also in order not to miss the great fun.

CENTRAL HOTEL, YABA
(under new management)
264, HERBERT MACAULAY STREET, YABA.
Enjoy yourselves in the air-conditioned & open-air Restaurants serving Nigerian & European Foods,
DON'T MISS THE SPECIAL EXCLUSIVE ATTRACTIONS FROM MONDAY 23RD TO THURSDAY 26TH JANUARY 1967 PRESENTING THE "ROLLING BEATS" OF GHANA
Backed by the music of:-
GODWIN OMABUWA AND HIS CASANOVA DANDIES
(Nigeria's only Calypso & Maharani Resident Band)

OBA Oyekan (third from left) at last night's impressive ceremony. On the Oba's right is Chief Ishola Bajulaiye, the Eletu-Odibo of Lagos, while Alhaji H. A. B. Fasinro, acting Town Clerk of Lagos sits on his left.

'SPORTS UNITE NATIONS'
— Oba Oyekan

"TODAY, a large number of our young people are interested in lawn tennis, but with the acute shortage of land in Lagos, it has not been possible to provide enough Municipal Courts to satisfy this vital need.

"However, now that two courts are built on this site it should be possible for those who have had to travel all the way to Lagos to cut their journey to play here."

That was Oba Alaiyeluwa Adeyinka Oyekan II, of Lagos officially opening the magnificent new tennis courts at Rowe Park in Yaba last night

The two courts built at a cost of about £1,800 took only three months to complete and they are built to be highest modern standards.

Amenities

The Oba continued: "For many decades, the only Municipal tennis courts are those at Onikan on the Island ... I would like to see the people of Ebute Metta and Yaba old and young, turn out in large numbers to play on these courts.

"The council will not charge exorbitant fees beyond the reach of the average person. I therefore urge everyone to avail himself of this amenity.

"...I feel sure that other parts of the City, Apapa and Surulere, to mention a few, will be borne in mind so that when finances permit, amenities like these could be brought easy reach of all".

He recalled the tennis glories which former greats like Chief Ayo Williams Mr Ishola Williams, Dr. Kwao Sagoe, Mr. G. Percy Savage, Mr. J. Seyton-McGregor, Chief J. O. Laniyonu and Mr. Etim Ironbar, among others had brought the nation.

In an informal speech, Oba Oyekan remarked that sports unite people of different tribes and nations together, because on the field of sports, whether athletics or cricket — people come to the same levels.

Oba Oyekan, who was accompanied by several White Cap Chiefs, was loudly cheered as he officially declared the courts open.

◆ Then the stars tried out the new courts.

Current Lagos and National singles king Lawrence Awopegba paired Segun Akantaku against Matthias Nwabunor and Joe Njoku-Obi The latter pair won 6-3 in the single set decided

◆ Alex Taiwo and Emerich Hidas pair were level 7-7 with Nsekpong Ekong and Cornelius Sanwo when play was halted.

Then, in a mixed-doubles match, Mrs. Schiff and Njoku-Obi beat Awopegba and Mrs. Kay McGlach 6-4.

LAWRENCE Awopegba in action on one of the new courts last night.

Okezie robbed by referee?

JOE Okezie, Nigerian lightweight was beaten in the fourth round by Jim Revie of Bermondsey, London, at the World Sporting Club in London.

Revie, who was favourite to win last year's ABA featherweight title but had to withdraw with a cut eye had the better of the first two rounds scoring well with his southpaw right jabs.

But the Nigerian came back well in the third round He trapped Revie against the ropes and caught the Londoner with several good hooks to the head.

First time

In the fourth round Okezie got on top at the start but half way through the Londoner managed to land a hard right and left to the chin and although the Nigerian did not seem to be badly hurt the referee stopped the fight.

Afterwards Okezie said- "This is the first time I have been stopped for a year and I certainly could have lasted out in this one."

◆ On the same bill, Maurice Cullen, the British lightweight boxing champion, was knocked out by Marshall of the United States, in the ninth round of a scheduled ten-round lightweight contest at the World Sporting Club also in London.

Ride
Rabbit
for COMFORT
LUXURY
LONG-LIFE
Rabbit
... THE SCOOTER OF THE FUTURE!
See all the new models at:
ABC
A. BRUNNSCHWEILER & CO. LTD.
29/31, Balogun Street, P.O. Box 576, Lagos.
Branches: Ibadan, Port Harcourt, Onitsha.
Agents: Benin.
JOIN YOUR RABBIT SCOOTER CLUB today!

Fig. 2. A photograph of the late Jide Sode. Published in the *Daily Times* on January 21, 1967.

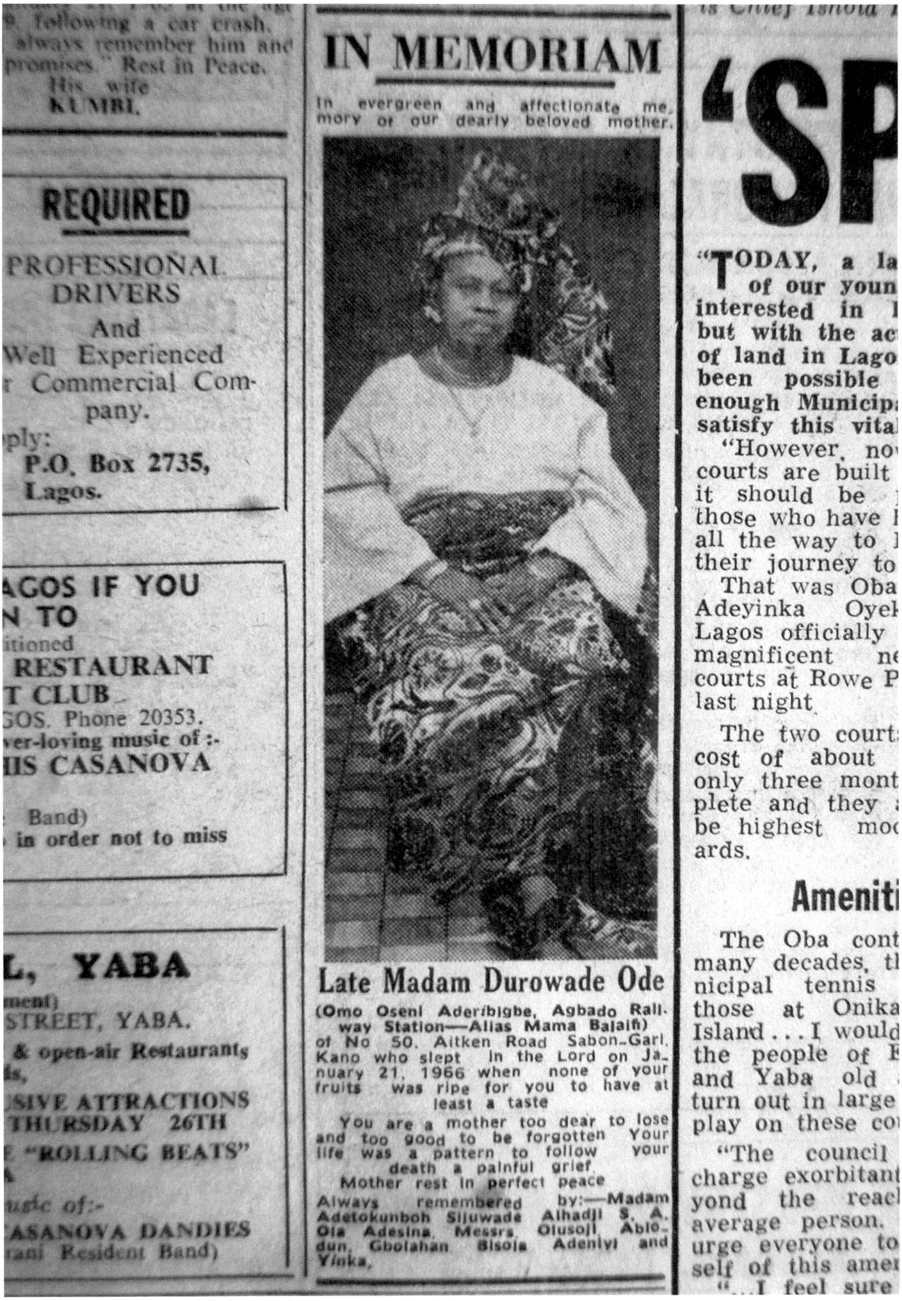

following a car crash.
always remember him and
promises." Rest in Peace.
His wife
KUMBI.

REQUIRED
PROFESSIONAL
DRIVERS
And
Well Experienced
r Commercial Com-
pany.
ply:
P.O. Box 2735,
Lagos.

AGOS IF YOU
N TO
itioned
RESTAURANT
T CLUB
GOS. Phone 20353.
ver-loving music of :-
HS CASANOVA
Band)
in order not to miss

L, YABA
ment)
STREET, YABA.
& open-air Restaurants
ds,
USIVE ATTRACTIONS
THURSDAY 26TH
E "ROLLING BEATS"
usic of:-
CASANOVA DANDIES
rani Resident Band)

IN MEMORIAM

In evergreen and affectionate memory of our dearly beloved mother.

Late Madam Durowade Ode

(Omo Oseni Aderibigbe, Agbado Railway Station—Alias Mama Bajaih) of No 50. Aitken Road Sabon-Gari, Kano who slept in the Lord on January 21, 1966 when none of your fruits was ripe for you to have at least a taste

You are a mother too dear to lose and too good to be forgotten Your life was a pattern to follow your death a painful grief.

Mother rest in perfect peace

Always remembered by:—Madam Adetokunboh Sijuwade Alhadji S. A. Ola Adesina, Messrs Olusoji Abiodun, Gbolahan Bisola Adeniyi and Yinka,

'SP

"TODAY, a la
of our youn
interested in l
but with the ac
of land in Lago
been possible
enough Municipa
satisfy this vital
"However, no
courts are built
it should be
those who have
all the way to
their journey to
That was Oba
Adeyinka Oyek
Lagos officially
magnificent ne
courts at Rowe P
last night.
The two court
cost of about
only three mont
plete and they
be highest moc
ards.

Ameniti

The Oba cont
many decades, th
nicipal tennis
those at Onika
Island . . . I would
the people of E
and Yaba old
turn out in large
play on these co
"The council
charge exorbitant
yond the reach
average person.
urge everyone to
self of this amen
"...I feel sure

Fig. 3. A photograph of the late Madam Durowade Ode (Omo Oseni Aderibigbe, Agbado Railway Station—alias Mama Bajaih). Published in the *Daily Times*, January 21, 1967.

economic ladder and gain the financial means for public visibility. In this era, obituaries started to record funeral details and interment plans more swiftly, so that it became common for families to announce the passing of their loved ones through these notices well before the actual burial. Nzeribe's obituary (Fig. 4) includes a distinct section specifically focused on the funeral logistics, a new development as compared with earlier eras.

The aspiration for public visibility was further fueled by the efforts of the corrupt political elite, who printed magazines and campaign posters with well-decorated photographs to woo voters (Nwafor 2021, 132). Prominently situated in public spaces, the posters launched an obscure political figure into public renown while simultaneously concealing the politician's questionable character. Over time, families recognized the poster's potential to amplify an advertised persona, leading many to adopt this strategy for promoting their deceased relatives. Obituary posters started appearing in southern Nigeria in the 1970s. The posters were usually life-size or above life-size and printed on A1 paper with a photo of the deceased. The posters also contained information about the burial and funeral. By the 1980s and 1990s, the traditional roles individuals played in their families and communities were beginning to be reimagined in visual culture. For most families, deceased family members were regarded as accomplished and heroic individuals who toiled to raise families, survived the civil war, or confronted the economic challenges and instabilities of the postcolonial state. Thus, the posters were decorated to reflect local nuances of prestige, honor, and respect and were captioned in phrases such as "exit of a hero," "exit of a legend," "exit of an icon," and so on.

It became commonplace for mourners to craft posters and other funeral items where the deceased's photo appeared with appropriate phrases that they believed would inscribe the body into the realm of befitting immortality and ancestry. Delaplace (2008, 333) has suggested that "photographs are used precisely to achieve a transformation of the deceased into an 'icon.'" The use of "icon," "legend," "hero," or "enigma" to caption certain obituary posters by southern Nigerians reflects the reverence accorded the departed. To the deceased is ascribed an omnipotent status, like that of an iconic ancestor. According to one mourner I interviewed, "The dead will be happy wherever he is that he was buried well." I use the words "icon," "exit," and "hero" to examine various manifestations of the obituary photograph and their idiosyncrasies within the narratives of heroism and fame, on the one hand, and regret and loss, on the other. In particular, the word "icon" featured prominently in most posters I examined. It becomes necessary to situate this word within a larger theoretical discourse.

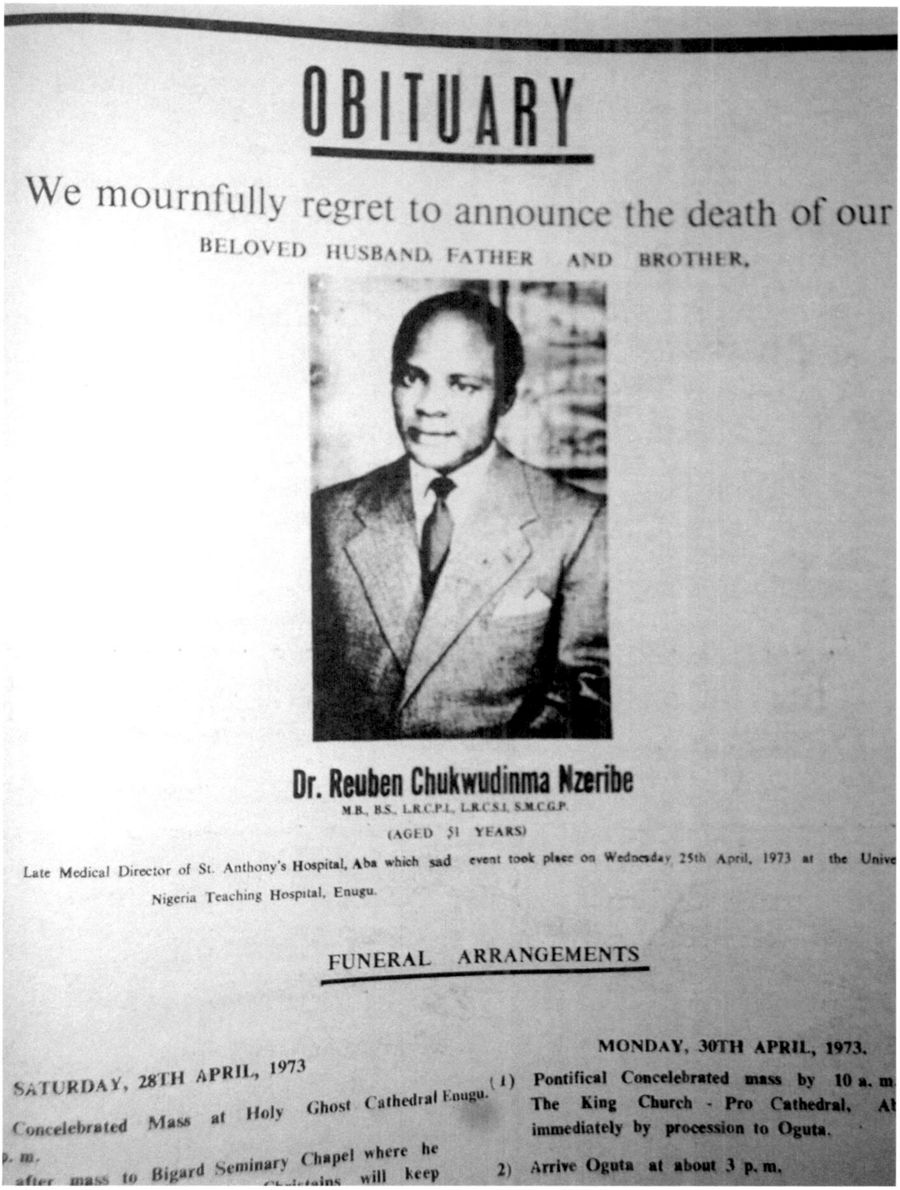

OBITUARY

We mournfully regret to announce the death of our

BELOVED HUSBAND, FATHER AND BROTHER.

Dr. Reuben Chukwudinma Nzeribe

M.B., B.S., L.R.C.P.I., L.R.C.S.I., S.M.C.G.P.

(AGED 51 YEARS)

Late Medical Director of St. Anthony's Hospital, Aba which sad event took place on Wednesday 25th April, 1973 at the Unive

Nigeria Teaching Hospital, Enugu.

FUNERAL ARRANGEMENTS

SATURDAY, 28TH APRIL, 1973

(1) Concelebrated Mass at Holy Ghost Cathedral Enugu.

p. m.

after mass to Bigard Seminary Chapel where he ... will keep

MONDAY, 30TH APRIL, 1973.

(1) Pontifical Concelebrated mass by 10 a. m. The King Church - Pro Cathedral, Ab immediately by procession to Oguta.

2) Arrive Oguta at about 3 p. m.

Fig. 4. A photograph of the late Dr. Reuben Chukwudinma Nzeribe. Published in the *Renaissance Newspaper* of April 28, 1973.

THEORIES OF ICONIC REPRESENTATIONS

The simultaneously banal and reverential use of "icon" by southern Nigerians to address their deceased is subtly suggestive of the broader theoretical concerns of the photographic icon. In his examination of the uses of icons in medieval Europe, Belting offers insights that could be equally applicable to understanding the role of photography within Igbo culture:

> Authentic images seemed capable of action, seemed to possess *dynamis*, or supernatural power. God and the saints also took up their abode in them, as was expected, and spoke through them. People looked to such images with an expectation of beneficence, which was often more important to the believer than were abstract notions of God or an afterlife. (1997, 6)

Belting's theory of the icon is deeply rooted in his broader work on the anthropology of images, which approaches high-art and popular images on an equal level. He argues that icons should be understood not merely as art objects but as entities with their own agency and presence. He emphasizes that icons historically served as mediators between the divine and the human, embodying a spiritual presence that transcended their material form. Belting's approach thus disrupts the conventional art historical view that confines images to mere aesthetic appreciation. He advocates for understanding icons within their authentic religious and cultural milieus, where they serve as dynamic agents in devotional activities and foster a profound connection between the observer and the divine.

Bringing the idea of iconicity beyond strictly Christian art contexts, Ryzova (2015) has argued that we tend to attribute iconic value only to prominent individuals or events that have a significant aesthetic impact, but she insists that, in fact, all photographs are potentially iconic objects. Iconicity means the capacity to transport meanings across a broader reach beyond indexical referents. In de-emphasizing the content of the photograph, iconicity interfaces the image with social and religious values. Iconic photos are thus appreciably more symbolic than referential and act as outlets for values, dogmas, mindsets, curiosities, and obligations.

In this chapter, I argue that obituary posters captioned with "exit of an icon" act in a similar way for their viewers. Like the icon, photographs of the deceased in Igboland uncover windows through which we see the spiritual, ancestral realm. Also, and not insignificantly in modern-day mediatized everyday life, obituary posters can work to reposition an unknown individual or family among the mourners in a local society. Markers of fashion and accomplishment allow the image to confer status upon the mourning family.

IKENGA: OBITUARY POSTERS AND THE HEROIC FIGURE

In the 1980s, photographs were first incorporated into television announcements of death. Families bought air spaces on the Nigerian Broadcasting television station, where death was announced over a photograph of the deceased (see Gore 2001, 330), conveying that the deceased lived a heroic life worthy of public approbation. As time progressed, and to make a more impactful public presence of the deceased on television screens, families replaced the still photograph with videos of the deceased in their finest moments, with music and narration that highlighted their achievements, status, and influence (see, for example, Nwoye 1993; Sprague 1978, 54; Gore 2001, 330). The video was believed to consolidate the deceased's social relevance in their communities. Many individuals who could not afford radio and television advertisements reimagined their deceased in other visual forms that deployed photographs to reinscribe the memory of the deceased into the center of the public sphere. Obituary posters became a more affordable means through which the dead were transformed into heroic icons. Obituary posters are more than just a way of informing the public about death; they are a powerful expression of how the deceased lived, loved, and left a legacy. By adorning the posters with symbols of honor, achievement, and identity using digital technology, families and communities celebrate the lives of their deceased and affirm their own sense of belonging and purpose. These posters thus also reveal the cultural fantasies and anxieties that shape the perception of social status.[2]

The visual heroization of deceased figures in traditional Igbo society has a long history. In Igbo cosmology, the hero is seen as a person who uses more than his God-given powers to achieve extraordinary deeds. Mastering the supernatural determines true heroism and distinguishes the hero from the ordinary everyday person. Heroism was often invoked during wartime, and it sometimes paralleled the Western concept of heroism in certain aspects, the difference being that a hero in Igbo cosmology held sway among his contemporaries even in death. Death entrusts the status of ancestorhood to certain persons. And ancestorhood is associated with heroism because of its omnipresent, omnipotent cosmological amplification. Sculptural figures often represent heroic images of ancestors. For example, the Igbo Ikenga sculptural figure is a spiritual and physical embodiment of the heroic persona. This heroic persona is evident in ways in which the Ikenga sculpture was revered: Ritual sacrifices and libations were poured on it daily to animate its supernatural powers. Ikenga figures, seen as possessing a live soul that listened and responded to its custodians, were revered in most clans as the iconic embodiment of the spirit of the dead. There are many types of Ikenga, but the most famous variety is the "warrior," which depicts a well-developed human figure with horns and a fierce expression (Fig. 5).

To understand fully the relationship between Ikenga and heroism in Igbo cosmology, one must comprehend the relationships between the object and the life process of its owner. Reincarnation is a central belief in the Igbo worldview. After death, a person, provided that he lived an appropriate life and was properly buried, returns to the land of the spirits, *ala muo* (Stevenson 1985). The Ikenga is closely associated with the *Ogbo na uke*, which stands for aspects of man's identity that are not confined to predestination. The warrior Ikenga corresponds to the stage in life when men are expected to demonstrate their military and heroic prowess, and they are owned by many young men. Ikenga depicts the ideal young man: robust, wearing the warrior's grass skirt, and holding a knife and a severed human head, all symbols of heroism. This pose used to be seen in warrior groups when they performed dances (Basden 1938, opp. 401).

The knife is always held in the right hand, called *aka Ikenga* (the Ikenga hand), and the Ikenga is also called a shrine to the right hand. In many Igbo communities, those who killed in wars were admitted into a lower level of the complex set of title societies. This grade was known as *ogbu mmadu*, "man killers" (Talbot 1926, 3:828; Basden 1921, 256). Recently, the overt violent visual element has been de-emphasized, and the knife and head have merely become metaphors for aggression.

The above clearly illustrates how "icon" and "hero," used in the captions of obituary posters in contemporary Igbo society, allude to the Igbo quest for achievement as encapsulated in the warrior Ikenga. In funeral posters, we see the Ikenga knife and the head replaced by chieftaincy paraphernalia and emblems of authority such as a feather and an elephant tusk or other types of staff (Fig. 7), as well as other signs of wealth suggestive of family and personal accomplishments. The most characteristic of all the iconographic elements of the Ikenga, the horns (*opi*), also carry the connotation of achievement through aggression or boldness. An Igbo proverb says, "The ram goes into a fight head first" (*Ebuli ji isi eje ogu*); that is, one must plunge into a venture in order to succeed (Chukwuma 1974).

The epithets "icon," "hero," and "legend," among others, fundamentally underscore the Igbo quest for heroic exploits and titles. Titles allow the Igbo man and, to some extent, woman to express their achievements in the socioeconomic sphere and to convert them into culturally acknowledged forms of prestige and political power (Bentor 1988). Throughout his lifetime, an upwardly aspiring man is expected to acquire increasingly higher titles through his own achievements, for most titles are not hereditary. So an obituary poster announcing "Exit of an Icon" or "Exit of a Hero" suggests that the family did not inherit heroism but toiled to earn it. Each title has its own price, significance, and insignia (Basden 1938, 135–140). By adopting a befitting title of heroic significance for their loved ones' obituary posters, survivors demonstrate that the Igbo's quest for achievement has been fulfilled.

In his description of the historical relationship between the image and individual self-realization in Igbo land, Behrend remarks:

> In the Ikenga carving we find an example of local self-evaluation, a kind of materialized double of the successful person which had to be cared for, had to be fed, sacrifices etcetera. The Ikenga represented an accumulation of success, as well as the new composition of the represented person—the quantitative as well as the qualitative changes in a man's life—in one double, in one carving or representation. Thus, the statue allowed the man a reflexive attitude towards himself; however, it did not so much serve to produce self-knowledge as give visual representation to the social success and prestige of its owner. (2002, 48)

An Igbo proverb says, "As long as my Ikenga is active, I can wrestle in the land of the dead" (*Ikengam di ile, njee mgba na ana mmuo*); another says, "An Ikenga that is inactive, cut it for firewood" (*Ikenga adigh ile, awaa ya nku*) (Agbogu 1974, 51–53). The warrior Ikenga corresponds to the phases of the personal development process when men are required to demonstrate their aggressive preparedness for personal accumulation and heroic accomplishments. A careful study of the obituary poster reflects the above qualities as well and suggests that while the Igbo concept of achievement presents itself as an evolving project of modernity, it retains the fundamental elements that inform heroism in traditional Igbo society.

I participated in about one hundred funeral ceremonies, where I joined photographers to select photographs for the obituary posters. The choice of

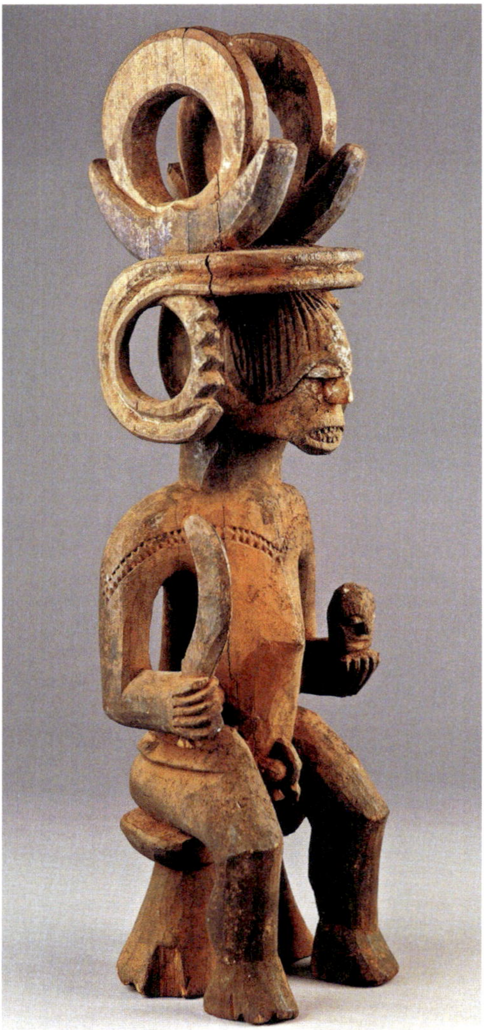

Fig. 5. Ikenga wooden sculpture displays different attributes of a heroic persona in the Igbo society

photos in family albums reflected conventions where a cap is especially seen as a mark of honor and prestige. Most photos chosen for obituary posters either showed the individual dressed in traditional attire with a befitting cap and staff or a religious attire with a befitting religious cap. In the absence of photos that include such honorific elements, individuals adorn their deceased using Photoshop. In recent times, while Ikenga has transformed into an artwork representing cultural authenticity as defined in terms of a static traditionalism in museums and cultural institutions around the world, I argue that the Ikenga symbolism of heroism and achievement has evolved into the modern form of the obituary poster.

PHOTOGRAPHIC REPAIR: CREATING VISIBLE SIGNS OF HEROISM

The use of state-of-the-art photo-editing software to create obituary images that are suitably heroic epitomizes the evolution of this form into the present. In one of my encounters with Chidi, who was preparing a poster for his late father's funeral, no photograph of his father was befitting of the obituary poster. At some point, Chidi took selected photos of his father to Chidimma Okoye, a computer technician working in a digital lab at Awka, Anambra State. Chidimma explained: "I employed the digital tools of Adobe and CorelDRAW to repair the broken photos of Chidi's father. Customers bring old, broken, and damaged photos of their late relatives and ask me to repair them. Most times when I repair them, they look more beautiful than the original photos. I wear them a different dress requested by the families" (author's interview, 2021). In interviews with fifteen computer technicians, this concept of "repair" was central. Again, my interactions with some other family members of the dead were revelatory. For example, Uche Onwusi remarked, *Papa chiri echichi, o ga-eyibe ya akwa isi agu*, meaning "Dad was a titled chief so she [the photo editor] should adorn him with *isi agu* dress." Onwusi said that his initial fear of printing his father's damaged photo was allayed when the photographer told him that he would repair the damaged part and clothe him in a chieftaincy dress. "She indeed repaired them," said Onwusi, pointing at the facial distortion of his father's photos and the *isi agu* dress. Likewise, Madam Ikeokwu remarked, *ntupo nile juru Nnem n'ihu puchara*, which translates as "All the pimples in my mother's face disappeared." A few individuals expressed concerns, in local Igbo parlance, about the tendency toward *ichofe ya mma oke*, "over-beautification." However, this worry was not expressed by many.

From the editor's perspective, Chidimma said that she has a primary responsibility to make "ugly" photos look "beautiful" and to elevate the status of the deceased through dress. The "repaired" photo would eventually appear on the poster. Chidimma said that sometimes the deceased had only one surviving photograph that was severely damaged by time and weather, which the owners requested her to "repair." Obituary photographs are thus enhanced through digital manipulation in ways that bring attention to their constructed artificiality. The families create a fantasy impression of the actual family situation. The image looks airbrushed, skin tones are too even, limbs elongated, and, as a result, the image of the deceased becomes a "synthetic ideal" (de Perthuis 2008, 171). By the same token, underachievers are technologically heroized.

It is important to recall that the concept of repair features prominently in the funeral business in southeastern Nigeria. Morticians also "repair" damaged bodies to get them ready for burial. Meanwhile, the family's public image likewise undergoes a repair, as the family endeavors to repaint and redecorate their houses and the surrounding area before the funeral. A typical example is seen in Figure 6 during the burial of the late Mrs. Christiana Nkechi Okaphor in Adazi Nnukwu of Anambra State. The children contracted a local event manager who decorated the entire premises. The dusty brown floor was covered with an artificial green rug, while every other surface, including the chairs, walls, and tables, was bedecked with decorative pink-and-white silk cloths.

There is a local belief that a corpse must not be brought into an unkempt compound. Before the corpse is brought home for burial, the entire family convenes a meeting to renovate old buildings and, in certain instances, build a new house. The old life is renewed for the eventual arrival of the dead. Everything about the corpse is renewed—it is dressed in its best clothes before being placed inside the coffin—while the photos are beautified, in other words, mounted with decorated frames (Figures 7 and 9). The repaired family image that is thus enabled allows the family name to be inscribed within the honorific realm. Here repair is both physical and powerfully symbolic.

While the quest to enact repair is pursued through the beautification of the material surface of architectural edifices, it is also pursued through the reconstruction of the material surfaces of photographs. In Belting's analysis of photo retouching, "Digital construction of body images via data set abolishes all resemblances to a real body and, as a result, the distinction between death and life." He further states that "electronic images . . . exchange the mortal body for the invulnerable body of simulation, which conveys immortality upon us. But this immortality is only a new fiction with which we conceal death" (2011, 122). However, I would argue that in appropriating the digital software of CorelDRAW or Photoshop to actualize the Igbo sense of achievement in the obituary poster, a new visual language of beauty is enacted. In making the funeral poster of the late Nonso Nnabuife, the computer tech-

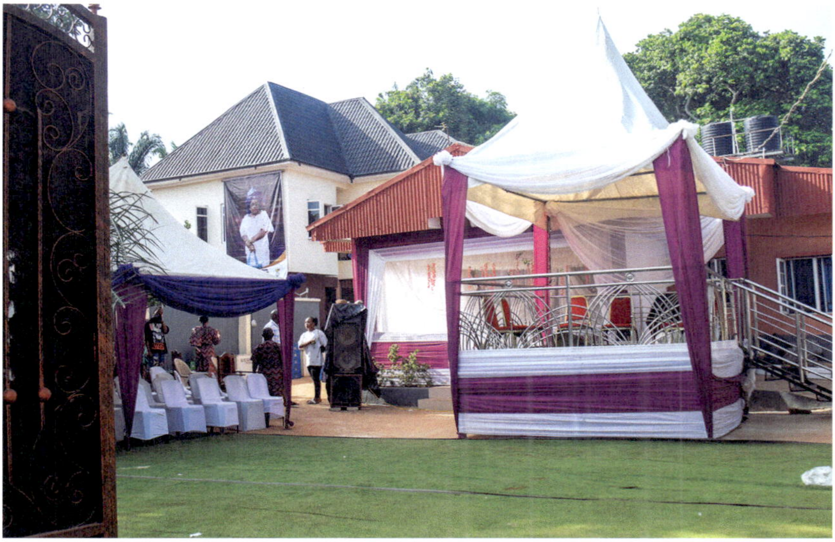

Fig. 6. The entrance of the house was decorated for the funeral of Mrs. Christiana Nkechi Okaphor in Adazi Nnukwu, Anambra State

nician states, he "repaired" the photo to eliminate skin blemishes; he photoshopped the dresses and bodies in a resplendently decorative style that aimed to advertise the family's credentials. The computer technician believes the late Nnabuife's family credentials must be defined by sophistication and elegance—especially because of Nnabuife's career as a professor—which must be advertised on the obituary poster by imbuing it with a heroic significance.

Generally speaking, for both men and women, two different photographs are needed for the obituary poster: first, a photo of the dead in their youth and, second, a photo at an older age. Both photos must be fashionable and must reflect the reigning styles of each epoch.

The younger photos are usually superimposed in front of the older photos. A remarkable difference between men's and women's photographs is that the men are dressed in Western suits in their youthful photos, while women wear so-called traditional clothing in both their youthful and older photos. In some of my interviews, smiling photographs are given high priority.[3] If a funeral is described as *ogara ofuma, mmadu abiaka*, meaning, "It went well, many people attended," then the assigned task of repair was well enacted and consummated. In her research on "changing perceptions

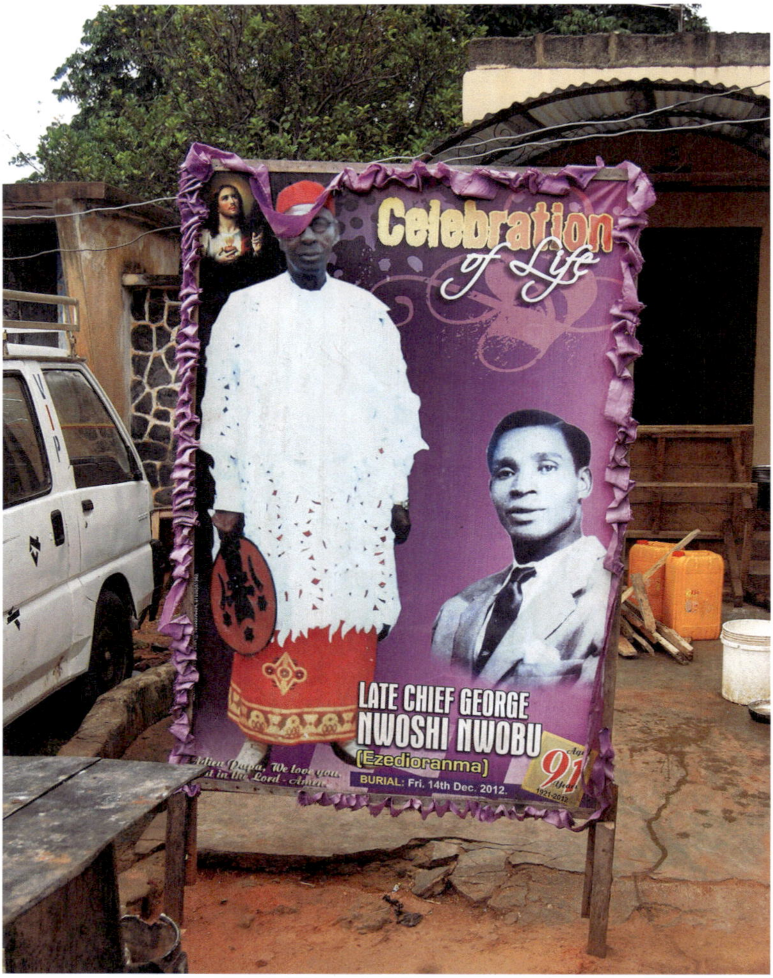

Fig. 7. Obituary poster of Chief George Nwoshi Nwobu at Awka, Anambra State

of death and burials in Nigeria," Ogbuagu (1989, 98) notes that many individuals engage in extravagant funerals "in order to look 'good' before their friends, relations, and workmates." This behavior suggests that "social considerations tend to overshadow those of the future economic welfare of the individuals and their families."

Returning to the Ikenga figure earlier discussed, one may observe that Ikenga is not supposed to be an image of verisimilitude; by representing the self in a state of fulfillment, it is a shapeshifter that helps to mediate the passage of the dead from this earthly world into the next. It is the repaired image of impure and battered personhood, a visual transformer of the invisible persona. Likewise, in obituary photos, imperfections that would potentially ruin the transfigurative process are redeemed. In the new performative fiction of the obituary photos, we find the repaired image of the dead, whereby a patch from the past is stitched to the fabric of the future. In the obituary poster, the dead are reinvented to assume a new role in the world of imagined heroism, sartorial elegance, and spiritual transcendence.

SOME CASE STUDIES

Late Chief John Iliemenam Nwabude

The production of the late Chief John Iliemenam Nwabude's obituary poster (Fig. 8) is described by Jude, the computer technician:

> I noised the photograph to remove all the pimples and blemishes. I removed all the wrinkles. I even wore him *isi agu* cloth because the children said they want him to look beautiful. In fact, any photograph that is not "pimped" and treated would be deemed imperfect and bad by the owner. (Author's interview, August 2014)

From Jude's narrative, it seems an index of the Nigerian, and perhaps technology-driven, society that a shabby, scraggy-looking world must be substituted with a world complete with simulated images of dainty dresses, unblemished skin, and effusive displays of wealth. Indeed, in certain situations, such attributes lie beyond the realistic realm of the dead individual. In Figure 8, it can be seen that Jude's expertise seems to have constructed an artificial body inserted into an artificial background to announce that the subject has transited into eternity. Jude photoshopped the late Chief John Iliemenam Nwabude with a red cap, eagle's feather, and *isi agu* dress. *Isi agu* dress translates as "the dress with the lion's head" and is seen as an expression of heroic exploits in Igbo society.

Ogbu agu means a lion killer, referring to a typical heroic achievement in traditional Igbo society. Adorning the deceased with *isi agu*, therefore, suggests a visualization of the heroic persona upon death.

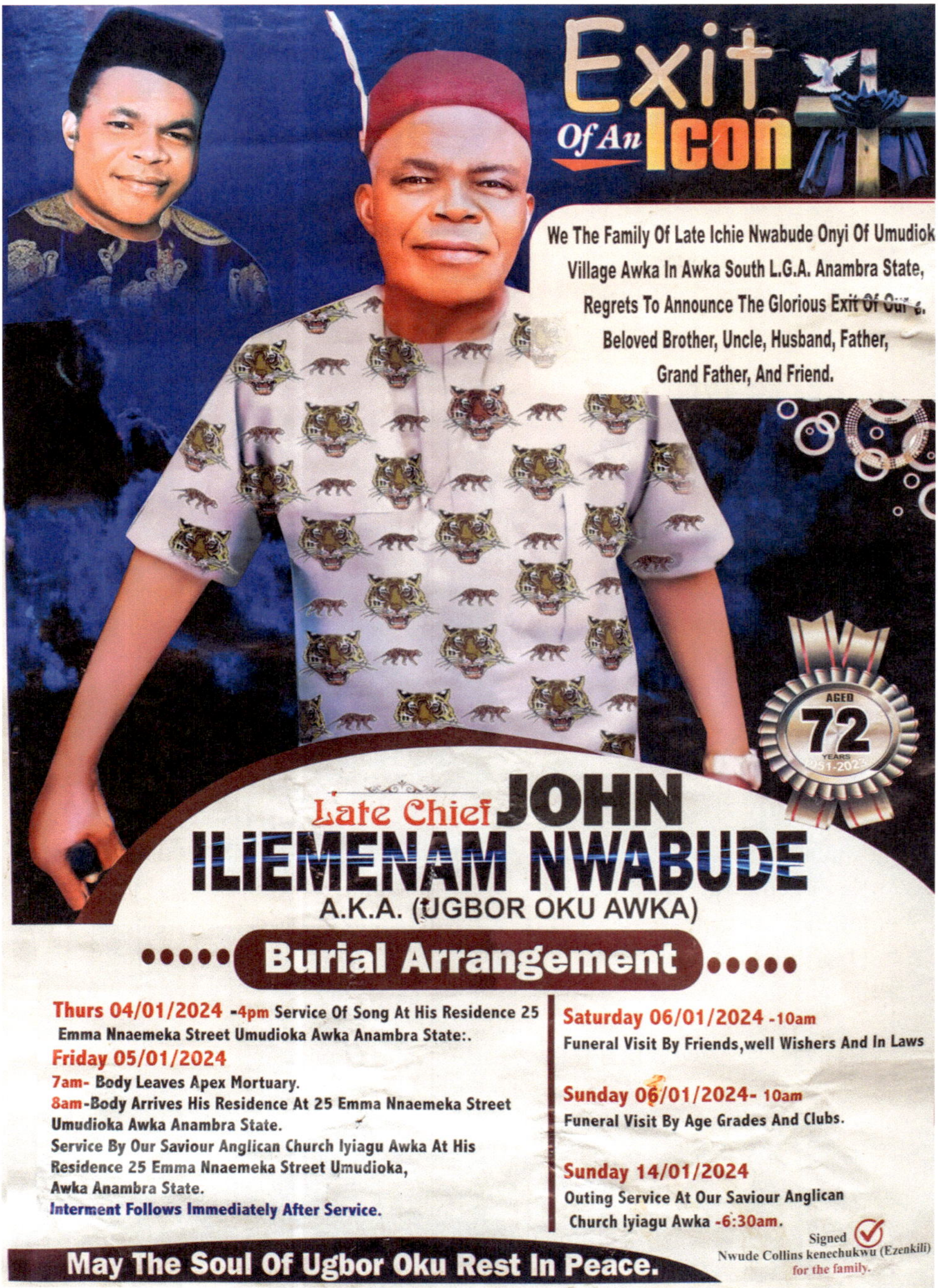
Exit Of An Icon
We The Family Of Late Ichie Nwabude Onyi Of Umudiok
Village Awka In Awka South L.G.A. Anambra State,
Regrets To Announce The Glorious Exit Of Our
Beloved Brother, Uncle, Husband, Father,
Grand Father, And Friend.
AGED 72 YEARS 1951-2023
Late Chief JOHN
ILIEMENAM NWABUDE
A.K.A. (UGBOR OKU AWKA)
Burial Arrangement
Thurs 04/01/2024 -4pm Service Of Song At His Residence 25 Emma Nnaemeka Street Umudioka Awka Anambra State:.
Friday 05/01/2024
7am- Body Leaves Apex Mortuary.
8am-Body Arrives His Residence At 25 Emma Nnaemeka Street Umudioka Awka Anambra State.
Service By Our Saviour Anglican Church Iyiagu Awka At His Residence 25 Emma Nnaemeka Street Umudioka, Awka Anambra State.
Interment Follows Immediately After Service.
Saturday 06/01/2024 -10am
Funeral Visit By Friends,well Wishers And In Laws
Sunday 06/01/2024- 10am
Funeral Visit By Age Grades And Clubs.
Sunday 14/01/2024
Outing Service At Our Saviour Anglican Church Iyiagu Awka -6:30am.
Signed
Nwude Collins kenechukwu (Ezenkili)
for the family.
May The Soul Of Ugbor Oku Rest In Peace.

The Late Ajie Cletus Onwuha Ochije

Just like the Ikenga, where a similar heroic tendency is exemplified in the dress and forms of the sculpture, this quality is observed in the funeral poster of the late Ajie Cletus Onwuha Ochije, aged ninety-five years (Fig. 9). This poster, titled "Glorious Exit of an Icon," exemplifies some of the most visible attributes of the Igbo hero seen in Ikenga. The computer technician said of the poster: "I brightened it and noised the body. I added the staff and wore him the *aka* [beads] and the *isi agu* [the dress with the lion's head]. I also added the staff to his right hand." Again, the right hand, referred to as *aka Ikenga* in the Ikenga sculpture, is the manifestation of the spiritual and physical force required to conquer. For this reason, in some Ikenga, the right hand is exaggerated to visually launch that force. To substantiate the belief that a heroic hand cannot be left empty, Ochije is handed a staff, which is also a contemporary equivalent of the machete held in the right hand of the Ikenga figure. Ikenga (literally "place of strength") has also been described as "an Arusi and a cult figure of the right hand and success found among the northern Igbo people. He is an icon of meditation exclusive to men and owners of the sculpture dedicate and refer to it as their 'right hand,' which is considered instrumental to personal power and success" (Basu and Chika-Kanu 2020).

As in the case of Chief John Iliemenam Nwabude, the computer technician photoshopped the *isi agu* dress onto Ochije's body and attached the eagle feather to his red cap. When we compare the Ikenga's horns and Ochije's eagle feather, we see two upward projections that signify an elevated status for a titled individual. The eagle feather, known in the Igbo language as *ugbene ugo*, refers to the rare feat of killing an eagle, accomplished by only few hunters. The lion and the eagle are the two most powerful animals signifying heroic achievement in Igboland; the lion is represented by the *isi agu* dress, while the eagle is represented by the *ugbene ugo* (the eagle's feather) on the cap. The two mark a consummation articulated in visual form with the Photoshop tool. The photoshopped lions on Ochije's *isi agu* dress are presented in regal golden color against a black background and complemented with beaded necklaces. Ochije's shadowy photograph lurks behind his original photo to suggest the incarnation of a spiritual essence; according to the technician, the editorial process aimed to achieve a double. Most funeral photographs I encountered passed through this editing process, all in an attempt to enact

Fig. 8. Funeral poster of John Iliemenam Nwabude at Awka, Anambra State

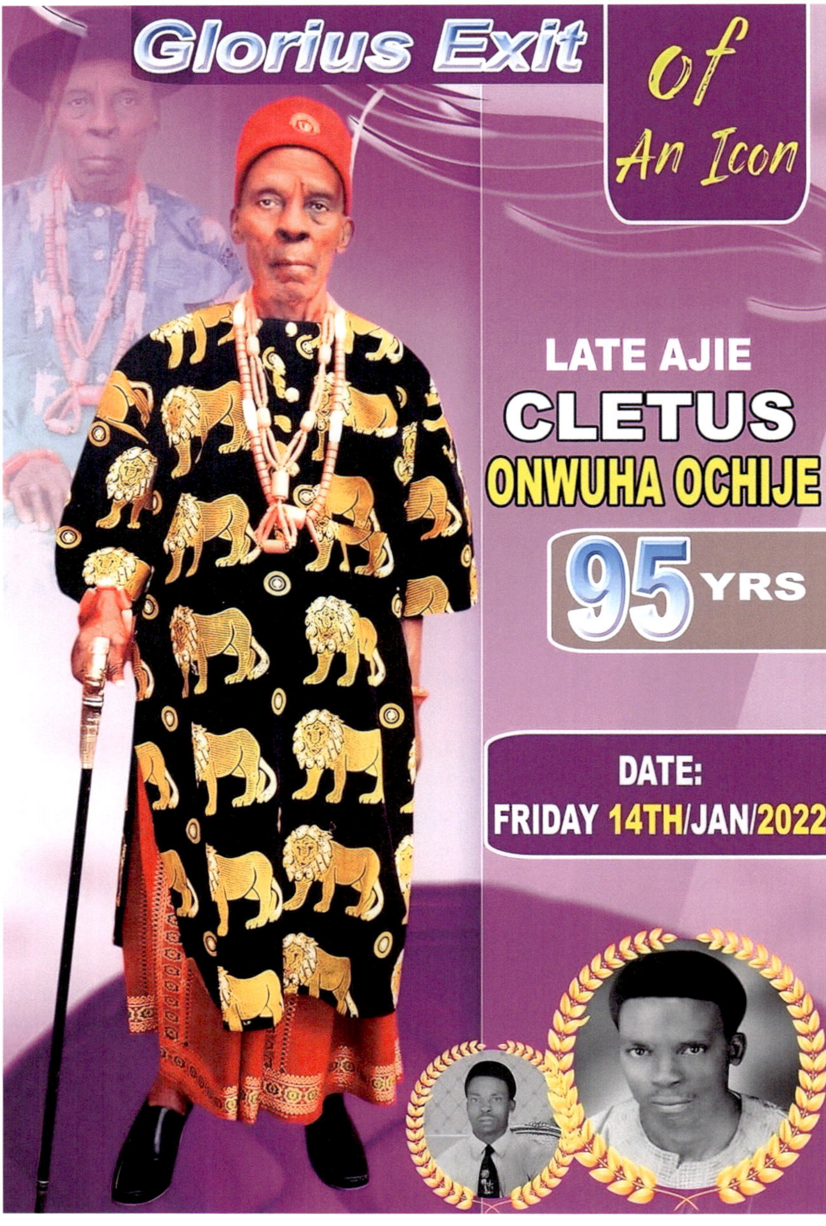

Fig. 9. A photoshopped funeral poster of Ajie Cletus Onwuha Ochije

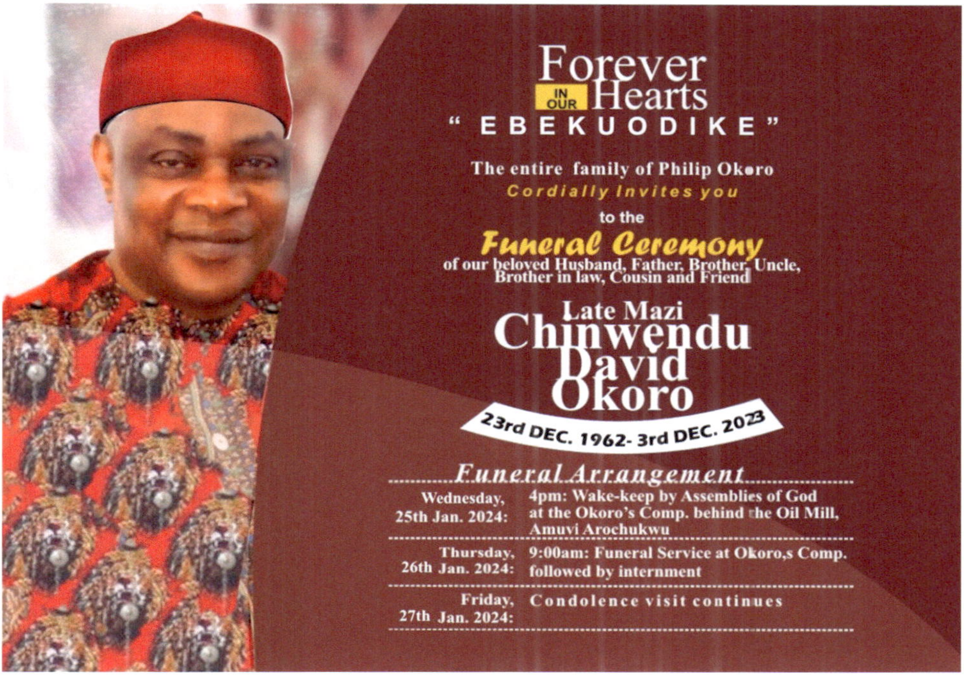

Fig. 10. A photoshopped funeral poster of Mazi Chinwendu David Okoro

a consummate image of the deceased and align with the dual perception of beingness in the Igbo cosmology, especially enunciated in the phrase *ife kwulu ife agwudebe ya* (When something stands, something stands beside it). Ikwuemesi (2023, 127) articulates this as "a symbolic verbalization of the dual essence of being." Beingness in Igbo cosmology transcends mere existence through the dual and balanced complementarity inherent in Igbo thought, as exemplified, especially, by the interplay of two fundamental forces: *enu* (sky) and *ani* (earth). *Ani* shapes the very essence of reality and constitutes a more significant force in the discourse of spirituality. This explains why the traditions are known as *omenani* or *omenala* (literally: that which happens on the ground) as against *nso ani* (literally: that forbidden by Earth), that is, taboo or abomination (Nwafor 2014).

In another related case, Chief Okoro's family crowned him as chief by photoshopping the red cap and the *isi agu* dress (Fig. 10). While the late Okoro did not receive any chieftaincy title in the traditional institution, the entire community believed he deserved to earn the title, and thus everyone called him chief. Upon his death, a segment of his family decided that he would be adorned with *isi agu* as a parting gift and an endorsement by the community.

THEORIZING THE POSTER'S DIGITIZED PUBLIC PRESENCE

It is possible to insist, unarguably, that we are witnessing in recent times what one can call the indigenization of the new digital technology: that is, the development of locally specific photographic practices by individuals who have adapted and domesticated new digital technologies. Joanna Sassoon (2004, 198) described acts of "translation" achieved in the process of digitizing analog photographs. In her view, "The nature of the photographic object and institutional practices that surround it means that translation from the material to the digital becomes a cultural, rather than simply a technological process." This cultural process is seen throughout this book in the editing mechanisms adopted by individuals to fulfill the cultural and the religious, as well as the social and civic responsibilities, to the deceased. Sassoon invokes Benjamin's notions that "no translation would be possible if, in its ultimate essence, it strove for the likeness of the original." In other words, there is a silent, universal consensus that fundamental changes occur during the translation process and that successful translation serves to express the "central reciprocal relationship" between two products (Benjamin [1968] 1985c: 73, 72). It is my argument that in this process of translating a personal analog photograph to a commemorative digital photo intended for public viewing, mourners also (re)shape the public sphere as a meeting place between the living and the dead, in which their own relatives—however ordinary—become worthy of fame.

When I visited the photo editor Jude in his studio, he emphasized that skin retouching helped to produce an effect of beauty. This warrants further analysis. In fashion photography, sign systems communicate the image of a person's status without regard to whether it is real or a kind of disguise (Evans and Thornton 1989). In their catalog accompanying the exhibition *In/sight*, a survey of African photographers from 1940 to the present, Okwui Enwezor and Octavio Zaya write of photography's "false sensation of presence" as well as the "fallacy of photographic images as stable, fixed information" (1996, 21). The authors note, with respect to the commercial photographer Seydou Keïta, that his "portraits foreground the fallacy as a fallacy. Models do not stand as illusorily clear iconic objects within colonial systems of race, sex, and gender. Instead, photographers and models engage in the open-ended ambiguous play of revealing and masking quotidian and fantasy identities" (see also Keller 2008, 102; 2013; Pinney 2003b, 215). Although Keïta had a unique vision, his work can be seen as representative of the development of studio portraiture in mid-twentieth-century West Africa and therefore serves as a suitable context for the obituary photographs in our study. Here the surviving relatives and a group of individuals collaborate to enact a false impression of death. Death is presented in an image that brims with life, or we can argue that, as Belting would put it, "we mask death's visage with an image of life" (2011, 122). The obituary photographs are made to smile, to look gorgeous and accomplished, by concealing physical along with biographical imperfections. Quotidian identities are masked so that the fantasy identity of heroism can be revealed; the heroic mask is unveiled following the event of death. As the product of the efforts of a team composed of the family members and photo editors, the obituary photograph is presented as the dead's final public show of greatness, splendor, and fashionability. Belting (2011) describes the photographic image as part of the cult of the dead and as a medium that reestablishes the presence of the deceased. In the context of public display, the bereaved do not perceive the picture as a mere representation of the deceased. Instead, they continue to engage with it as if it were a heroic, living entity deserving of the same respect and discretion accorded to the living. Belting asserts that the image is endowed with the power to replace the physical body, thereby acquiring a form of "Being" as a surrogate for the corporeal presence. Consequently, the image transcends its role as a mere substitute for loss, embodying Being through its representation of the body (Belting 2011, 87). In the communities under examination in southeastern Nigeria, the positioning of heroic images of the dead in public space makes the elevation from individual to abstract embodiment of Being into a public phenomenon.

At an intersection in Umubelle village at Awka, southeastern Nigeria, well-framed posters of the dead were mounted days before the burial ceremony. Passersby and the public were thus invited to partake in a public photo exhibition (see Fig. 11).

Some passersby who beheld the photos for the first time stopped and took a glance or a more prolonged study of the photographs (a practice typical of art exhibition halls). During this process, some of them expressed shock. They asked questions about the dead, pertaining to their family background and networks, when they died, and general information about the funeral as spec-

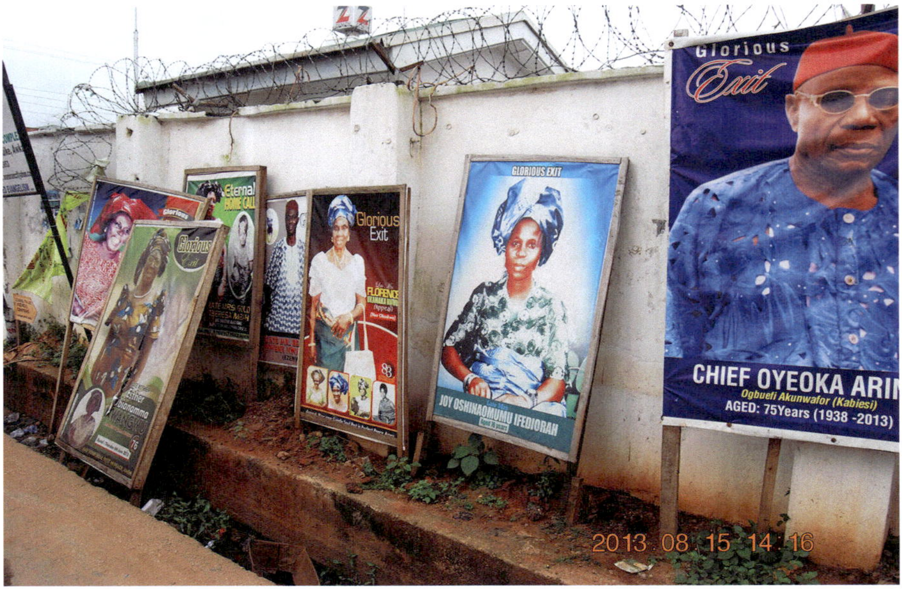

Fig. 11. Obituary posters mounted at Umubele village intersection, Awka, Anambra State

ified in the poster.[4] On public display at the village intersection, the transformed image of the deceased retains its embeddedness in everyday life. It is important to mention that such exhibitions adorn almost every major intersection in eastern Nigeria. The images of the deceased are no longer contained within the home; now they are "at large." The ubiquity effect is enhanced by the printing of the image on many other items that mourners carry with them away from the funeral. In recent times, with the help of modern digital and printing technology, there is no limit to where the deceased's photo can be printed, including clothes, ballpoints, handkerchiefs, plates, and umbrellas. Through the ubiquity of their image, the deceased can be felt to have attained a spiritual omnipresence that is simultaneously "hereafter" and "here."

In mobilizing discourses of life and death, the photos of the dead are often dislocated formally from the earthly realm and shifted unto the heavenly abode or embedded in a timeless backdrop suggestive of immortality. One interesting aspect of these photos is their rejection of the chronotropic interiority of the surface (Pinney 2003). The refusal of depth by the monochromatic background achieves a suspended movement purposefully designed to signal a transition, specifically, the end of the earthly voyage and entry into the spiritual realm. The photographs thereby simultaneously evince sociality and a ghostly detachment.

Returning to the poster of Chief George Nwoshi Nwobu (Fig. 7), we see that in the younger photo Nwobu is presented as a cosmopolitan youth, while he is shown as having climbed the ladder of success in the older photo, in which he is dressed in white lace and a red cap, with a titled fan. A picture of Jesus Christ has been inserted on the flat background at the top left corner. The poster conveys Nwobu's dual identity as a distinguished figure in his native Igbo society, evidenced by his titled attire and the alias of *Ezedioramma*, meaning "the king with unanimous approval," and a faithful adherent of Christianity, represented by the image of Jesus. A well-dressed Nwobu represents himself when he inhabited the social world of the living on earth, at two distinct and mutually distant points in time, while a sea of monochromatic background represents the timelessness of eternity.[5] This composition enacts the Igbos' sense of cosmic duality: the mutual independence between *ndi di ndu* (the living) and *ndi nwuru anwu* (the dead) or between *ana mmadu* (the land of the living) and *ana mmuo* (the land of the dead).

THE EVOLUTION OF A NEW PUBLIC IMAGE IN OBITUARY

By 2021, a new form of photo exhibition was introduced in funeral photography. When I attended the funeral of the late Professor Tina Okoye of Agulu in Anambra State, I discovered that the sitting room and the adjoining entrance were dedicated to her photo exhibition (Fig. 12a).

Tina's children selected photographs that heroized their mother's accomplishments across different facets of life. The photos were digitally printed, and an illusion of decorative wooden frames was created with Photoshop. The photos were mounted on the walls of the sitting room. In a small adjoining room, three photographs were also displayed, one of which at the entrance showed Tina adorned in her PhD gown. A similar pattern is seen at the funeral of the late Mrs. Christiana Nkechi Okaphor (Fig. 13). The late Okaphor's portraits conferred upon the formerly battered walls a facade of reverence, although they could not conceal the underlying decay. Okaphor stands in the photo, symbolically framed and decorated with purple, brown, and yellowish backgrounds, gazing meaningfully at the compound she left behind. In two of the photographs, she wears a long blue-green gown, a yellow or white blouse, a white or yellow headscarf, and carries a handbag, but

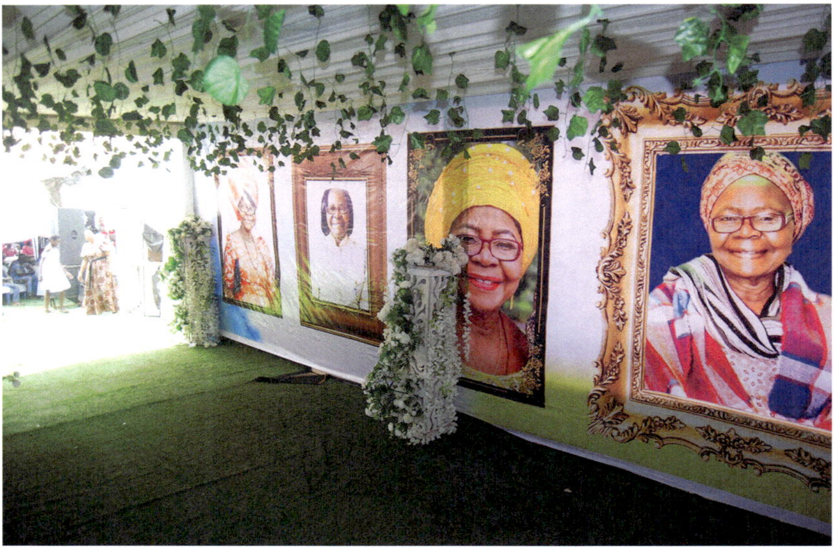

Fig. 12a. Funeral photographs of Professor Tina Okoye. The photoshopped photographs were displayed on the walls of the house.

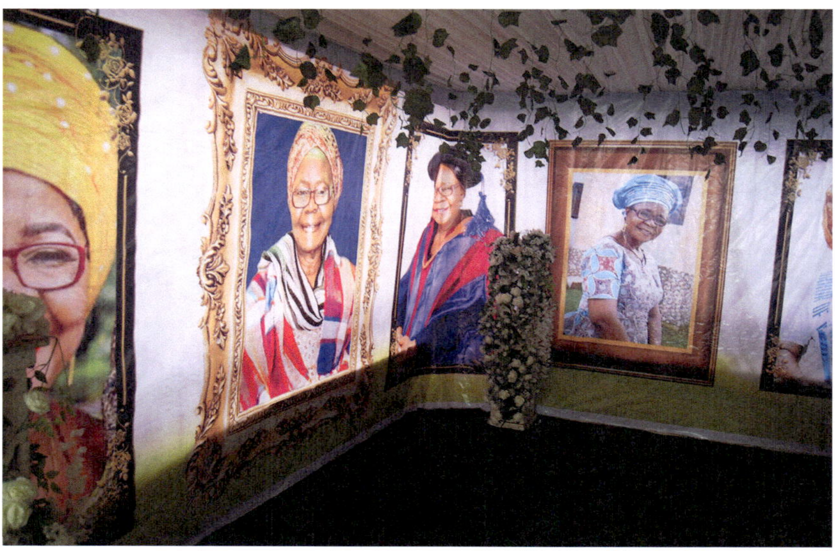

Fig. 12b. Funeral photographs of Professor Tina Okoye. The photoshopped photographs were displayed on the walls of the house.

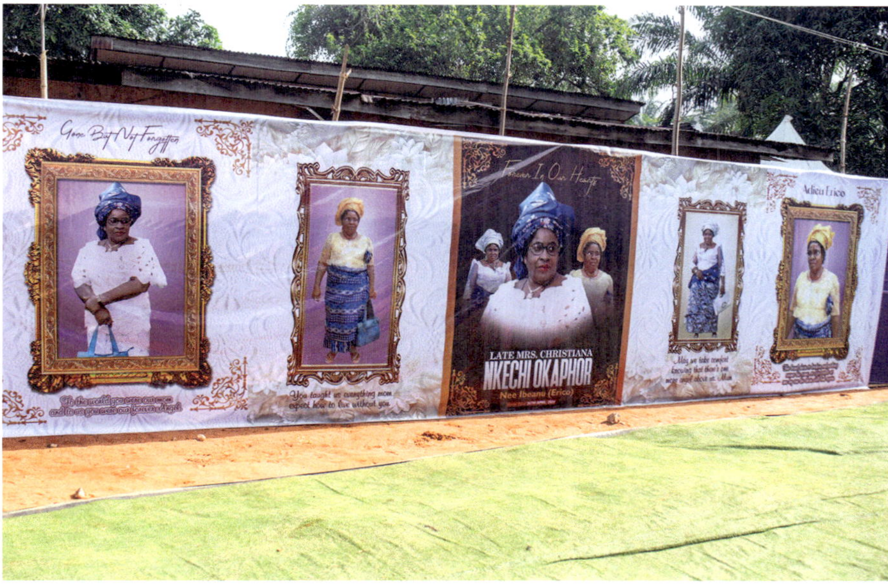

Fig. 13. Funeral poster of Mrs. Christiana Nkechi Okaphor at Adazi Nnukwu, Anambra State

photography has uprooted her from the earthly space and suspended her in a purple or golden background to appear like one about to rapture to heaven. In the other photograph in the middle, a dark, brownish, cloudy background envelopes three images. As images at the center of a public event, Okaphor's photographs are no longer ordinary photographs tucked inside an album. The photographs are now extraordinary images of exceptional import and elevated stature. In the previous case as well, the oversized photographs of Tina Okoye seem to enlarge the respectability and social relevance of the Okoye family.

Indeed, the technologically mediated obituary photo recasts the "Igbo" funeral as a constantly evolving project of modernity that gets entangled in the cultural crisis of digital identities, self-invention, and the social world. The rise of such visual expressive forms and their increasing technological mediation in cultural practices such as funerals are aspects of a more general shift toward what Keane (2002, 65) describes as a new "representational economy." To fully grasp this idiosyncratic accent of digital visuality in Igbo funerals, it is important to reflect on the relationship between the postcolonial state, photography, and society (Buckley 2006; cf. Comaroff and Comaroff 2001) and between politics and performance (cf. Gunner 2001). For, as I argue, the art of digitally reworked obituary photos is a political, technologically mediated, and visually spectacular act emerging from crises of self-invention. Here I am interested not merely in the reasons behind the rise of obituary posters in Igbo funerals per se but also, above all, in how these posters are articulated as public visual spectacles: drawing motley curious crowds at various village intersections, with an unusual capacity to push their visual expressive forms into a somewhat increasingly photography-conscious public (including market women, farmers, and passersby, among others), evoking a discourse that resonates beyond the spheres of the funeral.

TRIUMPHANT ENTRY INTO THE PUBLIC SPHERE THROUGH OBITUARY BILLBOARDS

After my interviews with ten family members who mounted giant billboards of their deceased in Anambra State, I discovered that such giant billboards were inspired by the families' desire to position their deceased within an expensive and exclusive realm. In Igbo cosmology, the public space is an exclusive space where only heroes make a triumphant entry. According to Ugwuanyi and Schofield, the Igbo public space, also known as the village arena, "was in the past and (in some places) is at present the centre for political, cultural, religious and economic meetings and a meeting point for human and spirit, for the dead and for the living" (2018, 11).

As one of the most important spaces in the framing of the Igbo landscape architecture, the arena has been constituted as a complex space for social and political alignments that is key to the existential survival of any Igbo community (Ugwuanyi and Schofield 2018; Aniakor 1984, 2002). Encompassing multifaceted dimensions of the Igbo social existence, it has become a dynamic space where the interplay of communal and individual agency converges and where the invocation of ancestral powers resonates across time and tradition. It is a space where familial bonds are strengthened, ritual oaths administered, masquerade performances reenacted, and judicial and religious obligations enforced (Aniakor 1980, 2002; Okolie 1992; Anigbo 1996; Ajaegbu 2014; Achebe 1958; Nwabueze 1984; Shelton 1971; Onyeozili and Ebbe 2012). J. Kelechi Ugwuanyi and John Schofield have conceptualized the Igbo public space as a combinatory force or power negotiated between permanence and temporality, a dialectic that unfolds within the liminal states of transition, where the intangible and the material converge. The concept of *iputa n'ogbo* in Igbo refers to "the act of making a giant and heroic leap into the public space." Those who summoned the courage to take the leap earned a triumphant ovation from the crowd. Making a giant leap into the public space entailed fulfilling certain onerous tasks that only those considered heroes could fulfill. However, it is important to note that the death of certain underachieving individuals instantaneously elevates them to a dignified, transcendent, and heroic stature.

To become like an ancestor that is spiritually ubiquitous, the dead must also make a ubiquitous presence through many spectacularly visual avenues, such as obituary billboards. From this elevated position, the dead person is ready to receive public offerings that will usher her or him into a glorious ancestral realm. My interviewees repeatedly alluded to one point: Their deceased were heroes and must be treated as such. For example, with the assistance of the commissioned photographer who edited their mother's photos, Nwudi's family selected many photographs of their mother from across many years. The final production of their funeral billboard and posters revealed the inclusion of multiple photographs of their mother at different stages of her life (Fig. 14)—from the 1970s to 2013.

Likewise, Elizabeth, the daughter of one of the deceased whose gigantic billboard was mounted in Nnewi, Anambra State, says:

> My father's burial and funeral was one of the grandest in town and we are happy that we gave him a befitting funeral. We had a wonderful giant billboard. In fact, it is as big as Ngige's father if you know how big Ngige's late father's poster looks like. The grand occasion and the billboard confirmed that my late dad was an important person in my town. The billboard could be seen from anywhere in the town.

The above narratives are quite expository of new modes of satisfaction derived from visibility. Chris Ngige was the former governor of Anambra State who had a society funeral for his late father. The obituary billboard of his late father was about sixteen feet wide, and it was positioned across the major cities in Anambra State. Elizabeth's competitive tendency with respect to the billboard's size indicates a widespread acknowledgment of obituary billboards as markers of affluence and prominence. In the case of the Nwudis, conspicuous insignia of wealth, as signified by fashion, were as important as the ubiquity and magnificence of visual display.

By 2020, obituary photographs became so magnificent that they com-

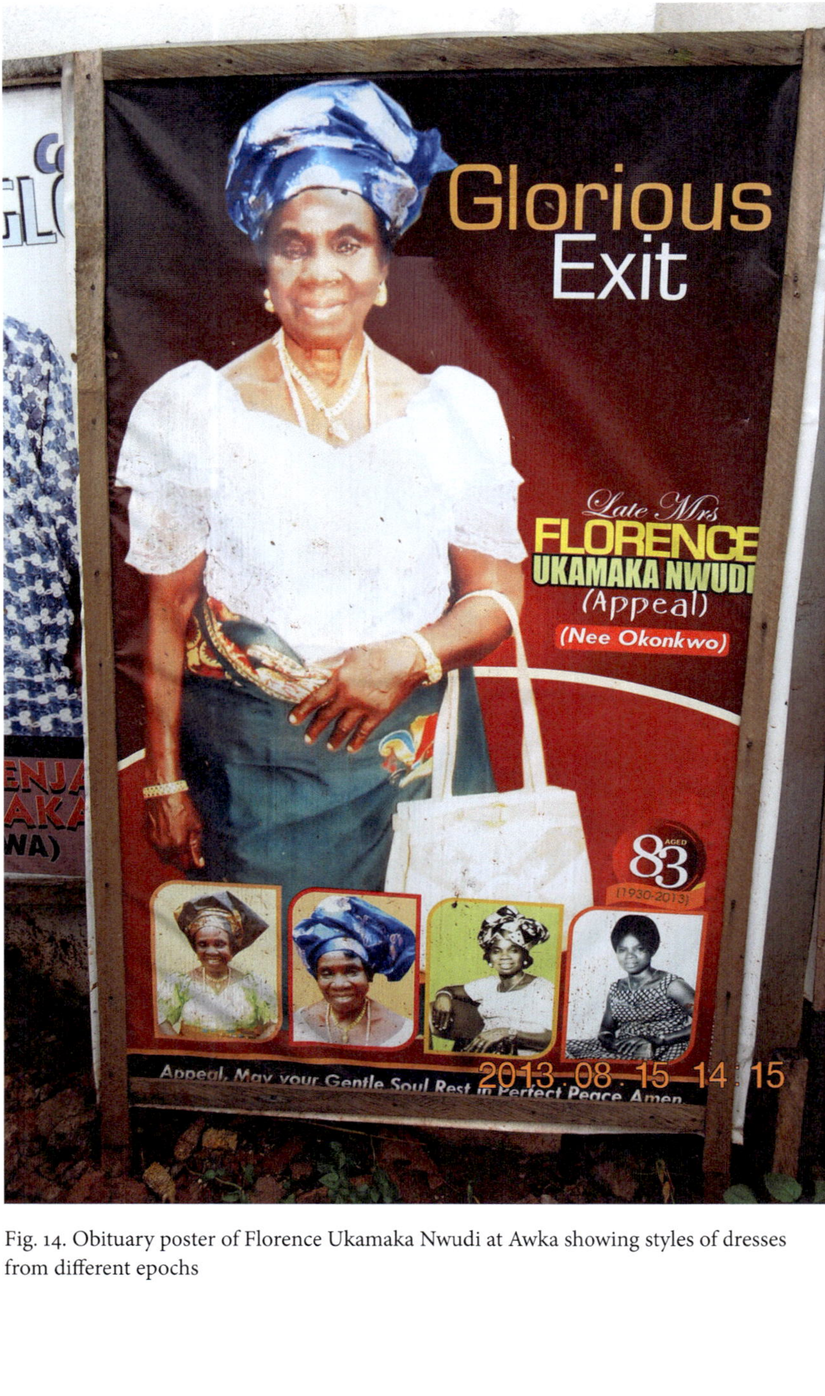

Fig. 14. Obituary poster of Florence Ukamaka Nwudi at Awka showing styles of dresses from different epochs

peted with giant political billboards in Nigeria. Political billboards gained currency in Nigeria during the 1980s when they were mounted to announce the imposing presence of a political contestant and attract followers to his or her candidacy. Vokes (2019b, 320) has described the emergence of billboards in Africa as a "new public political visual culture" with a proliferating impetus for photos across different visual media. In responding to the future aspiration of political modernization in Uganda, Vokes notes how billboards have enabled the image to become "more mobile and more easily mediated" (310). What is striking in Vokes's study is the identification of the potent force in "this new visual culture, with its ability to engender (or at least amplify) a sense of 'fantastic possibilities' that touches people within the most intimate arenas of their social life" (320). I want to suggest that obituary billboards as well employ "public visual artifacts as a means of generating an effective response to" a family's social aspirations (Vokes 2019b, 320). Obituary billboards are increasingly shaped by visions of postcolonial modernity in which families imagine progress as a grandiose project confirmed through photo promotion. In this reading, obituary billboards are a form of visual culture that has become publicly political, especially in how they attach an exaggerated importance to the socioeconomic influence of the families.

By turning over a page, a viewer not interested in a photograph can avoid viewing it in any print media. Similarly, while social media photographs can be intrusive to individual privacy, there is also a private mechanism to block such photos by unsubscribing, unfriending, disabling pop-up windows, or adjusting the spam settings on email. Viewers lack these amenable conveniences in obituary billboards. It is complicated to shut one's eyes each time one passes a dreaded obituary billboard, especially one that overly monopolizes public space. Photos of the deceased on gigantic obituary billboards become a visual strategy deployed by families to advertise their credentials unavoidably to many viewers. The obituary billboard of the late Herbert Kingsley Nnaedozie Ezisi was described by Ugochukwu, his townsman, as *Okwulu Okalisia* (the Igbo word for "one who is taller than everyone else when standing"). In other words, the billboard's gigantic size outcompetes any other structure around it. Encapsulated in the metaphor of *Okwulu Okalisia* is a seeming fact that, in obituary billboards, families and the deceased appear as big, important, and influential as possible in the public sphere. In *Okwulu Okalisia*, we see how the obituary billboard of Ezisi (Fig. 15) interrupted public visual traffic and, as such, attempted to command the public sphere in his community.

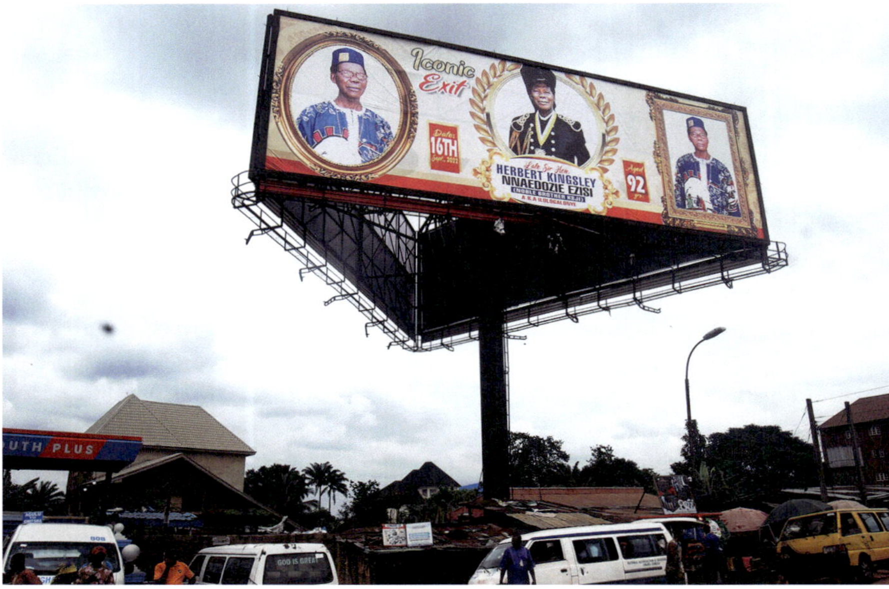

Fig. 15. A funeral billboard of Herbert Kingsley Nnaedozie Ezisi captioned "Iconic Exit." The billboard was mounted at an intersection in Agulu, Anambra State.

One can argue that according to the logic of *Okwulu Okalisia*, Ezisi's wealth can be assessed by the grandiosity of his obituary billboard, its aesthetic embellishment, and its photographic idealization. Therefore, in obituary billboards, one can argue that families vie for the political offices of visibility. Visibility and ostentation thus constitute salient features of obituary billboards. As previously discussed, in Igbo society, seeing and being seen are designed to launder not only the image of the dead but also that of the families of the deceased. Wealth is not only interpreted in terms of one's material possessions; it is also translated in one's capacity to achieve imposing visibility in the public arena. As with obituary posters—and to an even larger extent—mounting obituary billboards in public spaces extends death into the public sphere. This process stands in stark opposition to the tendency in Western societies to deny the fact of death, so that public expressions of grief are essentially taboo and death is sequestered, removed from the public sphere into the individual's private world (Giddens 1991; Mellor and Shilling 1993). Death in Africa on the other hand is an occasion for public mourning; it is an invitation to see and be seen. The public square becomes a space where the dead are positioned as public monuments or altars where mourners traverse and pause to pay homage.

Funerals, like any other rituals in the southeastern part of Nigeria, have entered the conspicuous consumption discourse of contemporary Nigerian society. Photography essentially fits into the discourse of conspicuous consumption such that Heike Behrend (2013) deployed the term "conspicuous display of wealth and prestige" to describe the photographic ritual among the people along the Kenyan coast of Mombasa. It was generally agreed among many of my respondents that the degree of wealth expended on a funeral determines the level of bliss the dead will enjoy in the hereafter. If enormous wealth is lavished at the funeral, the dead rejoice, but if there is moderate spending, the deceased grieve in the grave. The circulation of such popular narratives helps to substantiate the compelling influence notions of wealth have had on southeastern Nigerian Christian funerals. By late 2000, not only were funeral invitation cards a general practice, they defined the taste and glamour of contemporary southeastern Nigerian funerals and symbolically placed the survivors and celebrants on a pedestal of affluence.

It is widely understood that the inclusion of photos in funeral items comes with extra monetary charges. Again photos seen on funeral items enact certain idiosyncratic "bourgeois" disparities when individually analyzed. For example, an invitation card or a T-shirt of the dead devoid of a photo suggests a parsimonious celebration. In contrast, those imprinted with a photo are highly regarded as a mark of class. Likewise, colored or black-and-white photographs are assessed in terms of the family's financial accomplishment.

CONCLUSION

At the end of Nnabuife's funeral, Ezimma, his wife, remarked, "Nonso will be happy in his grave." This statement recurs in most Igbo funerals that are considered successful. And this confirms my submission that the dead are never dead if happiness can be ascribed to them (see, for example, Stevenson 1985). The living deploy all the processes mentioned above to negotiate their own forms of existence. If the dead are seen to partake in such negotiations, then the dead are never dead. The deceased is perceived as a silent observer.

Indices of wealth delineate and divide contemporary southeastern Nigerian funerals into classes. Funeral posters and billboards with befitting photographs have become one of these indices that help individuals to imagine their social world, measure their financial worth, and reclaim their fashionable status in the public consciousness. While funeral posters and billboards herald the entry point of such reclaiming, invitation cards and other items imprinted with the photo of the dead feature as their enduring index. This chapter has thus challenged the internal contradictions in these funeral posters and billboards, transforming them from something that merely documents the momentous periods of the dead's life into something that actively performs a role in conspicuous consumption and the assertion of heroism. Every funeral object is seen as a surface where the image of the dead can live a consummate unique social life. From obituary posters to billboards, brochures, and caskets, from stickers pasted on almost every object to invitation cards, the obituary photograph seems to have transformed itself into a ubiquitous image. This tendency toward ubiquity emerged among southeastern Nigerians to define new paradigms of elite consumption in funerals. While it is becoming increasingly fashionable to stage a befitting funeral ceremony, it seems such funerals are considered unduly parsimonious without an effusive overflow of photographic images.

In this chapter, the shifting aesthetics in the commemorative visual culture reflect an intensification of the Igbo cultural aspirations through funeral posters. Here, as funeral photographs navigate the sociopolitical and cultural evolution in the public sphere of posters, billboards, walls, and other surfaces, they become mobile surfaces where the complex metaphors of heroism, beauty, novelty and sartorial discourses are creatively inscribed. In the next chapter, these complex metaphors of heroism and the public sphere will be further pursued within the context of the funeral booklet.

CHAPTER 5

The Funeral Booklet

Documenting Heroic and Worthy Lives

This chapter asserts that funeral booklets serve as significant cultural artifacts that transform private family narratives into public memorials using intermediality. These booklets not only document and celebrate heroic and worthy lives but also reflect the complex interplay between traditional and modern practices, social status, diaspora experiences, evolving print technology, and family dynamics. The public life of the booklets allows the deceased to forge new subjectivities, becoming socially itinerant actors that provoke further inquiries and shape identities across family, communal, national, and international networks.

HISTORICAL EVOLUTION

The concept of a funeral booklet seems like a print culture popularized by colonial modernity. For example, Brown (2012) has noted the prevalence of privately printed memorial books in the Christian tradition during the nineteenth century in Western Europe. These memorial books typically included a photograph in the frontispiece, either a tipped-in original photograph or reproduction, along with some combination of texts that might include a biographical sketch, sermon, and recollections from friends and family. Brown argues that these works use texts, not pictures, to narrate the life of the departed. Only one image is needed to evoke their memory. Even though these printed works were shared with many mourners outside the family circle, they still expressed personal and intimate grief. This practice of documenting the dead seemed to be exported to the colonies in the wake of the colonial encounter. In the *Lagos Weekly Record* of November 4, 1893, on page 2, the only semblance of what appears to be a funeral booklet was referred to as an "In Memoriam address." The newspaper stated that it had received from the author, Rev. William Vivian, "a copy of an 'In Memoriam address' bearing the above title and delivered at the unveiling of the Truscott Memorial Tablet in Centenary Tabernacle Church, Sierra Leone." According to the article, the address contained a beautiful photograph of Reverend Truscott on its opening page, while the last page displayed an illustration of the Memorial Tablet "erected by the Native Christians among whom he laboured." It was noted that the "In Memoriam address" also contained a biography of Reverend Truscott as well as his "work and worth." The newspaper recommended that its readers purchase the address at "the Methodist Book Room, Broad Street, and at Mr. S. A Cole's, opposite Tanimehin House." Even before its publication in November 1893, incessant demands for the "address" had necessitated an advert by the publisher in October issue of the *Sierra Leonean Weekly News* to state that the "address" was not ready: "Beloved Truscott: The Memorial Address by the Rev. W. Vivian is not ready. Contains a fine portrait of The Late Rev. Thomas Truscott and a photogravure of The Memorial Tablet. Price Three pence. To be had at the Mission House" (8).

ON INTERMEDIALITY

By analyzing the funeral brochure of the late Rev. Thomas Truscott within the context of the historical development of a new visual culture surrounding death, we can begin to elaborate a theoretical foundation for understanding photographic practices as they expand beyond the conventional paradigms of studio photography. Individuals select preferred photos of their deceased from old analog family photo albums for inclusion in funeral booklets. The concept of intermediality enables understanding of how photos previously hidden in family albums reappear in funeral booklets. Scholarly texts on family photo albums in Africa have centered on the social meanings surrounding their collective and individual circulation in weddings or other social functions (Buckley 2000–2001; Mustafa 2002, 2005–6; Buggenhagen 2014, 82–84; 2023). None has examined the rising practice of the inclusion of family album photos in funeral booklets. Intermediality, a term that has been used by scholars working in cultural studies and media theory to describe relations of explicit inter-referentiality between and across media, has been theoretically expanded by Jenifer Bajorek in her study of photography in West Africa. Bajorek calls for shifting the discourse of intermediality away from "an overwhelming concern with two-dimensional images toward a much broader understanding of photography and its histories" (2020, 99). These histories involve the relationship between photography and other "specific spheres of artisanal production" in West Africa. However, while Bajorek specifically considers the reciprocal transactions between tailors, photographers, and printed textiles, she also notes the presence of a "much broader field of intermediality than has typically been acknowledged in dominant histories of photography" (103).[1] It is in this broader field that I would locate the journey of a photograph from a family album in the living room into the public view of the funeral booklet.

The concept of intermediality has enabled commemorative photography in Africa to be deployed in the political bureaucracy of nation-states and institutions. For example, Gore (2001) examined how the commemorative photographs of Oba Ovanranwen Nogbaisi taken by J. A. Green were mass-produced to address multiple concerns within the administrative authority of the royal institution. Oba Ovanranwen Nogbaisi ruled Benin from 1888 to 1897 until the British "punitive expedition," when Oba Ovonranwen was eventually captured and the photographs were taken. The photographs were "subsequently reproduced across a variety of mediums, including posters, calendars, almanacs, cups, plates, and commemorative cloths issued by the royal family" (Gore 2001, 325). The use of commemorative photographs is here seen through the prism of mass production in various media and their efficacy in the political discourses of nation-states. Oba Ovonranwen's commemorative photograph became a source of legitimation for the subsequently reigning Oba, who is identified with the achievements and exertion of the political and ritual authority of his predecessor. Gore (328) argues that "these processes of conflation in the articulation of the Obaship of the Edo Kingdom are a key aspect of the commemoration through which memory and the past are constituted." Werbner describes this as "the ongoing processes of memory work" (1998, 2). Commemorative photographs of Oba Ovonranwen invest the next Oba with a legitimacy that predates both colonial and postcolonial states. Thus, photographs taken in the event of conquest transform into instruments of royal legitimation and empowerment. To compare a modern example, I have observed Nigerians sharing old memorial photographs of nationalists on three Nigerian Facebook pages ("Nigeria Nostalgia Project 1960–1980," "Tudun Tsira," and "Asiri") to engender a new online history that provokes substantial popular responses (Nwafor 2024). Similarly, Oba Ovanranwen Nogbaisi's photographs taken during the punitive expedition have also generated interesting online debates that persistently question the role of visual evidence in historical inquiry. No known scholarship has investigated the social media responses Oba Ovanranwen Nogbaisi's photographs have generated. Overall, there is a significant scholarly gap with respect to the intermedial dialogue ensuing when analog photos are scanned into online media.

Yékú and Ojebode (2021) delve into the intersection of digital technologies and photographic practices, focusing on "the reproduction of historical memory, and the transmission of personal memories and collective nostalgia." Their examination of the Nigeria Nostalgia Project (NNP) highlights its role as a platform for reconstructing history through photographs. As photos shift from one medium to another on NNP, the stories evolve from individual and private into a collective narrative within the public sphere. Yékú and Ojebode (2021) have underscored the significance of this kind of public sphere by illustrating how citizens use photographs and videos to "resist the politics of forgetting" imposed by the Nigerian state (see Yékú 2022, 510). Instructively, these authors identify the public sphere of the NNP reconstituting commemoration as a form of solidarity and respect for the dead while serving as an arena for the critique of state power and decentered spaces of activism.

John Peffer studied how South Africans used commemorative portraiture to invert the repressive identification performed by the state in apartheid passbooks. The same identifying photographs were revalorized into memorial honorific pictures through enlargement and overpainting with props and colorful, fine clothing. Peffer argued that this mode of photographic practice opposed the sociopolitical history of the apartheid period (2015, 118). In the insistent reappearance of images originally intended for bureaucratic control, photography appears, in the words of Bajorek, as a "historical force in its own right, one that is not confined to the sphere of the image or even . . . to the field of the visual" (2012, 140). In a different cultural context, Michelle Caswell (2014, 7) likewise describes "a new archive of responses" related to archival photographs from the Khmer Rouge era in Cambodia. Caswell explores how the mugshots taken at the Tuol Sleng prison evolved over time from mere administrative records to potent tools for memory, justice, and human rights advocacy. The above-mentioned theoretical ideas suggest a radical transformation of the "original" photographic records into objects with complex social lives, or what Eric Ketelaar describes as "dynamic objects in motion," which continue to shift with each new use and contextualization. Ketelaar (2001, 138) uses the term "activation" to refer to the consistent human mediation of historical photographs, whereby the photographs acquire new meaning and new social lives.

As a black-and-white photograph taken in the twentieth century is juxtaposed with the colored digital print in the pages of a funeral booklet in the twenty-first century, the material and technological progression of the historical photograph is implied. The photograph's changing social life is clearly evident in its new role in the funeral booklet. When photographs transition from family albums to funeral booklets, I suggest, they negotiate new social spaces, construct novel subjectivities, and provoke inquiries into family dynamics, aspirations, and moralities (cf. Werbner 1991, 2002). Additionally, they influence community and national networks and mobilities within the Atlantic visualscape (cf. Schneider 2018). Especially, funeral booklets play an important role in shaping family histories and demonstrating prestige.[2]

A VISUAL AND VERBAL HISTORY OF THE PUBLIC FIGURE

In this chapter, I examine the funeral booklets that share features similar to Reverend Truscott's "address." These features include textual documentation, a biographical narrative, and photographic images. While Reverend Truscott's "address" contained only one portrait photograph, the funeral booklets I analyze in this chapter demonstrate an enchantment with multiple photographs taken from the family photo album of the deceased.

The text in the booklet confers a heroic and biographical quality to the photograph. In addition to mourning the dead through published tributes, mourners also deployed their own personal photographs to suggest intimacy by bringing their own subjectivity into the booklets. Viewing the funeral booklet as a public space to announce one's existence, mourners thus also pursued recognition and visibility.

The recent funeral booklets I study have their roots in the nineteenth century, but they also draw from the innovations in print technology that emerged after the 1890s. These advances enabled the creation of a distinctive style of the booklet that connects the past and the present. As suggested in chapter 3, the complex practice of seeking renown through newspapers by Nigerian nationalists during the early twentieth century also informs the current practice. In the 1970s, funeral booklets were presented as mere pamphlets of a few pages shared at the burial and funeral to give information about the deceased (Lawuyi 1991b; Omoruyi 1988; Aronson 2017).[3] Lawuyi explored the complex interplay of religion, culture, and society in Yoruba funeral biographies. The absence of photographs in the above authors' analyses suggests that these visual elements were either rare or nonexistent in the funeral pamphlets they examined. Authors of more recent studies, instead of looking at the photographic aspect of the booklet, tend to continue to study the texts in funeral pamphlets as "a useful historical source" (Adotey 2018, 60) or a source of biographical information (Adjah 2007). Building on their fascinating insights, this chapter pays special attention to family photos as they transition from the private spaces of family albums to the public sphere of funeral booklets. The photos in the booklets transcend their visual form: They contain narratives of lives lived, the legacies of loved ones, and expressions of selfhood. As quotidian snapshots of ordinary lives elevated to extraordinary public figures, they reveal the unique ways that the dead are commemorated and the living are consoled.

In chapter 4, I argue that contemporary obituary posters comprise an evolution of the traditional sculptural form of Ikenga. Likewise, the obituary booklet can be seen to have evolved from the Nigerian praise singing tradition, which in Yoruba local parlance is known as *oriki*. It would be necessary to explore the Yoruba *oriki* and see how this might have shaped a contemporary resurgence of such practice among the Igbo of southeastern Nigeria. Karin Barber in her outstanding study *I Could Speak Until Tomorrow: Oriki, Women and the Past in a Yoruba* (1991)[4] shows how Yoruba commemorative poetry connects the dead with the living. According to Barber (1991, 20), "By keeping alive the memory of your predecessors, you ensure that your successors will keep alive the memory of you." *Oriki* serves the preservation of communal bonds, facilitating both the recalibration and consolidation of affiliations within the sociospiritual matrix. *Oriki* is therefore at the center of a crucial political process, one that reveals a multilayered framework instrumental in the rise of "big men" in traditional Yoruba society. It also gives narrative form to memories of big men and reinforces the centrality of this dynamic of class relations to Yoruba communal existence. According to Barber (1991, 213), "Everyone had a different set of big men in memory. A few built themselves up so conspicuously that they were remembered by many people." Numerous others attained a fame that was more circumscribed and localized, celebrated primarily within their immediate social circles and family units.

In this depiction, a competitive landscape is populated by "a multiplicity of individuals" striving for self-establishment, as opposed to a "clearly defined universally recognized category of big men and another category of followers." *Oriki* fundamentally supports and channels the culture of bigmanism. It is invested in a fluid blend of heroism and remembrance. *Oriki* of big men is essentially an oral praise-singing that draws on commemorative poetry and chants to reinforce notions of the "elite" in the Yoruba context. Traditional Yoruba thought, according to Adeboye, (2003, 283) emphasized the possession of *ola*, which translates as "honor." While the ultimate in individual social aggrandizement in precolonial Yorubaland was to attain a position of *ola*, there were several mediating social categories between the masses and *olola* (possessor of *ola*) (283). These categories included the *Borokinni/Gbajumo* (celebrities), *Oloro/Olowo* (men of wealth), *Ologun* (powerful warriors who came into the limelight in the nineteenth century), and *Oloye* (titleholders) (283). Barber (1991, 203) has observed that in terms of individual social advancement in the traditional Yoruba society, what men hoped to achieve was "not wealth as such or power as such, but a total state of sufficiency and command over their social environment, a state called *ola*. *Ola* is [a] complex, composite, shifting, and sensuously realized concept . . . [It] is ultimately the capacity to attract and retain the gaze of other people." While Barber identifies the elements of self-sufficiency, social command, and public acknowledgment in *ola*, she leaves out an important aspect of *ola*, which is splendor. The splendor of *ola* transcends all that is mean, poor, obscure, or inadequate and rises above the inhibition of powerlessness or low esteem (Nwafor 2021). It is simultaneously self-assured and magnificent. In certain respects, the concept of the elite in Western philosophy corresponded to the notion of *olola* (and *ola*) in traditional Yoruba thought. Underlying both concepts are principles of high class, social influence, social superiority, and public acknowledgment. As a dynamic category, values associated with eliteness are often modified and appropriated within its limits as a response to changing times. In the case of Lagos eliteness, many changes were foisted on it, not only in the realm of values but also in lifestyle and consumption (Mann 1985, 284; Cole 1975, 63, 170, 199).

In colonial Lagos, those who constituted the elite comprised several categories. There were the chiefs, whom we could call the traditional elite; wealthy individuals who corresponded to the commercial elite; and the first-generation educated intelligentsia, whom we could call the educated elite (Mann 1985, 284). During the decolonization period, a new set of individuals acquired elite status. These were the politicians (284). Although educated, their ticket to elite status was more attributed to the leadership role they played. There were also elites comprising religious leaders in traditional religion, Islam, and Christianity. Many of the prominent individuals in Lagos had numerous wives and, thus, children, whom they had an obligation to care for at every special social occasion (284). Although polygamy was a common practice in traditional Yorubaland, it acquired a wider appeal to the nouveau riche in the twentieth century. According to Okediji and Okediji (2012 19), "Although polygamy was valued in traditional Yoruba society for social and economic reasons, it did not appear to be the preferred form of marriage for many except those who were relatively affluent, and hence, were in a strong position to maintain a big household." Hence, polygamy constituted a significant force in the *oriki* of big men and also emerged as a symbolic desire by many families upon death, especially in narratives involving family expansion. This will be shown in subsequent discussions where funeral booklets became a space and occasion to amplify family pedigree, expand class, reinforce self-sufficiency, and underscore the tenets of *ołola* via photographic representations of kinship networks.

Following Barber, Adeleke Adeèkó deploys the concept of "visuality in Orality" to demonstrate that the Nigerian *Ovation* magazine, in existence since the 1990s, "reworks the Yoruba *oriki* praise chants into the photographic medium" (2012, 332). After *Ovation*, there was an unprecedented proliferation of similar magazines, each emphasizing photographs over printed words. They covered mainly social events such as weddings, funerals, and birthday parties by deploying only photographs as instruments of communication (Nwafor 2021). In the photographs, "Funerals of the old are depicted as culminations of high achievement, and the rare representation of the death of the young often laments the unfortunate abbreviation of an unfolding greatness" (Adeèkó 2012, 337). *Ovation* emerged to satisfy the yearnings of the wealthy in such a manner that bodily and moral imperfections were erased through a photographic endorsement. This tendency clearly reenacts Barber's notions of *olola* in *oriki*.

Adeèkó suggests that the evolution of a hybridized visual form of praise-singing in Lagos can be attributed to the inherent adaptability of Yoruba panegyric traditions. However, it is imperative to consider the manner in which the increasing cosmopolitanism of Lagos in the 1980s and 1990s influenced lifestyle and aesthetic practices. In this context, *oriki* underwent a transformation into an urban cultural phenomenon, entwined with the patronage-driven prebendal politics characteristic of that era. It emerged as a cosmopolitan urban genre utilized by residents of diverse ethnic backgrounds within Nigeria to maneuver through the class war exacerbated by the ethical decay associated with military dictatorship. In other words, the "infiltration of praise-singing into Lagos-based popular culture" may not be solely interpreted within the context of Adeèkó's affirmative extension of the traditional Yoruba panegyric form. Although Adeèkó's model of praise-singing could be a useful conceptual model to approach the emergence of funeral booklets in 1990s Nigeria, one must carefully reflect on other possible influences on this practice. One particular influence is the impact of the dwindling oil economy.

The decline in oil revenue in the 1980s resulted in the introduction of the Structural Adjustment Program (SAP) in most developing nations, forcing governments to cut budgetary spending and introduce austerity measures. In Nigeria, for example, the Nigerian military introduced many counterproductive economic reforms that served as an avenue to enrich corrupt military cabals and their cronies. This strategy impoverished the larger population and eroded the middle class. However, while the middle class was occluded in the struggle to access the economic benefits of the nation's resources, the rich continued to expand their economic base and social capital through their connection with the military. In essence, the rich monopolized the economic means and political connections required to inscribe one's social presence, especially through the preponderant visual media of television, newspapers, and magazines. Photographs may also have gained increasing recognition across different social settings due to the influence of emerging print capitalism and the ubiquity of handheld cameras, as well as the rise of Igbo highlife music in the 1990s.

In the wake of the economic meltdown of the Structural Adjustment Program, Igbo highlife music celebrated the rich, announced their presence, and endorsed their reckless and extravagant lifestyles. In their songs, highlife musicians such as Oliver de Coque and Osita Osadebe adopted a style that expanded and entrenched the social capital of the rich through praise. Given that songs travel extensively beyond one's immediate space, the flattery style of these musicians helped consolidate the social dominion of the rich in the public consciousness of Nigerians. Such increasing urge for material and visual extravagance was irresistible and soon trickled down to the commons, where it appeared as photographs printed on various occasions in different formats, including as funeral pamphlets. In the early 2000s, funeral pamphlets had a few photographs aiming to imitate the photos of the wealthy in *Ovation* and other high-profile magazines.

The pamphlets were initially produced in black and white and contained the funeral order of service along with a few black-and-white photographic prints of the deceased. By the mid-2000s, relentless in their effort to confront and contest the unequal visual representation championed by the rich, the middle class further attempted to reinscribe their social presence into the public sphere. Soon, the funeral pamphlets graduated into a more elaborate booklet containing a few colored photographs. The photos in these booklets perform the conscious function of presenting to the public a flawless body and soul of the dead, along with a fulfilled, progressive family. Perhaps in recognition of the above changes across space and time, the question could still be, "What does family photography do? And what happens when its images enter the public sphere?" (Rose 2016, 4). Numerous questions concerning the role and place of family photos need to be addressed as they enter the public domain: questions such as "What can the images in the albums tell us about their owners, taken either as individuals or as belonging to a local culture? How have the albums been used? What have they meant to their owners?" (Sandbye 2014, 12). Bazin (1967, 14) sees the family photo album as a space where "photography does not create eternity, as art does; it embalms time, rescuing it simply from its proper corruption."

Family photo albums have been central to the construction of family togetherness in Africa by serving as a material embodiment of the self as well as a site for the production of narratives of the self (Vokes 2008, 2012).[5] In her work on photography in Dakar, Hudita Nura Mustafa (2005) observes how photographs constituted part of the mutual material exchange among women. Taking photographs dressed in sophisticated and dainty attires, building photo albums, and exchanging photos among family and friends became part of the sartorial modernity that enabled Senegalese women to engage in self-performativity (*sañse*) often associated with concepts of gender decorum and honor. Edwards (2005) has argued that as material objects, photographs possess relational and experiential qualities, enabling them to provoke empathy among humans. Through the photograph's multiplicity of possible interpretations, photographic identities are unstable and open to critical reflection (Behrend 2013; Mustafa 2005; Vokes 2008). Richard Vokes and Darren Newbury (2018, 2) have interpreted these complex photographic identities as constituting a social world shaped by "fantasies, imagination, and projections." This social world is inherently irreducible and possesses a multidimensional social agency characterized by its reproducibility, exchangeability, and circulation (Smith and Vokes 2008).

In the current social context in which the photograph has become a radically manipulable technological device, Kratz (2012), following Appadurai (1986a), has argued that photographs have social lives (Kopytoff 1986; Pinney 1997; Hoskins 1998; Harris 2004). To fully understand what certain family photo albums do and what they mean to different families, it is important to examine their participation in the funeral booklet. The following section is drawn from my study of one hundred funeral booklets, although six are cited specifically. The selection was carefully made to reflect the generic pattern adopted by the rest.

THE STRUCTURE OF THE FUNERAL BOOKLET

A typical funeral booklet comprises fifty to one hundred or as many as three hundred pages, divided into five or more segments: the cover, the biography, the order of church service, the family photos, and the tributes. The one hundred funeral booklets I studied retained most segments, with slightly different arrangements. In some, the family photos came before the tributes or vice versa. For example, the funeral booklet of the late Ozo Chief Oyeoka Offodile (1917–2014) is eighty eight pages long and made up of four sections. Pages 1 to 6 are Ozo's biography, pages 7 to 22 are the order of the funeral mass, pages 23 to 37 comprise the family photo album, and the last segment, pages 38 to 88, is devoted to tributes. All the segments have photographs on some pages to support some textual narratives. In the funeral booklet of the late Nonso Nnabuife (1949–2017) (Fig. 17), the biography comes first, followed by the family photo album and tributes. In the case of Nnabuife, the order of funeral mass was printed as a separate booklet. In the funeral booklet of Madam Elizabeth Onuigboegbunam Emoh (sixty-eight years old), the biography comes first, followed by the order of the funeral mass, the tributes, and then the family photo album. Photos of the deceased are printed on the cover and back pages of almost all the booklets.

Nnabuife's and Ozo's booklets are printed with more expensive paper and would be regarded as booklets of more affluent families. Less expensive booklets are produced with ordinary paper and the photographs appear in black and white to save cost. The photos are also printed in miniature size and packed into a few pages to save costs. Typical examples are the booklets of the late Madam Anna Nwadi Okon-Obiorah (seventy-nine years) and her late husband, Okon-Obiorah (Figs 23 and 24). In Okon-Obiorah's booklet, twenty-nine photographs are crammed into four pages. From these characteristics, the wealth of each family can be determined.

THE COVER PAGE

The cover is one of the most crucial aspects of the funeral booklet. The cover pages of both Nnabuife's and Offodile's booklets have their names written in full with their religious titles, KSM, meaning Knight of St. Mulumba of the Catholic Church. In the case of Offodile, an additional national award, MFR, is added, which is one of the merit awards of the Nigerian presidency in recognition of an individual's contribution to national development. While Offodile has the title "Ozo" prefixed to his name, Nnabuife has his academic title, "Prof," in his name (Figs. 16 and 17).

"Ozo" is the highest title among male age grades in Igboland, while wealth is the first benchmark in the stages of *Ozo* title-taking. According to one saying, *Ichi ozo bu maka ndi ogadagidi*, "Taking the Ozo title is an affair for superior beings." In some communities, one seeking such title is expected to deposit a minimum of three million naira ($7,000) to the institution responsible for the title-taking. This money excludes the celebrant's financial expenditure on food, entertainment, and incidentals that, in most cases, cater to the daily meals of an entire community for at least one month.[6] In more than sixty booklets I examined, the traditional institution is emphasized, and the *Ozo* title is prominently reflected on the cover pages in the names of the deceased. The exorbitant financial demand of the *Ozo* title-taking and its accompanying grandeur make it an enviable position in elite society. Therefore, the title and its accompanying visual attributes must be exhibited on the cover of the booklet as a reflection of the late individual's importance according to community discourses of achievement. Ozo Chief Elias Oyeoka Offodile thus belonged to the enviable society.

In another booklet of the late Innocent Ofor (1929–2013), the cover is captioned "Chief Innocent Ezeanyaku Ofor, KSM" (Fig. 18). It is noticed that Ofor's cover has a photograph of him dressed in his Knight of St Mulumba (KSM) attire. Even though Ofor's name on the cover page is written with his title of "Chief" in recognition of his accomplishment in his community, his photo shows him in his KSM attire to underscore that he also achieved a religious title. A similar format was adopted in the late Chief George Nwabueze Onwuegbune's funeral booklet (Ogbuefi Nwachinemelu) (Fig. 19). While

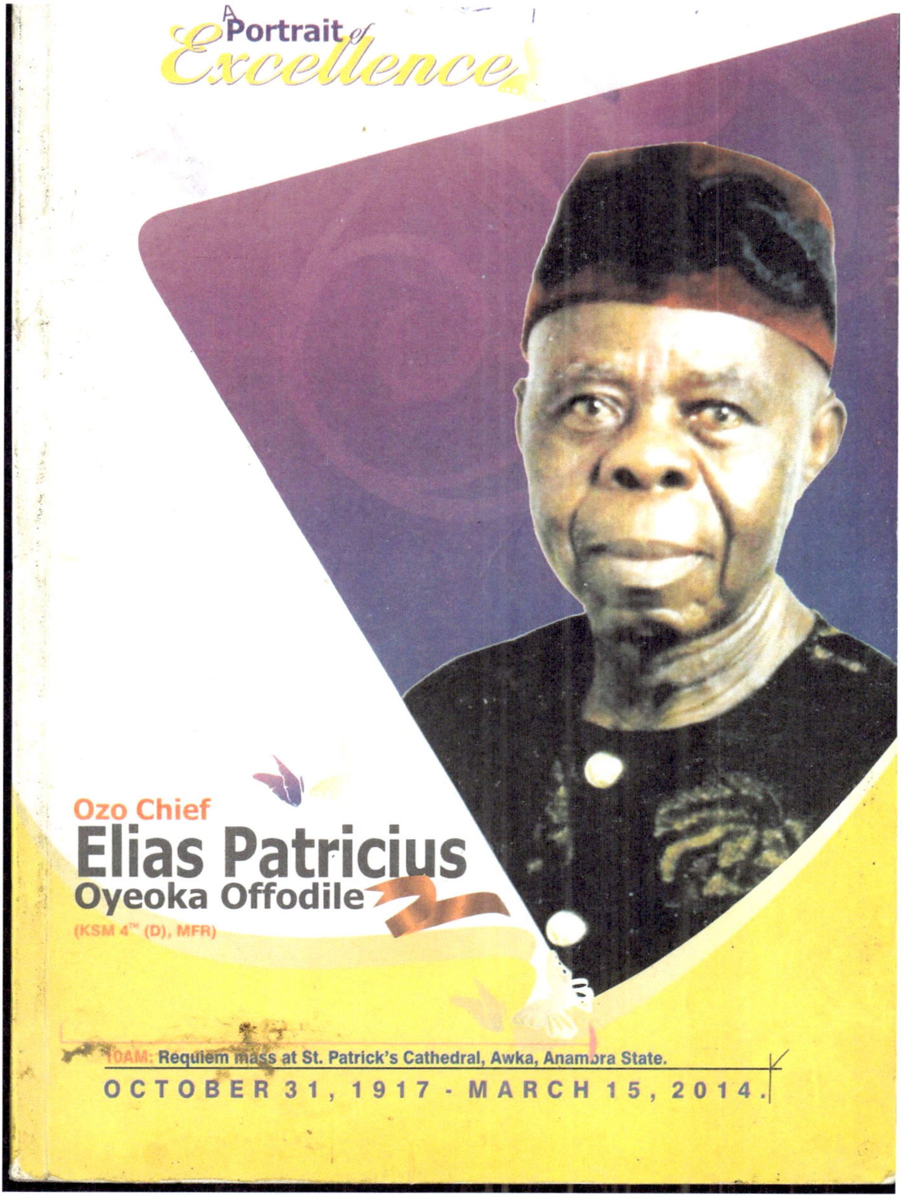

Fig. 16. Funeral booklet of Ozo Chief Elias Patricius Oyeoka Offodile at Awka, Anambra State

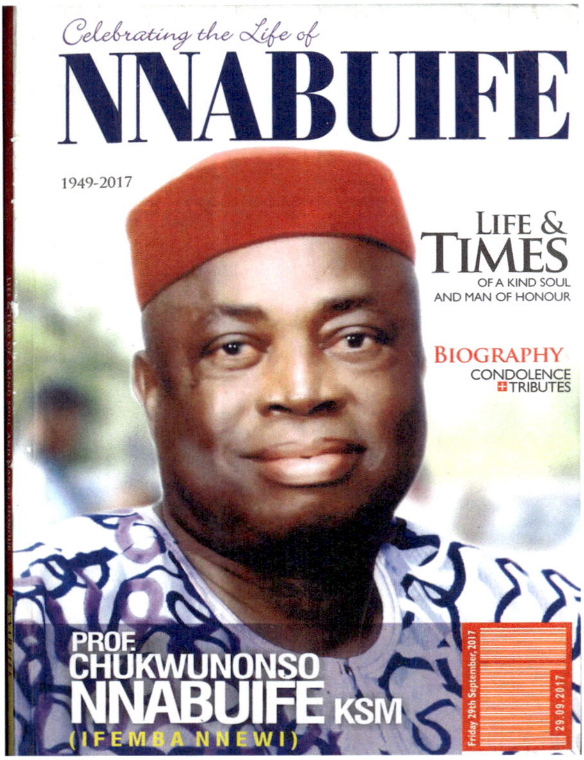

Fig. 17. Funeral booklet of Professor Nonso Nnabuife at Nnewi, Anambra State

Onwuegbune is dressed in his Catholic Men's Organization (CMO) uniform, he wears a red cap decorated with an eagle's feather and holds a chieftaincy fan and an elephant tusk, four symbols of a titled chief in Igbo traditional institution. Because it is unlikely that one wearing a CMO uniform would simultaneously flank emblems of traditional institutions, I made an effort to track the computer technician who designed the photograph, and she revealed that the elephant tusk and the Ozo-titled fan were photoshopped. In her account, she was instructed by the children to create a photograph that would capture all the attributes of their late father to exemplify completeness in religious and traditional institutions. In chapter 4, we saw a very similar artistic style where the Ikenga sculpture was armed with an elephant tusk, a horn, and a matchet. The computer technician has become a contemporary version of the traditional sculptor, using Photoshop in place of sculptors' tools. Both aspire for one thing: to pronounce the heroic attributes of an accomplished life.

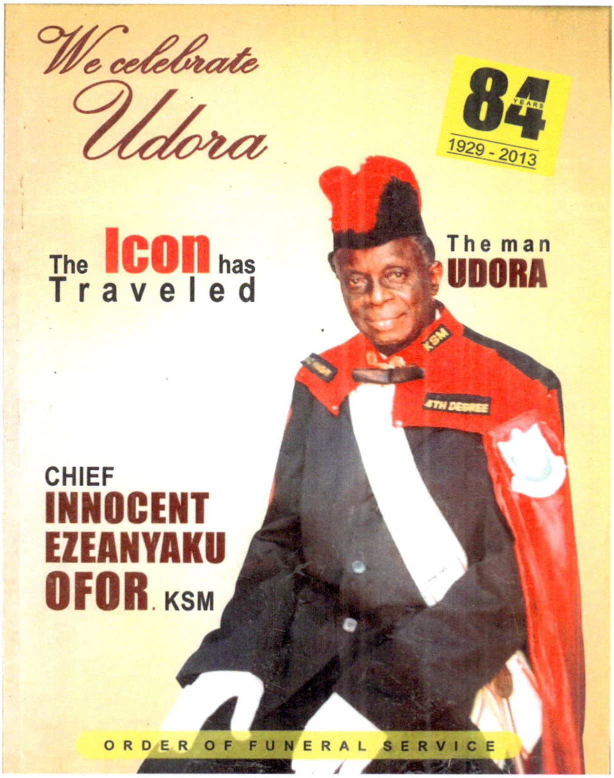

Fig. 18. Funeral booklet of Chief Innocent Ezeanyaku Ofor, KSM

The magisterial radiance of Jesus's image, directly enclosing Onwuegbune's photo, powerfully conveys the message of "transition to glory"—the ultimate destiny of every faithful soul. Juxtaposing this photo is another portrait-sized photo of Onwuegbune in his red cap, traditional white dress, and a chaplet hung over his neck. In Ofor's cover, "Chief" and "Knight" address two enviable positions; "Chief" is traditional and conveyed in a written text, while "Knight" is religious and conveyed through his well-robed figure, while Onwuegbune's cover presents a visual convergence of cultural and religious identities, encapsulated in a single photographic frame. This synthesis is materially articulated through the sartorial ensemble: the Catholic Men's Organization (CMO) attire, the emblematic red cap, the eagle's feather, the chieftaincy fan, and the elephant tusk—all of which collectively signify a negotiated identity grounded in indigenous authority and Christian symbol-

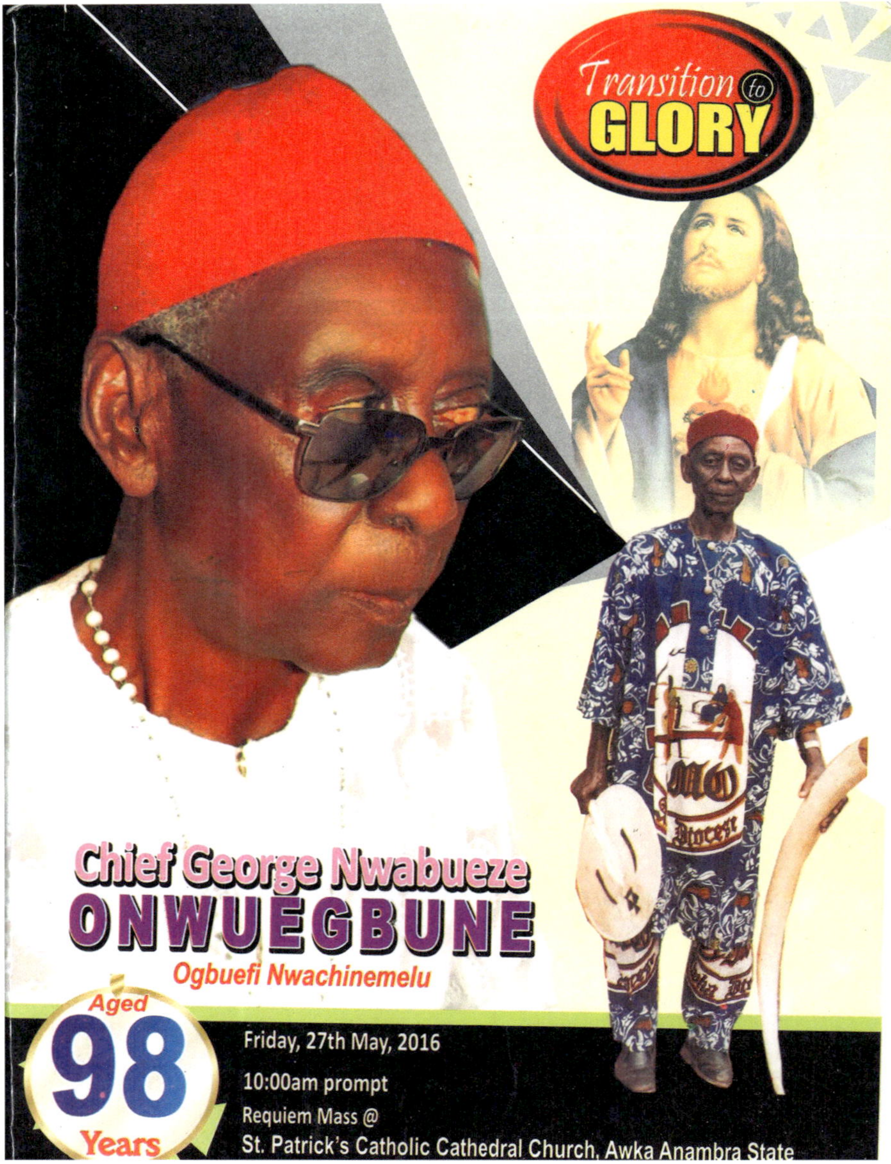

Fig. 19. Cover of Chief George Nwabueze Onwuegbune's funeral booklet. Chief George Nwabueze Onwuegbune is shown robed in traditional and Christian attire at the same time.

ism. As in the funeral posters examined in chapter 4, here the photograph is used to communicate social position with the help of Photoshop.

All the cover pages of the one hundred booklets I studied bear the dates of the church service, with the respective ages of the deceased written beneath the photos. On the cover of seventy-five of the booklets, the deceased are dressed in their traditional attires, while in ten, they are dressed in their academic gowns; the remaining fifteen have them in their religious dresses and Western suits. The back covers of the booklets have photos of the deceased, either in their younger or their older ages and dressed in their traditional, religious, or other attire. For example, while the overleaf of Offodile's cover page has a photo showing him dressed in an ash-colored Western suit and tie, the overleaf of Nnabuife's cover page shows him dressed in traditional attire.

These photos show how the cover pages of funeral booklets are important spaces for public exhibition of the deceased's most striking credentials. The first public impression of the deceased's most sterling accomplishments in fame and character is formed by the cover photo and its accompanying titles. It can therefore be said that without a befitting photograph, the cover page of a funeral booklet is incomplete. My interviews with eighty-eight family members who own the booklets I studied overwhelmingly point to one fact: They selected the best photos for the cover of the booklet from their family albums to visually accentuate the beauty, grandeur, greatness, and achievements of the deceased.

Ekemma said, "It took us more than one week to get the best photo for this cover; the printer eventually collected all the photos and later sent the one he thought was the best. That was the one where Papa dressed in his Ozo titled costume." Likewise, Uchenna narrated how his family could not choose a befitting photo of their late mother for more than five days, but eventually "settled for the picture where mum dressed in her traditional outfit." More than twenty individuals told me that the printers and photographers eventually chose what they thought was a befitting cover photo for them. In comparison, thirty individuals told me it was a painstaking process of negotiation among their siblings who made different choices. Ejike said: "Searching for Mama's photos was not so easy; the photographer who printed the booklet eventually advised us to use a picture where Mama dressed in her PhD graduation gown, which everyone accepted." Photographers have functioned in dual or multiple capacities as printers of booklets. Some of them take up the role of middlemen, while some are graphic designers and photo editors who complete the designs and then take them to a printing press for the final production. Many of those I interviewed said that the photographers contracted to photograph the funeral also produced funeral posters and booklets. This is akin to what Liam Buckley observed among the Gambians.

Charles Ogu told me that he didn't bother to select any photo for the cover of his dad's funeral booklet and that "the printer did the entire selection and placement in relevant places." This statement is reminiscent of the quiet confidence sitters reposed in photographers during the early days of photography: photographers directed the sitters' poses, decorated them with cosmetics, and then determined when the occasion was ripe for a photo shoot. That some families allowed the photographers and printers to choose the best photo for the cover pages of their deceased's funeral booklets indicates that many families are still confident in the photographer's curatorial infallibility beyond the studio spaces. It speaks to the type of influence wielded by photographers even in death.

In most Christian funeral masses I attended, once the booklets were distributed inside the church, most individuals made a prolonged study of the cover page. My conversation with some mourners afterward revealed that the cover photos elicited a strong emotional reaction. I watched as some women looked at the cover photo and sighed painfully. The cover photo, therefore, affords the mourners an opportunity for instant pictorial assessment and emotional reaction. In my subsequent interviews with fifty individuals who attended burials and got funeral booklets, they mentioned that they first studied the cover by reading every word in it, viewed the photo to understand who the deceased was, what he or she achieved, the deceased's age, and what the deceased represented to the surviving families. Many I interviewed harped on the suitability of the cover photo. One said, "I always recognize a less affluent family through the photos in the booklet. Once the photos are in black and white, few and blurred, I don't need anyone to tell me that the family is not so rich." In this way, photographs in funeral booklets embody and disseminate sentiments of wealth and prestige. Recognizing these impactful nuances of the cover photo, families attempt to launder the reputation of their deceased using photographs and textual inscription with Photoshop software. For example, the children of the late Ozo Offodile titled the cover of his booklet "a portrait of excellence" (Fig. 16). Excellence is presented as an all-embracing portfolio of achievement encapsulated in the singular portrait photo of Offodile on the cover. Excellence is also exuded in the striking, high-quality print.

BIOGRAPHY

As with the photo selection and editing, the biography section of the booklet can also be an occasion for the consultation of professionals. For example, Nwamaka sought help from a professor who, in addition to being a friend of her late husband, is also a writer. Nwamaka provided the professor with her late husband's curriculum vitae. According to Nwamaka, while writing the biography, the professor occasionally called her to seek clarification. Forty other families also confirmed that they did not write their deceased's biography but sought professional writers' services. Twenty-one families composed the biography by themselves. Some were written by educated children and others by spouses who could write very well. Chinwoke, an administrative staff member at Nnamdi Azikiwe University, told me that he could not articulate a compelling biography using the appropriate vocabulary that would be attractive to readers, so he sought the services of his friend, who is an accomplished writer in the English Department of Nnamdi Azikiwe University. Overall, it is evident that surviving relatives take biography seriously. The text is broken into many sections: birth, education, career, religious life, community life, marital life, retirement, ailment, and death. For example, Ozo Offodile's biography contained the following sections: "Childhood & Education," "Career," "His Community and Social Life," "Intellectual Works," "Married Life and Family." Innocent Offor's biography was divided into "birth," "academic achievements," "some of the posts held," "spiritual life," "family life." The late Emoh's biography included "birth," "Marriage & social life," and "Christian Life." While the late Mrs. Belinda Obele's biography was captured in just one page without any subheadings, each paragraph highlighted the salient aspects of "birth," "family life," and "Christian life." All one hundred booklets I studied give more sustained attention to the section on the Christian life than to any other category. In the one hundred biographies, there is no mention of the personal flaws or shortcomings of the late individual. Instead, every narrative pointed toward life's achievements. Obstacles were narrated as an obstruction to the late individual's noble ambition and were eventually surmounted. For example, for most of those who lived from 1960 to 1970 in eastern Nigeria, their biographies describe how the Nigeria-Biafra civil war of 1967–1970 briefly truncated their careers. Such impediment was recorded in the biography of Madam Emoh as follows: "The outbreak of hostilities and the eventual pogrom which preceded the Biafran/Nigerian Civil war made mama and her entire family return to the Eastern part of Nigeria and settled in Onitsha. When Onitsha was finally captured by the invading Federal troops, the family fled for safety, with Mama carrying her sewing machine and some few valuables to Nsugbe." In the same vein, in the late Nnabuife's biography, the event of the war years was captured thus: "As was the case with many of his contemporaries, this academic period was truncated by the civil war of 1967–1970, and in 1970 he went back to Colliery and completed his studies with Grade I WASC." While the war was not directly reflected in Offodile's biography, its consequence was captured in the statement that "his career was brought to an abrupt end with a forced retirement, on March 1, 1971," by the same federal government that decorated him with the highest national award. The reason is easily inferred: The Nigerian-Biafran civil war ended in 1970, and Offodile, coming from embattled Biafra, perceived as secessionist, was unjustly forced to retire. In the middle of Offodile's biography, ten photographs were inserted to enhance the narrative in different sections. They included a photograph showing Offodile and his thirty-two classmates at Christ the King College, Onitsha, in 1938 (Fig. 20), and Offodile in his Ozo attire and knight regalia, among others. The inserted photographs illustrate sections of the biography that refer to the depicted events. For the late Nnabuife, a photograph of him dressed in his academic gown and another in a mutual embrace with his wife were inserted in the middle of the biography.

Most of the biographies show a predilection for dates, suggesting that the bereaved are all conscious of the historical moment. The dates of important events such as birth, marriage, the receipt of important recognition in society, and death were all strictly captured. For example, in Offor's booklet, the dates and the landmark achievements were itemized and numbered as follows: "1. Elementary Education at St. Mathew's Umuchu and St. Charles Achina, 1937–1945," "2. Teacher's Grade II at St. Thomas Ibuzo, 1947–1951," "3. G.C.E. 'O' level and 'A' Level, 1955–1957," among others.

The conscious attention to historical dates suggests how "biographies can never be divorced from their temporal or spatial contexts [since] the individual is always within the historical web, not without it" (Rotberg 2010, 306). Biographies can be a tool to put "human lives into history, and history into human lives" (Perry 2017, 336). As such, they can be linear and readable and still show the complexities of individual lives by studying them in "dialectical relationship to the multiple worlds they inhabit, social, political, and cultural" (Sorin 2012). As one consequence, it is impossible to record every detail of a subject's life.

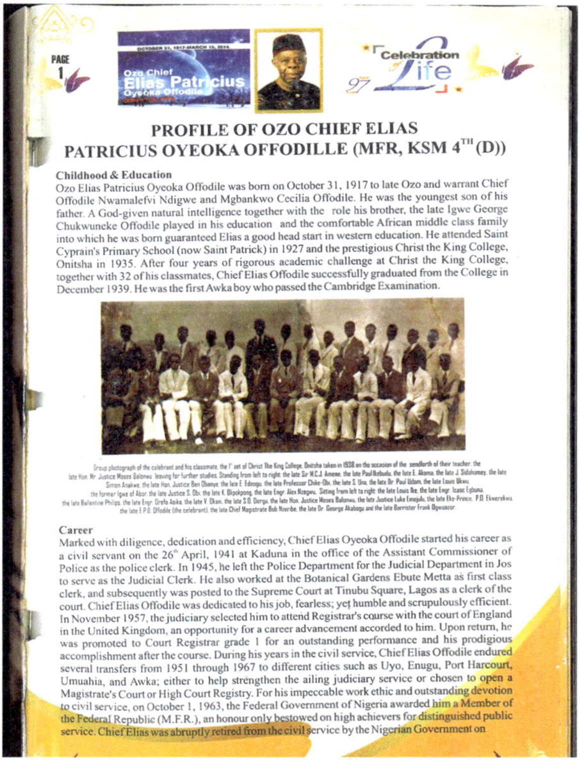

PAGE 1

OCTOBER 31, 1917-MARCH 15, 2014.

Ozo Chief Elias Patricius Oyeoka Offodile

Celebration of Life 97

PROFILE OF OZO CHIEF ELIAS PATRICIUS OYEOKA OFFODILLE (MFR, KSM 4TH (D))

Childhood & Education

Ozo Elias Patricius Oyeoka Offodile was born on October 31, 1917 to late Ozo and warrant Chief Offodile Nwamalefvi Ndigwe and Mgbankwo Cecilia Offodile. He was the youngest son of his father. A God-given natural intelligence together with the role his brother, the late Igwe George Chukwuneke Offodile played in his education and the comfortable African middle class family into which he was born guaranteed Elias a good head start in western education. He attended Saint Cyprain's Primary School (now Saint Patrick) in 1927 and the prestigious Christ the King College, Onitsha in 1935. After four years of rigorous academic challenge at Christ the King College, together with 32 of his classmates, Chief Elias Offodile successfully graduated from the College in December 1939. He was the first Awka boy who passed the Cambridge Examination.

Group photograph of the celebrant and his classmate, the 1st set of Christ The King College, Onitsha taken in 1938 on the occasion of the sendforth of their teacher, the late Hon. Mr. Justice Moses Balonwu leaving for further studies. Standing from left to right: the late Sir M.C.J. Amene, the late Paul Ikebudu, the late E. Akoma, the late J. Sidohomey, the late Simon Anakwe, the late Hon. Justice Ben Obanye, the late E. Edeogu, the late Professor Chike-Obi, the late S. Una, the late Dr. Paul Udom, the late Louis Ukwu, the former Igwe of Abor, the late Justice S. Obi, the late K. Okpokpong, the late Engr. Alex Nzegwu. Sitting from left to right: the late Louis Ike, the late Engr. Isaac Egbuna, the late Ballentine Philips, the late Engr. Orefo Asika, the late V. Okani, the late S.O. Dorgu, the late Hon. Justice Moses Balonwu, the late Justice Luke Emejulu, the late Eke-Prince, P.O. Ekwerekwu, the late E.P.O. Offodile (the celebrant), the late Chief Magistrate Bob Nzeribe, the late Dr. George Akabogu and the late Barrister Frank Ogwuazor.

Career

Marked with diligence, dedication and efficiency, Chief Elias Oyeoka Offodile started his career as a civil servant on the 26th April, 1941 at Kaduna in the office of the Assistant Commissioner of Police as the police clerk. In 1945, he left the Police Department for the Judicial Department in Jos to serve as the Judicial Clerk. He also worked at the Botanical Gardens Ebute Metta as first class clerk, and subsequently was posted to the Supreme Court at Tinubu Square, Lagos as a clerk of the court. Chief Elias Offodile was dedicated to his job, fearless; yet humble and scrupulously efficient. In November 1957, the judiciary selected him to attend Registrar's course with the court of England in the United Kingdom, an opportunity for a career advancement accorded to him. Upon return, he was promoted to Court Registrar grade 1 for an outstanding performance and his prodigious accomplishment after the course. During his years in the civil service, Chief Elias Offodile endured several transfers from 1951 through 1967 to different cities such as Uyo, Enugu, Port Harcourt, Umuahia, and Awka; either to help strengthen the ailing judiciary service or chosen to open a Magistrate's Court or High Court Registry. For his impeccable work ethic and outstanding devotion to civil service, on October 1, 1963, the Federal Government of Nigeria awarded him a Member of the Federal Republic (M.F.R.), an honour only bestowed on high achievers for distinguished public service. Chief Elias was abruptly retired from the civil service by the Nigerian Government on

Fig. 20. Offodile and his thirty-two classmates. A page of his funeral booklet shows Offodile and his classmates at Christ the King College, Onitsha, in 1938.

BIOGRAPHY AND PHOTOGRAPHY

I propose an analogy between the representation of the deceased's character as performed in the biography and in the image section. By curating the most favorable images of the deceased for the photo album, the photographer and the families construct an idealized public persona, as do the biographer and families in shaping the narrative of the life story. In both cases, the most admirable aspects of the deceased's life are extracted, and key moments are pinpointed. The photographer and the biographer thus assume the responsibility of curating the public life and history of the deceased.

The point of biography is to teach the reader which actions should be praised. Photography and biography shape the public subject. Virginia Woolf made this very point in her 1939 essay, "The Art of Biography" when she stated that the biographer has to "sift the little from the big, and shape the whole so that we perceive the outline" (Woolf 1939; Bradshaw 2008, 116). Likewise, the photographer edits, enlarges, and prints a "big image" from a small image of the individual. Bowker argues that "any given biography will embody the vision, prejudices, stock of knowledge and critical disposition of the biographer" (Bowker 2006, 15, in Lenta 2007, 98). In the same way, every photograph also reflects the critical disposition of the photographer who selects, edits, and places it in context. Kalugin (2015) notes that "The hero of a biography is a man who has exerted influence on the fates of "a nation or of humanity" or is famous for "an extraordinary peculiarity of character or way of life" (49). On the other hand, however, biography "legitimates an interest in the everyday life of successful individuals, identifying and affirming the social merits that aid in the attainment of public recognition" (347). In the production of funeral booklets we observe a process of consensus-building among the family and consultants with respect to which achievements are worthy of public notice.

At the same time, the booklets I studied in southeastern Nigeria unfailingly recognize the tension between traditional institutions and Christianity and aspire to assuage this tension by acknowledging them as having attained the pinnacle of both institutions. In other words, successful individuals use their unrivaled position and role to reconcile this tension.

PHOTO GALLERY

The photo gallery section is put together by selecting images from the family album of the deceased. Many families adopted similar patterns when selecting photographs for this section. Charles Ogu told me that he searched for his late father's photographs from the earliest days of his life to old age. This span in the selected photographs, representing the lifespan itself, was typical of the booklets I studied. For example, the printer for the funeral booklet of the late Nnabuife said: "We often aim to show how the life of the deceased was spent in the photographs, so we must start from the beginning of their life to the end. Majority of the older parents we printed started with black-and-white photographs and ended with colored photographs" (author's interview, 2017). In the juxtaposition of outmoded black-and-white and modern colored photographs, a chronological transition is demonstrated that recognizes the essential role of history in articulating a visual biography. More insights were provided by those who attended funerals. Okagbue Ezemuo (age seventy)

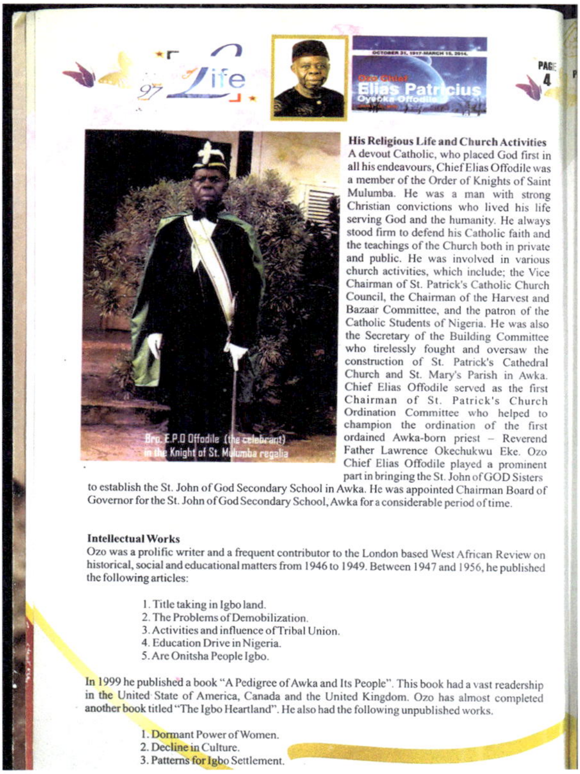

97 Life

PAGE 4

OCTOBER 21, 1917–MARCH 15, 2014.

Ozo Chief Elias Patricius Oyeka Offodile

Bro. E.P.O Offodile (the celebrant) in the Knight of St. Mulumba regalia

His Religious Life and Church Activities

A devout Catholic, who placed God first in all his endeavours, Chief Elias Offodile was a member of the Order of Knights of Saint Mulumba. He was a man with strong Christian convictions who lived his life serving God and the humanity. He always stood firm to defend his Catholic faith and the teachings of the Church both in private and public. He was involved in various church activities, which include; the Vice Chairman of St. Patrick's Catholic Church Council, the Chairman of the Harvest and Bazaar Committee, and the patron of the Catholic Students of Nigeria. He was also the Secretary of the Building Committee who tirelessly fought and oversaw the construction of St. Patrick's Cathedral Church and St. Mary's Parish in Awka. Chief Elias Offodile served as the first Chairman of St. Patrick's Church Ordination Committee who helped to champion the ordination of the first ordained Awka-born priest – Reverend Father Lawrence Okechukwu Eke. Ozo Chief Elias Offodile played a prominent part in bringing the St. John of GOD Sisters to establish the St. John of God Secondary School in Awka. He was appointed Chairman Board of Governor for the St. John of God Secondary School, Awka for a considerable period of time.

Intellectual Works

Ozo was a prolific writer and a frequent contributor to the London based West African Review on historical, social and educational matters from 1946 to 1949. Between 1947 and 1956, he published the following articles:

1. Title taking in Igbo land.
2. The Problems of Demobilization.
3. Activities and influence of Tribal Union.
4. Education Drive in Nigeria.
5. Are Onitsha People Igbo.

In 1999 he published a book "A Pedigree of Awka and Its People". This book had a vast readership in the United State of America, Canada and the United Kingdom. Ozo has almost completed another book titled "The Igbo Heartland". He also had the following unpublished works.

1. Dormant Power of Women.
2. Decline in Culture.
3. Patterns for Igbo Settlement.

Fig. 21. Offodile referred to as the celebrant in the funeral booklet by his children

said: "I cherish those black-and-white photographs once I see them in the booklets. They remind me of the good old days and help me connect to the era when we used to go to the photo studios" (author's interview, June 10, 2019). Bright Uzoukwu also said, "I struggled to get the booklet each time I attended a funeral mainly because of the photographs. You see, those photographs tell a lot about the person's life and the struggles of human life. Sometimes, I see how much work some people have done in this world and still end up in the grave. This makes me think that the whole effort is worthless" (author's interview, July 20, 2019). More than eighty persons I interviewed emphasized that the photo gallery was the main attraction in the obituary booklet.

In traditional Igbo society, families would present photo albums to their guests as part of the hospitality practices known collectively as *oji*, or "kola nut," which stood metonymically for the respect and cordiality extended to visitors. Frequently, visitors viewed the photo albums in the company of family members, who invariably offered explanations for the photos and identified people the visitor didn't recognize. This moment of viewing a photo album was always anticipated by every visitor and typically afforded an exciting opportunity to learn about family genealogies, networks and affiliations, and individual and collective modes of subjectivity. The traditional Igbo family photo album was thus itself a semipublic artifact that was mediated in conversation. When photos move from the family album to the funeral booklet, they go through a higher-level selection process that ensures the selected photos are the most suited for the public eye.

In the funeral booklets I studied, the bereaved indicated that some of the photos in the booklets were carefully chosen from the hundreds of photographs in the family photo album. The photo gallery section was crafted in a manner that depicted the deceased in different capacities as one who fulfilled the conditions of a successful individual in society: the family, the church, the traditional institutions, the community, and the nation at large. "This is one of the factors that determine the type of photograph that will be included in the booklet" (author's interview with Mrs. Anachebe, daughter of the late Chinwike Okeke, January 5, 2021). The photo gallery section also typically contains photos of the deceased during some of their visits to their children's families in the diaspora, especially in the United States and Europe. For example, in one of the late Offodile's photos, he was shown playing with his grandchildren in a park in Georgia (Fig. 22).

Again, photos showing the deceased participating in public and social events were included on some of the pages. Remarkable events in the life of the deceased were included. For example, a photo of Offodile's retirement send-forth party in 1974 was juxtaposed with a photo of one of his community's Association. Juxtaposed with the photos of numerous personal, family, and social engagements is a chronological display of the deceased's children, each with their own families. This is seen as a family roll call whereby the number of the deceased's children and grandchildren and their social standing can be made somewhat familiar to outsiders. Images of Offodile's affluent family occupy about forty pages of high-quality and superbly printed photos. Less affluent families aspire to this benchmark, although in an essentially more modest manner. An example of a modest photo gallery by a not-so-rich family can be found in the booklet devoted to Okon-Obiorah (Fig. 23). This booklet has only two pages of photos depicting the deceased with his family and a few church activities.

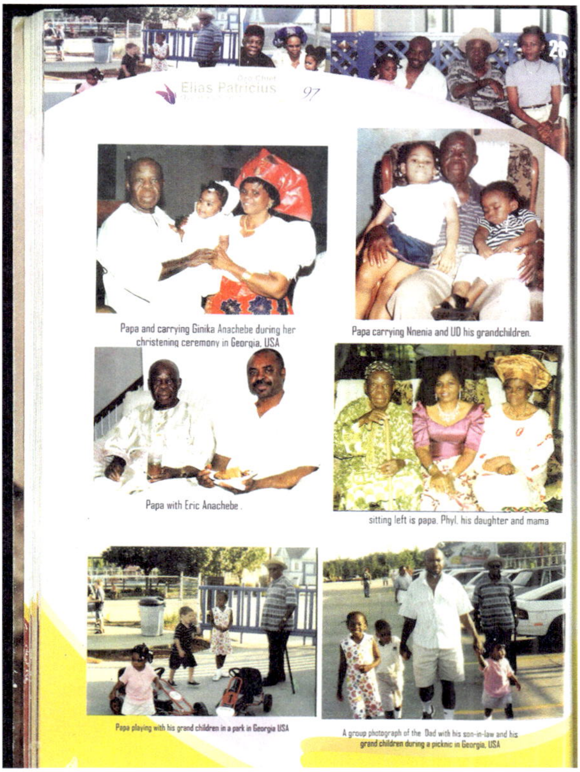

Fig. 22. Offodile playing with his grandchildren in a park in Georgia

It is instructive that the photos that represent Okon-Obiorah's family also include church members. Perhaps the expense of reproducing photographs compelled them to select the photos they considered most important, so that they prioritized their late father's church activities. In Figure 23, nine photographs are cropped into one page, unlike in Offodile's, where each page contains, on average, two photographs, in some instances, one. Whereas Offodile was visibly represented in the traditional institutions and community, no such photographs can be found in Obiorah's album. Two of the photos in Figure 24 captured Obiorah with two different reverend fathers and three different Catholic church groups. Others showed him with his late wife at their son's wedding. The rest are portraits of himself, his late wife, son, and daughter-in-law. While Obiorah's booklet could be seen as deficient in announcing his accomplishments across community, state, and national institutions, one sees

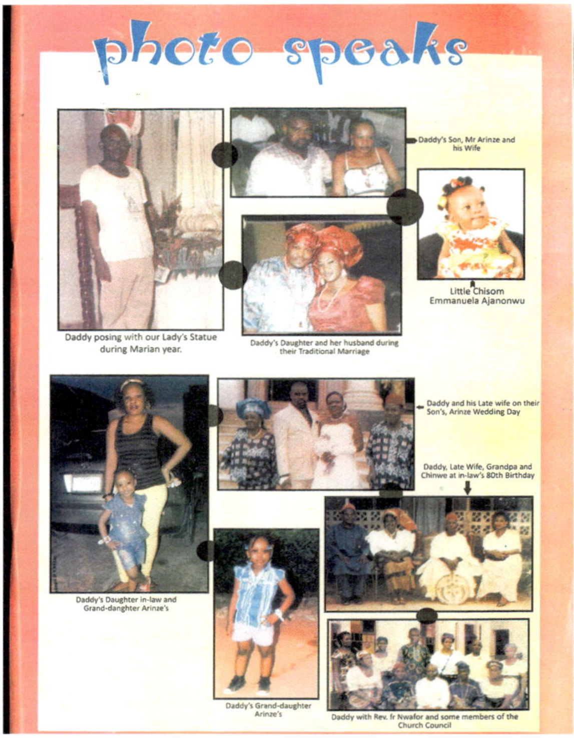

Fig. 23. Funeral booklet of Mr. Okon-Obiorah

that it pursues interests similar to Offodile's, especially in its inscribing the individual within a code of the heroic norm.

In the funeral booklet of Chief Boniface Okonkwo Nkwuaku (Ezebunachi) (1930–2012), the middle pages are introduced with a cover captioned "Photo Speak." Six pages in the middle are dedicated to family photographs of the late Nkwuaku. Photos showing him with his children's families feature more prominently than any other photograph. A photograph shows the late Nkwuaku posing with one of his daughters during her graduation from the University of Nigeria, while another one shows the late Nkwuaku's own wedding. It is titled "Dad's wedding day. B. O. Nkwuaku." Similarly, in the funeral booklet of the late Lady Victoria Nneka Ndinechi (1955–2007) the middle page is also titled "Photo Speak" and is introduced with photographs of the late Ndinechi's wedding with her husband.

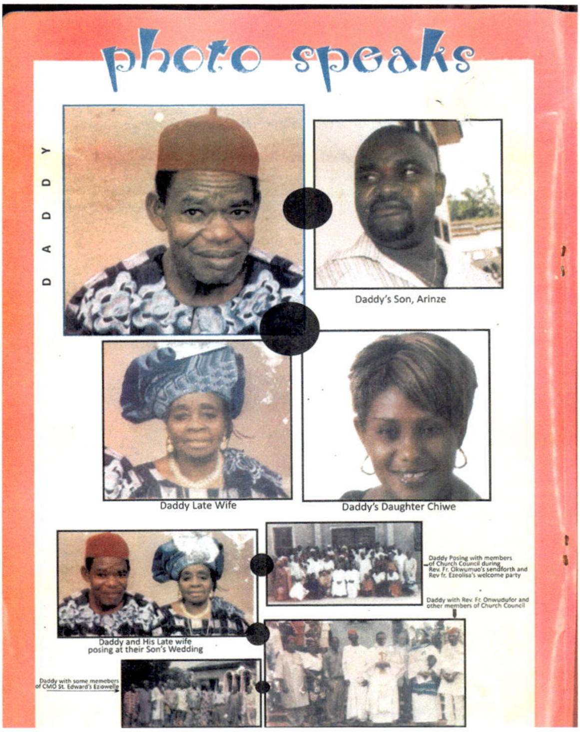

Fig. 24. Funeral booklet of Mr. Okon-Obiorah

THE PHOTO GALLERY AS THE PURSUIT OF ELITE CONSUMPTION

Most booklets have a section specifically titled "Photo Gallery." The concept of the gallery here metaphorically announces a public space where the public is expected to view the carefully curated life history.

The rising demand for the inclusion of family photos inside funeral booklets illustrates the pursuit of elite consumption and a need to publicize heroic achievements by the bereaved. On page 34 of Offodile's funeral booklet, just above the photo of his retirement send-forth party in 1974, is a photo titled "Group photograph of Mr. E.P.O. Offodile (the celebrant) with members of Njikoka Judiciary staff" (Fig. 25).

A close study of this photograph reveals many layers of personal and sartorial histories as well as the stages of photographic convention in the region. Most funeral booklets I studied included similar photographs. In Figure 25,

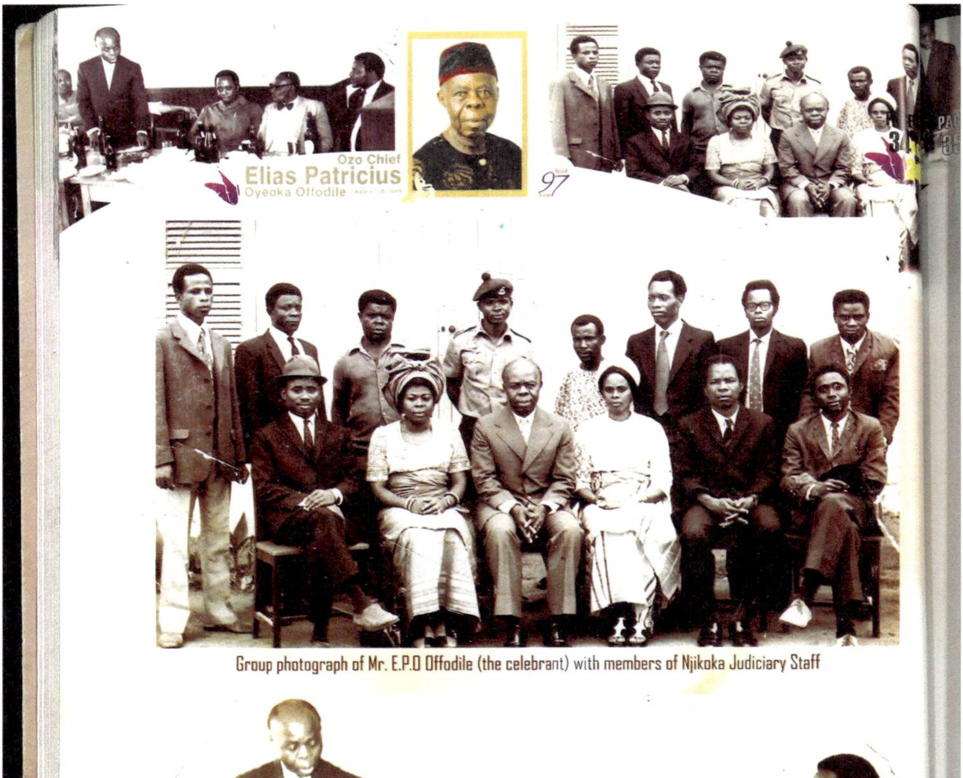

Fig. 25. Chief E. P. O. Offodile (the celebrant) with members of the Njikoka Judiciary staff

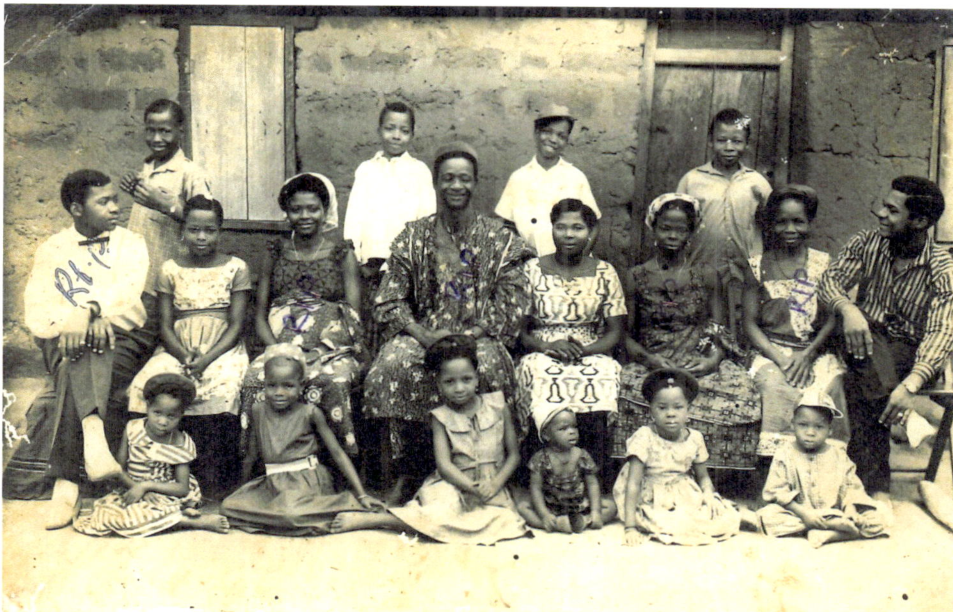

Fig. 26. Memorial photograph of Nwankwo Nwafor (Okachamma) of Mkpoghor village, Ndiukwuenu Town, Orumba North LGA of Anambra State

most of the men are dressed in Western suits and ties. The two men sitting on the extreme right ends adopted a similar sitting style, with one leg crossed on top of the other and their arms resting on their knees. The same sitting arrangement is adopted by Ifeatu and his late younger brother (both sitting on the extreme ends of the front row) in Figure 26. This photograph was published in the memorial booklet of Ifeatu's late father, popularly known as Okachamma. As mentioned earlier, the sitting arrangement is typical of mid-twentieth-century Africa and an emulation of the early twentieth-century Europeans. In Figure 25, the two women sitting in the middle of the front row may have also been positioned in the same way to achieve balance. The men standing behind could be seen to adopt the same systematic arrangement: Those in dark suits and ties were positioned to achieve uniformity at the extreme ends of the photo as they symmetrically enclosed those in mufti to create a balance. Such careful arrangements were performed routinely in the early days of photography. Figure 25 is seen as a total deviation from today's posing style where photographers, confident in the user-friendly manipulation offered by digital software, abandon the painstaking drudgery of fixing the sitter's pose as undertaken by earlier photographers.

Ifeatu told me that he was working in the Ministry of Treasury when the photograph in Figure 26 was taken. His brother was also a civil servant in Onitsha, eastern Nigeria. Thus, Figures 25 and 26 reveal how the state civil service forms a distinct class of elite identity, reflecting a certain sartorial convention whereby the Western suit was predominantly adopted by men as the official dress code in government offices. There is a marked deviation from this dress style in present-day Nigeria's political and civil service institutions, where less emphasis is laid on Western suits in favor of "traditional" dress or informal clothes such as jeans and T-shirts. In effect, the photo gallery allows for a chronological narration of elite styles as well as belonging to specific groups and state institutions. The albums consummate the elitist narrative of texts in the booklet, by pairing each achievement with a corresponding photograph.

In more than sixty of the booklets I studied, some of the selected photographs of the deceased in their youthful age seem to reflect the style of what was then considered a bourgeois pose in Western European convention. For example, Offodile's sitting arrangement in his youthful photographs is very much connected to the mid-twentieth-century pose among African nationalist elites, in which the search for sartorial identity revealed a conflict between identity and mimicry (Bhabha 1987).

A very important aspect of the photo gallery is the manner in which the diaspora is narrated. For example, three photos of Offodile with his children in Atlanta, Georgia, were cropped and used to form a repetitive design that runs through the upper part of the booklet (Fig. 22)—this type of frieze is a typical design strategy. By adopting this photo collage as the unifying theme across the entire booklet, it narrates the diaspora as a conquered space of heroic achievement. Silvester, Hayes, and Hartmann (1998, 17) describe how European colonialists deployed photographs of Africa's landscape to reinforce the notion of a conquered territory. Their images depict "idyllic rural homelands and timeless tradition where Africans are given culture but not history." I want to suggest, conversely, that in photo galleries such as Offodile's, depicting the subject's activities in the diaspora, the modernity of Africans in contemporary Western territories is projected through a photographic process that conceives time as fast-paced, radically futuristic, dynamic, and sophisticated. For Offodile, the mastery of American geography and temporality is a necessary component of the father's heroic life, which is inscribed in the photo gallery as worthy of public viewership.

In this manner, many photographic depictions of the deceased's visits to their children's homes in the United States or Europe announce a conquered geographic territory. The choice of this type of photo for inclusion in the funeral booklet over hundreds of other family photos suggests how the surviving relatives treasure their deceased's international experience. Well-traveled deceased individuals are positioned as international citizens beyond local and national narratives of heroism. In other words, internationalization is woven into the photo gallery as a trademark of a heroic and successful life.

In the funeral booklet of the late Lady Victoria Nneka Ndinechi, photographs that showed important family landmarks also emphasized the diaspora, such as a photo titled "Mum's first daughter Adaora and family at Raalu's baptism in U.S.A." In my entire study of more than one hundred funeral booklets, it became evident that the absence of a photograph of either the children or the deceased in the diaspora meant that none of the family members visited or resided there. For example, while the late Ndinechi did not appear in her daughter's American photographs, it was still deemed proper for the family to include them. Again, for the late Lady (Chief) Grace Ugonma Odibo, LAUX (Nne Muru Oha Nee Edom) (ninety-six years), none of the photos in the booklet were captioned except the ones she took with her children in the United States.

One would not expect individuals to use the space of funeral booklets to pursue certain ambitions. However, these booklets reproduce the cultural sign of one who has achieved in all fields of endeavor. The effect is a history that is collectively shaped and culturally legitimated, or what Pierre Bourdieu has termed "the essence of social memory" ([1965], 1978, 30), in sharp contrast to the idiosyncratic and singular memories that each individual possesses (Zuromskis 2013, 54). In other words, the booklets perform the work of shaping social memory (see Sandbye 2014, 12). The momentum of this process can be seen in the growing appetite for the production and consumption of obituary photo albums outside the old model of living room albums.

SELF-INSUFFICIENCY AS SELF-SUFFICIENCY IN THE PHOTO GALLERY

In viewing these photos, one senses the utter distaste for the insufficiency that must be transcended in the abundant display of signs of sufficiency. Photos of numerous children, grandchildren, and great-grandchildren are seen as strong signs of this self-sufficiency. Each booklet must visually amplify the larger family tree: nearly all the photographs emphasize not only the deceased but also their children and families. Interestingly, images of children receive more prominent attention than, in certain instances, those depicting the late parents. Lawuyi (1991a, 234) concludes that the "fertility potential of both men and women seems to be a widely publicized aspect of the funeral pamphlet."

Sufficiency is signified by togetherness, which can be both accomplished and communicated through the medium of photography in funeral booklets. In the Igbo worldview, a successful family life is one in which the family of the dead achieves collective intimacy. This is affirmed through marriage and often associated with a man who applied wisdom to avert family breakdown. One of the most important questions asked by elders to ascertain the successful admittance of young men into enviable elderly enclaves is *O na-anu nwanyi*? meaning, "Is he married?" and if the young man is married, the next task would be to adjudge whether he maintained a peaceful, happy home. The dishonor of a broken home is abhorred and redeemed through a photographic construction of family togetherness. Gillian Rose (2014, 76) states that "family photographs picture families together" and "photos as objects register 'togetherness' as a central quality." The passion for countering public opprobrium of disunity, where it exists, is seen in the seemingly unifying family photos inside the booklets. Even in certain cases of broken families, photographs are deployed to achieve a sense of unity and togetherness after death. In some cases, a divorced wife can be seen in the photo gallery together with her late husband and their children. The booklet, therefore, serves in some cases to reunite an estranged family life, also in cases not involving marriage. For example, some of Offodile's children living in the United States and elsewhere, including those who had not been together with their siblings for many years, sent their family photographs through email and WhatsApp for the unifying albums in the booklets. Rose (2014, 76) agrees that "sending photographs maintains familial affiliations and shows togetherness." Some of the photos in Offodile's funeral booklet were supplied by each of his children from their albums where Offodile appeared. As a selective record of a life, each of Offodile's children's photos makes a set of claims about who the child is. Each of the children constructs an autobiography of their separate families to produce a biography of their late father (see also Zussman 2006, 4). Then the narratives are merged in a way that suggests a family bond. Bourdieu describes a similar effect occurring in family snapshots, in that "each snapshot helps to establish and maintain a bond between family members" and "serves as an index for the degree to which families are 'integrated'" ([1965] 1978, 38–54, cited in Pauwels 2008, 35), but in this case, a reintegration occurs after death for the sake of public display. As criteria for a photo's inclusion in the funeral booklet, distinctive, cherished elements in these family photos either directly document or imply the following: that the deceased has conquered encumbrances to success within public and private spaces; can be located in an elitist circle; has acquired the material rewards of life such as cars, houses, children; and has transcended physical geographic barriers to emerge as an international citizen. In sum, while photo albums in funeral booklets can be seen as part of a broader strategy of rising visual modernity in southeastern Nigerian funeral activities, this convention at the same time bears strong resonance with traditional Nigerian praise-singing, in which the dead are described as inhabiting an ancestral afterlife that is holy, untainted, and saintly. A mourner during the funeral rites of the late Okeke said, *onye nwuo oburu ezigbo mmadu*, or "One becomes a saint upon death."

PICTURING A SAINTLY ANCESTRAL FIGURE THROUGH THE PHOTO GALLERY

Some contentions arose from the late Chinwike Okeke's funeral booklet and, equally, some other family booklets I studied. When Benson, Okeke's first son, demanded photographs from his siblings for inclusion in the photo gallery section of the booklet of their late father, he specifically mentioned "photos that would portray the family's prestige such as photos of remarkable achievements" (author's interview, January 5, 2021). Each of his siblings submitted photographs of their own families with their children. Benson told me that he only accepted photos that showed significant achievements of each of his siblings and relatives, such as photos of academic graduation, wedding, and other landmark achievements. He rejected a photo of his cousin with their late father during a public function. Benson informed me that the photograph's context was questionable and might not reflect their aspirations to be a perfect family. Benson, however, did not inform the cousin that this photo would not be included. When the booklet was printed, his cousin accosted him and demanded to know why his photo had been excluded. When Benson informed him of the reason, he was furious and, according to Benson, "threw the booklet at me and left in anger." His cousin claimed that excluding his photograph from the funeral booklet translated to excluding him from the funeral event.

As already suggested, in selecting photos from various members' albums, families engage in a political process and create a perfect vision of the family's cultural and social history. Certain gaps are widened, while certain affiliations are reinforced. Excluded family members, such as Benson's cousin, behold their own absence. This sense is especially acute when the dead are perceived to be great and effusively venerated through photographs. *Eji ya ama otu onye ha* ("You understand an individual's influence through the photos and tributes"), exclaimed Ike, a relative of the late Chinwike Okeke. The Okeke family's construction of a perfect persona of their father prompted the extended family members to identify with the family photos in the funeral booklet. This identification would not occur if Okeke were portrayed as a villain.

Chika's family printed a separate booklet of the church program and then printed a book that contained only photographs of the family without captions. According to Chika, "The bishop commended our family for not including the photographs in the church programme booklet. The bishop expressed joy that my family deviated from the convention," which was to merge family photographs with church program with result that church members usually flipped through the booklet and looked at the photographs during the mass, thereby getting distracted (Chika, author's interview).

Chika told me that by the same token, the family didn't want to compromise the high regard they had for their dad by distracting people from enjoying and appreciating his family's visual history. She said her father loved education, and that was why they chose mainly graduation photographs of most of his children. Chika said they also included their father's religious photographs because he was at the forefront of the establishment of Ikeduru Diocese and eventually became the first church patron. Their father cherished those activities, and they selected photographs that represented them.

The authority ascribed to the selected photos validates each family's process of self-making. At some point, the family photo gallery in the booklets constitutes a shared space for family members and their relatives. Families share the spaces of the albums by enacting a collective definition of what must constitute their past, a shared interest in the importance of the family's history, and a shared sense of prestige that defines their collective self-perception. But we also need to ask, with Benson's cousin, "What is not there?" In other words, how do such acts of exclusion participate in constituting cultural realities? The definition of family can be seen to collapse when some of the members are unable to connect with the visual praises presented in the booklet.

Some scholarly accounts have centered on the implications arising from the displacement of family snapshots as they are recontextualized from their traditional contexts within albums and domestic spaces to the public sphere of museums or galleries (Langford 2001; Batchen 2008). Beyond a mere archival function, the album, as argued by Langford, assumes a performative role within the domestic setting. The spoken word, manifested through narrative exposition and reflective recollection, which coexists with the presentation of photographic albums, constitutes an indispensable facet of the viewing ritual. Langford writes that "voices must be heard for memories to be preserved, for the album to fulfil its function." Because of this, the preservation of an album in a public museum "suspends its sustaining conversation, stripping the album of its social function and meaning" (2001, 5). Batchen identifies a similar tendency in a wave of major art exhibitions focused on snapshots over the last decade or so. Separated from the stories that would contextualize it, the snapshot image becomes a static art object, overlooking its most important characteristic as "a complex social device and a personal talisman" (Batchen 2008, 133). I argue that the photo gallery section of the funeral booklet resurrects and reanimates conversation around family photographs as they undergo rejection or selection and finally achieve new publicity in the funeral booklets. This is significant in an age when digital photo practices seem to disrupt the flowing conversations of the analog photo album in an interesting intermedial dialogue.

CONCLUSION

Offodile's booklet designates him prominently and repeatedly as "the celebrant." This term is also used in the traditional Ozo title-talking ceremony, in which the celebrant achieves the highest status in his community. The caption of "celebrant" in all the photos throughout the booklet might suggest, at first glance, that this event was photographed while Offodile was alive; he seems to have been reanimated. Many individuals I interviewed recognize the prevailing and rising demand for the "celebration" of death rather than "mourning." This sense of celebration is created largely through photographs in the gallery, which, I have argued, re-form the traditional oral praise-singing into visual praise-singing.

In migrating from family albums into funeral booklets, photos demonstrate political agency by promoting membership in certain institutions and social groups within and beyond community, state, and nation. In this way, family visual (auto)biography is grafted onto the community, state, and national narratives of heroism and prestige. This chapter has tracked the trajectory of commemorative photographs within funeral booklets, revealing their crucial impact on the Igbo contemporary lives in culturally, economically, and politically significant ways. It has also demonstrated how this transition has reconstituted the public sphere of the deceased and their surviving families. In the next chapter, I examine a related transition of commemorative photographs into social media, examining its implications for the emerging theoretical directions in the discourse of African photography and social media.

CHAPTER 6

Social Media and the Heroic Significance of Online Commemoration

Facebook was established in 2008, and many Nigerians began to join. However, some individuals opposed posting their photographs there, due in part to the superstitious concern associated with evildoers' spiritual manipulation of photographs. I interviewed fifty individuals on their use of photographs on Facebook. More than thirty people between forty and fifty years of age said they were wary of posting their photographs on Facebook when they joined it between 2008 and 2009. Seven other individuals in a younger age group, between thirty and fifty years old, who joined Facebook between 2011 and 2012 said they were not scared of any spiritual manipulation of their photographs. The remaining interviewees, still younger individuals who joined Facebook between 2015 and 2019, didn't believe that someone could manipulate their photos on Facebook. Among the thirty older respondents who were wary of posting their photographs, seven said they did not post their photos initially for fear of evil manipulation. When I asked them to explain in more detail, one of them said, "In those days, you know that evil people use other people's photographs to commit evil by taking their photo to the witch doctors who use such photos to invoke the actual person through spiritual incantation. They would insert your photo inside a bowl of water that was spiritually charged, and once your picture is inside the water, you will be summoned to appear, and you will appear. Once that happens, the evil person can stab you to death."

Another individual said, "I know that some people searched for my photo on my Facebook when I joined it in 2009 so that they can use it to kill me through witch doctors. I started posting my picture on Facebook recently because I know that most of those evil people have died."

These individuals' fears suggest a certain socially acceptable feeling that the photographic material can be animated even in the virtual spaces of social media. As Arnold et al. (2018) argue in their book *Death and Digital Media*, social media photos of the living and the dead evoke a sense of presence and connection that transcends time and space. In this regard, one may argue that a photograph has become a new version of the human being on social media. Some individuals I interviewed strongly believed that any spiritual harm done to the photograph translates to harm to the real human body. This chapter explores how social media photos of the dead shape the public discourses of mourning and commemoration in southern Nigeria. In Igbo cosmology, the spiritual is held sacrosanct in the commemorative ritual, whereby the absent body is evoked through words and images. This practice found a ready extension in social media, as mourners maintain constant ties with the dead through various practices that rely on the photographs of the dead.

THE EVOLUTION OF COMMEMORATIVE PHOTOGRAPHS ON THE IGBO SOCIAL MEDIA

Digital technology has activated new uses for photography (Stylianou-Lambert and Widmaier 2023; Gomez et al. 2012; Miller and Edwards 2007; Van House et al. 2005). Certainly, photo sharing on social media deviates markedly from its offline predecessors. For example, Amanda Brown (2012) notes that existing traditions of displaying photographs of the dead have become more conspicuous and less socially labeled in social media (Cann 2014). Social media-specific sharing practices are also evident in a range of new image genres, such as the selfie, photobomb, and duckface. Early studies of online mourning examined Web 1.0 memorial sites as emerging spaces of consolation, while later research explored how social media enables distant and performative expressions of grief and attachment to the deceased (Moss 2004; Roberts 2004; Marwick and Ellison 2012; Fiefer 2013; Gibbs, Carter, et al. 2014; Lofland 1985). Here the living and the dead meet in and inhabit the same space. The image of the deceased wanders around the rooms in the same manner that the image of the living does; in fact, both migrate like a ghost ship in cyberspace (Péne 2011).

Eva Anyaeze, a lecturer at Nnamdi Azikiwe University, Awka, south-eastern Nigeria, posted a photo of his late brother, Tony, on Eva's Facebook wall, lamenting that Tony had just passed away and saying that his death

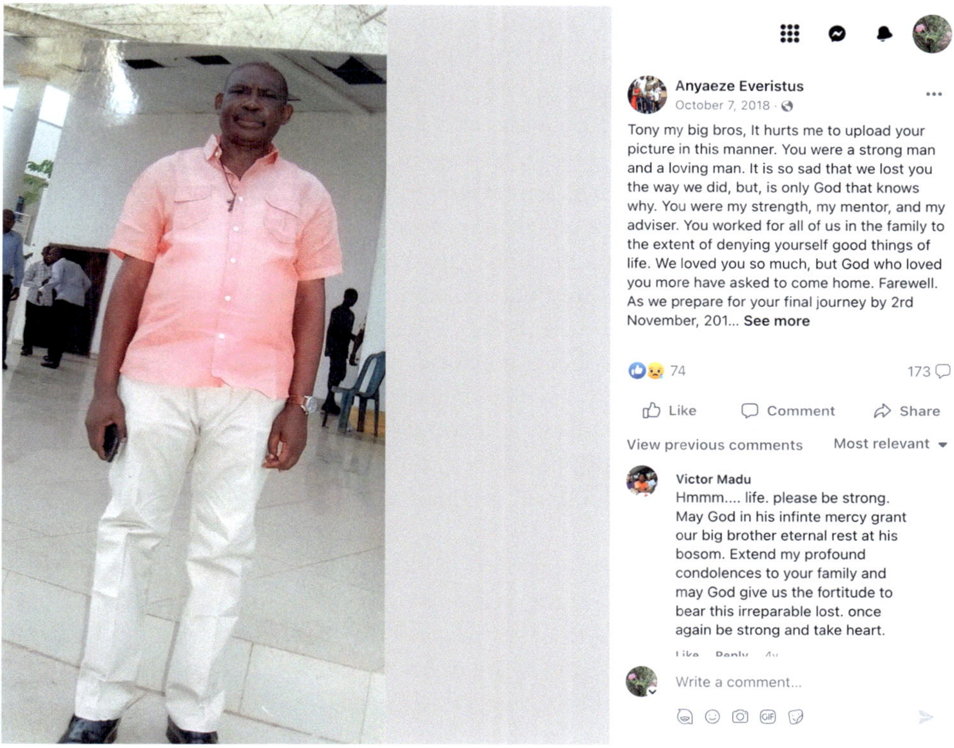

Fig. 27. Evaristus Anyaeze shared a photo of his late elder brother, Tony Anyaeze, on his Facebook wall.

evoked challenging memories of his goodwill (Fig. 27). Eva noted how emotionally difficult it was for him to post the photo. Finally, he praised Tony for living a worthy life. The comments accompanying Eva's post were expressed in the same mournful tone. Many commenters pleaded with God to accept Tony's soul in peace, while others charged Eva to be strong and "take solace in the Lord."

Following most deaths in southeastern Nigeria, and likely elsewhere globally, posts similar to those by Eva frequently emerge on Facebook walls. Typically, these mark the first appearance of the deceased's postmortem photograph on social media. Eva's lamentations also included the dates of the burial and funeral: "As we prepare for your final journey by 2nd November 2018, I pray that the good Lord will keep you in his bosom." My interview with Eva revealed that he lifted this photo from his late brother's Facebook wall. This same photo of Tony, which sparked a lively and joyful conversation on his own Facebook wall prior to his death, now adorns Eva's wall, accompanied by sorrowful lamentation. This example shows how a single image can inhabit multiple temporalities and elicit contrasting reactions: on Tony's wall, the photo participates in an ongoing social exchange, while on Eva's wall, it signifies a final exit. Tony stands with his two hands suspended beside his body while holding a mobile phone and gazing meaningfully at the public. The photograph evokes public affect and transforms into a mnemonic object. It inhabits the threshold between two opposing notions: the harsh truth of his bodily absence and the recognition of his enduring presence in memory, as enabled by such a memorial, in which he gazes at us and bears witness to us eternally in the digital public sphere of social media. The Igbo culture's valorization of death as a socially conspicuous event in the public sphere might have shaped its online counterpart of publicly monumentalizing the deceased. Death (*onwu*) becomes a clarion call (*oku*) for community participation.

Among southeastern Nigerians, I identify three different stages in the photographic evolution of the deceased in social media's public sphere. The first is a post of the photo of the deceased by family members and friends immediately after the death, to announce that the death has occurred. This photo is usually lifted from the deceased's social media photo archive, either on the Facebook page or elsewhere, just as we saw in Eva Anyaeze's case. In traditional Igbo society, the first reaction to death is to visit the bereaved at home and express one's grief with a loud, uncontrollable cry (*mkpu akwa*). This ritual is mirrored online by visiting the deceased's social media page and downloading their photo or leaving a tearful emoji. In the Igbo variation, a tearful emoji would mean *mkpu akwa*. In the Facebook posting shown in Figure 30 a mourner responds to the death of Ijeagbala with tearful emojis along with the spelled-out cry, "ewooo!" The deceased's social media page becomes a house, just as in traditional Igbo society, and a site of collective mourning, as swarms of mourners arrive to lament and console the family. The deceased's photos are copied and posted on walls with emotional eulogies. Yékú (2022, 102) has argued that "the 'social' in social media highlights the emergence of a vibrant virtual public sphere, where regular citizens from diverse social backgrounds engage in cultural practices aimed at political structures." While Yékú focuses on political structures, I would add that in the context of commemoration, the political assumes a ritualistic dimension. In this digital space, the shared use of emoji tears symbolically manifests a collective empathy, bridging the gap between physical absence and emotional presence, and enabling mourners to convey their condolences and support in a universally understood language.

The second stage in this photographic evolution is posting a funeral poster and invitation card bearing the photo of the dead. In these images, as we have seen in previous chapters, the deceased's photo has been extracted from the human world and now sails through a shadowy, illusory space made possible by computer technicians, suggesting that the dead has departed from the living. In the last stage, the photo of the dead is posted weeks, months, or years after the funeral to mark a memorial: This photo looks dead yet refuses to die; it is everywhere. The reinterpretation of these photographs, from images of mortality and finality to narratives that embrace diverse facets of life through online public interactions and performances, demonstrates a social media public sphere whose veneration process is immortal, dynamic, omnipresent, and technologically glorifying. At the same time, we find a clear manifestation of the Igbo culture of ancestor worship, where the dead still live among the living. Indeed, for the Igbo, social media becomes the ancestral realm where the public comes to pay homage to the dead. Here the dead are constantly invoked to partake in the daily cultural life of the people.

Of course, this commemorative public space encompasses other social media platforms as well. On WhatsApp as well, individuals post photos of dead friends, relatives, or any other person as soon as the death occurs. For example, on a group WhatsApp page of Nnamdi Azikiwe University, known as NAU Staff Community, a member once posted a photo of another late staff member and wrote, "Choky is gone." Choky was about forty-five years old and himself the son of an important former staff member of the university. The comments that followed the post ranged from expressions of shock to questions about what happened, such as "What do you mean, what happened?" and "Biko how manage? Was he sick?" and numerous others. Many individuals responded instantly, suggesting that the photograph enabled immediate recognition and spontaneous emotional reaction.

The second stage in the evolving presence of the deceased's photos on social media involves posting the funeral poster. This stage marks the photograph's transition into eternity. As previously discussed, this is usually achieved through a digitally reworked graphic editing process that prepares the photograph, just as morticians prepare the physically dead body for the funeral. For example, in the editing of the late Angela Nwudu Obiweluozo Ijenwogo's funeral photo by her son (Fig. 28), Angela's photograph

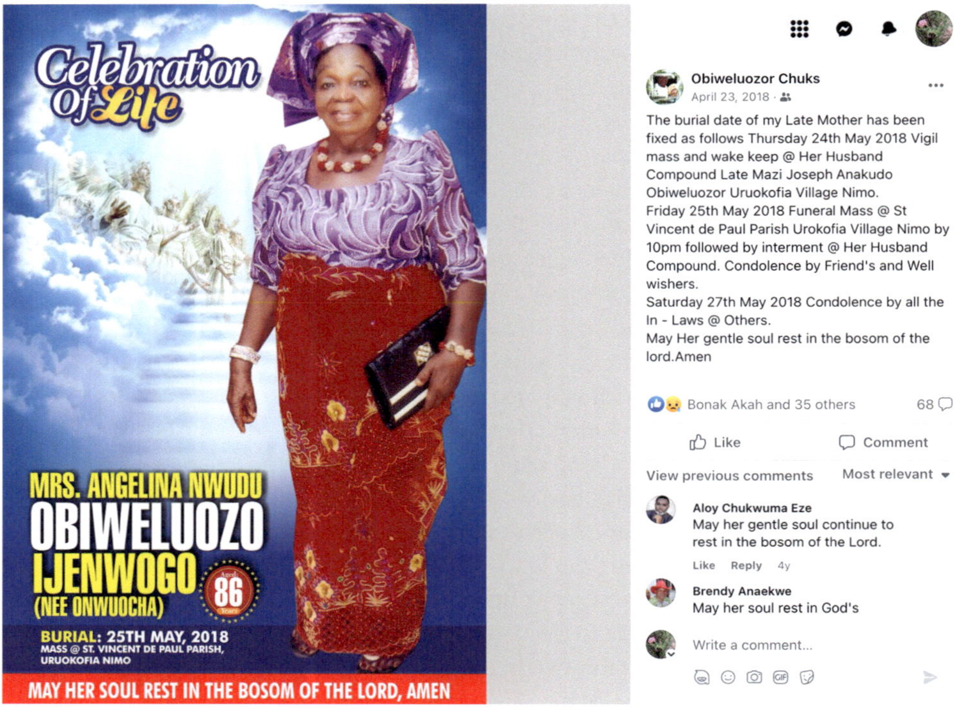

Fig. 28. Mrs. Angela Nwudu Obiweluozo Ijenwogo (née Onwuocha). Chuks Obiweluozor shared the funeral poster of his late mother on his Facebook wall.

was detached from the human world by means of Photoshop software and inserted into the celestial realm depicted in the funeral poster. Her son then posted the poster on his Facebook wall to announce to the world that Angela had commenced the eternal journey. Angela's funeral poster provides comprehensive details including: the dates of birth and death, the funeral date, information on the final church service, and the venue. The transition of Angela's funeral poster to her son's Facebook wall symbolizes the extension of remembrance beyond the immediate physical world. It suggests that through digital sharing, her memory transcends traditional boundaries and enters a space where time and presence are fluid. Here Angela is not confined to the past; her digital perpetuity challenges the finality of death, offering a space where she continues to exist within the collective consciousness of the online community so that she remains an active participant in the human world, albeit in a different realm. In Figure 28, both the Facebook wall and the photoshopped blue background seem to locate the late Angela within immortal space; a technological dislocation may be seen to occur on two counts: first, through photoshopping and, second, through importation to Facebook.

When Angela's figure is decontextualized from a familiar spatial backdrop and inserted into a bluish, cloudy background, then made to wander on Facebook wall spaces, I suggest, her photo assumes the status of a spirit. Her photograph's transition from a physical print to a digital entity reflects a profound transformation that can be seen as a liberation from material constraints, allowing it to exist in a more "spiritual" form, free to interact with viewers across time and space, much like the Igbo ancestral spirits or the Holy Spirit in Judeo-Christian eschatology, which is described as a guiding living force, omnipresent and immortal, floating around earthly spaces; it is present in the world but not confined to any single place or object.[1] In essence, the photograph becomes a noncorporeal entity that embodies memory, emotion, and history, transcending its original form to become a part of the collective digital consciousness. In other words, the photograph's editing and its insertion—for eternity—into social media imbues it with an aura of immortality.

To once more invoke Joanna Sassoon's concept of "translation," as explored in chapter 4, the digitizing process is no longer just about turning a photograph from material to pixel; instead, it is a complex cultural translation, shifting between different forms of representation (2004, 198). Sassoon believes that translating photographic images into digital form standardizes them, abolishing the distinct physical characteristics of diverse photographic formats. Thus, a once three-dimensional object translates into a one-dimensional, frail digital proxy, losing its original tactility and materiality and assuming a transient and otherworldly nature. Angela's "original" three-dimensional photograph has undergone a translation into a new mode of existence. Following Sassoon, we can say that it has lost all evidence of its other lives such as dirt and damage, among others. Batchen (1997, 2) therefore believes the translated photograph has lost its "aura of originality, volume, opacity, tactility and a physical presence in the world that all emanate from the complexity of the original photographic object." I argue, instead, that a new auratic quality is regained in the circulation of digital copies, especially in the context of commemorative photographs. This auratic quality is specifically sustained by the immortality the photograph achieves online. In the case of Obiweluozo's digital photographs, the translated image acquires auratic significance not only through its explicit reference to the heavenly realm but also through its ability to evoke awe when shared online. It garners reverential and dignifying comments akin to those directed toward a spiritual entity. The frequent allusions to the spiritual realm by numerous commenters, who consistently refer to the photograph in the present tense, indicate that their engagement with the image transcends the boundaries of mortality.

In another photographic manifestation of the dead on social media related to this second stage, photographs of the funeral ceremony are also posted. Here photos of the dead are occasionally interposed with those of the living. Ogochukwu Okafor, for example, posted several photos of her mother's funeral on her Facebook wall (Figs. 29a and 29b). In Figure 29a, Ogochukwu carries a framed photo of her late mother and dances around the funeral arena. Her relatives flanked her. The photo is posted for a specific reason, according to Ogochukwu, "to show the world that a dream of a successful funeral has been accomplished." When we look at how Ogochukwu and her mourners pose on her Facebook wall, it becomes clear that Ogochukwu relished how her late mother's funeral transcended the boundaries of the physical space into the virtual technology of Facebook, even in death, so that her late mother's funeral can be ongoingly venerated in a manner that is technologically significant. In the image, she carries her mother's photo while posing for the camera. The image of her mother's photo, along with her and her fellow mourners trailing behind, embraced the immortal moment on the Facebook wall. Multiple such photographic moments are frozen on the screen and made to resist the erasure of physical death. Virtual immortality is achieved, and her mother is permanently reunited with the community in one frame. Here the Facebook wall acts as another photographic surface that unites virtual bodies.

In another photographic encounter, Jude Ilozumba posted a funeral poster of his late mother, Ijeagbala, on his Facebook wall with the caption, "Please honor us with your presence as we bid our dear mother and Matriarch farewell to eternal glory on 1st September 2022" (Fig. 30).

Jude used the same photo, in which his late mother wore a smiling countenance, as his profile picture, as well as for the funeral poster and a large banner that was mounted at the funeral arena during the funeral proper. I had accompanied Adaobi (Ada) Osunkwo, Jude's cousin, to the funeral ceremony. Also in our company were Ada's mother—the sister of Ijeagbala—and father. The funeral took place at Obeledu in Anambra State, eastern Nigeria. At the commencement of the funeral, Ada and her parents, in the company of their kindred, visited the funeral altar, where they performed the official

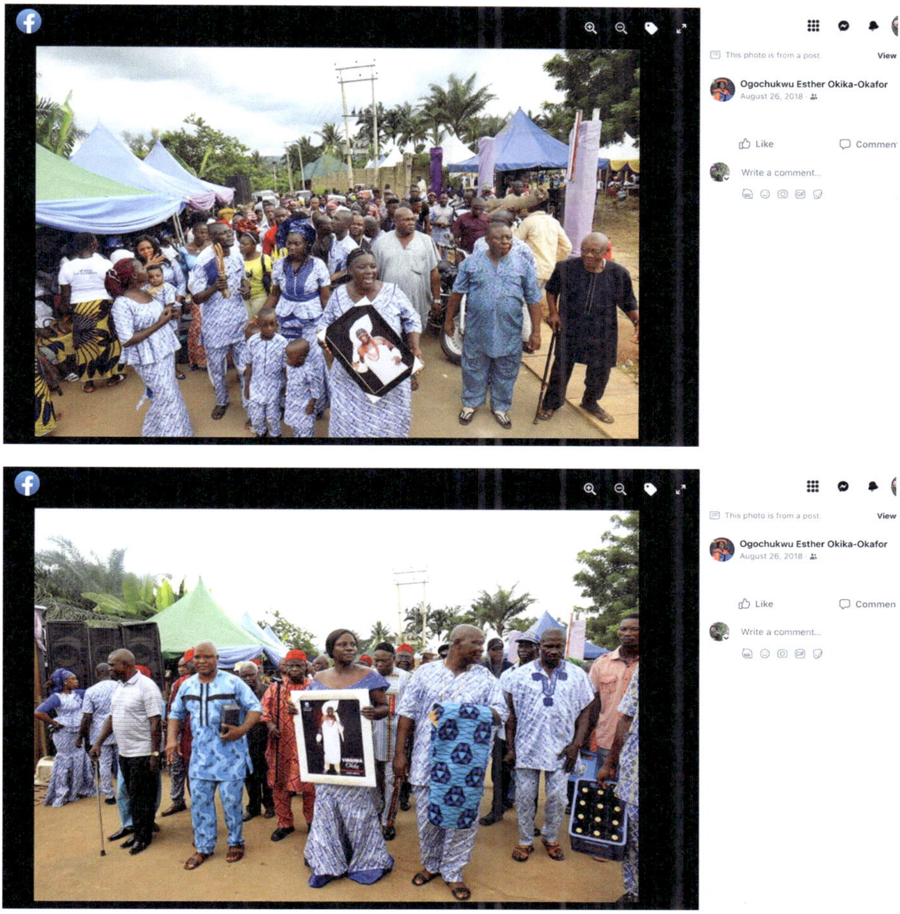

Fig. 29. Ogochukwu Okafor's Facebook photo of her mother's funeral. The photo conveys a sense of a heroic and successful ceremony.

funeral rites by offering the bereaved the usual funeral gifts of drinks, clothes, and money.

Jude gave Ada a laminated paper on which was written "Gate Pass," which would allow us entry into a canopied shelter built in the corner of the funeral arena, with the bold inscription "V.I.P." The VIP canopy was reserved for important individuals with an intimate relationship with the family, including prominent, eminently distinguished, and respectable members of the society, such as politicians, chiefs, clergymen and women, or traditional rulers. The

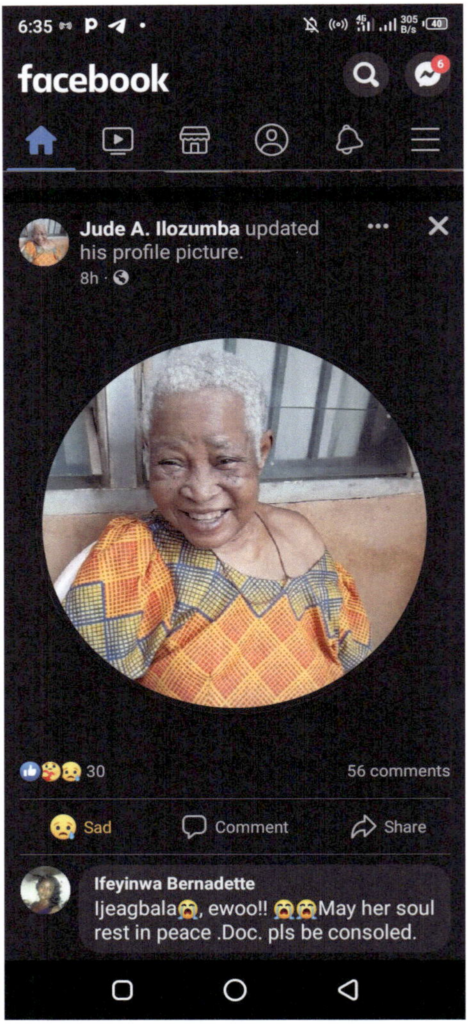

Fig. 30. Jude Ilozumba used a photo of his late mother as his Facebook profile photo and posted the same photo on his Facebook wall, inviting friends and well-wishers to the funeral event.

canopy provided catered food and drinks, with standby bartenders to serve the mourners. I joined Ada and others in the VIP canopy. The bouncers prevented anyone who did not show a gate pass from entering. We were served food, drinks, and other nourishments while we sat inside the hall amid the din of the DJ's raucous music reverberating through the loudspeakers. When we ate the first round of dishes, Ada brought out her Android phone, drew her seat closer to mine, and took a selfie, capturing herself beside me. She stood up and took shots of all those seated inside the VIP canopy, after which she also shot short videos. "I hope you got me and your dad clearly?" asked Ada's mum. "Yes, I will post it on our family WhatsApp," Ada replied. As soon as Ada finished shooting her photos and videos, she shared them on her family WhatsApp, uploaded them immediately on her Facebook page and tagged me, and sent them to me on WhatsApp (since we are Facebook and WhatsApp friends)

As soon as we were done at the VIP canopy, Ada said, "Mummy, please let's go and take photos with Ijeagbala outside." A life-size image of Ijeagbala was mounted in front of the funeral arena. Ada assisted her mum and dad, positioning them on both ends of the photograph, and then took their snapshot (Fig. 31). "Those at home would see you guys immediately," Ada told her parents.

All along, Ada was confident that the funeral outing wouldn't serve any purpose without the photographs. Ada's Facebook and WhatsApp enabled instant transportation of Ijeagbala's funeral to the global community, announcing that we were attending it. Ada's statement, "Those at home would see you guys immediately," embodies all the selling attributes and affordances of the Android camera phone that resonate with the Igbo notions of death and funerals. These three parts of speech, "those at home," "would see you," and "immediately," exemplify, first, the notion of distance and the significance of overcoming spatial constraints; second, the significance of seeing as a mode of knowing that confers epistemic authority to the visual; and third, immediacy. For the Igbo people, *onwu* (death) signifies *onwu ora* (public death), a communal event that transcends the individual. *Onwu ora* entails the constitution of the public by both the visible and the invisible, the living and the ancestral, who are obliged to partake in the ritual. Ikwuemesi (2018, 187) notes that "once someone dies[,] unless s/he or the family is estranged from the community, the ensuing grief is shared by a lineage of relatives and friends." To be sure, absentees from Ijeagbala's funeral must provide solid justification for their nonattendance. Otherwise, they face the cultural sanction reserved for *onye abiaghi uno akwa* (one who did not attend a funeral), which may entail fractured social relations. To bridge this gap of absenteeism and attain a comprehensive sense of being with those at home for good reason, social media become a ready tool. In the Igbo cultural context, funerary rituals are more than an expression of grief and mourning; they also constitute sites of amiable sociality, performative engagement, collective glamour, and self-fashioning. They offer opportunities for maximum socialization, where

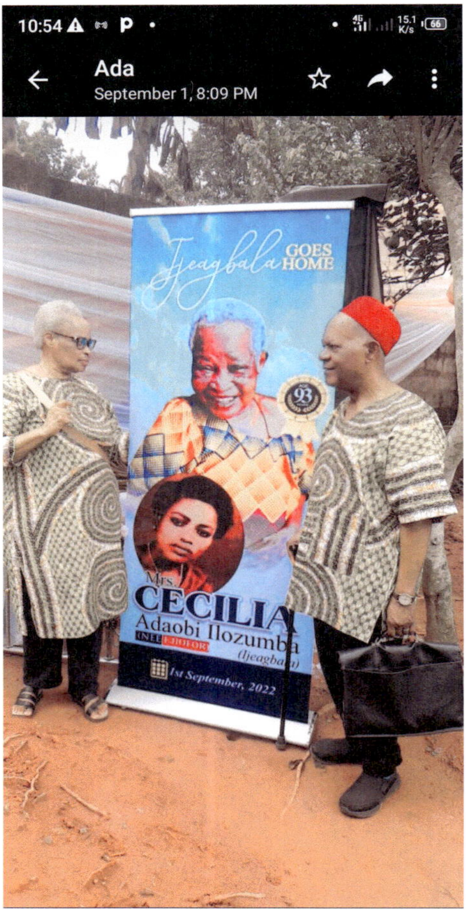

Fig. 31. A life-size poster of Ijeagbala, with Ada's mum and dad. Adaobi Osunkwo captured a photo of her parents standing next to the funeral poster of Ijeagbala in Obeledu, Anambra State.

severed ties are restored and old acquaintances and kin are reconnected. Ada's invitation to her parents to join the late Ijeagbala in a photo session presupposed that this was their final opportunity for a photographic moment with Ijeagbala, and that this act would create a closer bond with the departed. Hence, Android camera phones and social media platforms become integral elements of the funeral ritual, in guaranteeing the persistence of Ijeagbala's digital presence alongside her sister and her spouse. The invitation of her parents to pose for a photo with Ijeagbala—and the use of her name to refer to what is now only a photo—seem to reveal that the photo possesses an auratic quality similar at this moment to life or presence.

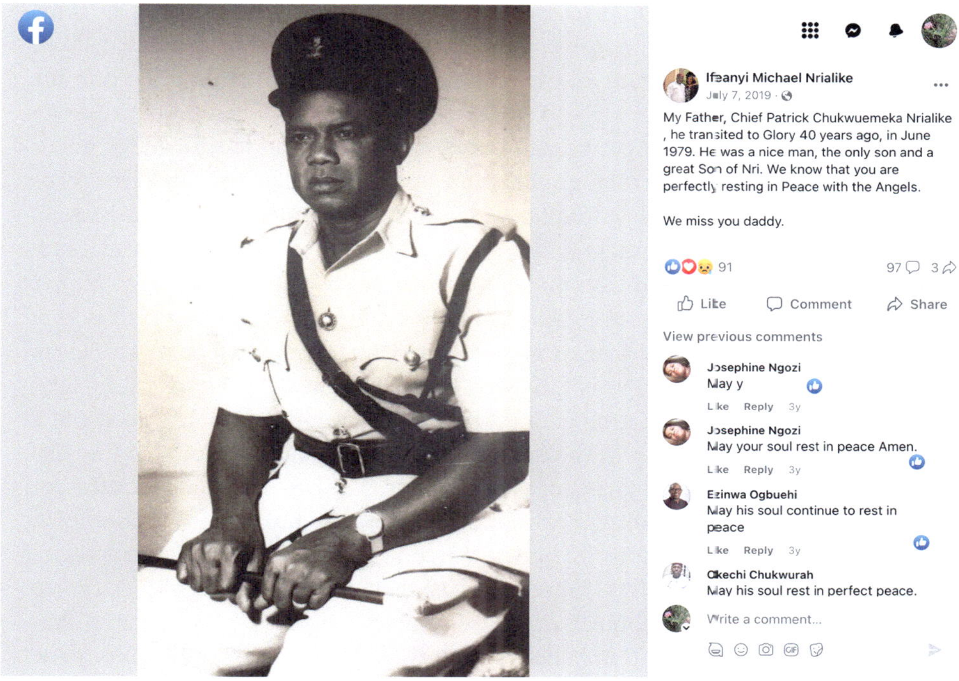

Fig. 32. Ifeanyi Nrialike's father on Ifeanyi's Facebook wall. The photo commemorates the fortieth anniversary of his passing.

In examining the last stage in the evolution of the deceased's photos in the social media public sphere, I will look at how, forty years after his father's death, Ifeanyi Nrialike shared the photo of his late father on his Facebook wall as a form of virtual homage and commemoration (Fig. 32). In doing this, Nrialike enabled his future generation to observe the remains of his father's presence (see, for example, Church 2013, 118). Facebook, in the manner Ifeanyi and others use it to commemorate death, serves as "mobile, computerized cemeteries" where "digital remains" pile high (Dilmac 2018, 288). Ifeanyi told me that his late father's children and generations celebrated him and the anniversary of his death after he (Ifeanyi) posted his photographs on Facebook and that this afforded other individuals who did not know his late father an opportunity to leave messages in his memory.

The reemergence of Nrialike's father on social media forty years after his death fulfills another funeral rite that is culturally socializing and that defies both time and space. Jurgenson (2019) has argued that "digitality in some ways has made the image more permanent: images of the deceased taken years ago can resurface and spread more easily now than they could in the past." Nrialike's father's photo seems to transgress death and time and serves as a disruptive element against decay, a witness to indestructibility, and a sign against death's total annihilation. Again, Nrialike's father seems to be communicating with his children, grandchildren, and great-grandchildren, thus enacting, quite suggestively, an old and unilateral form of Igbo ancestral communication, a conversation in which an answer is not expected in return. In the Igbo belief system, the continuous presence of the deceased is kept alive in the same manner social media have kept the continuous presence of Nrialike's father alive (see Lingel 2013). Again, just as on social media, Igbo ancestral communication entails a denial of severance from the dead and a continuous insertion of the deceased into the scheme of everyday life. The online public space does not conceal the earthliness of Nrialike's father or confine it to a final resting place; rather, the screen functions as a portal that brings his being and that of his contemporaries into a new mode of incessant interactivity. Lapper (2017) has remarked that "the interactivity of such shared information on Facebook is exactly what makes it different from printed obituaries—it invites an immediate response." In the Igbo worldview of ancestral veneration, interactivity ensures that death does not mark a definitive end but a transition to a different plane of existence, where the living and the dead maintain an ongoing dialogue.

Finally, in another form of photographic evolution, one finds many YouTube videos of funerals posted online. The video captures a significant part of the funeral celebration. For example, in a YouTube video of the funeral of Mrs. Okafor Oyekwe, there is a spectacular public display. The pallbearers, carrying the casket on their heads, danced in a circle accompanied by chanting and percussion as they marched from the church toward the deceased's home. The dance is a fast-paced, dynamically and dramatically choreographed show that features singing and some masterful drumming: they throw the casket in different directions and aim for a swift, uniform, entertaining body movement that draws the attention of curious onlookers. The pallbearers' performance was both videographed and photographed, as a photographer and the videographer joined the funeral entourage everywhere they went. However, the video posted on YouTube is not that of the paid videographer but instead had been taken by one of Oyekwe's children. Every year, when the children reposted the video on their Facebook wall to mark the late Oyekwe's remembrance, it gathered more comments and "like" buttons. The comments trickled in for weeks before the video disappeared, only to reappear again the following year. While this act of maintaining "continuing bonds with the deceased" is not novel if we consider, for example, the practice of constant annual visits to a loved one's gravesite (Moss 2004, 77), the novelty of these social media profiles and online memorials is the increased immediacy with which these bonds can seemingly be maintained, as well as the new forms of commemoration and engagement that emerge through the process. According to Favero (2017, 114), "With the help of photographs, we seem to constantly keep the door to the world of the dead open; reincorporating them in our lives, we also seem to be incorporating ourselves into their realms."

By means of the photographic and videographic representations of Nrialike Sr., Ijeagbala, and Madam Oyekwe, the yearly rite of their reemergence in social media public space is enacted, whereby their existences and those of their relatives are reinscribed into the lived contract of mutual coexistence. James Yékú (2022) has articulated the capacity of Facebook to reenact photographic memories of past events as a kind of recurring performance. He refers to what Schechner (2006, 28) describes as "twice-behaved behaviour" and to Bert States's description of "photography as the quintessential art of reproduction that survives only in the encounter and re-encounter of the spectator" (States 1996, cited in Yékú 2022, 157). Adenekan (2021), writing about African literary production, also specified how social media enact a networked community that fosters collaborations, alliances, and interconnections and how power is dynamically shifting with time. One thing is evident: Time and space are no barriers to the collective consciousness triggered by social media, whether in literary or other fields of endeavor, such as commemorative photography. This digital landscape fosters a vibrant space for community intervention, critique, and the generation of counternarratives. One pertinent idea that emerges from online commemoration is how it is constituted around notions of what Adeoba and Yékú (2024, 2) have described as "cultural netizenship," which "captures the aesthetic and cultural dimensions of visual popular media." Following Yékú and Adeoba, I want to propose commemorative netizenship as a subgenre of cultural netizenship that entails an immediate mode of platform grieving and mourning. If, as argued by Meese, Nansen, et al. (2015, 416), a "complex data economy assists in entrenching commemorative connection as a social practice," then commemorative netizenship is one way social media constitutes itself as an ontologically extractivist space, wherein users' posts are inherently vulnerable to social media algorithms and the Global North companies that control the platforms. In his seminal work on "knowing capitalism," Nigel Thrift (2005) introduces the concept of the "technological unconscious" and the "cultural circuits of capitalism," which he describes as the operation of potent and enigmatic information technologies that shape everyday life. Although it is acknowledged that these emergent forms of power do not obliterate historical power structures, it is compellingly evident that a society saturated with media translates into one where power is increasingly vested in algorithms (Lash 2007a, 71).

It is essential to understand how the concept of platform capitalism is fundamental to digital subjectivity, online public spheres, and the socialities that influence commemorative cultural practices. While I acknowledge platform capitalism as an agent of late capitalist economies, I theorize commemorative netizenship as part of the consumer behavior that contributes significantly to the success of platform capitalism. I draw a parallel between commemorative netizenship and what Carolin Gerlitz and Anne Helmond (2013) termed "the like economy," a concept that posits that social interactions hold significant economic value, as user engagements are immediately converted into quantifiable data and displayed to other users, thereby fostering increased traffic and engagement.

Thus, following Yékú, reposting commemorative photographs is a performative act that is constantly reenacted on Facebook. Although Facebook commemorative photos and obituary notices are global phenomena, the distinctiveness of Igbo commemorative photography lies in its dynamic online engagement. The photograph's multiple transformations—from the album to the poster to the funeral—are shared online where mourners perform active engagement. The social media public sphere serves as both a physical and a spiritual space, enabling interaction and communion among humans and ancestors.

The entire funerals of the late Madam Oyekwe and Ijeagbala are constituted by an overly visual spectacle: The videographer captured the entire activities, including the pallbearers and their band; three women danced with three different photographs of the late Oyekwe, the photographer shot the event, and a communal viewership by the entire village was enabled. After the funeral, the videographer and photographer returned a video CD and photo album to the family. While Ada posted images and videos on her social media pages, Oyekwe's children posted photos and uploaded videos to YouTube, their Facebook pages, and Instagram, among other sites.

In southeastern Nigeria, funerals conventionally entailed an outwardly effusive show of sorrow. Many individuals, especially elderly women, with kin affiliations to the deceased shed profuse tears at the burial venue to fulfill the ritual of sorrowful display.[2] Here on Facebook, individuals I interviewed claimed to have exhibited a similar emotional outpouring. They argued that their inability to be physically present at the funeral venue is redeemed by the expressive, tearful emojis, which to them are genuinely and demonstrably sorrowful. More than twenty individuals I met in the field confessed to me that they had responded to a photo of the deceased on Facebook with a tearful emoji without bothering to read the text accompanying the photo. Over thirty-five individuals also typed "RIP" without knowing who the individual was. They typed "RIP" or left a tearful emoji once they saw a photo on their friend's Facebook wall with sorrowful insignia such as "RIP" and tearful emojis. Of course, it is possible that the mere typing of three letters "RIP" may signify emotional distance from the deceased, while extensive, intimate comments may suggest a measure of closeness.

THE OBITUARY PUBLIC SPHERE OF FACEBOOK WALLS

The death of Ikeogu Oke, an Igbo poet from Ohafia, who had made a significant Facebook presence with his poetry while alive, sparked a wild and wide itinerary of photographs across social media.[3] There was a sudden rush of traffic to his Facebook wall and a consequent copying and wide distribution of his photos on virtually every Facebook wall of his family members and other friends. In fact, those who did not know Ikeogu beyond Facebook friendship also visited his Facebook wall and copied photos, tagged the late Ikeogu in the photo, and wrote a tribute. This illustrates how Facebook appears to mirror the collective rite of mourning in Igbo culture. Accessing Facebook walls and copying photos of the deceased is akin to the ritual of visiting the deceased's residence. Facebook allows users to tag and visit the profiles of the deceased, creating a virtual space for communal mourning and reminiscing (Kasket 2012).

After Ikeogu's death, I identified more than five thousand posts where friends and other individuals tagged his photos on Facebook. While most of the photos were lifted from his Facebook photo archives, a few were copied from online sites where Ikeogu had appeared in some of his public performances. In fact, Ikeogu's YouTube video of his BBC poetry reading was seen floating around Nigerians' Facebook walls, and shared on Ikeogu's and other people's

Facebook walls with an accompanying farewell note. During my ethnography, I discovered that while life's achievements could ignite such photographic traffic among Nigerian Facebook users, the spread is more rapid and profuse with death. The absence of the physical body on earth is redeemed by the proliferation of the body in virtual space. The above photographic traffic of the dead on social media seems to transcend traditional rites of passage in certain cultures. At the same time, I would argue that for the Igbo of southeastern Nigeria, it reinforces already primordial notions of immortality and temporality.

In the wide circulation of Ikeogu's photos on Facebook and social media, the accompanying mourning exchange moves beyond death to embrace heroic exploits. Likewise, when Ada posted her parents' group photograph with the framed photo of the late Ijeagbala, many instant comments not only expressed sorrow at Ijeagbala's death but remarked on the ebullient sociality exuded by her group photographs. Likewise, friends juxtaposed Ikeogu's photos with emotional and intimate narratives of their relationship with him. In fact, twenty of those I interviewed did not know Ikeogu in real life. Some were only friends with him on Facebook, while a few were not Ikeogu's Facebook friends, but simply admirers who visited his Facebook page, copied his photos, tagged him in the photo, and wrote a tribute. "I don't know him, but I thought he was a great writer, so I joined others to mourn him," said one user. Another user said that Ikeogu was a friend to his own friend on Facebook, and he followed his friend's praises of Ikeogu when the latter won the Nigerian Liquefied Natural Gas (NLNG) prize, "So I joined my friend to mourn his demise by sharing his photo and tagging him." Ikeogu's photos that spread around Nigerians' Facebook walls emphasized one important fact: that he won the NLNG award a few months back. NLNG is Nigeria's biggest literary award, with a $100,000 cash prize. That Ikeogu won this award a few months before his death intensified the traffic of his photo across Facebook and other social media platforms. Surely, this traffic in death exceeded what his photo could have accomplished when he was alive. This posting of Ikeogu's photos across social media was not solely a reflection of sorrow and grief but also a celebration of his remarkable achievement as a poet.

SOCIAL MEDIA WALLS AS EVOLVING TEMPORALITIES

One user who shared Ikeogu's photos told me that he "admired his talent and what he achieved in life" even without knowing him. Here social media seem to redefine the public space: This time, photos of the departed, which were once hung on the walls of Glover Memorial Hall in nineteenth-century Lagos, or featured in brochures and posters in recent times, are now exposed to the eyes of all through social media. I would like to consider the contrast between the communal funding of obituary photographs on the walls of Glover Memorial Hall in the nineteenth century, explained in chapter 3, and the digital appropriation of images from the deceased's Facebook walls in the contemporary era. According to Navon and Noy (2021, 2911), online memorials transform the deceased into symbolic figures, introduce a novel dimension by extending their public presence, and actively promote their broader social significance and impact (Walter 2015; Walter et al. 2012).

As gatekeepers of immortality, walls of both Glover Memorial Hall and Facebook serve as embodied platforms for commemorative photographs. They are sanctuaries where commemorative photographs allow us to traverse the fluid boundaries between the tangible and the intangible. In real life, the walls of Glover Memorial Hall could be constituted as spaces where mourning expresses loss and irrevocable absence, but on Facebook walls, the deceased's body is constantly exposed through the persisting image, which achieves a sort of virtual immortality. In addition, on Facebook walls, the memory of the departed is kept fresh among the present and living, enjoying the same responses. For example, social media users post photos and captions of their cherished moments with their deceased loved ones, especially on their birthdays, death anniversaries, and Christmas, just as they do with images of the living. Many scholars have observed that the internet allows funerals to reach more people and create new forms of social interaction and mourning (Thimm and Nehls 2017; Van Dijck 2007, 2008; Church 2013; Brubaker et al. 2013; Walter et al. 2011; Welling et al. 2011). Online photographs of the dead are a crucial part of this process, as they integrate memorialization with everyday communication.

As previously stated, Ikeogu's photos posted on his family's and friends' Facebook walls are used not just to announce his death or express sorrow but also to announce his (recent) heroic achievements while alive. Thus, Facebook walls enable constant communication with the dead, creating hope for "digital resurrection" and challenging the notion of death as an end. These walls also allow people to participate in funerals, celebrate the achievements of the deceased, and make political statements through photos of the dead (Navon and Noy 2021; Meese, Nansen, et al. 2015; Casilli 2010). Hence, online photographs of the deceased remain a persistent agent in familial, social, and civic exchanges. Walls are malleable artifact that contest and disrupt the course of mortality, interweaving discourses of life and death.

VISITING AND DIALOGUING WITH THE ANCESTORS ON SOCIAL MEDIA

In Okachamma's family's WhatsApp, a conversation erupted regarding the use of photographs of their grandfather for the group's icon. Sunday Jude, one of the wife's children, suggested that those who have the photos of their grandfather should post them to the page so that they could be used as the group's photo icon. Some posted, and there were further discussions over the most appropriate photograph. In the end, a smiling photo of the late Okachamma was chosen and used for the group icon. No photographs of other late family members were included except Okachamma's.

All of Okachamma's surviving children from his seven wives were represented in the group icon photo. The act of cropping these photographs alongside Okachamma's photo, positioned as the central image, bears significant implications for the interpretation of Igbo ancestral veneration. Okachamma's reintegration into the familial context, nearly four decades after his death, serves to reaffirm the enduring intergenerational bonds inherent in Igbo ancestral practices.

In a remarkable Facebook post, Chijioke Onuora commemorated the ninth anniversary of his father's passing by sharing a series of photographs of his grandfather's family and his deceased dad, accompanied by eloquent descriptions of their admirable and fulfilling lives. These photographs were also featured in his father's memorial service program. He arranged the photographs chronologically, beginning with the oldest one, in which Joshua Onuora, his father, posed with his own siblings in 1953 (Figures 33 and 34).

Figure 33 depicts Joshua Onuora sitting next to his father (Chijioke's grandfather) with his two siblings, a boy and a girl, behind him. Their pose adheres to the mid-twentieth-century photographic convention, where age determined the pose: Children either stood or sat on the bare floor, while elders and young adults sat on chairs. Onuora's father, dressed in a flowing agbada, places his two hands on his knees and gazes directly at the camera. With his amply flowing dress and pose, he seems to align with Stephen Sprague's (1978) version of the Yoruba sitter in Ila-Orangun during the 1970s. Joshua's hairstyle is an angle shaving, while his younger brother's hair is styled

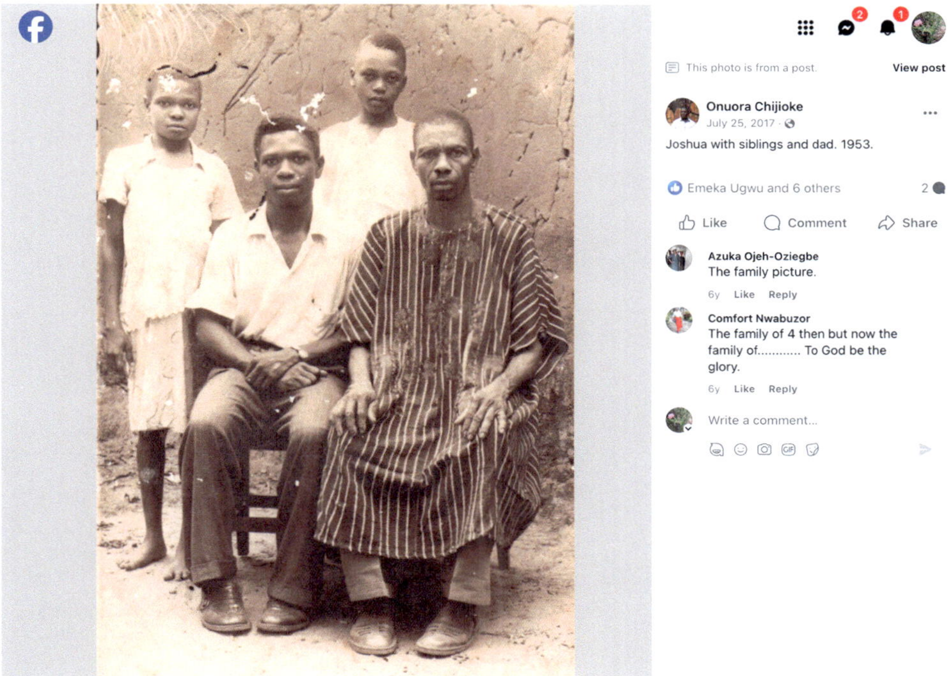

Fig. 33. Chijioke Onuora shared a photo of his late father and his family on his Facebook wall. The photo commemorates the anniversary of his passing.

differently. His attire, consisting of a white shirt, a watch, a pen tucked inside the upper pocket of the shirt, shoes, and trousers, signifies his alignment with the fashion and culture of Western modernity, in contrast to his father, who wears no watch or accessories, only his agbada, sandals, and trousers. This is similar to the visual representation in Okachamma's photographs discussed in chapter 5, where Ifeatu like Joshua wears Western-style clothes, while his father wears traditional attire (see Fig. 26).

Thus, the 1950s appear to construct a consistent narrative of children as agents of Western modernity within their families. Onuora's family photo captures meaningful gazes and poses and provides profound insight into the fashionable trends that characterized Nigerian society in the 1950s.

Chijioke's father's expression conveys the seriousness of parental responsibility in the 1950s, which the camera helps to fix. The whole atmosphere lacks any informal conviviality and presents Joshua's father as an emotion-

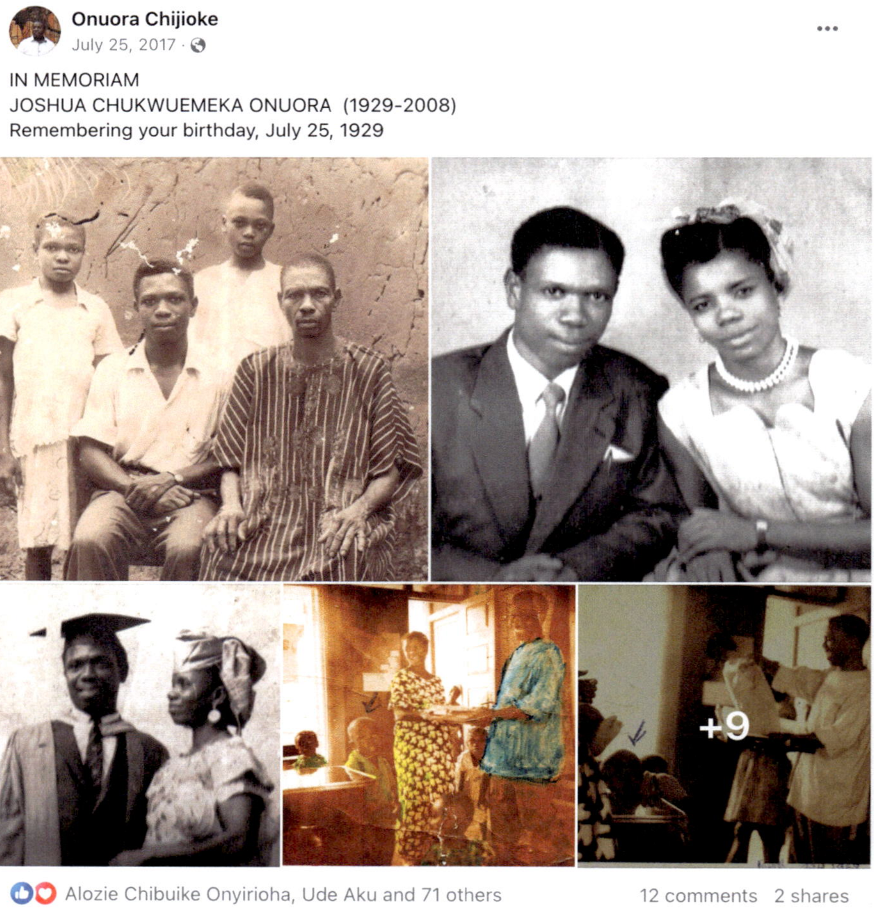

Fig. 34. Chijioke Onuora shared a photo of his late father and his family on his Facebook wall to commemorate the anniversary of his father's passing

less, austere disciplinarian. This characteristic demeanor of the father figure in Igbo society must be culturally fixed by the camera. The camera emerges as a potent instrument of behavioral, moral, and affect comportment, a medium that pays ritualistic attention to posture. In Onuora's photograph, the camera forecloses the possibility of familial joviality during photography sessions and instead records the solemn atmosphere that pervades the father-son relationship in the 1950s Igbo village, where the father's expression, if I may borrow from Chinua Achebe (1956), was "strict, severe and harsh." Thus, we see that when Onuora's family assembled for a photographic session, they complied with the strict rules of traditional social demeanor, which the camera required to capture a successful family occasion.

Chijioke wrote on top of this photograph: "In Memoriam, Joshua Chukwuemeka Onuora (1929–2008), Remembering your birthday, July 25, 1929." The contrast between Onuora's Facebook "In Memoriam" and for example, J. Bolaji Olukolu's "In Memoriam" from the *Lagos Weekly Record* (Fig. 35) of July 25, 1910, reveals a profound transformation of the public sphere. Olukolu's "In Memoriam" is devoid of any photograph and instead provides one line of prose and two of verse: "In ever Loving Memory of My dear beloved Father. The height that great men reached and kept / Were not attained by sudden flight."

However, in 2017, Onuora's "In Memoriam" on Facebook featured nine photos of him and his loved ones. To compare the middle of the intervening century, in the *Daily Times* newspaper of January 26, 1967, out of the three "In Memoriam" notices on page 19, only two included photographs of the deceased, Mr. J. F. Obi and Mrs. Omolara Adewakun (Fig. 36).

In contrast to the early twentieth century and the 1960s, when newspaper "In Memoriam" columns were unable to quench the readers' appetite for the visual history of the dead, Onuora's Facebook wall facilitated a visual genealogical reconnection through nine photographs (Fig. 34). These photos attracted comments from friends and family members who were excited to witness such ancestral communion in line with Vokes's (2008, 356) assertion that "the photograph preserves the subject as a living image, one that will outlive the subject him- or herself." By offering nine photographs of the late Joshua Onuora, the commemorative practice is transformed into a dialogic visual encounter that transcends temporal boundaries. A half-century span of Joshua's life is revealed to Chijioke's friends, who observe the transformation in his father's bodily features and appreciate his sartorial choices. They also discern his personal interests and the occasions that he deemed worthy of preserving through the photographic lens. Among the photographs, one depicted Joshua's graduation ceremony in 1965; in another, Chijioke's mother presented Joshua with a birthday gift on July 27, 1967, while Chijioke himself appeared as a young child. In this photograph, Joshua held up the gift of a shirt and expressed his gratitude with a radiant smile while his wife and Chijioke positioned themselves on opposite sides. The commenters remarked, "Never seen this before" and "It's a packet shirt, love in action." Another

WEEKLY NOTES

In view of the importance attaching to short-hand writing and the increased and increasing demand for clerks who are proficient in short-hand writing, it is a wonder the programme of subjects of examination for First Class Clerkships in the Public Service does not include this subject. The inclusion of the subject would stimulate endeavour to acquire a knowledge of it and especially if the marks were fixed high.

The exceptional good produce season in the yield of palm-oil and palm-kernels, does not appear to have affected the Central Province very much, for despite the yield from Warri, Sapele, and Benin showing an increase from January to the end of May, the increase is not sufficient to counterbalance the decrease in export from Forcados and Onitsha, and the Province shows a falling off for the period as compared with the corresponding period in 1909 of 362,580 gallons. The season is marked however in the case of Lagos and the Eastern Province. The returns for Lagos showing an increase for the period as compared with the previous year of 1,300,725 gallons palm-oil, and 13,381 tons palm-kernels. The returns for the Eastern Province show an increase over the previous year of 922,650 gallons palm-oil and 2,015 tons palm-kernels.

It is to be hoped the Maize crop will turn out to be as good as the palm crop. Maize has been exceedingly dear for some time past while there is no sign of any abatement in price. The new corn is just coming in, but it will take some time before the freshly gathered crops become sufficiently dried for purposes of local consumption or export. There is the hope however, that as the local market is not so fastidious as the foreign, the former may be served before the latter at a reduced price and to the relief of the local population.

We find from the *Sierra Leone Weekly News* that the complaint is being made, as is done here, of the railway not conveying foodstuffs from the Interior to the town at rates that would attract such traffic and thus prevent a dearth of foodstuffs in the town. During a dearth the Governor of Sierra Leone was so considerate as to have foodstuffs brought by the railway into Freetown from the Protectorate free of charge. We have passed and are still passing through a similar crisis in Lagos, but we have yet to experience such thoughtfulness and consideration for the people on the part of our Executive, although we feign would hope that humane feeling is not a monopoly of the Executive of Sierra Leone. What we would particularly urge however, is that a sort of business and benevolence plan should be introduced into the working of the railway in this respect, and foodstuffs transported at rates which would cause such produce to become a staple item of traffic, feeling sure that the railway management could effect this without hurt to the other traffic, and which would mean increased business and increased profits for the railway.

German shipping has been distinguished by a notable increase in the river of late, and which is probably due to the good produce season and consequent increase of trade. Unfortunately it is spirits more than anything else that the German ships bring, and so increase of trade in this direction does not spell as much advantage to the native as it would if German trade consisted less of spirits. Of course there are those who try to make us to believe that the trade in spirits is not harmful to the native. We suppose the same argument was adduced when the drink traffic had not reached the alarming proportions it has now attained in Europe; and when its effects were not so frightfully pronounced as they are at present. The effects of the drink traffic and which have aroused a national effort in both Europe and America to abate such effects, divests the profit-maker's cry of all meaning when he proclaims his trade is not harmful. If not harmful whence comes the problem of drunkenness confronting the countries where the trade obtains—a problem entailing the most gigantic and strenuous efforts to suppress it. With such lurid facts outlined in bold relief before him it is an insult to the intelligence of any native to suggest that the drink traffic is not harmful.

The communications from the Secretary of the Aborigines Protection and Anti-Slavery Society which we publish shed a lurid light upon the methods of commercial exploitation nowadays. It matters not where the country or who the people engaged in such pursuits, the methods are uniformly the same and involve an abnegation of moral and human codes alike, while it is to men who are civilised and christianised that the honour belongs for such methods, and engendered under the *regime* of high enlightenment and civilisation supposed to distinguish the nineteenth century. And what stamps the methods more as the product of civilisation is the inability or unwillingnes of the civilised governments to interfere to suppress them. The atrocities perpetrated in the Amazon region will in all probability share the fate of the atrocities carried on in the Congo, the hue and cry raised against them exhausting itself in academic display. But does this not spell moral weakness and ineptitude the a kind, character and fate that stand out so luminous on the pages of the world's history? It would be well if the civilised world paid more attention to this symptom and do not suffer it to gaugrene into the fatal canker which has eaten out the life of nations in the past and strewn the long path of time with the ashes of empires.

The assemblies were engaged last night mainly with foreign missions. They were calling for more missionaries to blacks. Would it not be more like the thing to get a few black missionaries brought here? As far as we can make out, the black man puts the white to shame. This applies to Church members and even to ministers. Is proof required? It will be found in statements made publicly in the Assemblies yesterday. Take the ministers first. Are they of blameless walk and conversation? Here is Professor Curtis, of Aberdeen, at the Auld Kirk Assembly, telling his brethren of the cloth how far they are as a class from what is expected of them. "He did not know in Christendom a Presbyterian Church so small a proportion of whose ministers were total abstainers, or a Presbyterian Church—and he added it with all seriousness and grief—which had within its record the story of so many painful cases of discipline in their own ranks in past generations." From what Professor Curtis said, the necessity for ecclesiastical discipline is not by any means extinct, even to-day. That is said about a Christian ministry specially favoured and endowed to uphold national religion in this la[illegible] Now turn to the blacks. Here is a mission[illegible] from Old Calabar at the United Free Asse[illegible]y. What does he say? "They had not a me[illegible]ber in full communion who was not a pledged [illegible] to taller." More can be said for those black [illegible]en and women of Old Calabar than for the [illegible]gy of the Church of Scotland! Old Calabar [illegible] not exceptional. The next speaker was from L[illegible]gstonia. "Every Church member and every [illegible]dherent in the statistics sent home were [illegible] abstainers." Those are the people we look do[illegible] upon as belonging to inferior races. They can give an example. Christianity can do in Darkest Africa what it cannot do, or at any rate has not yet done, here in this enlightened Scotland. At the very doors of the Assembly there are to be witnessed scenes of degradation that would make the people of Old Calabar ashamed. To that we have the testimony of the Master of Polwarth, also at yesterday's Assembly. "He felt often as he went down that street that the sights which they saw there and in these closes were a disgrace to a Christian country." Does it not seem a queer contrast, that Christian teaching within, perhaps a matter of fifty years, has made the negro temperate and self-respecting, while after a thousand years of religious ordinances, the shadows of our city churches fall on Scottish men and women to whom temperance is a thing unknown? The negro with his dusky skin, may be, like Gunga Din, "white, clear white, inside," and the white of skin may be the moral black. If the converts of Old Calabar got hold of our Assembly reports, what would they think of us? They would say and say with justice: "If this is the best Christianity can show at home, it is high time we set out to convert the Christians—commencing with the Auld Kirk ministers."—*Edinburgh Evening News*

NEWSPAPERS AND LIBEL ACTIONS.

TO LORD MERSEY OF TOXTETH, LONDON.

DEAR LORD,—The subject of the present law of libel as it affects newspapers is one of the sorest which can be mentioned to the average newspaper proprietor. It keeps him in a hot sweat all the day and a cold sweat most of the night; and therefore I am sure he will thank you from the bottom of his palpitating heart for what you said to the Newspaper Society the other evening. It is not as easy to conduct a fearless-speaking journal as it is to poke one's neighbour's fire, my lord; it only appears so. Some of your old colleagues of the Bench have so frightened newspaper proprietors by their dicta and their denunciation that many of them dare not even speak disrespectfully of a blackbeetle. The result is that hundreds of scoundrels known to be trading on human credulity escape exposure.

Your Lordship spoke of some libel actions against newspapers being systematised blackmail. Does your lordship know that there is a species of law shark in London whose sole occupation is to search papers with the object of subsequently inducing people to commence libel actions on the chance of winning damages and being free, or all but free, of the costs if they lose? As for libel actions with legitimate cause, it is not too muce to say that porobably most of them could be privately settled in a fair basis if the grievances were not swollen to colossal proportions in the offices of the legal profession. I agree with your lordship that "if upon proper material brought to the notice of the judge at the commencement of an action a case can be made out for ordering a plaintiff to find security for costs it would be a very good thigg." At present the speculative lawyer and the blackmailing plaintiff have all the best of the law between them. Any assistance your lordship can give in your new capacity as legislator in the adjustment of the law of libel as it unfairly affects the public press I shall gladly receive and carefully consider.

But just one word more. I do not seem to recall that your lordship was quite so outspoken on the subject whilst you were on the Bench. Why was that? JOHN BULL.

SIR ALFRED JONES CHARITY FOR AFRICA

The Editor of the "Lagos WEEKLY RECORD"

Sir,—I send for consideration a oopy of an article of mine recently published in the "African Mail."

It is a matter of opinion whether a large sum of money about to to be devoted to West African Education would be best applied by division between several bodies, or by concentrating it almost all on one central institution on the lines indicated:—

Might I suggest your opening your columns to correspondence on the question, and sending a resume of the matter to the following:

W. O. Harrison Williams, Esq.
Elder Dempster Shipping. Ltd.
Colonial House Water Street, Liverpool.

He is the sole executer under the will of the late Sir Alfred Jones. Also to.—

The Tutor,
Fourah Bay College, Sierra Leone.

He is making representations to the former gen[illegible] College and the [illegible]urham University, I am informed.

Yours faithfully
G. ROME HALL [illegible]

IN MEMORIAM.

In ever Loving Memory of my dear beloved Father.

The height that great men reached and kept
Were not attained by sudden flight.

J. BOLAJI OLUKOLU.

EPITOME OF NEWS

[illegible] following were passengers [illegible]go by th[illegible] leeward and sailed North on Tuesday:—Dr. H. R. Ellis, Captain A. H. Blair, Messrs. A. Densham, H. N. Thompson, W. Ralston, G. R. Smith, P. L. H. Archer, W. Bellamy, J. Rafter, Mrs. P. L. H. Archer, and Miss. R. M. Vecock, for England. Mrs. C. W. Domingo, and Miss. Jane to Sierra Leone.

Captain L. C. H. Humfrey has succeeded Captain A. H. Blair, as Commissioner at Ilesha; the latter having proceeded on furlough by the Falaba.

An official notice dated the 20th instant, cancels the notification declaring the port of Sekondi to be infected with yellow fever.

The published returns of the export of palm oi and palm kernels for the Colony and Protectorate for the period from January to May, show the exports of palm-oil for the present year to amount to 11,032,395 gallons and the export of palm kernels to 67,653 tons as against 9,171,700 gallons palm oil and 51,489 tons palm kernels exported in the preceed year.

It is announce that His Excellency the Governor has been to pleased recognize the appointment by the Alafin of Oyo of Bale Apanpa of Ibadan to be Bashorun.

The death is announced as having occurred on or about the 2nd June, of Aladesonmi, the Ewi of Ado.

We glean from the *Gold Coast Leader* that of the eight medical men composing the expedition organised by Sir Rupert Boyce, and including himself, to investigate the outbreak of Yellow Fever, six are for Sekondi and four for Sierra Leone.

We learn from Liberia of the death in his 78th year of Dr. G. W. Gibson, ex-President. The deceased was a prominent citizen of Liberia, and had filled important positions in the Church and State. He was one of the Commissioners sent recently by the Liberian Government to the United States.

photograph captured the wedding of Chijioke's father on January 2, 1960, eliciting a comment that praised his youthful and attractive appearance and reflected on the brevity of life. Hence, the commemorative photograph ceases to be a solitary entity, secluded and forsaken in mute archives; it transforms into a catalyst of reflections and an emotionally stimulating object. It brings together the owner and the visually inquisitive public, generating inquiries, provoking interest, and inviting critiques; in other words, it becomes a dialogical entity. It provokes "interactivity," which has been hailed by Haskins (2007, 406) "as a democratizing attribute of new media." Haskins argues that interactivity embodies "one of the biggest potentials of cyberspace." The online commemorative photograph introduces new grounds for nostalgic contemplations, assuaging the thirst of starving eyes while receiving accolades and affirming its own perpetual presence among the living. In fulfilling some of these promises, in 2020, three years after his father's passing, Onuora paid tribute to him on his Facebook wall by uploading his picture and placing it side by side with a picture of his younger brother, who adopted a pose akin to his father's. He sought to demonstrate their remarkable resemblance in this commemorative juxtaposition.

In Igbo society, it is common to invoke the ancestors through daily prayers as well as on almost every special occasion: rituals, child dedication, marriage, and housewarming, among others. Such ancestral invocation is seen as a daily form of commemoration. Prayers are not considered efficacious if a form of supplication or homage is not paid, mainly through the pouring of drops of wine or other drinks on the floor, in libation, to seek the ancestors' protection. As Ebere and Shehan (2016, 2) note:

> Anthropomorphically, ancestors are ascribed both bodily and spiritual characteristics, including the ability to hear, feel, and express emotions; to monitor events and activities on earth; to exist anywhere; to consume food and drink; to enter into and to possess human individuals or brute animals; and to maintain the greatest interest in the affairs of humans, particularly those of their immediate family.

Ebere notes that though essentially a religious phenomenon, ancestor worship has a social function, in that it sustains interdependence and ensures

---

Fig. 35. "In Memoriam" of J. Bolaji Olukolu. The "In Memoriam" was published in the *Lagos Weekly Record* of July 25, 1910.

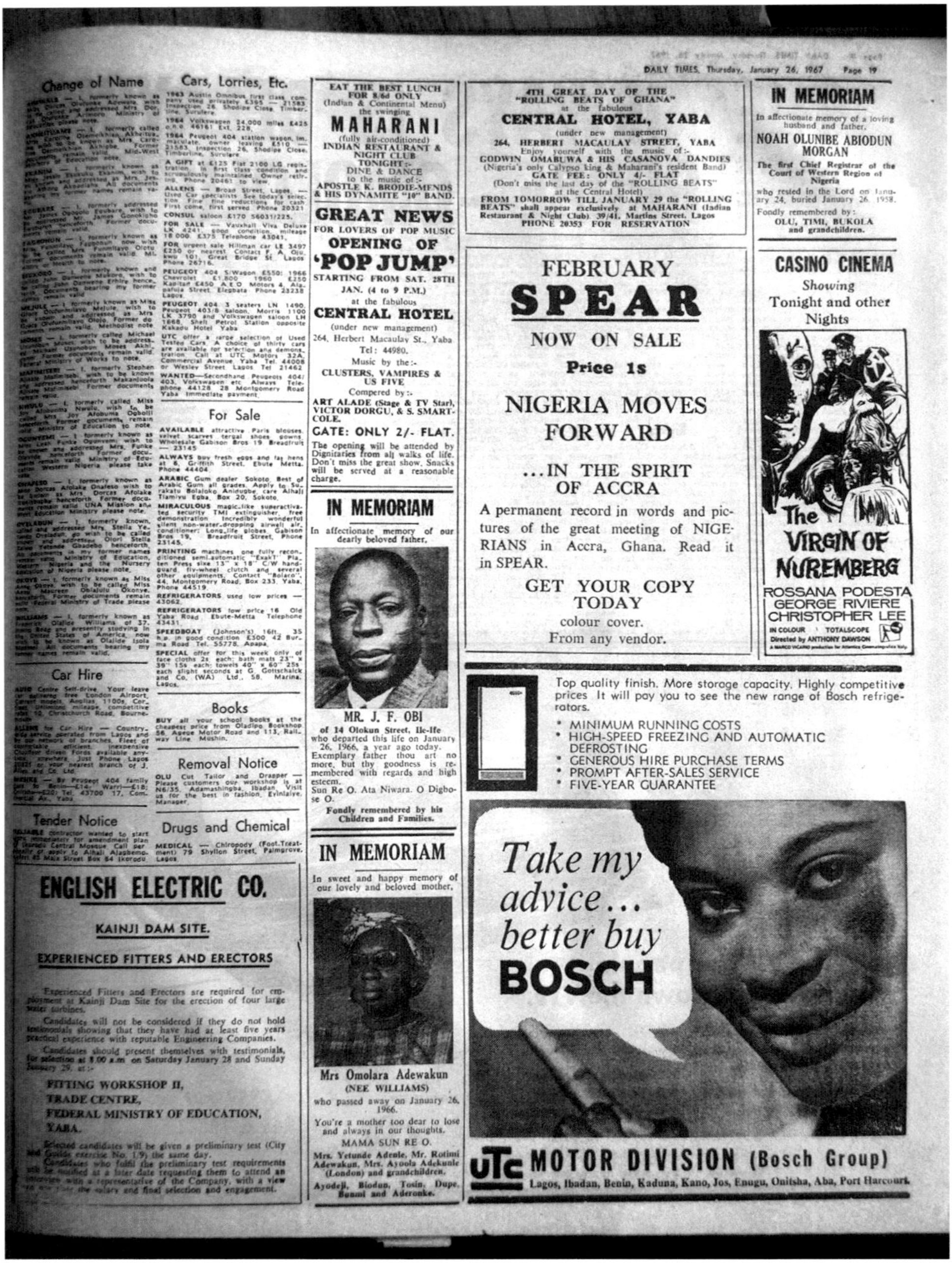

DAILY TIMES, Thursday, January 26, 1967 Page 19

Change of Name

Cars, Lorries, Etc.

For Sale

Books

Removal Notice

Drugs and Chemical

Car Hire

Tender Notice

ENGLISH ELECTRIC CO.

KAINJI DAM SITE.

EXPERIENCED FITTERS AND ERECTORS

Experienced Fitters and Erectors are required for employment at Kainji Dam Site for the erection of four large water turbines.

Candidates will not be considered if they do not hold testimonials showing that they have had at least five years practical experience with reputable Engineering Companies.

Candidates should present themselves with testimonials for selection at 8.00 a.m. on Saturday January 28 and Sunday January 29, at:-

FITTING WORKSHOP II,
TRADE CENTRE,
FEDERAL MINISTRY OF EDUCATION,
YABA.

EAT THE BEST LUNCH FOR 8/6d ONLY (Indian & Continental Menu) the swinging

MAHARANI
(fully air-conditioned)
INDIAN RESTAURANT & NIGHT CLUB
TONIGHT:-
DINE & DANCE
to the music of:-
APOSTLE K. BRODIE-MENDS & HIS DYNAMITE "10" BAND.

GREAT NEWS
FOR LOVERS OF POP MUSIC
OPENING OF
'POP JUMP'
STARTING FROM SAT. 28TH JAN. (4 to 9 P.M.)
at the fabulous
CENTRAL HOTEL
(under new management)
264, Herbert Macaulay St., Yaba
Tel: 44980.
Music by the:-
CLUSTERS, VAMPIRES & US FIVE
Compered by:-
ART ALADE (Stage & TV Star), VICTOR DORGU, & S. SMART-COLE.
GATE: ONLY 2/- FLAT.
The opening will be attended by Dignitaries from all walks of life. Don't miss the great show. Snacks will be served at a reasonable charge.

IN MEMORIAM

In affectionate memory of our dearly beloved father,

MR. J. F. OBI
of 14 Olokun Street, Ile-Ife
who departed this life on January 26, 1966, a year ago today. Exemplary father thou art no more, but thy goodness is remembered with regards and high esteem.
Sun Re O. Ata Niwara. O Digbo-se O.
Fondly remembered by his Children and Families.

IN MEMORIAM

In sweet and happy memory of our lovely and beloved mother,

Mrs Omolara Adewakun
(NEE WILLIAMS)
who passed away on January 26, 1966.
You're a mother too dear to lose and always in our thoughts.
MAMA SUN RE O.
Mrs. Yetunde Adenle, Mr. Rotimi Adewakun, Mrs. Ayoola Adekunle (London) and grandchildren,
Ayodeji, Biodun, Tosin, Dupe, Bunmi and Aderonke.

4TH GREAT DAY OF THE "ROLLING BEATS OF GHANA" at the fabulous
CENTRAL HOTEL, YABA
(under new management)
264, HERBERT MACAULAY STREET, YABA
Enjoy yourself with the music of:-
GODWIN OMABUWA & HIS CASANOVA DANDIES
(Nigeria's only Calypso king & Maharani's resident Band)
GATE FEE: ONLY 4/- FLAT
(Don't miss the last day of the "ROLLING BEATS" at the Central Hotel)
FROM TOMORROW TILL JANUARY 29 the "ROLLING BEATS" shall appear exclusively at MAHARANI (Indian Restaurant & Night Club). 39/41, Martins Street, Lagos
PHONE 20353 FOR RESERVATION

FEBRUARY
SPEAR
NOW ON SALE
Price 1s
NIGERIA MOVES FORWARD
...IN THE SPIRIT OF ACCRA
A permanent record in words and pictures of the great meeting of NIGERIANS in Accra, Ghana. Read it in SPEAR.
GET YOUR COPY TODAY
colour cover.
From any vendor.

IN MEMORIAM

In affectionate memory of a loving husband and father,
NOAH OLUNIBE ABIODUN MORGAN
The first Chief Registrar of the Court of Western Region of Nigeria
who rested in the Lord on January 24, buried January 26, 1958.
Fondly remembered by:
OLU, TIMI, BUKOLA and grandchildren.

CASINO CINEMA
Showing
Tonight and other Nights
The VIRGIN OF NUREMBERG
ROSSANA PODESTA
GEORGE RIVIERE
CHRISTOPHER LEE
IN COLOUR · TOTALSCOPE
Directed by ANTHONY DAWSON

Top quality finish. More storage capacity. Highly competitive prices. It will pay you to see the new range of Bosch refrigerators.
- MINIMUM RUNNING COSTS
- HIGH-SPEED FREEZING AND AUTOMATIC DEFROSTING
- GENEROUS HIRE PURCHASE TERMS
- PROMPT AFTER-SALES SERVICE
- FIVE-YEAR GUARANTEE

Take my advice... better buy BOSCH

UTC MOTOR DIVISION (Bosch Group)
Lagos, Ibadan, Benin, Kaduna, Kano, Jos, Enugu, Onitsha, Aba, Port Harcourt

Fig. 36. "In Memoriam" of Mr. J. F. Obi and Mrs. Omolara Adewakun. The "In Memoriam" was published in the *Daily Times* of January 26, 1967.

the strengthening of kinship and communal identity. The reverence accorded to parents, grandparents, and other elder relatives extends beyond their lifetimes, enduring as a vital aspect of ancestral veneration and cultural continuity (Bae 2008, 54). Although this practice of pouring libations to invoke the spirit of dead relatives is deemed animistic and crudely paganistic by Pentecostal Christians, its profound essence as a means of reaching dead relatives and ancestors has not been undermined. The ancestors are "honored" as the unseen heads of their lineages (Uchendu 1964, 31).

Facebook, YouTube, WhatsApp, and Instagram, among others, could be seen as means of reaching dead relatives and, as I argue, act as a more contemporary form of the Igbo practice of ancestral veneration and visual praise-singing. Following Giaxoglou (2014, 15), who states that mourning on social media is "a reconfigured rather than an entirely new form of mourning," I argue that these social media visual practices, acting as globally circulating image technologies, have successfully reinforced localized forms of Igbo ancestral veneration and ritual. Photos of the deceased on Facebook walls construct mourning and commemoration as socially continuous processes, like ancestral veneration, which are inscribed into everyday life rather than processes that terminate, as in traditional burial rites.

Considering Chijioke Onuora, Ikeogu, and others, it could be suggested that social media reinforce the Igbo understanding of the grave not as a final resting place but as a site of perpetual presence and interaction (Gibbs, Meese, et al. 2014; Carroll and Landry 2010; Williams and Merten 2009; Brubaker et al. 2013; Dourish 2013; Church 2013). Online commemoration through photos and videos disrupts the boundaries of death and creates a shared space of ongoing social interaction and identity formation (Walter et al. 2011; Veale 2004; Kern et al. 2013; Dourish 2013; Carroll and Landry 2010). Photos of Okachamma, Onuora, Nrialike, and Ikeogu attained digital mobility and triggered familial conversation, escaping temporal and spatial boundaries (cf. Rigney 2005).

Facebook, with over two billion users, offers a rare opportunity to study how people use social media to maintain bonds with the departed and express their collective grief (Blaha 2012). Pictures previously circulating in family albums, funeral brochures, posters, and billboards have been assigned a new value in a process that can be considered as recycling, reinterpretation, or reframing to re-echo Fahd (2023, 111) observation that "in this digital age of networked sociality, family albums are now online." While the analog photos in the family photo albums, brochures, and posters are tangible objects, the digital photos as intangible objects defy containment once they enter the global space of social media. As intangible objects, they can be worked on and distributed within a global public space. They act as spirits and souls of ancestors wandering in spaces of eternity. As Derrida argues, "Modern technology, contrary to appearances, although it is scientific, increases tenfold the power of ghosts" (Derrida and Stiegler 2002, 15).

In a more political vein, the recent commemorative photographic practice on social media may be seen as a means through which the Nigerian poor challenge the elite privilege of photographic visibility that was once established by elite magazines in the 1990s, as described in chapter 5. Previous studies have indicated that the pursuit of family honor and distinction is a significant factor behind the ostentation exhibited at many African funerals in the present day (van der Geest 2000; Arhin 1994). While these writers are referring to the material consumption of food and display of wealth, I have argued that there is a new trend to visual ostentation, in various formats including social media. Through the digital dissemination of commemorative photos and their accompanying textual narratives on social media platforms, Igbo families enact their rites of bereavement while simultaneously affirming their social capital and cultural identity—for substantially less money than is spent in the production of posters and booklets, to say nothing of billboards.

People are also able to learn the number of individuals who visit their wall and see their posted photos. They feel a sense of satisfaction to observe that their photos or videos are being viewed by as many individuals as possible, proof that "he or she exists through 'catching the eye' of others" (Gozlan and Masson 2013 cited in Dilmac 2018, 284). This process reveals the tension between the quest for visibility and the commodification of social relations in the contemporary world. Online reputation is based on how many people view, follow, and comment on one's photos or pages, which makes everyone into a brand whose value is measured by its popularity (Rosenbaum 1998). This is a strange kind of connectivity because it relies on others to prove that they viewed your photo. Haroche (2011) argues that many online viewers visit, scrutinize, analyze, and admire your photos only to eventually abandon you. Some respondents also pointed out that they were forced to remember the deceased as soon as their photos popped up on Facebook. Remembrance for them is no longer a matter of choice but becomes automatic or compulsive. Yet one cannot dispute the fact that online visibility brings with it the capacity to reach a greater number of viewers, and—with relevance to diaspora members—at greater distances than analog visibility. I aim to incite a deeply critical examination of the capitalist ramifications inherent in this online practice, transcending its interpretation as merely an evolving cultural peculiarity of the Igbo. It could be argued that this online commemorative revolution is driven by the prevailing capitalist paradigms of both established and emerging software algorithms. The result is a convergence of technology and human agency, which Lash (2006, 581) describes as a collapse of "ontology and epistemology" in the following remark:

> What may be happening in the information order is such a collapse of ontology and epistemology. Ontology itself is increasingly epistemological. And of course the notion of information implies this. What else could informational being be? But equally epistemological or modes of knowing are increasingly also modes of being. Being always necessarily shifts over into modes of classification.

Reflecting on Lash's significant insight, Roger Burrows (2009) contends that the distinction lies in the role of information technologies, which now "comprise" or "constitute" our lives rather than merely "mediate" them. Burrows argues that the stuff that makes up the social and urban fabric is now driven by complex social interactions that are constituted by software and code. While I do not wish to diminish the influence of algorithms and data capitalism in shaping contemporary social life globally, I also seek to highlight the unique creative potential of Igbo commemoration and its ritual dynamics in deploying social media to transcend spatial and temporal limitations. Social media have thus empowered the Igbo to reimagine their commemorative practices, enriching their perceptions of heroism and the public sphere. Accordingly, the next chapter leverages the theory of "Storytelling" to show how I moved from pervasive social media indulgence toward a renewed engagement with funeral photographers. I will show, in line with Walter Benjamin, that a ubiquitous social media practice might have occasioned a decline in the human capacity to narrate the social lives that commemorative photography so dominantly captures. Through this strategy, I will reflect on what I call a "meaningful gaze at death" to reinvigorate the theoretical premise of African photography.

CHAPTER 7

Photographing the Igbo Funeral

The Materiality of Its Performance

This chapter is a reengagement of my visual odyssey, verbal dialogues, texts, and proceedings that I have undertaken during my participation in multiple burials, funerals, and commemorative events in the past ten years of this research in southeastern Nigeria. Responding to the emergent demands of communal and social responsibilities, the chapter is the result of a gradual, thoughtful process that I progressively explored as I went through my photographs, diaries, and interviews. I thought that scholars of funerals and burials in Africa had missed an exciting opportunity to tell the stories of the funeral photographers and the photographs of the dead. This chapter is an exploration of a unique methodology in visual history where I attempt to understand what it means to photograph a funeral in eastern Nigeria. In my further attempt to examine the multiple meanings that can be derived from funeral photographs, I deploy storytelling as an essential ingredient to arrive at a robust theoretical argument in my ethnography.

A VISUAL ODYSSEY

This chapter explores the many meanings that can be read from the art of photographing burials and funerals in the Igbo region of Nigeria. It builds simultaneously on my practice as an ethnographer, a visual historian, and an artist. Being an auto-ethnography of burial and funeral, this chapter follows what John Dewey (in Stoller 1989, 152) describes as "negative capability." This is a form of "immediate, sensuous, and poetic" (1989, 152) reflection that is essentially impulsive and innate. This chapter is a reengagement of the visual odyssey, verbal dialogues, texts, and proceedings that I have undertaken during my participation in multiple burials and funeral services in the past years in southeastern Nigeria. Responding to the emergent demands of communal and social responsibilities, it is the result of a gradual, thoughtful process that I progressively explored as I went through my photographs, diaries, and interviews. I assimilated my thought processes into the photos that I gathered during the funeral services I attended. I further articulated my ideas on paper, transmitting them to my computer. For every subsection of this chapter, I contemplated every encounter with my participants and the grave significance of life and death. I thought that scholars of funerals and burials in Africa had missed an exciting opportunity to tell the stories of the funeral photographers and the photographs of the dead. This chapter is an exploration of a unique methodology in a visual culture where I attempt to understand what it means to photograph a funeral in eastern Nigeria. In my further attempt to examine the multiple meanings that can be derived from funeral photographs, I rely on storytelling to develop a nuanced ethnographic analysis. Favero (2022, 74) argues: "Storytelling is, for me, not a tool for communicating already preconceived knowledge. Rather it is a producer of knowledge." Indeed, Favero (2022) approaches storytelling as "a participatory, open-ended process, an opera aperta" (see also Eco 1989). Storytelling is a contextual art (Benjamin [1968] 1985a). It reinvigorates itself by adjusting to a system that begat it. It negates the rigid criteria that inform novel writing by constantly searching for new meanings and transcending the norms of letters during its endless journeys across space and time. This is the fundamental methodology I deploy in this chapter. This is my attempt to understand the local nuances of image-making in death. Photographs have become agents and curative materials used to transform contemporary life into a ritualistic event and initiate a new dialogue between the living and the dead.

In this chapter, I investigate the role of photography in the funeral proper. I argue that photography plays multiple roles during and after the funeral. For example, photographs serve as the material endorsement of the funeral ritual by freezing culturally specific functions of the Igbo funeral; they serve as objects used during dance performances in Igbo funerals; they enter the deceased's afterlife as a material trace of death and a commemorative object of value. It is generally believed that a successful funeral outing must be extensively documented through photography. It is also believed that the camera must capture participants in various performative gestures to be able to fix the funeral ritual in time and space. Through photography, funerals have come to be symbolized by a new materiality: one that reinscribes the dead back into the ancestral afterlife with an omnipresent significance for the living. I observed these transformations while participating in more than seventy burial and funeral ceremonies in eastern Nigeria.

At certain points, photography transforms the severe pains of loss into an embodied experience of joy for the bereaved. This is emphasized by Ikwuemesi (2013, 139), who notes, "As an embodiment of art, funerals harbour elements of entertainment, and entertainment can culminate in 'jollity' or sorrow. The implicit interface of 'mirth' and 'sorrow' is part of the theatricality and artistry in Igbo funerals. Influences of Christianity and modernization (Westernisation) have not changed the pattern very much, as can be deduced from contemporary Igbo funerals." Photographing the entire funeral event evolved in different contexts around the world (Ruby 1984; de Witte 2001, 2003; Hartmann 1998). For example, Sigurjón Baldur Hafsteinsson (1999) notes how amateurs in Iceland began to take pictures of the "entire funeral process," from placing the deceased in the coffin to the memorial reception after the ceremony.

JOURNEY TO THE MORTUARY

When preparations had been concluded for the burial and funeral of the late Nwachukwu Okafor Nwosisi of Umuawulu in Awka South Local Government Area of Anambra in eastern Nigeria, the business of the hired photographer commenced. Nwoye, the hired photographer, accompanied the entire family to the mortuary. He photographed the commencement of the journey to the morgue to fetch the corpse. The family members were photographed, followed by the undertakers and their hearse, where the funeral poster was pasted. A motorcade accompanied the hearse. I was among the team of mourners traveling in one of the vehicles. The photographer went ahead of the motorcade and photographed from the front. When we got to the mortuary, I observed as the undertakers brought out the casket from the morgue, placed it inside their hearse, and commenced the journey to the church, where a final church service would be held. In the church, I observed the pattern of photography. I observed how the photographer focused his lens on family members and the pulpit. Women were shown dressed in white mourning uniforms as men while sitting separately from men. A collective photo session showed the women and a more detailed aspect of their faces.

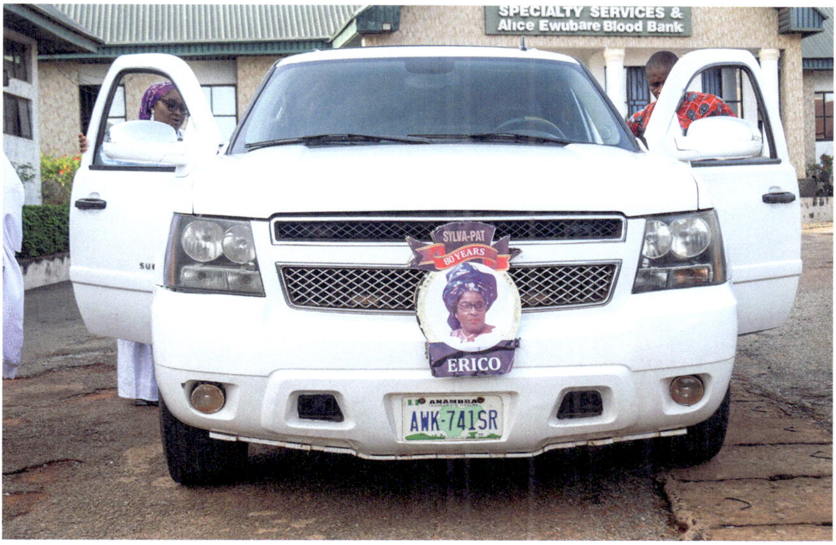

Fig. 37. The late Mrs. Christiana Nkechi Okaphor at Adazi, Anambra State

The same style was adopted for men. From the church, Nwosisi's coffin was taken back home for final burial.

People in the motorcade disembarked as we got some distance from the deceased's home. The undertakers grabbed the coffin from the hearse and started dancing with it toward the deceased's residence. The photographer captured the dramatic choreography. When we arrived at the deceased's home, I saw how the photographer captured the final disembarking of the coffin into the sitting room. Inside the sitting room, the coffin was unveiled, and the family members, all dressed in white uniforms, gathered around. Amid tears of sorrow, each family member brought a textile fabric and deposited it on the casket. I observed how the photographer photographed the deceased inside the coffin.

On another journey to the mortuary to fetch the corpse of the late Mrs. Christiana Nkechi Okaphor (Fig. 37), Nwoye, the photographer, symmetrically framed the car and the passenger and the driver as they opened the door simultaneously. While Nwoye, the photographer, did not consciously set out to achieve the compelling creative impression of this photo, we see how the photo of the late Okaphor, her nickname, Erico, and her age, "80 years," are pasted in front of the car to underscore her importance. The main emphases of this photograph are the image, the nickname, the age, and the car. The photographer had waited for this crucial moment when the two occupants, the driver and the passenger, would open the door simultaneously to ensure that their bodies were hidden from these influential signifiers of the late Okaphor's presence. Going to the mortuary thus becomes another means to photographically frame the dead to reemphasize their influential presence in a moment of undeniable absence called transition.

This postmortem photography of the late Nwosisi and Okaphor is a practice that has undergone tremendous changes in southeastern Nigeria over time. For example, I observed a marked difference between the postmortem photographs of Nwosisi and Okaphor from those of the late Chief Okachamma taken in 1986 (Fig. 38a). According to Ifeatu, the first son of the late chief, there was a makeshift arrangement for a photographer who photographed the body immediately after the chief died in 1986 and shortly before he was interred. The need for an immediate photo of Chief Okachamma's remains was informed by the fact that the family wanted an immediate interment. They did not want to deposit the corpse in the mortuary. The need for a material trace and a final visual account of Okachamma's last earthly journey occasioned a postmortem photographic documentation. All Okachamma's family members gathered beside his corpse for the group photograph (Fig 38b). It was assumed that this would be the last group family photograph of the late chief and his family (see, for example, de Witte 2003, 546; Wendl and du Plessis 1998). For many other families, similar postmortem photographs most likely became the last group photograph with their dead relatives. More than seventy funerals I studied revealed this often-overlooked photographic practice.

While postmortem portraiture seems to be a colonial import that came with the invention of the camera, Nigerians have utilized its visual affordances to perform specific culturally prescribed roles. For example, the late Nwosisi's daughter was photographed as she cried beside her father's coffin and was comforted by one of her siblings. This is one of the culturally significant roles postmortem photography is desirably utilized for in Igboland: to pepper funerary rites with pictures that attest to the ostentatious nature of sorrow. Sorrow in Igbo cosmology cannot be secretly contained, and an absence of the grandstanding appeals of sorrow implicitly denies the funeral its most profound essence. In principle, burials and funerals must be conspicuously photographed and visualized. This excessive attention to the visual is a cultural attribute that recognizes the attention-seeking aspect of sorrow as one of the most critical components of the funeral. That was why it is important for the photographer to capture the performative gestures of sorrowful displays such as that of Nwosisi's family.

By the mid-twentieth century, postmortem portraiture was already popular in Nigeria, such that by the late twentieth century, it was characterized by a certain informality that greeted the arrival of hand-held cameras. A typical example was the remarkable casualness that informed Okachamma's postmortem photograph, which deferred markedly from that of Nwosisi, taken in the twenty-first century.

Chief Michael Nwankwo Nwafor, popularly known as Okachamma, was a paramount ruler of Ndiukwuenu community in Anambra State. He had seven wives with many children, grandchildren, and great-grandchildren. He died in 1986 at his home in Mkpoghor, Ndiukwuenu, Orumba North Local Government of Anambra State. The children traveled to Awka, the nearby city, and bought a casket and other necessary materials to prepare his body for final interment. The eldest son, Ifeatu, invited a photographer whose studio name was simply identified as Sammy from a neighboring village known as Akpugoeze, to take photos of all the family members as they gathered around Okachamma's coffin (Figs 38a and 38b) (interview with Sunday Jude, 2020).

In this postmortem photograph (Figs 38a and 38b), the expressions on the faces of the family members were those of grief and sadness. According to Ifeatu, "Then photography was not so common like the camera phones; we waited for some time to get the photographer. We gathered everyone who was around in the village for this shot. Watching this photograph every time reminds me of the sad event, but at the same time, it allows me to reflect on a life well lived by Papa" (author's interview, 2020). To Ifeatu, the photograph is a spiritual link between him and his late father. The photograph thus ensures the continuation of a material connection between the living and the dead. This is akin to what Igbo ancestral masks do. Ikenga, for example, serves as a spiritual link between the owner and his *chi* (god).

In a similar encounter, I attended the funeral ceremony of Nwosisi of Umuawulu village in Anambra State, where I found a situation different from Okachamma's. When Nwosisi died, the children took his corpse to the morgue, where it remained for a while. That morgue interval allowed the children ample time to prepare for Nwosisi's burial. Their family home at Umuawulu was repainted. Nwosisi's children engaged the services of a professional photographer. The difference between Okachamma's postmortem photo and that of Nwosisi lies in the decorative style current in postmortem photography. There was no decorative casket for Okachamma: he was buried

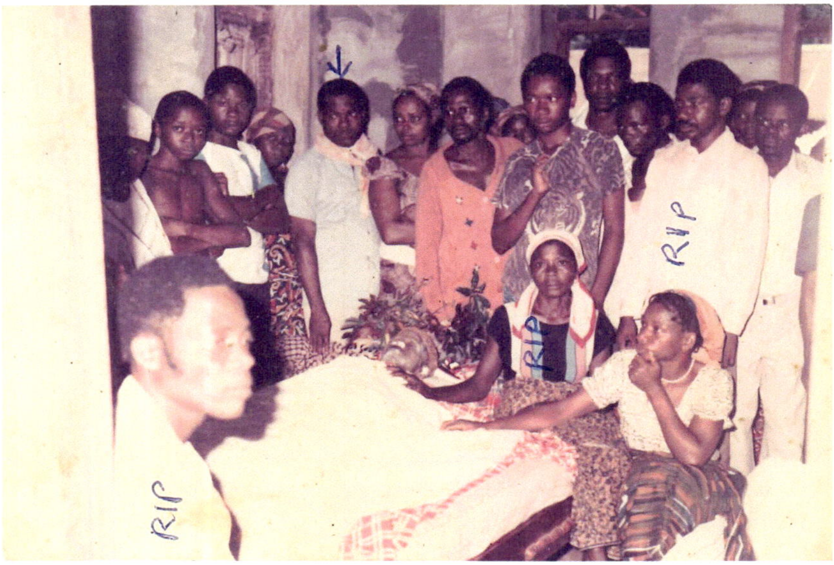

Fig. 38a. Postmortem photograph of Chief Michael Nwankwo Nwafor (Okachamma). Ifeatu preserved the photograph of his late father, who passed away in 1986 at Mkpoghor, Ndiukwuenu, Anambra State.

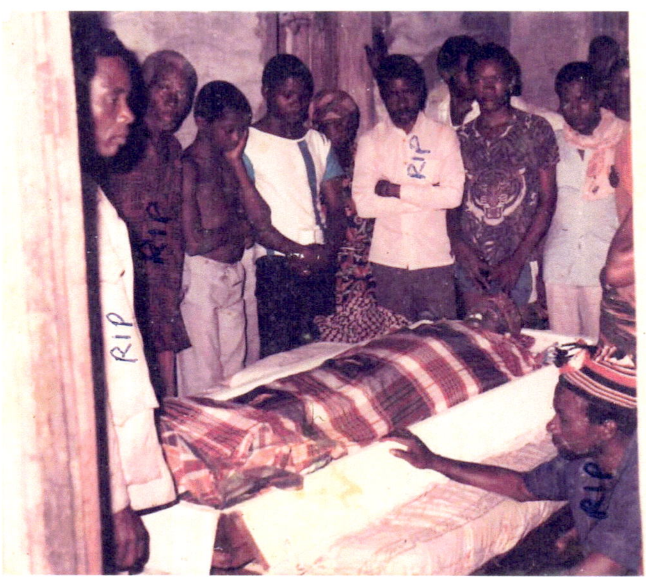

Fig. 38b. Postmortem photograph of Chief Michael Nwankwo Nwafor (Okachamma)

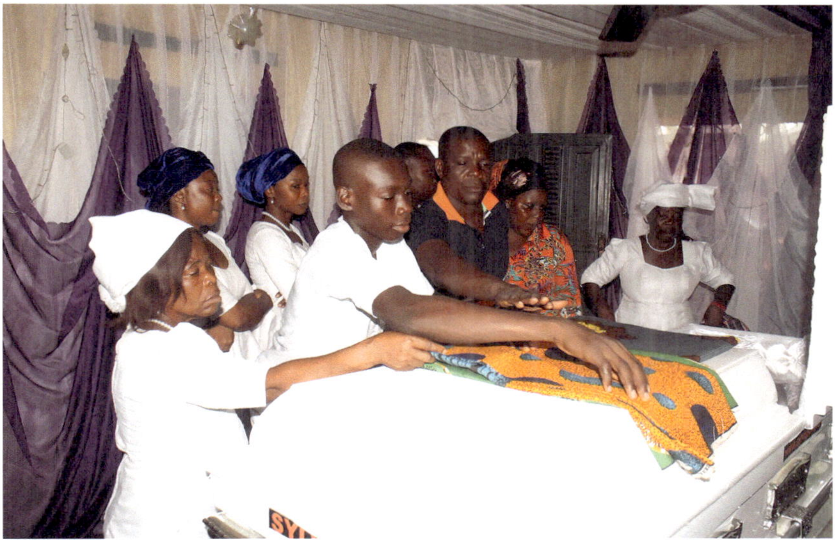

Fig. 39. Postmortem photograph of Nwosisi at Umuawulu. The photograph depicts Nwosisi's children placing textiles over his coffin at Umuawulu, Anambra State.

immediately after death. In most contemporary postmortem Christian photography, such as that of Nwosisi, there is always a well-decorated coffin and a well-decorated corpse.

THE EXHIBITION OF SORROW

In exploring the culturally significant roles played by postmortem photographs, I observed how Nwosisi's children took turns to bid their late father a final farewell. They held the coffin and cried. The photographer captured their emotional facial expressions as evidence of the ostentatious affectations that attend funerals. A camera could be seen from the left side of the photograph, indicating that more than one photographer was covering the occasion. Other close family members also came to bid Nwosisi their final farewell, most of them placing pieces of textile materials on Nwosisi's coffin (Fig. 39). The placing of textiles, as well as the stretching of arms to touch the coffin, is a cultural ritual that must be documented by the camera. This is because the ritual significance of *ikpu akwa* (clothing the dead), when captured in a photograph, is a subtle reminder of the inseparability of material textiles and humans. In most local contexts, textiles must accompany humans on the eternal journey to show that even though humans journeyed into the world unclothed, their singular toil fetched them wealth, symbolized by textiles. Such photographs of *ikpu akwa* are held sacrosanct by the bereaved, kept in a safe place, and used to revisit local beliefs in immortality: that the dead must travel to the next world well clothed.

One thing is pertinent from our initial journey to the mortuary and back home: There was an imposed pretentious, emotional performativity that took place throughout the entire journey. Starting from a group photograph of the pallbearers to the live band that accompanied the motorcade home, each segment unfolded with well-orchestrated performativity. Everyone looked forward to the photographic moment when the camera would capture their faces as a compelling testament to this poignant performative ritual. Again, the performative dimension of the funeral that has been escalated by photography lies in such Igbo saying as, *I jebe uno akwa chefuo anya mmirri, Iyota mmadu*, meaning, roughly, "If you attend a funeral and forget your sorrowful tears, you can borrow tears from someone at the scene of the burial to enable a visual documentation of your sorrowfully performative role." For example, the photograph of Nwosisi's daughter crying beside the coffin shows how photography has captured this saying. It is expected that even strangers should perform this emotion-laden ritual to justify the pain of loss. De Witte (2003, 195) has argued in relation to Ghanaian funerals that "the decorated and ritually displayed dead body on the bed becomes like an altar, mediating between the visible and the invisible. It connects the metaphysical and the physical person. The tears and lamentations at the bedside, then, are like an offering by the mourners to the deceased person, whose spirit is still felt to be present, through the fixed and idealized image of his/her body." These postmortem photos act as the initial signifiers of a materialized funeral ritual whereby the textiles that were hung on Nwosisi's body, as well as crying family members, are captured in both instances, fixing the material emblems of ritual in time. This practice is somewhat missing in many texts on funeral photography, perhaps because most postmortem photographs are not advertised like the photos of the living.

The materiality of Okachamma's and Nwosisi's corpses finds its double in the photograph as an object. Here their corpses are susceptible to decay, a death surrounded by a temporality that suggests the natural annihilation of human life. However, the presence of Nwosisi's photo and of Okachamma's after more than forty years, their capacity to survive the ravages and vagaries of time, imbues their bodies with a spatiotemporal dimension and existence

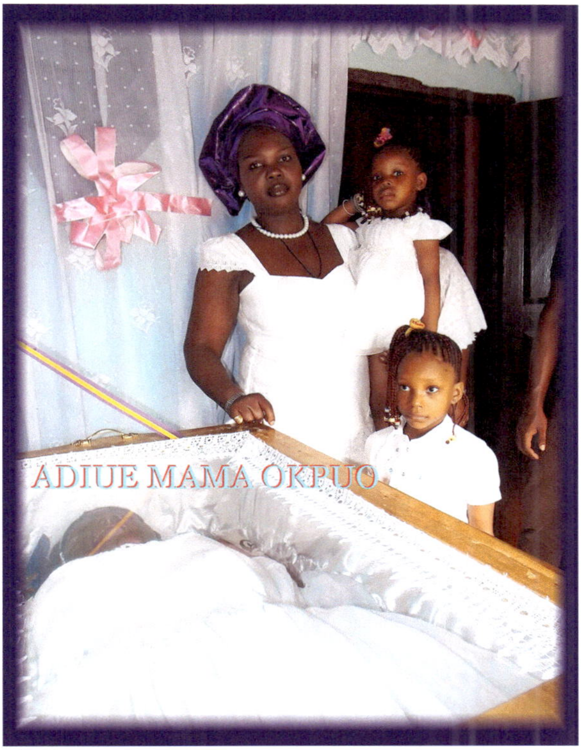

Fig. 40. Postmortem photograph of Mama Okpuo. Mama Okpuo's daughter, in the company of her children, stretches out her hand to touch the coffin of her late mother.

that is beyond history. This effect finds an explanation in the autonomous life of the image, bridging the gap between human and nonhuman, reality and imagination, and ultimately returning the viewer's gaze.

POSTMORTEM PHOTOGRAPHY AND THE SOCIALIZATION OF DEATH: CASTING A MEANINGFUL GAZE AT DEATH

I had the opportunity to encounter Mama Okpuo's funeral in 2014. Before interment, her children swarmed around her coffin and performed the traditional ritual of clothing her with different textile materials. They had invited a photographer who captured this moment. The photographer also captured the coffin, the textiles, and their different poses beside the coffin. One of the daughters brought her children to view their grandmother's corpse (Fig. 40).

In a similar manner, Ejike Okaphor brought his children to witness the last

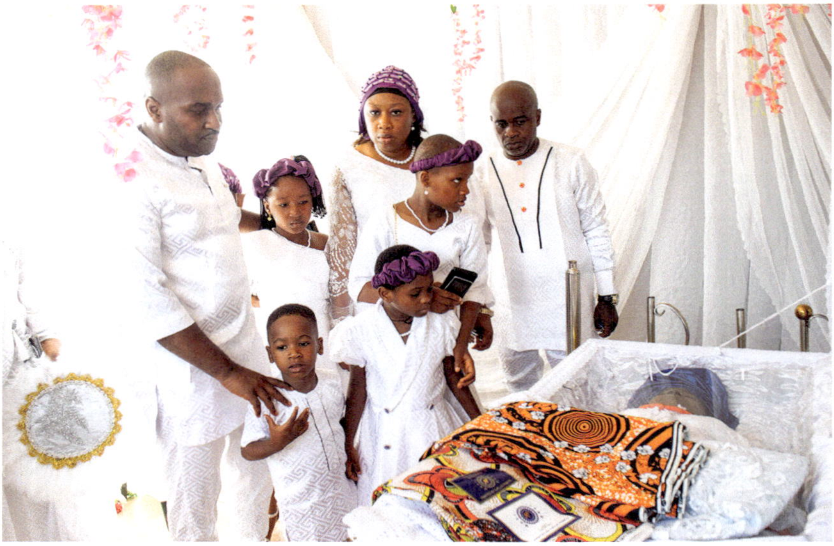

Fig. 41. Dr. Ejike Okaphor and his family with Mrs. Christiana Nkechi Okaphor. Dr. Ejike Okaphor and his family are shown with the remains of his late mother, Mrs. Christiana Nkechi Okaphor, in Adazi, Anambra State.

moment with their grandmother, the late Mrs. Christiana Nkechi Okaphor (Fig. 41). In Ejike's photo, there are multiple gazes at work. While some gaze at the corpse of his mother, one of his children gazes at the camera lens. Consequently, the camera serves a dual purpose: It is a distractive object, yet simultaneously it is a critical apparatus that captures what I describe as "a meaningful gaze at death." The camera fixes this significant contemplation of mortality. Without the camera, this meaningful gaze and such profound contemplation would be lost.

Similarly, the "meaningful gaze at death" is seen in Figure 42, where Ejike's sister, Dr Oby Ruphina Ezimora, performs the typical "coffin pose." Ruphina stretched out one hand to touch the coffin, lowered and bent her head slightly, and then cast a meaningful gaze at the coffin. Her gaze is a performative one that seems to demand a reciprocation from a nonexistent thing. It is not entirely an exercise in futility or a seeming pursuit of an elusive entity because it is a gaze that we recognize as meaningful because the camera captured it. McGrath (2020, 189) argues that "the photograph itself is a locus of 'intersecting gazes'" (see also Lutz and Collins 1991). McGrath's statement is captured most vividly in Figures 38a and 38b, where Okachamma's household casts a meaningful gaze at death. Each person casts a subjective gaze, either at the

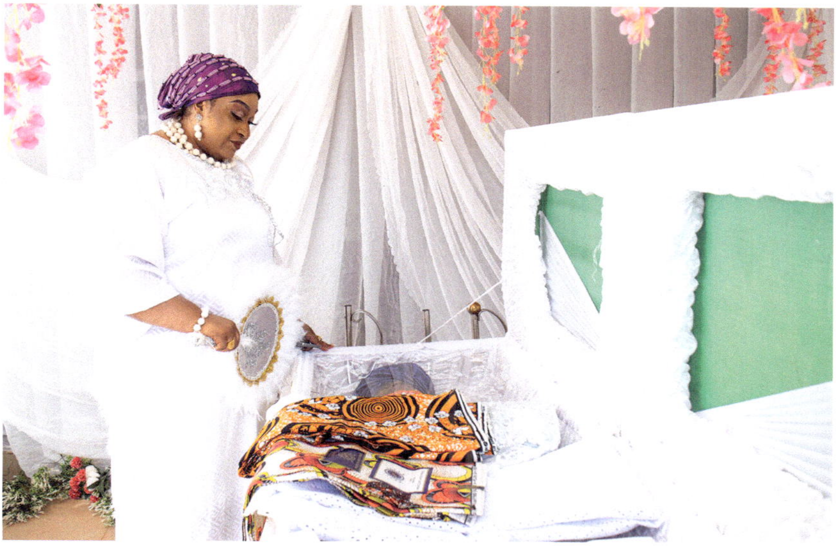

Fig. 42. Dr. Oby Ruphina Ezimora casting a meaningful gaze at her late mother, Mrs. Christiana Nkechi Okaphor at Adazi, Anambra State

coffin or into a void. Here I suggest we recover what is left out in photography theory: the distinction between a photograph of death (a postmortem photograph) and a photograph of life (such as a wedding photograph). This is a task left for photography theorists. In the photograph of death, gazes are complex, disaggregated, yet deep and subjective (Fig. 41), while in the photograph of life (such as a wedding photograph or another photograph taken outside the realm of death), gazes are collective and geared towards a mission and a focus to counter sadness; here, the camera lens becomes the target of gazes. These gazes evoke what Azoulay (2015) terms "civil gazes," situated within her expansive theoretical framework of the political ontology of the photograph. This concept underscores photography's ability to forge connections among the photographer, the photographic subject, and the spectator, fostering open-ended relationships of mutual responsibility that resist preemptive totalization. In my exploration of the meaningful gaze at death, I move away from Azoulay's (2015) political ontology of the photograph to enact a photographic system that derives significance from the circuits of peaceful family transition.

In Figure 41, the camera lens becomes the avoidable thing, the abhorrent target of gazes. Even where the camera lens is the target of the gaze, it is a gaze at a void (Fig. 43), something deeper than the camera lens or an invis-

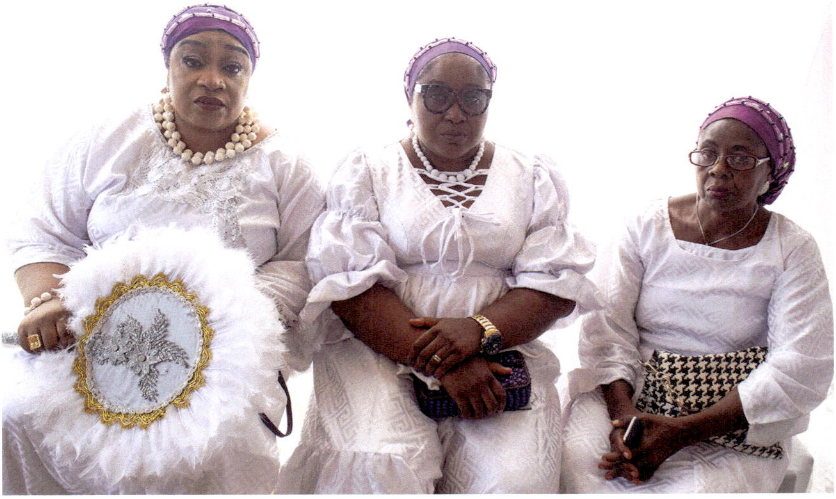

Fig. 43. Dr. Oby Ruphina Ezimora and her relatives during her mother's funeral

ible entity. Like a fetish, the photograph is "a substitute for an object that is missing, and yet we believe that the photograph is the object that it is not" (McGrath 2020, 194). Belting (2011, 85) contends that "an image finds its true meaning in the fact that what it represents is absent and therefore can be present only as image. It manifests something that is not in the image but can only appear in the image." This notion provides a compelling lens through which to interpret the prevalence of photography at Igbo funerals. The act of photographing may thus be seen as an attempt to capture the intangible—the presence of an absence. The photographer becomes instrumental in documenting "what is not there," "that which is absent in person," and yet whose "unbearable absence was made good by the presence of images" (Belting, 2011, 85). On another note, one could argue that the postmortem camera seems regimental, like the colonial camera that enforces what Tina Campt (2017) describes as "stasis" in the photographed. Campt suggests that the stasis of the photograph "requires us to listen to the infrasonic frequencies of images that register through feeling rather than vision or audible sound." In this instance, to listen to the feelings of postmortem photographs is like "friction that requires us to read their stillness, their taut demeanor as an active, tense, and expressive practice of both restraint and constraint" (Campt

2017, 57). Borrowing from Campt, one can say that each of the photographed appears to hold back something too difficult to grasp, call it hysterical grief or tears. I suggest that the photographed are embroiled in an economy of gazes enacted not only by their emotional states but by a combination of cultural and technological contexts of their creation. This subscribes to the popular definition of 'stasis' as "a state of balance between various forces."

In "Right in the Eyes," his brief critique of Richard Avedon's work, Roland Barthes examines the complex layers of gazes. First published in 1977, Barthes separates the threefold essence of a gaze: It serves as knowledge, as a mutual interaction, and as a form of control or understanding. Through this exploration, Barthes navigates us from the detached act of seeing (opsis) to the intimate act of connecting (hapsis), employing linguistic routes (see McGrath 2020, 192). He contrasts the detached nature of vision, in which the photograph functions as a mediating artifact rather than a site of direct engagement ("The gaze informs, I see and I know"), with the immediacy of touch where the photograph is refigured as an extension of the sensorium—an almost second skin that blurs the boundary between image and body ("I touch, I attain, I seize, I am seized") (see Barthes 1985, 238). Barthes guides the viewer from an initial position of epistemological certainty—where the photograph appears to function as incontrovertible evidence ("here it is," "I see," "I know")—to a more ambiguous terrain in which the distinctions between subject and object, self and other, begin to dissolve (I seize, but I am also seized by it). This is exactly what we see as the power of the image in the meaningful gaze by Ruphina Ezimora. According to Roberta McGrath (2020, 192), "It has a hold on me; I am arrested by it." For Barthes, "The gaze seeks something, someone, it is an anxious sign . . . its power overflows it" (1985, 238). The gaze is always in excess of simply looking or seeing; it provokes anxiety. This stems from the fact that we can see only from one point, and we do not know when others may be looking at us. We never see ourselves as others see us.

Figures 40, 41, 42, 43, and 44 illustrate the distinction between the camera's fleeting capture and the profound nature of the gaze. For instance, Ruphina Ezimora's "meaningful gaze at death" exemplifies the depth of "the gaze" in contrast to the superficial "look." Roberta McGrath (2020) suggests that the gaze extends along a continuum, abiding and deep, drawing us into a prolonged contemplation that merges deliberate focus with a dreamlike state of mind. It is an extension of sight and perception, transitioning from the camera's ephemeral snapshot to a deliberate and detailed observation, inspection, and even surveillance.

Ruphina Ezimora's profound contemplation of mortality presents a stark contrast to the fleeting nature captured in her photograph (Fig. 42). Foucault (1976, 121) articulates this idea, stating that the gaze penetrates directly to its target. Ezimora's own gaze in the photograph extends through time, signifying a profound absence. Roberta McGrath (2020) interprets this absence as a certain "something" that is no longer present, a void that connects Ezimora's intense gaze with the photograph itself. The photograph (Fig. 42) serves as a stand-in for this void, representing what used to be visible to the camera's lens—whether it actually existed or not—but has since vanished. The emptiness in Ezimora's eyes evokes the loss of her mother, an entity that is no longer there.

Let us reflect on another photograph (Fig. 43) that embodies this meaningful gaze at death. Figure 43 includes Ruphina Ezimora and her sisters-in-law, Maureen Ugonwa Anietoh and Ngozi Anietoh, gazing at the camera lens. The photograph embodies the essence of photography: capturing a subject or an event in its most crucial state—the quintessential moment. In this photo, we observe Ruphina, Ngozi, and Maureen, familiar figures whose attention is fixed on something beyond our view. This act of gazing signifies an acceptance of the visual frontiers they encounter, compelling us to ponder their continued, meaningful gazes. It is now certain that the camera lens captures the meaningful gaze in the event of death. Their contemplative gaze introduces an element of uncertainty and inexplicable encounter with a void. Even though they gaze at the camera lens, it is a gaze that is "understood as some "thing" that is missing, and it is this missing "thing" that links the gaze to the photograph . . . what was once there in front of the camera (or now perhaps never was), but no longer is" (McGrath 2020, 194). In contrast to their searching gaze, the photograph itself (Fig. 43) does not simply reflect the world as it is. Rather, it represents a thoughtful idea, a tangible result, a condensed visual representation of a distinct body of knowledge, shaped within a particular visual context during a unique time and crafted with a specific intent.

Thus, capturing these multiple gazes, the camera ensures that the essence of mortality is perpetually encapsulated within the confines of time. In Figure 44, the first in-law to the deceased, known as *Onye isi ogo* in the Igbo language, Chief Engineer C. Y. Anetoh (president general of Adazi-Nnukwu Community), performs the *ikpu akwa*. He is accompanied by his brother Chief Gabriel N. Anetoh. We see a young man with a camera phone capturing the ritual of *ikpu akwa* by these two chiefs. Chief Anetoh quietly rests the textile on the plastic covering of the coffin. While other standing individuals

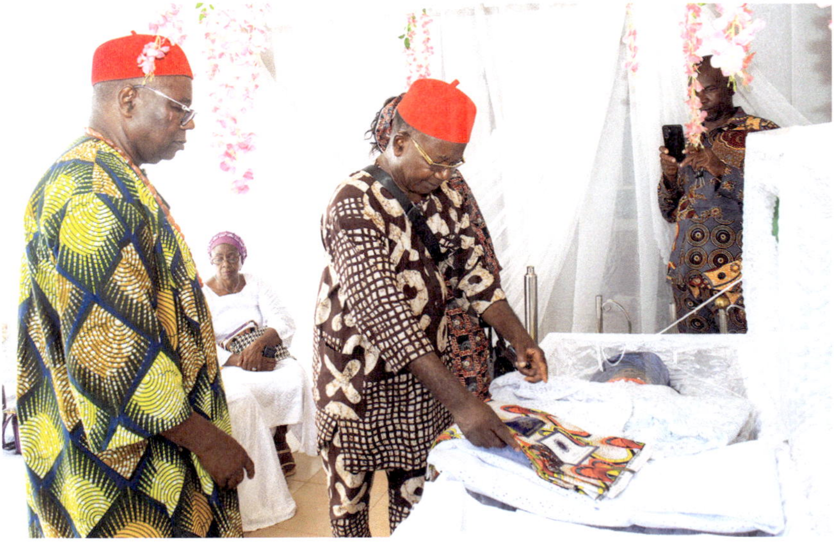

Fig. 44. The in-laws performing the ritual of *ikpu akwa* for Mrs. Christiana Nkechi Okaphor at Adazi, Anambra State

wear wax print textiles, it is evident that the two camera lenses (that of the young man with camera phone and the photographer in Fig. 44) capturing the man placing the textile reflect a crucial dimension in viewing the corpse: that textiles are inseparable from the photographic display. In the ritual of postmortem photography, textiles and the camera are mutually exclusive, as will be shown in subsequent discussions.

Ada Okpuo and her siblings, as well as Ejike and his own siblings, described their last moment with their mother as a moment of beatific delight, relishing their crucial encounter in the group photograph with their mother's corpse inside the coffin. They each stretched their arms, held the coffin, and expressed the joy of a last opportunity to feel the warmth of their mother's presence (Figs. 40, 41, and 42). Mama Okpuo's daughter stood beside the coffin and spoke to her mother's dead body: *Nne Jee Nke oma*. She spent about ten minutes muttering emotional words and consoling the dead. She created a conversational mood around the coffin to suggest a dialogue. I observed as the photographer captured the entire process in stills and video. The photographer inscribed a written text, "Adieu Mama Okpuo," on the surface of each of the printed photos to consummate the entire process with textual evidence.

Ruby (1995) notes how photographing the dead in American tradition has been reimagined in recent times, perceived as strange and insensitive and a weird interference with the sacrosanct order of existence. In many Igbo postmortem photographs, the case is different. As I observed the processes involved in photographing Mama Okpuo's and Christiana Okaphor's dead bodies, it became obvious that death is still resocialized as part of the embodied reality of human existence in Igbo society. In Belting's terms, "we give the dead an immortal body in the image: that is a *symbolic body* in which they are resocialized while their mortal body dissolves into nothing" (2011, 85). Here, the presence of the dead body gathers mourners, enables communal relations, and provokes the performativity required to reinscribe the presence of the deceased into the human world. In the end, more than two thousand copies of the photographs were printed by the photographer.

Mama Okpuo's and Christiana Okaphor's bodies and their photographs constitute part of the social ritual of death in Igbo society. As a result, the index of the postmortem photograph performs two important functions: first, to reinsert the embodied nakedness of the corpse into its humanized social reality, representing death and presence at the same time, and second, to mark the event of death, which (Fernandez 2011, 309) characterized as "a historical moment in time to be stored as a socially sanctioned form of mourning" with a specific ritualistic configuration. While the body disappears as an object associated with the corpse's mortal identity, the photograph ensures that the corpse's presence is not completely erased from the realm of the living. This parallels the function of Ikenga in the Igbo ancestral practice.

Okachamma's, Nwosisi's, Mama Okpuo's, and Christiana Okaphor's photographic presence and influence occupy an important space in their families' conceptualization of death. This space constitutes an ancestral presence. The ancestral presence is an omnipresent, looming presence. In recent times, this ancestral influence has emerged as an innate aspect of the photograph that challenges fixed social canons through its excess value. The excess value here refers to the ability of the photograph to serve as a polymorphic object. A photograph records more than the eye can objectively perceive, and as such, its power as an image does not solely rely on human agency (Fernandez 2011). In effect, the Igbo postmortem photograph does not detach itself from a chronological sense of Igbo time because, through its very existence, it places itself as a thing that is dependent on its referent and its historical context. In this way, the Igbo postmortem photograph can be said to possess "life." As a material object, the postmortem photograph embodies multiple life cycles:

an extended presence of its material body in its ability to recall the past and reintegrate it into the reality of the present. In Igbo cosmology, the ancestral presence is extended beyond the temporal space, recalled in constant everyday events.

Okachamma's, Nwosisi's, Mama Okpuo's, and Christiana Okaphor's postmortem photographs feature them as they are entrenched in their domestic surroundings: Their corpses feel almost evanescent and part of the domestic realm of the living. One is most astonished by the photograph's ability to bring the romanticized images of their corpses into a confrontation with the living. The social identity is sentimentalized and deployed to conceal the moment of death. Rather than deep sorrow, we witness the overwhelming materiality of the photogenic corpse, contemplated as a key moment in the process of mourning. The four anxious bodies invite us to contemplate the obduracy of their physiognomic gazes. The photographs' raw, barefaced portrayal of death begs for a narrative of an entire lifespan condensed into a single photographic moment, disrupting our conceptualizations of time as linear. While these postmortem photographs compel us to ponder the body as frail, in Igbo cosmology, the photographic bodies aim to fix the shadow eternally. The spatiotemporal space of the image is consistent with social time and narratives of history. More than anything, the excess value of postmortem photographs conflates the space between past and present and closely adjoins the realms of the living and the dead.

In the Igbo mourning ritual, funeral services are interactive, with individuals being photographed during staged performances, such as dancing with the photograph (Fig. 50). During the funerals of Mama Okpuo, Nwosisi, and Christiana Okaphor, photography and videography were employed to fix the event in time. The spectacle of Igbo funeral resists the dissimulation of death and allows the survivors a sense of permeability. It represents the imposed victory of the dead to indulge in certain warmth with the human world. The bereaved stretch their hands to touch the corpse and mutter some words of encouragement to the dead and the living. This postmortem photographic pose of stretching out the arm to touch the corpse is equally observed in Figures 38a and 38b. This transformation of the funeral as an event of the dead expands the influence of the corpse pervasively. In Mama Okpuo's and Christiana Okaphor's postmortem photographs, the staging of the funeral event takes place with an overwhelming reference to their corpses. The majority of activities comprising the ritual of the final viewing process promote the interaction of the mourners with Mama's body and their material testimonies, such as clothing the corpse with textiles (*ikpu akwa*). The presence of the corpse marks an important narrative in the event of death. In recent Igbo practice, the viewing room serves as a space where social ties are reinforced and rekindled. For instance, the ritual emphasizes the connection among members from different spheres of the deceased's life who commingle to "catch up" or relate stories of their interaction with the deceased. In the cases of Mama Okpuo, Nwosisi and Okaphor, their children contracted the decoration of their dead bodies to funeral contractors who dressed them before they could confront the camera. The photographer then photographed the process before embarking on the morgue. This aspect of decoration is survivor-oriented and entangled with the more material aspects of death.

The decoration of Mama Okpuo's, Nwosisi's, and Okaphor's bodies and the process of photographing them affirms both the social identity and the material entity that their bodies transform into after the moment of medical death. The return of attention to the corpse as an independent material entity is evident in the postmortem photographs of Okachamma, Nwosisi, Mama Okpuo and Okaphor. In this case, the liminal presence of the corpse occupies a permanent space; the homes of Okachamma, Nwosisi, Okpuo and Okaphor represent a waiting room for their presence to be reinscribed into daily social interaction. The interplay of photographic work and ritual performance offered new modes to articulate sociality (Heidemann 2022, 85). Here photography emerges as a distinct social arena with its own identity. The teeming humans surrounding the corpse reemphasize the substance of the corpse, turning the funeral event into an experiential stage that unveils the reality of death through the exposure of the shadow. Here we fully witness the socialization of the corpse (Hallam et al. 1999).

Mama Okpuo's daughter stood still, placed her hands on her mother's dead body, and gazed fixedly at her mother's stone-cold face, and said, *Mama Lote kwa anyi biko. Echezokwana anyi, asi m kwuo ika anozugakwuo*, which translates: "Mama remember us. Please don't forget us. In my mind, you should have stayed longer." While Mama Okpuo's daughter chanted incantations and called on Mama Okpuo to rethink her departure, we witness a conversational mood that recognizes the deceased's family ties and social identity. Mama Okpuo's corpse seems to return her daughter's gaze, that which enjoins most Igbo people to meditate on their own corporeal existence as individuals who cannot be denied their own continuing life cycle and presence on earth. In the Igbo cosmology, through careful orchestration, the living expands the influence of *ndi nwuru anwu* (the dead), shifting icon, index, and symbol from death to a social event invested in accepting mortality through restoration and social conformity. This represents the active corpse, raw, naked, secured, that symbolizes traditional, ancestral death. The living insists on a continual conversation with the dead, and this must be documented visually, just like the communication with the living.

The rising ubiquity of postmortem photographs in Igbo society makes death an over-represented phenomenon. As Bauman concludes, "It deprives mortality of its vile terror by taking it out of hiding and tossing it into the realm of the familiar and the ordinary—to be practiced there day in, day out. Daily life becomes a perpetual dress rehearsal of death" (1992, 187). While Bauman equates death with the spectacle and the performative, we find that death has been domesticated through the photograph and its material emblems. The dead body ceases to be a corpse upon death because the photograph has transformed it into a material that can provide succor to the living. The fact that Okachamma's great-grandchild preserved his postmortem photograph for more than forty years and engaged it makes us contemplate postmortem photograph as a new factor of social modernity used to resist death. Bauman describes this process as the relentless "emancipation" of humans from "constraints" (1992, 49). This may be seen as the creation of new technology to prolong material life. There seems to be a collective obsession by humans to conquer the cause of nature and free themselves from the shadow of death. Modern dying as a process does not require distance. It resists invisibility, and the corpse is not silenced from the conversational spaces of humans; the corpse's engagement with the viewer's imagination is not suppressed but reinforced through photography.

I observed how the photographer captured the lowering of the late Nwosisi's coffin inside the grave. After the coffin had been lowered, the photographer captured the ritual of family members pouring red earth with a shovel into the grave before the final concealment of the grave with red earth (Fig. 45). As soon as the coffin was covered with mounds of red earth, the family mounted a condolence altar, which signaled the official commencement of the funeral ceremony. This particular tradition is one of the most controversial aspects of the burial ritual. In some Igbo communities, women were prohibited from pouring red earth into their dead husband's graves. In Awka, Anambra State, southeastern Nigeria, it has occasioned some of the most violent clashes between traditional worshippers and Christians that led to deaths; it has remained an unresolved component of Igbo burials in some of the Igbo states.

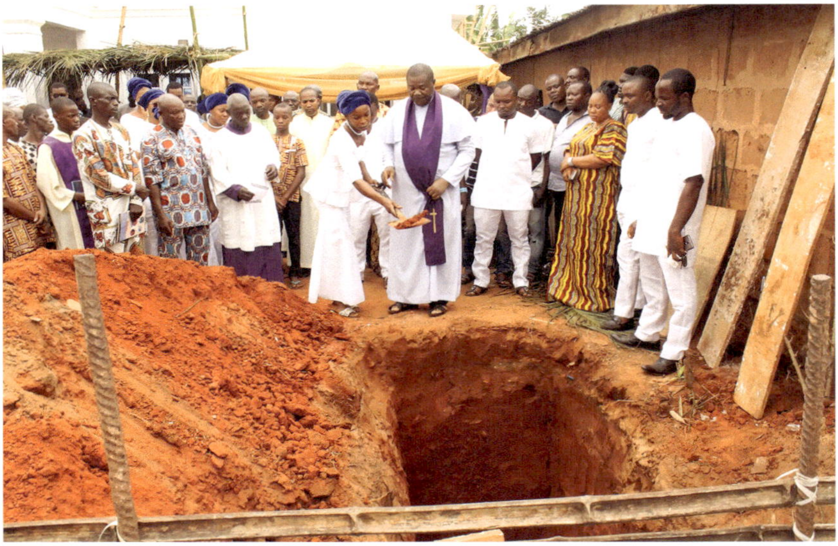

Fig. 45. Nwosisi's interment at Umuawulu. Nwosisi's daughter performs the *ikponye aja* ritual (pouring of red earth into his grave).

THE CONDOLENCE ALTARS

In this section, I have formulated the concept of the condolence altar to contextualize contemporary condolences in line with a historical understanding of Igbo aesthetics. In the case of Nwosisi's funeral, a typical condolence altar comprises a table upon which is placed a booklet (Fig. 46). A hierarchy of family membership comprising only men known as *umunna* (kindred) ranging from *Onye isi Umunna*, known as the eldest member of the kindred, to *diaokpala* (first son) and others, sat around the table. *Umuada*, women, were not allowed to sit on this altar. In the case of the late Nwosisi's widow (known now as *Nwanyi ajadu*), another form of condolence altar was mounted specifically for her. This altar was ensconced at the rear corner of the main altar, in a space immediately before the entrance to the main house. This altar, considered more sacred, usually has a rope barricade around the widow.[1] In Figure 47, Nwosisi's widow is seen seated inside this altar, barricaded with a white rope and a bucket for collecting monetary gifts from mourners.

She is surrounded by *Umuada* (female members of the kindred) who provide emotional succor to her heavy grief.[2] She was not allowed to touch the

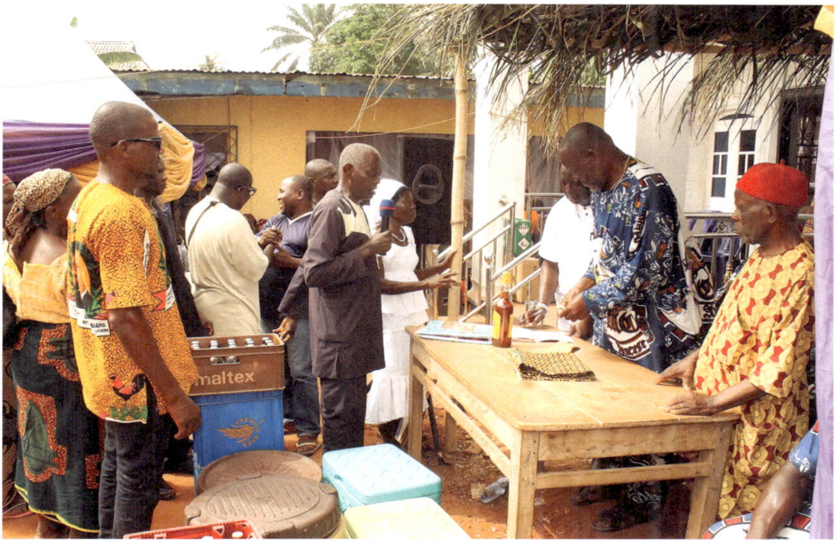

Fig. 46. The condolence altar of Nwosisi before the condolence at Umuawulu. The photoograph of the condolence altar is taken before the condolence ceremony proper, showing the table empty.

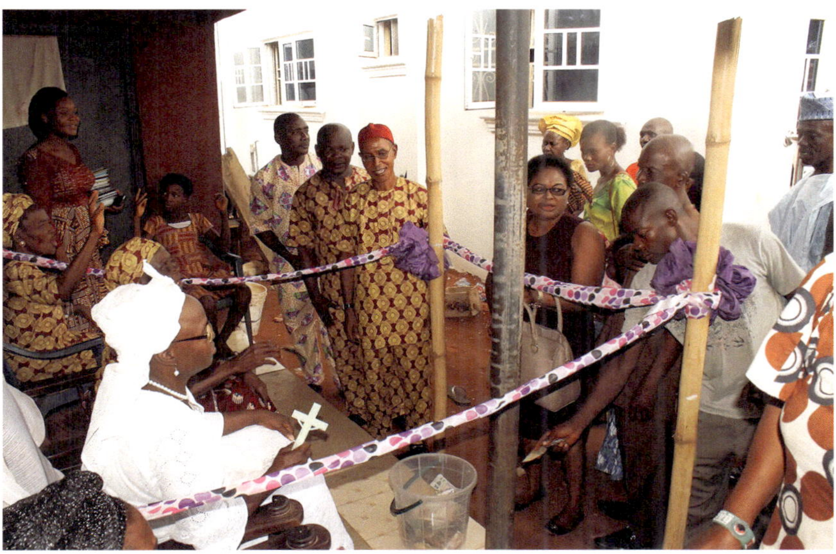

Fig. 47. Nwosisi's wife in a corner of the entrance to the house. The photograph of Nwosisi's altar shows his wife secluded from visitors in a corner near the entrance to the house.

monetary gift donated by mourners, nor were visitors allowed to touch her. In the photograph, she is seen as being in a state of solitary confinement and only allowed to listen without responding in a clearly overt manner to sympathetic gestures. All the monies collected inside the bucket placed in front of her belonged to her, while those collected at the main altar where men sat belonged to *Umunna* (male kindred). In front of the men's altar is also mounted a framed portrait of the late Nwosisi. Textiles brought by visitors are also placed on top of the table.

Attention to this condolence altar may provide a space for deeper reflection on the configurations and possible discursive contexts of contemporary funerals in the southeastern Igbo region of Nigeria. The altar serves as the reception point where visitors and mourners are received. A visit to the altar marks the consummation of the condolence ritual by anyone. The altar serves as the point of physical and spiritual encounters between the living and the dead. It is at the altar that the community's last conversation with the dead takes place, a place of last tribute by all visitors. While the funeral altar can be described as a sacred place of respect and utmost purification from all forms of impure acts, it begs a curious question of how it parallels some contemporary orthodox Christian altars where women are not allowed to constitute part of the spiritual ritual.[3] A visit to the altar must be photographically documented both by the attendees and by the mourners. In more than one hundred funerals I attended with mourners, they said that photographic documentation is necessary to prove their presence during the funeral.

A visit to Nwosisi's condolence altar by his in-laws was accompanied by obligatory funeral goods. These goods, which distinguished the condolence visit by Nwosisi's in-law from others, included a piece of textile material, crates of drinks, bottles of whisky and wine, cows, and envelopes of cash. Each of these items is a symbolic gesture of a farewell wish. As mentioned earlier, the presentation of textile is referred to as *ikpu akwa*, meaning "clothing the dead." The eldest member of the family seated at the table receives the gifts. While other visitors to the altar may bring different gifts and drinks, envelopes of cash are seen as compulsory gift items that most visitors to the altar are expected to bring. Visitors are asked their name and the name of their family, and they are recorded in a notebook on the table. This notebook is important because it is eventually kept for future reference in identifying those who attended the funeral. Sometimes a law of reciprocal transaction is played out using this notebook. When a member of the community is bereaved, the family refers to the notebook to ascertain whether the bereaved family attended their own funeral. If their name is missing from the register, then there will not be a collective family condolence visit to the family. In such cases, individual family members may attend, but a unified, organized extended family condolence will be denied that family.

Recently, the camera has been used to complement the work of the note-book by capturing everyone who appeared on the condolence altar. These photographs assist family members in easy recognition. Battaglia (1990, 10) has argued that the "production" of memory out of images of the body is a ritual strategy for overcoming futility. Futility in this context can be seen as the act of forgetting. Images of the living are deployed to avert the futility of forgetting. Photography fixes the materiality of the ritual in time. The materiality of the altar must be fixed to enable memory to be recovered.

It is necessary to highlight a dimension of funeral photography that has been largely neglected but can constitute the locus of real aesthetic and ritual experience and value. This dimension concerns the performative process of documenting the dead and the sorts of artistic performances and aesthetic experiences that this process may entail. The condolence altar presents an aspect of this aesthetic experience. The materiality of the funeral ritual is seen on the altar, which acts as an installation in conceptual art terms. Before the commencement of the late Nwosisi's condolence, the table of the altar was empty, but by evening, when hundreds of visitors had turned up, the table was filled with various forms of materials (Fig. 48). In Figure 46 the table is virtually empty, while in Figure 48 various material gifts from mourners have covered it. The ropes represent the number of cows that were brought. In the past, live cows were brought to the funeral arena by visitors. Recently, the cow has been replaced by a symbolic rope, and an accompanying envelope of cash is the monetary equivalent of the cow. Cows are compulsory funeral gifts that must be brought by the in-laws, especially that of the first daughters. It is not compulsory for other visitors, who may, on their own accord, come with a cow depending on their relationship with the deceased.

The dramatic dimension to the photographic process here is almost non-existent in the literature on funerals in Africa, and thus a need arises to highlight them. Funeral photography's dimension of the dramatic, performative process (and its potential for enhanced postmortem aesthetic experience) is occluded by our one-sided concentration on the figure of the deceased itself. The altar exemplifies the level of success recorded at the end of the funeral. The number of cows, textile materials, drinks, and other goods on the funeral altar suggests whether a befitting funeral took place. The members of the altar

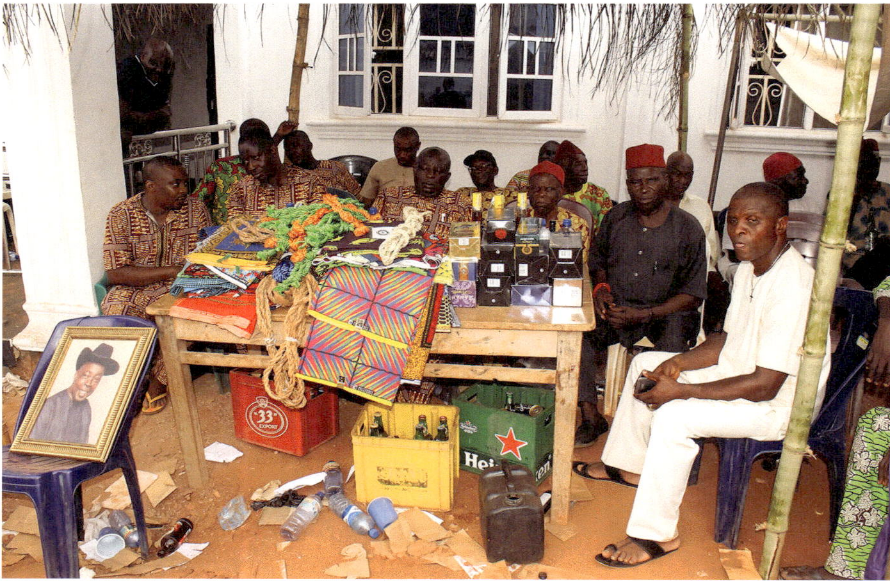

Fig. 48. The condolence altar of Nwosisi after the condolence. The photograph captures the condolence altar now adorned with textiles and drinks following a successful condolence ceremony.

often record these items as mourners arrive and, in the end, take stock of the materials and modalities of sharing them.

FROM MOURNING TO CELEBRATION

By the evening of Nwosisi's funeral, photographs depicted expressions of joy that mediated the pain of loss. Seemingly losing focus on the brutal fact of death, post-funeral photos show individuals engaging in a drinking spree and wearing smiling countenances (Fig. 49). Evening banters around tables of wine and beers deviated significantly from discourses of death and grief seen in the morning. At this point, photography is seen to assume a different role: a role of transfiguring sad faces into smiling countenances. Richard Shusterman (2012, 69) speaks of how the "photographer's quality of attention and presence infects the photographed subject as well, thus raising her quality of presence that can then be captured in the resulting photograph, a pres-

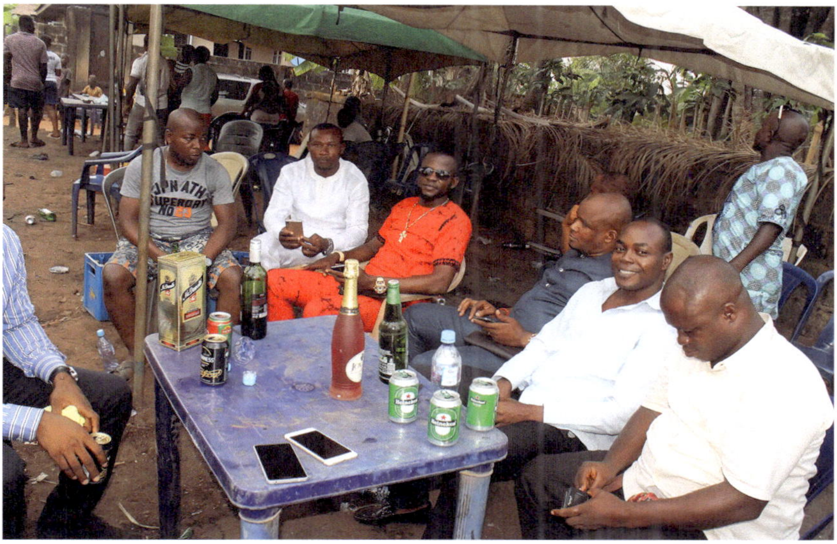

Fig. 49. The condolence arena of Nwosisi at Umuawulu. In Nwosisi's condolence arena, mourners and well-wishers engage in heartfelt and joyous banter as the evening draws the condolence to a close.

ence that transfigures even ordinary faces into beautifully expressive ones." Here the photographer influenced certain photographic poses and demeanor. During Nwosisi's funeral, the photographer requested those in Figure 49 to smile. By provoking a happy mood at the funeral, the photographer disrupts the dominant tropes of despair and converts them into a conscious image of systematic happiness.

In the initial photographic process at the beginning of the funeral, most of the photographs were captured without the conscious physical attention of the photographed. The images at this stage constituted a reason why individuals cherish funeral photos: to know those who are in the photos and to reveal the hidden momentous gaiety embodied in sorrow. However, while these initial photos were mainly taken without the conscious observation of some of the photographed, most photos taken toward the end of the funeral were posed for and self-conscious. Sontag (1977) believes that people display a different demeanor when they know they are being photographed and that there is something awkward, artificial, or false about it.

Notwithstanding the photographer's skills in ensuring that the photographed maintains his or her natural mien, the photographed requires some degree of personal courage and skill to do so (Shusterman 2012). Roland Barthes emotionally acknowledges his own complex problems as a posing subject. As soon as he realizes that he is "observed by the lens," he feels the need to reconstitute himself, "in the process of posing. . . . I instantaneously make another body for myself, I transform myself in advance into an image" (1981, 10).

The Igbo person's belief in accomplishment is found in Nwosisi's children's remark that the photograph showed that *mmadu abiaka* and *ogala ofuma*, meaning, "Many people attended" and "The funeral went well." As a matter of fact, the postmortem video and photographs are used to weigh the success of the funeral. Attention is paid to every detail and every individual and bodily gesture taken note of. For example, each member of the family got excited when they saw themselves in the funeral video, making excited remarks. A satisfactory feeling among the children while watching the video indicates how photography presents mourning as an accomplished event in which potent images effectively imprint a trace of achievement into the ego of the bereaved, thereby ensuring an enduring and embodied connection between the living and the dead. The Igbo believe in achievement in all ramifications. While going through the photographs, Nwosisi's children made constant allusion to the number of ropes and textiles on the table: *Anyi nwetekwara ego*, meaning, "We made a lot of money." This visual record of achievement extends the corporeal boundaries of the subject outward to encompass humans and the materials as yardsticks for assessing the success of the funeral. The logic of this is surely suggested by photography itself. Funeral photo albums returned by the contracted photographer at the end of the funeral permanently archive the funeral in family homes. They are viewed as material signifiers of a transition, sometimes consulted by family members to resolve the ambiguous family issue that concerns the funeral. If photos materialize success (in Igbo people's terms), then these acts of photographing funerals further imprint and fix the spectral in the fleshly materiality of the world.

The Igbos' belief in the dead person as a participant in his or her own funeral found a ready explanation in the dancing photograph. In most funerals, the bereaved believe that the deceased are the real "celebrants" in their own funerals, meaning that the dead partake in their own funeral celebration. In other words, a funeral ceremony is an event for the dead. This explains why a framed photo of the dead must be mounted in front of the condolence altar, indicating that the real owner of the condolence altar is deceased. Nwosisi's portrait photo was placed in front of the funeral altar. One may compare this practice with a Cantonese, Hakka family home, in which "during visitations when relatives, friends, and neighbors pay their respect to the deceased, the funerary portrait is centrally located for visitors to see in what is referred to as the *sang tang* (or *xiao tang*, "mourning hall")." Can this funerary portrait be seen as an iconic image of the deceased, hung in the living room for all to see when the deceased becomes an ancestor (which in China is part of the spiritual realm of the gods and the ghosts; see Wolf 1974).

Batchen argues that photography as a medium is privileged over other representations because the camera is touched by the subject of the photograph: "It is as if those objects have reached out and impressed themselves on the surface of a photograph, leaving their own visual imprint, as faithful to the contour of the original object as a death-mask is to the newly departed" (2001, 61). As a result, photographs portray the "truth" about the subject, being more than just a visible representation but rather an embodiment of the subject. This is a compelling argument, but one that is not consistent with my empirical evidence—historically sculpted funerary portraits mounted in front of the family house, still evident in the Igbo homeland, had the same function as funerary photographs. Funeral sculptures are spiritually potent figures that serve ancestral roles in many Igbo families. These sculptures stand as funerary icons. Icons possess power, as Tambiah (1984) argues, because they are objects imbued with charisma—photographs resemble charms and talismans, acting as the material embodiment of the prowess of a charismatic leader. These items with objectified charisma, according to Tambiah, allow for greater participation by people in the original charisma of the leader, such as the saint, and can renew or redirect the original charisma. Funerary photographs, therefore, can be seen as the objectified charisma of the ancestor, charged both by the act of photography and by its use in funerary rituals.

Thus, the potency of iconic images enacted here relies on the ability of Nwosisi's family, for example, to reinterpret the framed photo of their late father. Taking a photo with this framed photo is seen as initiating a member of the family into an intimate relationship with the iconic image of the deceased. It is assumed that they are snapping a photo with their living dad and thus building an intimate connection that is indescribable. For Nwosisi, each family member wished to experience this bond, and hence this explains why all of them posed and danced with a framed photo of the deceased. De Witte (2003) has argued that in Africa, funerary photography goes beyond the mere representation of the image but embodies the ambiance, the spiritual essence, of the human person, a practice that historically dates back to the use of ancient funerary terra-cottas and effigies of gods in traditional shrines. Charles Gore (2001, 332) has equally observed that, in Benin, "when the photograph of the deceased is positioned on the ancestral shrine, it has similar indexical linkage to the deceased, which relates the ancestors in the spirit world to their capacity to act in the material world, with its consequent implications for the welfare of the family." Gore draws this remote connection between the deceased's photographs and the welfare of the family in Benin, a connection also seen in Igbo funerals, where the photograph of the deceased is positioned within the spiritual realm of the ancestors. Positioning photographs within the spiritual realm has also manifested in more contemporary forms of visual media, ranging from the use of photographs in traditional healing practices, where the human spirit is commandeered through manipulating the photograph, or in Pentecostal Christianity, where the photographs of Jesus and "anointed men of God," among others, are believed to transmit miracles through the screen of the television and other media (see Bredenbröker 2024; Meyer 2006; de Witte 2003, 2005, 2010; cf. Behrend 2003).

In line with this, Nwosisi's children believe that taking a photo with the framed photo of their late father ignites a profound sense of connection with their father. I watched Nwosisi's daughter as she stood in front of the photograph and chanted a few incantations of reverence before grabbing it and dancing around with it (Fig. 50).

The materiality of the framed photo here invokes that tangible relation with life. The conversational chant between Nwosisi's daughter and the late Nwosisi's photograph seems to constitute the photograph as a kind of living-dead mediator that evaluates the way we visualize the world around us. Eck (1998) argues that images are "a matter of reciprocity," and that the act of looking is a two-way process: gazing and being gazed at, a constant inundation that ultimately leads to a total preoccupation of the viewer with the image. As Eck (1998, 46) argues, because the image can be likened to the Supreme Lord, it enables and boosts the close relationship of the worshipper of God. The close relationship between Nwosisi's daughter and Nwosisi's ancestral spirit has been boosted by the framed photo. Nwosisi's funeral portrait transcends itself, foregrounding instead the act of seeing as the fundamental principle of the spiritual activity. The centrality (and reciprocity) of the act of looking can be found in a number of African practices, underscoring "viewing as a spiritual act." Celebrating the synthesis of the viewer and the viewed, of the

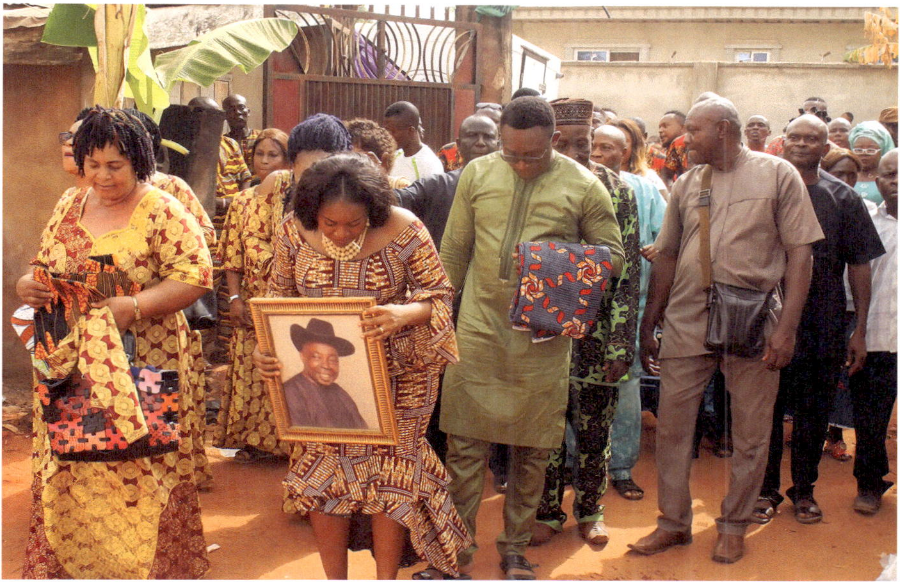

Fig. 50. Nwosisi's daughter dancing with Nwosisi's commemorative photograph

human and the godly, the divine and the mundane, Nwosisi's framed portrait materializes in a significant way the local indulgence in viewing as a spiritual act. For example, viewing an Igbo Ikenga sculpture is not just a memorial ritual; it is also a spiritual act. Ikenga serves not only as a commemorative image of veneration, but also as a potent image of devotion (see chapter 4). Such principles are equally found in popular Catholic imagery as well as in several contemporary hypnotic digitalized image-making practices, such as 360-degree cameras, photogrammetry technique, and light filter cameras that appear to emphasize a sense of tactility, mutuality, and reciprocity.

DANCING WITH THE PHOTO: THE MATERIALITY OF THE FUNERAL PHOTO

A dance with the framed photograph of the late Nwosisi reveals another performative role played by photography in Nwosisi's funeral. Nwosisi's children grabbed his framed photograph and took turns dancing around the funeral arena. Each dance provoked a participatory performance from other family members and the crowd. Individuals sprayed Nwosisi's daughters with money and textile materials. Again, when Nwosisi's in-laws arrived for the condolence, Nwosisi's daughters joined them and led them into the funeral arena with a dance while carrying a framed photograph of their late father (Fig. 50).

In considering the changing conception of the body's materiality Elizabeth Hallam and Jenny Hockey (2001) have demonstrated how the dead are given meaning through material culture. They interpret artifacts as relational constructs because of the mutual constitution of human beings and material objects, which in a roundabout way can animate those objects and give them agency, as has been argued by others (Gell 1998; Ingold 2011; Knappett 2016; Hockey et al. 2012; Miller and Parrott 2009). In Nwosisi's framed photograph used in this dance, we see how Nwosisi's body has become an artifact through technical and semiotic materializations that mediate life and death. Nwosisi's framed photograph confirms the fact that death rituals are constituted by material objects intended for preservation as records for the bereaved. In this regard, Alfred Gell's concept of "distributed personhood" (1998) might suggest how aspects of Nwosisi's identity are extended through their photographic representations.

Gell's distributed personhood implies a reciprocal relationship where external representations (indexes) not only reflect but also shape the individual's identity. In this dynamic interplay, it is possible to suggest that Nwosisi is no longer a singular entity but a "dividual" (Deleuze 1992), fragmented across various dimensions, identities, functions, objects, and texts. Thus, Nwosisi's photographic objectification persists beyond his life, continuing to influence and define his personhood. In fact, Hallam and Hockey (2001, 9) see funeral materials such as coffins as things that are "deliberately allowed to decay, having only a temporary role in the visual order of this rite of passage." This statement takes into account the fact that death relies on the visible and invisible to fulfill the rites of passage. While Hockey and Hallam's work emphasizes this relative significance of materiality, much work is needed to resolve the question of visible and invisible materialities, especially as can be seen from the framed photographs of late Nwosisi used by the surviving children. It is possible to conclude that while maintaining multiple lives as image and object, the photograph traverses temporal and spatial boundaries such as the sites of its production, consumption, duplication, and preservation to acquire new meanings as it experiences contextual transmogrification (Appadurai 1986a; Pinney 1997, 2004, 2011; Poole 1997).

In his study of nineteenth-century daguerreotypes Batchen (2004, 14) argues that "holding a photograph within a photograph answers to the need to include the virtual presence of those who are otherwise absent." Holding her late father's photograph within a photograph is a way Nwosisi's daughter "enabled life and death to stand side by side before the camera" (see Batchen 2004, 12). Nwosisi's daughter "turned the experience of being photographed into an explicit act of remembrance." Batchen states: "It is as if, in these pictures within pictures, the subjects want to draw our attention not only to the image they hold, but also to photography itself as a touchable entity to the comforting solidity of its memorial function" (2004, 14). Batchen's remarks reveal why this practice cannot be described as a peculiarly Nigerian phenomenon. Dancing with her father's photograph, Nwosisi's daughter shows how a funeral photograph can be constituted as a performative object. As Edwards (2001) has argued, photographs can be seen as performance in that in the context of social biography, "things" are active, not passive, in the making of meaning. She argues that this theatricality happens in two ways: in the intensity of its presentational form (as a framed fragment of reality, experience, etc.) and in its particular signifying properties. Thus, "Photographs have a performativity, an affective tone, a relationship with the viewer, a phenomenology, not of content as such, but as active social objects" (Edwards 2001, 18; Edwards 2021). Edwards, too, stresses the link between orality and a historical relationship with the photograph, as "people talk about photographs, with photographs and to photographs" (2001, 21), as seen in the manner Ada and Ifeatu spoke about Mama Okpuo and Okachamma's photographs respectively.

In the material culture of death, the entire photographic album of Nwosisi's burial and funeral can be understood as an embodiment of memory and a means of coping with loss. Each time the family came together during memorial services, the albums were revisited. There was always a profound attachment to the photo album as an object that is sometimes overvalued by some members who seem to prioritize it above the dead individual.

BEYOND GRIEF: STORYTELLING AND THE AFTERLIFE OF FUNERAL PHOTOGRAPHS AND VIDEO

Having previously concentrated on commemorative photographs that appeared in newspapers, booklets, posters, and billboards, I have devoted this chapter to storytelling around my physical encounter with photography, photographers, and the photographed. This is because Benjamin ([1968] 1985b) contends that the decline of storytelling can be attributed to the advent of print capitalism, particularly through the novel. Benjamin mentions the proliferation of newspapers, magazines, and other popular media forms as part of the causes of the decline of storytelling, which collectively eroded the foundation upon which wisdom is built.

Benjamin remarks that the true story is open-ended, so it provokes reflection and inspires recollection. The story of the deceased and their visual economy is never complete on the surface of print media or social media. I argue that the story must also be experienced, shared, and narrated, just as I have done in this chapter with the funerals I attended. Benjamin, writing in an era characterized by relatively modest information dissemination compared to today's sophisticated landscape, asserts that the primary challenge to storytelling is the prevalence of "information" ([1968] 1985b, 88). He argues that in our current age of information, communication predominantly involves the transmission of facts and reports, which are often accompanied by their own explanations or justifications. As Benjamin states, "Every morning brings us the news of the globe, and yet we are poor in noteworthy stories. This is because no event any longer comes to us without already being shot through with explanation. In other words, by now almost nothing that happens benefits storytelling; almost everything then affects information" (89). A crucial point in Benjamin's essay is his observation that we are losing the capacity to integrate and exchange personal experiences. Instead, our understanding is increasingly confined to information and factual explanations. Given the primacy of information, how can we understand our most profound experiences, which defy this model, and communicate them to others? How could I have understood the idiosyncrasies of the gaze in the commemorative visual culture of the Igbos? Benjamin's pursuit of genuine interpersonal exchange and the potential for true communication remains profoundly relevant. In his essay, he focuses on news reports, yet his insights are equally applicable to the electronic transmission of ideas, which similarly flattens our inner lives. Benjamin's essay is particularly pertinent to discussions of digital culture, which involves themes such as empathy, community, and embodiment. While Benjamin did not foresee contemporary developments, and, given his ambivalence toward popular culture, it is uncertain what he would have thought about the internet. Benjamin's apprehension about the expansion of information technology finds resonance in Jürgen Habermas's early critique of the digital public sphere. Habermas identifies the emergence of platforms as the defining organizational principle of digital communication and shows that their novelty lies in the bypassing of journalistic mediation and traditional programmatic structuring. Platforms, he argues, enable a diversified and decentralized form of communicative connectivity that fundamentally alters the architecture of public discourse (Habermas, 2022, 159). Although Habermas acknowledges the emancipatory possibilities embedded in interconnectivity as a central force in platformization, he maintains a critical stance toward the capitalist imperatives that underpin platform businesses. He argues that their market-driven logic compromises this liberatory potential by sidestepping any obligation to support meaningful civic discourse. Seemingly echoing Benjamin's lament over the erosion of storytelling, Habermas contends that the consumption of digital media contributes to a marked decline in reading and mass attention. This decline of sustained mass attention undermines cognitive depth, while the structural and institutional infrastructure of digital dissemination channels tends to privilege misinformation. As elaborated in chapter 6, this concern echoes the critique advanced by various scholars that the algorithm "embodies a certain view of the world as it should be, not just the world as it is" (Bar-Tura 2014, 212). One could argue that the digital culture we inhabit is an extension of the one Benjamin and Habermas heralded and critiqued, and their analyses remain remarkably insightful.

Extending Benjamin's analysis to the present, we can debate whether digital communities, such as Facebook, constitute genuine communities in a meaningful sense. One could argue that they are merely aggregations of isolated individuals who sacrifice personal encounters for online interactions. Consequently, these virtual associations may neglect and undermine authentic community life. According to White (2017, 9), "The Internet has brought amazing benefits, but it has also diminished our lives by disconnecting us from the direct experience of other human beings."

Benjamin observes that "the storyteller in his living immediacy is by no means a present force. He has already become something remote from us and something that is getting even more distant" ([1968] 1985b, 83). The essence of Benjamin's essay transcends a mere discussion of storytelling itself. It aims to illustrate that the decline of storytelling is symptomatic of a broader phenomenon: the seclusion of individuals in private life and the attendant inability to communicate experiences or attain wisdom—hallmarks of modernity.

In telling the story of my post-funerary encounters, I visited many bereaved families months after the funeral. Long after the photographer had delivered the funeral album and video, numerous families I visited derived profound joy from viewing them, experiencing a deep sense of nostalgic accomplishment. For example, when I visited Chike, one month after the funeral of his late father, he brought out the album from a bookshelf inside the parlor and showed me. Chike said, "Watching the video and seeing those I didn't expect to see in the funeral was a very emotional moment for me." Chike's father passed away in June 2022, and the funeral took place in August 2022. Chike told me that seeing some individuals who attended his father's funeral in the video and the photo album helped him heal further. Anabel, whose husband passed away in December 2021 and whose funeral took place in January 2022, said that she watched the video of her husband's funeral and saw a woman whom she didn't inform about her husband's death but who attended the funeral. The woman lives in Lagos and seems to have returned home for the December festive season. She decided to attend the funeral while she was still around during the January funeral. Jennifer, with whom I watched the video of her father's funeral in March 2022, showed me some friends in the video who, but for the video, she would have thought did not attend the funeral. She said, "Watching the video and the photo album made me feel that the sad feelings caused by the death of my father were replaced by the love of well-wishers." The video and the photo album are important materials used to articulate the role of photography in post-funeral encounters. They are not just critical to the healing process but function as visual roll calls of attendees to the funeral. The award-winning Nigerian artiste Teniola Apata revealed how she was able to record her award-winning song while watching her father's funeral video. According to Teniola, "When I was recording this song, I was sitting in my living room and watching my father's funeral, his body in the casket, my mother crying. I needed those emotions to be able to record that song in its true form. Everything I sang had to be from a place of truth."[4] Teniola's father was a retired Nigerian army brigadier-general, S. O. Apata, who was assassinated in 1995. Teniola was just three years old when her father died. Growing up to watch the video of her dad's funeral was a remarkable moment that allowed her to know who her dad was, an emotional experience that sparked and inspired her eventual rise to fame.

CONCLUSION

The art of postmortem photography in the Igbo region of Nigeria reveals that a photograph with the deceased parent always marks the last group photograph of the family. Photographs of mourners are used to activate memory in difficult times when families need to invoke the law of reciprocity before attending funerals. Photographs also provoke emotional memories and renew familial ties during funeral dances with the framed photograph. During lying-in-state, the ritual process of performativity, such as clothing the dead (*ikpu akwa*), around the coffin, is considered incomplete without photographic documentation. In capturing these performative acts by mourners and relatives around the coffin, photography extends the meaning of mourning to embrace visual evidence of the stark realities of loss. Photographic albums of funerals are regarded as a consummation of the ritual process and tangible materials of memory, sometimes consulted by relatives to settle an uncertain family matter that involves the funeral. These photos embody nuances of success (in Igbo person's terms), and the act of photographing funerals further inscribes and cements the ghostly in the corporeal reality of the world. Photographers induce a joyful mood at the funeral, thereby disrupting the prevalent tropes of sorrow to instigate a joyful mood. The mournful tears witnessed at the beginning of the funeral are replaced by a smiling countenance at its end.

Conclusion

Only several years ago, religious authorities in southeastern Nigeria deemed that the production of lavish funeral events and commemorative materials needed to be checked. On April 5, 2017, at the public hearing on the bill for a Law to Control Burial/Funeral Ceremonial Activities in Anambra State, the Catholic bishop of Awka Diocese, His Lordship Most Rev. Paulinus C. Ezeokafor, gave a presentation titled “Significance of Anambra Bill on Control of Funeral Ceremonies.” In the presentation, he stated:

> The extravagance displayed by our people during burial and funeral ceremonies in the State has reached such a point that there is a need for effective legislation to control it; otherwise, we leave our people in such a pitiable situation and bondage into which they have been trapped. The way our people degenerate from celebration of life to celebration of death is such that, if left uncontrolled and unregulated, we may likely sink into the hypothetical Hobbesian State of Nature, where life would become “solitary, poor, nasty, brutish, and short.” Therefore, I consider this bill as unqualifiedly and eternally significant to the citizens of the State and beyond. . . . In my Lenten Pastoral, I discussed the unwelcome wastage of money and resources through the printing of burial and funeral invitation cards, posters, billboards. I have already banned the production of brochures in the Catholic Diocese of Awka, with effect from 1 May 2017. . . . The money used for this could be better applied to helping the living. The faithful already know this, and I have received countless phone calls commending the move. The bill also covers this (clause 24), and it is a welcome aspect of the bill that would bring succour to many. (Ezeokafor 2017)

Quotation of this lengthy statement is necessary to underscore the tensions arising from not just expensive funeral ceremonies in southeastern

Nigeria but, more importantly, how the entire ostentation is crafted around the visual economy. Through his reference to funeral brochures, invitation cards, posters, and billboards, the bishop made clear his belief that the degeneration of society through this excessive ritual is propelled by the quest for visibility. The bishop's statement was confirmed two years later when Anambra State implemented a ban on funeral brochures, along with other restrictions related to burial and funeral ceremonies. According to the Anambra State Burial/Funeral Ceremonial Control Law, which was enacted on April 9, 2019, no funeral brochures are allowed except for the Order of Mass/Service 12. This law also includes other regulations, such as prohibiting billboards, banners, and posters for the deceased and limiting the duration and nature of funeral ceremonies.

These developments come as little surprise in the context of the Catholic Church's consistently adversarial approach to the traditional beliefs and practices of its indigenous communities. Nonetheless, communities themselves uphold the spirituality of their ancient ancestors even as they maintain devoted adherence to the Catholic beliefs that have been handed down for the past two hundred years. As we observed in chapter 5, funeral booklets in southeastern Nigeria typically present heroic images of the dead decorated with the titles and regalia of elite institutions, whereby Catholic and Igbo institutions are given equal representation. In some cases, titles and imagery, even costume elements, of both traditions appear on the same page. It could be argued that the perceived conflict between these two defining elements of contemporary Igbo culture comprises a primary obstacle that deceased individuals are portrayed as having heroically overcome.

Although the above bills were passed into law, they did little to deter the quest for visibility through photography at funerals. The defiant citizens still clandestinely print booklets and mount posters. As this quest for funeral posters continued unabated, in October 2023, the new governor of Anambra State, Chukwuma C. Soludo, realizing that the existing state law enacted in 2019 was ineffective, reminded the citizens that "the state's law on burial was still in force, warning that anyone who contravenes the law risks jail term" (Ujumadu 2023). According to the governor, among other listed bans, "No person shall erect any billboard, banner or posters of the deceased. Persons are allowed to erect only directional posts." This is a big blow to the Igbos of Anambra State seeking to announce their presence in the public sphere. A clash is evident between the modernity of the evolving leadership and entrenched cultural beliefs.

The new legislation has given more fuel to an already substantial trend: In seeking an alternative, hyper-visible public space for personal and collective aggrandizement, citizens continued to migrate to social media. Social media emerged to fill the void left by traditional funeral posters, banners, and booklets, serving as an alternative medium to evoke the lost hero image of the Igbo and reconstitute the embattled public sphere.

Especially in light of these recent attempts by the government to control this practice, which also serves to underscore its subversive power, the absence of African commemorative photography from scholarship is all the more glaring. In fact, photographs of the dead have been rarely discussed in general, not just in Africa but elsewhere. I started this conversation with the artistic evolution of the commemorative image from African figurative sculptures to contemporary commemorative photography. This shifted to the meanings of photographs in funerals and commemorations in southern Nigeria from the nineteenth century to the present. Colonial Lagos, which was a cosmopolitan urban center of multiple groups in Nigeria and West Africa, provided a historical context to investigate colonial relations. The scope then shifted to contemporary times in southeastern Nigeria, especially the Igbo region.

The impetus to launch this project was initially sparked by Peffer's concept of the "Àkan descriptions of funerary terracotta portraits (*mma*) as 'photos' of the deceased, capturing likeness as faithfully as a camera, understanding that these statements were made by individuals fully familiar with photographs" (2013, 320). Wendl's (2001) study of photography in Ghana was also an important factor. Wendl argues that Akan's standards for beauty and ethical uprightness, along with the visual conventions deployed to represent them, were slowly transferred from the traditional art form of sculpture to the emerging art form of portrait photography, facilitated by the alteration of photographic negatives. In Wendl's study, the analog camera and its technical processes were the major focus. I extended this conversation into Igbo funeral photography. The quest to produce a perfect body of the deceased is not just a personal aesthetic preference but a photographic project that aligns with Igbo sociocultural aspirations. Wendl observes with respect to Akan sculptures that "physical ideals of beauty have been carried over into the photographic portrait, enhanced by the photographer's manipulation of the image." In southeastern Nigeria as well, photography enabled many more people to have their portraits made than was the case historically when portraiture was the exclusive domain of the wealthy and important. Thus, commemorative photography became a new arena for image contests and a criterion for measuring the scale of influence and importance of individuals and families in the public sphere—with such success as to pose a threat to institutions of political and religious authority.

The Igbo public space continues to figure as a space where the interplay of communal and individual agency converges with the increasing influence of social media. Thus, the invocation of ancestral powers began to resonate more compellingly across time and space. It is a space where only heroes stand the test of might and wealth, where seeing and being seen are essentially envisioned as a negation of death. Here death as an end of visibility or presence is denied; instead, death is admitted as part of the sociocultural rituals required to elevate the family's prestige and status. By extolling the virtues of the deceased, families and communities reinforce their collective identity and existential ideals.

The inclusion of photographs within funeral booklets enabled families to reimagine a perfect family biography where togetherness is forged through a curatorial process between the families and photographers and where the bereaved deploy photographs to realize a unification of estranged family relationships. It also enables a visual canonization of the deceased, a transformation from fallible being to unimpeachable character who transcended public opprobrium to emerge as the saintly icon of the public sphere. Here photographs disrupt notions of underachievement, fallibility, and failed social performance. The virtual world offers even greater possibility for the invention of alternate lives and personal histories. Péne (2011) has argued that photos on individuals' social media pages are collages of various characteristics and personality traits that are then used to forge a new identity. Virtual bodies are produced bearing countless differences from the real bodies they represent, such as in chieftaincy attires, ethnic symbolisms, clothing, among others, through which new personas are invented (see, for example, Gozlan and Masson 2013 in Dilmac 2018, 284).

One of the most critical arguments of this book is how commemorative photographs reshape the linear meanings of family photo archives by making them readily available for public consumption via social media. In their social lives and viral journeys, these commemorative photographs help the public fashion nostalgia as a sentiment, implicitly evoking affective cultural criticism of the present. The deceased emerges as one who enjoys the acclaim of a global public sphere. Here the new meaning of the deceased's photograph as a fetishized hero of the social media public sphere who maintains a permanent presence in the lives of the living is underlined by the viral impetus activated by social media. Eventually, online photographs of the deceased marked a means through which individuals articulated a new digitized aesthetics of everyday ritual.

As we have seen, posters and booklet covers commemorating elderly individuals who died in the early 2000s tend to juxtapose a color photo taken in old age with a black-and-white one taken in young adulthood. Not only do such images document the subject's having lived through era-defining changes in technology, but the earlier photos also specifically index the period of optimism following Nigeria's independence in 1960. In my study of social media sites devoted to commemorating Nigerian nationalists, especially the Nigeria Nostalgia Project (NNP) Facebook page (Nwafor 2024), I observed that posted photos of nationalists from this period tend to serve as a starting point for debates around the nationalists' failed efforts to create an independent, unified Nigerian state. The continued placement of photographs from this era in the public sphere through the medium of commemorative images could therefore also be read as a collective insistence on the need to continue to hold up the ideals of the past against the shortcomings of the present.

In the Igbo region of Nigeria, a photograph with the deceased always appears as the last group photograph of the family. Photographs are also used to provoke emotional memories and renew familial ties during funeral dances with the framed photograph. I revealed these interesting episodes when I narrated my itineraries of funerals and burials with many photographers, including Nwoye. During this period, I witnessed lying-in-state and other events leading to interment and the funeral proper. I saw how performative ritual processes, such as *ikpu akwa* (clothing the dead), the funeral altars, or a dance with the photo, are considered incomplete without photographic documentation. In capturing these performative acts by mourners and relatives, photography captures new realities of the human gaze, what I call "a meaningful gaze at death." Photography (such as the photograph of Ruphina Ezimora) captures the meaningful gaze (Ruphina Ezimora's embodied act inside the photograph) or a mournful event in its most crucial state—the decisive moment. In this way, mourning and commemoration produce a unique kind of photographic experience, one that is meaningful yet focused on seeing what is no more (Ruphina's meaningful gaze at death), a gaze at a void, and a gaze at an empty space. The camera lens captures the contemplative gaze, which, as I argue, is a photograph that shows us two levels of vision: the vision of the photographic material itself (the photograph of Ruphina Ezimora) and the vision of its own embodied subjects (Ruphina gazing at her mother's coffin). One is longer, while the other is shorter. One is expressive, while the other is banal. One searches for a missing "thing," while the other captures the search for this "missing thing."

This book illustrates the power of interdisciplinary approaches in tackling complex issues in African studies. My work as a visual historian has enabled me to shift my engagement from closed textual analysis to more open and phenomenological embodiment. In this way, I have demonstrated in words of Victor Burgin that it is "necessary to 'think,' i.e., theorize, and also to historicize photography" (Burgin in McGrath 2020, 199), rather than approaching photographs as primarily aesthetic or documentary objects.

NOTES

CHAPTER 1

1. Newspaper and politics were intertwined in the collaborative efforts of anticolonial nationalism in Nigeria beginning in the 1940s Nigeria. Herbert Macaulay founded the first Nigerian political party, the Nigerian National Democratic Party, on June 24, 1923, and became the publisher of the *Lagos Daily News*, which ran until about 1940 (Omu 1978, 253). The *Nigerian Daily Times* (renamed *Daily Times* in 1948), supported by the colonial administration, resumed its publication on June 1, 1926, and did not support the nationalist party. The Nigerian Youth Movement, founded in 1936, used the newspaper *Daily Service*, founded in 1933, as its propaganda channel. Nnamdi Azikiwe (Zik), the political associate of Herbert Macaulay and cofounder of the National Council of Nigeria and the Cameroon, founded the *West African Pilot* on November 22, 1937, which became the leading newspaper that championed political independence in West Africa in the 1940s. In extending his political-journalistic enterprise, Zik's Press Limited, Zik also founded the *Southern Nigeria Defender* in 1945 and relocated it from Warri to Ibadan a few years later (Kunstmann 2014, 518; Duyile 1987, 143); Obafemi Awolowo established his newspaper, the *Nigerian Tribune*, on November 16, 1949, and founded the Western Region–centered political party Action Group on March 21, 1951.

2. Authors such as Rinhart (1967) and Welling (1978) believe that the postmortem phenomenon was an American invention, while Lesy (1973) attempts to understand the anthropological meanings of this practice.

3. The subject of the postmortem dates back to the Renaissance, when the deathbed became the preferred mode of displaying and portraying the dead. The invention of daguerreotype in the nineteen century was a turning point for memento mori. Reduced costs of photography made postmortem photographs readily available to ordinary people. From 1840, when the first postmortem photograph was taken, the popularity and profitability of postmortem photography became unquantifiable for photographers, a point endorsed by a *Humphrey Journal* report: "Gallery daguerreotypes for sale—the only one in the city of 20,000 inhabitants and where the photographs of deceased persons pay for itself all the costs" (*Humphrey Journal*, 1854, 33, cited in Borgo et al. 2016,

104). Such postmortem photographs became a misleading portrait of life and foregrounded as "the only portrait of the deceased person where there was no possibility of getting a photograph while the person was alive" (see Borgo et al. 2016).

4. Part of my investigation into the global cultural economy involves analysis of how Facebook and other social media platforms have enabled a virtual memorial and wider visibility of family photos beyond the immediate communities. It also looks at how these photographs on Facebook pages aid the processes of grieving and memorialization (see, for example, Carroll and Landry 2010; Degroot 2012; Robert 2006).

5. Some other authors have dwelled on the social contexts of private African photographs. For example, in her study of the historical and current uses of photographs in the Bamun Kingdom of Cameroon, Geary (2013) traces the highly mobile use of photographic images. A photographic image may find multiple uses and consumption in books, in the hand, as a postcard, as a personal memento, as an item of intimate exchange, in family albums, and as an ethnographic illustration, among other uses. These photographs have social lives (Kopytoff 1986; Edwards 2005) and biographies that can serve as reference points for multiple, diverse reflections. Furthermore, Isolde Brielmaier has shown how urban South Asian Africans have used photography to realize a transformation of local experiences into a global image world. They have refashioned a local experience relying on foreign aesthetics.

CHAPTER 2

1. On the negotiation of power in colonial African print, see Peterson and Hunter 2016; Hunter and James 2020; Krautwald 2021, 5–28; Newell 2013, 2020.

2. Some of these studies include, for example, Lee and Vaughan 2008. Both Charles Okigbo and K. Nwalo analyzed death and funeral advertisements in the Nigerian press and suggested that the obituaries pronounced the conspicuous presence of the individual by filling a vacuum created by lack. See Nwalo 1983; Okigbo 1987. Adebanwi has also shown that printed biographies were used to articulate the meanings of nationalism and heroism in his work on the biographical commemoration of Nigerian nationalists such as Nnamdi Azikiwe and Obafemi Awolowo. See Adebanwi 2008a, 2008b, 2016, 2021. See also Alali 1993; Togonu-Bickersteth 1986; and Adéèkó 2012.

3. These newspapers were accessed in the digitized newspaper collections of Readex's World Newspaper Archives.

4. Newell has suggested the existence of other public spheres in colonial Africa, such as "town and village associations, singing bands, church prayer groups, funeral cooperatives, masquerades, military groups, and a multiplicity of other social organizations that created spaces separate from the family and the state." She argues that many of the above-named public spheres predated colonialism and newspapers in Africa and were independent of chieftaincy structures (Newell 2013, 93; Little 1965; See also Kalusa and Vaughan 2013).

5. On the French Empire as an exception to this rule, see Cooper 2018.

6. For a detailed account of the African middle classes and the bourgeoisie in a global and other colonial context, see Dejung et al. 2018.

7. Coleman 1965; Benhabib 1992, 73–98; Fraser 1990, 56–80; Oke 2013, 29–56.

8. *Lagos Observer* (LO), September 14, 1882.

9. Some of these wars were reported in the same Lagos newspapers. For example, the *Lagos Times and Gold Coast Colony Advertiser* (LT) of 1881 reports: "From Abeokuta it is reported that the kidnapping and guerrilla warfare between the Egbas and Ibadans still continued. The king of Dahomey had sent messengers to the Egba Government, but these from political reasons had been ordered to remain at a suburban village (Ibara) where they would be communicated with." See LT 1881, 3; LO, September 14, 1882.

10. LO, September 14, 1882.

11. *Times of Nigeria* (ToN), February 23, 1920, 3.

12. ToN, March 2–6, 1915, 2.

13. This corresponds with Sawada's observation that "between 1890 and 1920, in order to insert one memorial advertisement (memorial poem or death notice), family or friends of the deceased paid between 4 and 15 shillings." See Sawada 2015, 169; Newell, 2022, 401.

14. ToN, February 23, 1920, 3.

15. ToN, November 15, 1915, 5.

16. ToN, February 23, 1920, 3.

17. *The Mirror*, December 24, 1887.

18. *Nigerian Times*, April 5, 1910, 1.

19. *Nigerian Times*, April 5, 1910, 1.

20. *Lagos Weekly Record* (LWR), June 18–25, 1921.

21. *Lagos Standard* (LS), February 20, 1895.

22. *Nigerian Chronicle* (NC), December 2, 1910.

23. NC, December 2, 1910.

24. On the relationship between the living and the dead in African cosmologies, see Mbiti 1990, 5–26.

CHAPTER 3

1. See Edwards and Hart 2004; Hoskins 1998; and Edwards et al. 2006.

2. Bourdieu 1965; Miller 2005.

3. See Don Ihde's concept of material hermeneutics in this regard (1999, 149–150); and Edwards and Hart 2004.

4. *Weekly News*, April 20, 1889.

5. ToN, December 1910, 2.

6. LWR, February 20, 1909, 7; LS, January 9, 1910, also remarks that the 1910 almanac contains the "pictures of Awujale of Ijebu Ode, the Akarigbo of Ijebu Remo, Prince Ajiki of Porto Novo, a map of Sierra Leonne."

7. LS, June 2, 1909, 3H.

8. LS, Wednesday, January 13, 1914.
9. LS, Wednesday, September 23, 1909.
10. LS, Wednesday, June 11, 1913.
11. LO, March 1, 1883, 2.
12. LWR, September 10, 1904, 1.
13. LWR, September 10, 1904, 1.
14. LWR, September 10, 1904, 1.
15. LWR, September 10, 1904, 1.
16. LS, Wednesday, February 14, 1912.
17. LS, Wednesday, February 14, 1912.
18. LS, November 27, 1918; See also *Sierra Leonean Weekly News*, December 7, 1901, 8, for similar news.
19. LWR, October 26, 1918, 6.
20. LO, December 3 and 17, 1885, 2.
21. LO, December 3 and 17, 1885, 2.
22. LO, December 3 and 17, 1885, 2.
23. LO, January 21, 1886, 2.
24. LO, January 21, 1886, 2.
25. LO, December 17 , 1885, 1 and 3.
26. *Eagle and Lagos Critic* [1882–88]; *Eagle and Lagos Critic*, October 24 and November 14, 1885, 2.
27. Sawada 2016; LS, November 15, 1899, 3.
28. *African Times*, February 23, 1866, May 23, 1966, February 23, 1967, August 22, 1968, October 2, 1982, February 23, 1866, May 23, 1866, February 23, 1867, November 23, 1867.
29. LO, November 19, 1885, 2.
30. LO, November 19, 1885, 2.
31. LO, November 19,1885, 2.
32. NC, March 6, 1914.
33. LWR, May 21, 1904, 3.
34. LWR, August 10, 1912, 3; LS, August 14, 1912, 3.
35. LWR, August 10, 1912, 3, August 24, 1912, 3; LS, August 28, 1912, 6.
36. LS, June 19, 1912, 5.
37. LWR, July 12, 1913, 5; August 16, 1913, 3.
38. NC, March 6, 1914, 3, 6.
39. See chapter 1 of this book for examples of portraits that served as ancestral memorials: for example, the *ndop* in Blier 1998, 233; the Okpella mask in Borgatti 1979; the Fante in La Gamma 2011, 77, to mention a few.
40. See LS, November 27, 1918.
41. LWR, September 3, 1892, 3.
42. LWR, October 21, 1905, 4.

43. It is unclear why the article made contradictory statements about the Child's rank as both 'Lieut,' and 'Captain.' LWR, February 10, 1917, 4.

44. ToN, November 15, 1915, 5.

45. ToN, November 15, 1915, 5.

46. ToN, November 15, 1915, 5. See chapter 2 of this book.

47. ToN, November 15, 1915, 5.

48. LS, June 1, 1910.

CHAPTER 4

1. Herbert Macaulay was the grandson of Samuel Ajayi Crowther. He established the first Nigerian political party, the Nigerian National Democratic Party, which successfully contested three Lagos seats in the Legislative Council. Macaulay, regarded as the "father of modern Nigerian nationalism," was among the most disliked by the British colonial authorities for his strong anticolonial politics.

2. De Witte notes how the social significance of rites of passage in Asante is materially constituted through conspicuous displays of money and wealth. The circulation and spending of money at Asante funerals do not just serve to symbolically mark the transition of the deceased from life to death, but make a strong social impact in the life of the living (see de Witte 2003).

3. This finding resonated with Audrey Linkman's study of Victorian postmortem photographs: "Photographs singled out for particular attention during the mourning period tend to be those in which the deceased appear happy or healthy, photographs that allowed the bereaved to transfer their thoughts away from the event of the death to a contemplation of the wider significance of the deceased's life" (2011, 152; see also Laderman 2003, 105–106).

4. Audrey Linkman has suggested that "photographs also provided an acceptable mechanism for friends and relatives to initiate conversations about the deceased's character and achievements" (2011, 152), while Favero notes that "for years to come, the images that accompanied a person's death will become key providers of stories. They will incite passersby to talk about the deceased in front of their graves and their home altars, making them share actual memories and often also inviting them to make up events and stories that never really took place" (2017, 100).

5. See Bredenbröker 2024. Geofrey Batchen has explored Christian visual elements in funeral photography. For example, in a piece from 1910 featured in the Van Gogh Museum's 2004 exhibition, *Forget Me Not: Photography and Remembrance*, photograph, text, and decorative elements such as flowers and taxidermied doves are used to create a memorial image. Writing on the piece in the exhibition catalog, Geoffrey Batchen notes: "Mingling Christian iconography—the dove of peace and resurrection, symbol of the Holy Ghost—with a secular, mechanical image—a photograph of the deceased—it speaks of death and mourning but also of the renewal of life. It seeks to

remember this man not as someone now dead, but as someone once alive" (2004, 82). With his reading of such vernacular photographs, Batchen rightly complicates Barthes's assertion that every photograph speaks of the death of the sitter, for in vernacular photographic practices, we often see the assertion of both life and death.

CHAPTER 5

1. According to Emily Keightley and Michael Pickering, "A further dimension of the amalgamation of old and new in the analogue/digital shift is the widespread practice of making analogue photographs digital by scanning them and storing them on a PC or uploading them to the internet" (2014, 583). In other cases where analog photographs have been digitized by users, all photographs are centralized, coexisting in one place on the PC. In this respect, personal collections give emphasis to the continuation of archiving photographs as family records and conveyances of remembering (Keightley and Pickering 2014, 583). Van Dijck (2007) highlights the intermedial character of photographic practice, contending that while new media elements can reshape our engagement with personal artifacts, intermediality also operates bidirectionally with newer elements being reconstituted by older ones.

2. For example, a theoretical model by Tom Nesmith (2005, 326) known as 'provenance' explicitly mirrors the intermedial dialogue when we analyze its definition as "the social and technical processes of the records' inscription, transmission, contextualization, and interpretation, which account for its existence, characteristics, and continuing history." Caswell (2014, 18) provides further analysis of provenance as "a new reconceptualization, an ever-changing, infinitely evolving process of recontextualization, encompassing not only the initial creators of the records but also the subjects of the records themselves, the archivists who acquired, described, and digitized them (among other interventions), and the users who constantly reinterpret them." Thus, intermediality seems a compelling means of articulating the social life of photographs.

3. Lisa Aronson (2017, 310) observes that "commemorative booklets and those produced to mark the installations of kings or chiefs also typically combine photographs with other images," referring specifically to the photographs of J. A. Green of Bonny in Rivers States. She refers to a 1978 commemorative booklet with three photographs, two of which were taken by Green, to visually assert Chief Samuel Will Braide's rightful claim to the throne. See Aronson 2017, 310–312.

4. *Oriki* is an inspirational literary chant of the Yoruba. It is usually declamatory and takes the form of poetry and praise songs. Settings include traditional wedding ceremonies, chieftaincy coronations, masquerading arenas, etc. In the case of traditional marriage ceremonies, some women chant praise poetry to inspire the bride, and the bride bursts into emotional expressions of joy often exhibited through tears. For the purpose of inspiration, the Yoruba people employ the use of praise poetry, songs and

sacred invocations, as well as inspiring names. Even as the name shows, *oriki* is a name or a praise poetry that "opens up" or "expands" a person's head. The etymology of the Yoruba word for inspiration reflects the belief of the people in Ori, i.e., the head. Furthermore, *oriki* praise song was "created in a situation where activities within the local community were all-absorbing. Little incidents, peculiar happenings, favourite remarks, were observed, discussed, taken up and commemorated in epithets" (Barber 1991, 203, 244).

5. Beyond the African examples cited above, Catherine Zuromskis has observed how the preparation of the family album requires an editorial process . . . that is expressive and full of crucial choices in the formation and representation of group identity. Annette Kuhn has criticized some of the scholarship on family photographs, saying that "cultural theory tells us there is little personal or private about either family photographs or the memories they evoke: they can mean only culturally" (2013, 397). This view is perhaps epitomized in the work of Pierre Bourdieu, who says of the family album that "all the unique experiences that give the individual memory the particularity of a secret are banished from it, and the common past, or, perhaps, the highest common denominator of the past, has all the clarity of a faithfully visited gravestone" (Bourdieu 1965, 44). The role of the family network in curating the family photos in the funeral booklets is decidedly normative one. Through production and various forms of consumption, familial groups curate and enforce cultural conventions by choosing when and how family photos are produced, which photos merit circulation and display, and who is granted access to them. See Zuromskis 2013; Bourdieu 1965, 30; Kuhn 1991, 17–25, 19.

6. During the Ozo title-taking of four Nwankwo brothers in the Enugwu-Agidi community in Njikoka Local Government Area of Anambra State, Ozo Fred Onubogu offered an insight into steps an aspirant for the Ozo title has to take before joining the exclusive league. According to Ozo Onubogu, "In the Ozo title-taking, before you step out to be an Ozo man in our place; you have to be prepared financially and otherwise. In our town, an Ozo man doesn't enter bike or tricycle because you must be in affluence. For those who want to belong, the first step is to host the group we call asaa mbu (the first seven), the person will host this group, fete them with abundant eating and drinking, including slaughtering of animals. Then the person will host the asaa nabo (the second seven) with their requirements too. After this, the asaa nabo will then inform the minor Ozo group of the aspirant's intention and they will be hosted again by the aspirant. After this, the aspirant will meet the table officers and settle them one by one, then the floor members also till the final day of the coronation. On the day, different groups will be invited, including the Uhie dance. All the Ozo title holders go home with a tuber of yam and a fowl at the expense of the new entrant while cows will be slaughtered among other heavy feasting and merriment." For a full description of the Ozo title and variations in different Igbo societies see Onwuejeogwu 1979, 25, 117–143.

CHAPTER 6

1. The Catholic religion believes that spirits are never dead, while in the Igbo concept of ancestor worship, the dead still live among the living.

2. De Witte has observed a similar practice in Asante funerals, where tears have become culturally obligatory. According to de Witte, "In Kumasi it is becoming the fashion to hire mourners to come and cry at your funeral to set the mournful atmosphere required for a good funeral. Certain funeral undertakers mediate between bereaved families and groups of women who 'know how to cry,' using the appropriate words, laments, gestures and body language to express the grief of others" (2003, 551).

3. A similar practice was observed about the death of celebrities in nineteenth-century Europe. Linkman (2011, 145) notes that the death of prominent political figures, such as Otto von Bismarck, Louis-Adolphe Thiers, and Prince Albert, sparked a high demand for their photographic portraits. Some photographers exploited this demand by taking unauthorized or exclusive pictures of the deceased and selling them for large profits. The fascination with nineteenth-century celebrity photos is similar to the obsession with today's online photos of the dead. However, today's fans need internet access to view their loved ones' photos after death. Here the use of internet access underscores a significant shift in the constitution of existential living. Scott Lash (2007) conceptualizes this shift as a "new new media ontology," where the double emphasis on "new" underscores an increasing apprehension regarding the profound impact of software on the very fabric and dynamics of everyday life (Dodge and Kitchin 2008, 2). This phenomenon vividly illustrates the pervasive infiltration of software into nearly every facet of daily life, seamlessly embedding itself into the unnoticed backdrop of our routines (Thrift and French, cited in Thrift 2005, 153).

CHAPTER 7

1. This altar is also seen as an isolation space for wives. Bess Reed and Benjamin Hufbauer remark, "Wives go into a period of isolation to prove to the community that they had no hand in their husband's death, although husbands do not do so when their wives die, probably an expression of the priestly nature of fathers and of the masculine prerogative in Igbo society" (2005, 144).

2. Umada has been described by Reed and Hufbauer as "a daughter's council, which is a political body that is meant to provide a forum for the resolution of women's concerns" (2005, 149).

3. There are examples of the existence of similar altars in some cultures. For example, photographs of family members—living and dead—feature prominently together with holy statues, religious pictures, and other assorted objects in the home altars that survive today in rural areas of Mexico. These altars have a spiritual function as the sacred site of interaction between the human and divine, and a commemorative function in which the memory of ancestors is honored and a family history is articulated through

the display of trinkets, treasured mementoes, and family photographs. These home altars are constructed and maintained continuously throughout the year, but special, more elaborate displays are created for important annual festivals such as Easter, Christmas, and the weeklong Day of the Dead celebration, which coincides with All Saints and All Souls Days in the Christian calendar. In Mexico, El Día de los Muertos (Day of the Dead) is the most important festival, when the spirits of the dead return to the family home to commune with their living relatives and feed together on the food laid out for them on the altars. In some areas of Mexico these altars are constructed at cemeteries. Photographs of dead relatives and items that once belonged to them feature prominently on the home altar at this time, acting both as a spiritual presence and an aide-memoire. Their association with holy images links the dead with the realm of the saints, and highlights their role as intermediaries who can intercede on behalf of the living. During this festival, the home altar brings together the divine, the dead, and the living in an effort to create a model of beneficial and productive relationships. Claire Harris has also noted that Tibetan exiles use photographs to build altars whereby the photograph is regarded as a sentient being, enthroned, sheltered by a canopy, and adorned with a ceremonial silk scarf (2004, 147). The materiality of the photograph becomes a reflection of the articulated and embodied personhood. According to Harris, "The photographic record of that body therefore becomes a positive affirmation of an ongoing stream of presence rather than a memorial to absence" (145).

4. Jayne Augoye, 2021. "I recorded 'Dad's Song' while watching my father's funeral—Teni." Premium Times. https://www.premiumtimesng.com/entertainment/music/music-interviews/450920-i-recorded-dads-song-while-watching-my-fathers-funeral-teni.html. Visited August 16, 2022.

BIBLIOGRAPHY

Abiodun, Rowland. 1976. "A Reconsideration of the Function of Ako, Second Burial Effigy in Owo." *Africa* 46, no. 1: 4–20.

Abiodun, Rowland. 2013. "Àkó-Graphy: Òwò Portraits." In *Portraiture and Photography in Africa*, edited by John Peffer and Elisabeth L. Cameron, 237–242. Bloomington: Indiana University Press.

Achebe, Chinua. 1958. *Things Fall Apart*. London: Heinemann.

Adebanwi, Wale. 2008a. "The Cult of Awo: The Political Life of a Dead Leader." *Journal of Modern African Studies* 46, no. 3: 335–360.

Adebanwi, Wale. 2008b. "Death, National Memory and the Social Construction of Heroism." *Journal of African History* 49, no. 3: 419–444.

Adebanwi, Wale. 2016. "Colonial Modernity and Tradition: Herbert Macaulay, the Newspaper Press, and the (Re)Production of Engaged Publics in Colonial Lagos." In *African Print Cultures: Newspapers and Their Publics in the Twentieth Century*, edited by Derek R. Peterson, Emma Hunter, and Stephanie Newell, 125–148. Ann Arbor: University of Michigan Press.

Adebanwi, Wale. 2021. "Burying 'Zik of Africa': The Politics of Death and Cultural Crisis." *Comparative Studies in Society and History* 63, no. 1: 41–71.

Adeboye, Olufunke. 2003. "Elite Lifestyle and Consumption in Colonial Ibadan." In *The Foundations of Nigeria: Essays in Honour of Toyin Falola*, edited by Adebayo Oyebade, 281–304. Trenton, NJ: African World Press.

Adéèkó, Adélékè. 2012. "From Orality to Visuality: Panegyric and Photography in Contemporary Lagos, Nigeria." *Critical Inquiry* 38, no. 2: 330–361.

Adenekan, Shola. 2021. *African Literature in the Digital Age: Class and Sexual Politics in New Writing from Nigeria and Kenya*. Suffolk: Boydell & Brewer.

Adeoba, Gbenga, and James Yékú. 2024. "Cultural Netizenship as Platformization of Popular Culture in Nigeria." *International Journal of Cultural Studies* 28, no. 1: 260–277.

Adjah, Olive Akpebu. 2007. "Ghanaian Funeral Brochures: An Unexplored Rich Source of Biographical Information." *African Research and Documentation* 103: 33–44.

Adotey, Edem. 2018. "Where Is My Name? Contemporary Funeral Posters as an Arena of Contestation and (Re)negotiation of Chiefly Relations Among the Ewe of Ghana and Togo: Critical Historiography." *History in Africa* 45: 59–69.

Adu-Gyamfi, Paul. 2010. "Observable Artistic Changes in the Funerals of Adanse Traditional Area." MA thesis, Kwame Nkrumah University of Science and Technology, Kumasi.

Agbo, George Emeka. 2018. "The Struggle Complex: Facebook, Visual Critique and the Tussle for Political Power in Nigeria." *Cahiers d'études africaines* 230: 469–492.

Agbo, George Emeka. 2019. "Challenging the Frivolities of Power: The Ubiquitous Camera and Nigerian Political Elites." *Africa* 89, no. 2: 286–301.

Agbogu, Herbert Tagbo. 1974. "The Art of Nri." BA thesis, University of Nigeria, Nsukka.

Ajaegbu, D. I. 2014. "African Democratic Heritage: A Historical Case Study of the Igbo of Nigeria." *IOSR Journal of Humanities and Social Science* 19, no. 4: 17–23. https://doi.org/10.9790/0837-19481723

Alali, A. Odasuo. 1993. "Management of Death and Grief in Obituary and In Memoriam Pages of Nigerian Newspapers." *Psychological Reports* 73: 835–842.

Altheide, David, and Robert P. Snow. 1991. *Media Worlds in the Postjournalism Era*. New York: Aldine de Gruyter.

Aniakor, Chike C. 1980. "The Concept and Symbolism of the Centre in African Architecture." In *Traditional and Modern Culture*, edited by E. Ihekweazu, 29–49. Enugu: Fourth Dimension Publishers.

Aniakor, Chike C. 1984. *Igbo Art: Community and Cosmos*. Los Angeles: Museum of Cultural History, University of California.

Aniakor, Chike C. 2002. "Igbo Architecture." In *A Survey of Igbo Nation*, edited by G. E. K. Ofomata, 272–299. Onitsha: Africana First Publishers.

Anigbo, O. A. C. 1996. "Commensality as Cultural Performance: The Struggle for Leadership in Igbo Village." In *The Politics of Cultural Performance*, edited by D. J. Parkin, V. Caplan, and H. J. Fisher, 101–114. Oxford: Berghahn Books.

Appadurai, Arjun. 1986a. "Introduction: Commodities and the Politics of Value." In *The Social Life of Things: Commodities in Cultural Perspective*, edited by Arjun Appadurai. 6-63. Cambridge: Cambridge University Press.

Appadurai, Arjun, ed. 1986b. *The Social Life of Things: Commodities in Cultural Perspective*. Cambridge: Cambridge University Press.

Appadurai, Arjun. 1990. "Disjuncture and Difference in the Global Cultural Economy Theory." *Culture & Society* 7: 295–310.

Arhin, K. 1994. "The Economic Implications of Transformations in Akan Funeral Rites." *Africa* 64, no. 3: 307–322.

Arnold, Michael, Martin Gibbs, Tamara Kohn, James Meese, and Bjorn Nansen. 2018. *Death and Social Media*. New York: Routledge.

Aronson, Lisa. 2017. "Green's Photos and the Visualizing and Reinventing of Ijo Histories." In *African Photographer J. A. Green: Reimagining the Indigenous and the*

Colonial, edited by Martha G. Anderson and Lisa Aronson, 299–333. Bloomington: Indiana University Press.

Azoulay, Ariella. 2014. *The Civil Contract of Photography*. New York: Zone Books.

Azoulay, Ariella. 2015. *Civil Imagination: A Political Ontology of Photography*. Translated by Louise Bethlehem. 2nd ed. London: Verso.

Bae, Choon Sup. 2008. *Ancestor Worship: The Challenges It Poses to the Christianity Mission and Ministry*. Saarbrücken: VDM Verlag.

Bajorek, Jennifer. 2012. "Ca bousculait! Democratization and Photography in Senegal." In *Photography in Africa: Ethnographic Perspectives*, edited by Richard Vokes, 140–165. Rochester, NY: Boydell & Brewer.

Bajorek, Jennifer. 2020. *Photography and Decolonial Imagination in West Africa*. Durham, NC: Duke University Press.

Bajorek, Jennifer. 2023. "Studio Portraiture and the Postcolonial Archive." In *A World in Common: Contemporary African Photography*, edited by Osei Bonsu, 31–38. London: Tate Modern.

Barber, Karin. 1991. *I Could Speak Until Tomorrow: Oriki, Women and the Past in a Yoruba Town*. Washington, DC: Smithsonian Institution Press.

Barber, Karin, ed. 2006. *Africa's Hidden Histories: Everyday Literacy and Making the Self*. Bloomington: Indiana University Press.

Barber, Karin. 2007. *The Anthropology of Texts, Persons and Publics: Oral and Written Culture in Africa and Beyond*. Cambridge: Cambridge University Press.

Barber, Karin. 2018. *A History of African Popular Culture*. Cambridge: Cambridge University Press.

Barthes, Roland. 1981. *Camera Lucida: Reflections on Photography*. Translated by Richard Howard. New York: Hill and Wang.

Barthes, Roland. [1980] 1985. "On Photography." In *The Grain of the Voice: Interviews, 1962–1980*, translated by Linda Coverdale, 353–360. New York: Hill and Wang.

Barthes, Roland. 1985. "Right in the Eyes." In *The Responsibility of Forms: Critical Essays on Music, Art and Representation*, 237–242. Oxford: Blackwell.

Bar-Tura, Asaf. 2014. "Habermas and Public Reason in the Digital Age: Technology and Deliberative Democracy." PhD Dissertation, Loyola University, Chicago.

Bascom, William. 1951. "Social Status, Wealth and Individual Differences Among the Yorubam." *American Anthropologist* 53, no. 2: 490–505.

Basden, George T. 1938. *Niger Ibos*. London: Seeley.

Basden, George T. [1921] 1983. *Among the Ibos of Nigeria*. Lagos: University Pub. Co.

Basu, Paul, with Glory Chika-Kanu. 2020. "Dibia, Nzu, Orhue, Sacred Chalk." *Re-Entanglements*. https://re-entanglements.net/tag/dibia/

Batchen, Geoffrey. 1997. *Photography's Objects*. University of New Mexico Art Museum, Albuquerque, NM, August 26 to October 31.

Batchen, Geoffrey. 2001. *Each Wild Idea: Writing, Photography, History*. Cambridge, MA: MIT Press.

Batchen, Geoffrey. 2004. *Forget Me Not: Photography and Remembrance*. Amsterdam: Van Gogh Museum Amsterdam; New York: Princeton Architectural Press.

Batchen, Geoffrey. 2008. "Snapshots: Art History and the Ethnographic Turn." *Photographies* 1, no. 2: 121–142.

Battaglia, Debbora. 1990. *On the Bones of the Serpent: Person, Memory, and Mortality in Sabarl Island Society*. Chicago: University of Chicago Press.

Bauman, Zygmunt. 1992. *Mortality, Immortality and Other Life Strategies*. Cambridge: Polity Press.

Bazin, André. 1967. *What Is Cinema?* Translated by Hugh Gray. Berkeley: University of California Press.

Behrend, Heike. 2000. "Feeling Global: The Likoni Ferry Photographers of Mombasa, Kenya." *African Arts* 33, no. 3: 70–96.

Behrend, Heike. 2002. "Ritual Enactment of Achievement: 'Ikenga' Symbol in Igboland." *Paideuma* 48: 47–62.

Behrend, Heike. 2003. "Photo Magic: Photographs in practices of Healing and Harming in East Africa." *Journal of Religion in Africa* 33, no. 2: 129–145.

Behrend, Heike. 2013. *Contesting Visibility: Photographic Practices on the East African Coast*. Bielefeld: Transcript Verlag.

Belting, Hans. 1997. *Likeness and Presence: A History of the Image before the Era of Art*. Chicago: University of Chicago Press.

Belting, Hans. 2011. *An Anthropology of Images, Picture, Medium, Body*. Translated by Thomas Dunlap. Princeton, NJ: Princeton University Press.

Belting, Hans. 2017. *Faces and Masks: A Double History*. Princeton, NJ: Princeton University Press.

Benhabib, Seyla. 1992. "Models of Public Space: Hannah Arendt, the Liberal Tradition, and Jürgen Habermas." In *Habermas and the Public Sphere*, edited by Craig Calhoun, 73–98. Cambridge, MA: MIT Press.

Benjamin, Walter. [1968] 1985a. *Illuminations: Essays and Reflections*. Edited by Hannah Arendt. Translated by Harry Zohn. New York: Schocken Books.

Benjamin, Walter. [1968] 1985b."The Storyteller." In *Illuminations*, edited by Hannah Arendt and translated by Harry Zohn, 83–109. New York: Schocken Books.

Benjamin, Walter. [1968] 1985c. "The Task of the Translator." In *Illuminations*, edited by Hannah Arendt and translated by Harry Zohn, 69–82. New York: Schocken Books.

Benjamin, Walter. [1968] 1985d. "The Work of Art in the Age of Mechanical Reproduction." In *Illuminations: Essays and Reflections*, edited by Hannah Arendt and translated by Harry Zohn, 217–252. New York: Schocken Books.

Bentor, Eli. 1988. "Life as an Artistic Process: Igbo Ikenga and Ofo." *African Arts* 21, no. 2: 66–71.

Bhabha, Homi. 1987. "Of Mimicry and Man: The Ambivalence of Colonial Discourse." In *October: The First Decade*, edited by Annette Michelson et al. Cambridge, MA: MIT Press.

Bhattacharya, Neeladri. 2005. "Notes Towards a Conception of the Colonial Public." In *Civil Society, Public Sphere and Citizenship: Dialogues and Perceptions*, edited by Rajeev Bhargava and Helmut Reifeld, 130–156. New Delhi: Sage.

Blaha, C. 2012. "Technology." *Technorati*, March 7. Visited August 15, 2022. http://technorati.com/technology/article/over-30-million-accounts-on-facebook/

Blier, Suzanne P. 1998. "Kongo and Kuba: The Art of Rulership Display." In Blier, *The Royal Arts of Africa: The Majesty of Form*, 229–248. New York: H. N. Abrams.

Blyden, Edward Wilmot. 1887. *Christianity, Islam and the Negro Race*. London: W. B. Whittingham.

Borgatti, Jean M. 1976. "Okpella Masking Tradition." *African Arts* 12, no. 4: 24–33.

Borgatti, Jean M. 1979. "Dead Mothers of Okpella." *African Arts* 12, no. 4: 48–57, 91.

Borgatti, Jean M. 1990. "Portraiture in Africa." *African Arts* 23, no. 3: 34–39.

Borgo, Melania, Marta Licata, and Silvia Iorio. 2016. "Post-Mortem Photography: The Edge Where Life Meets Death?" *Human and Social Studies* 5, no. 2: 103–115.

Bourdieu, Pierre. 1965. *Photography: A Middle-Brow Art*. Translated by Shaun Whiteside. Stanford, CA: Stanford University Press.

Bowker, Gordon. 2006. "Nuts About St Cyps: Lessons and Quarrels in the Lives of George Orwell." *Times Literary Supplement*, September 15, 13–15.

Bredenbröker, Isabel. 2024. "Advertising the Ancestors: Ghanaian Funeral Banners as Image Objects." In *Death's Social and Material Meaning Beyond the Human*, edited by Jesse D. Peterson, Natashe Lemos Dekker, and Philip R. Olson, 83–99. Oxford: Bristol University Press.

Brody, Hugh. 1974. *Inishkillane: Change and Decline in the West of Ireland*. Harmondsworth: Penguin.

Brown, Amanda. 2012. "The Way She Looked the Day She Died: Vernacular Photography, Memory, and Death." The Art of Death and Dying Symposium, University of Houston, Houston, TX, October 25–27. Proceedings published in Texas Digital Library 1 http://hdl.handle.net/10657/3002

Brown, Spencer Hunter. 1964. "A History of the People of Lagos, 1852–1886." PhD dissertation, Northwestern University.

Brubaker, Jed R., Gillian R. Hayes, and Paul Dourish. 2013. "Beyond the Grave: Facebook as a Site for the Expansion of Death and Mourning." *Information Society* 29, no. 3: 152–163. https://doi.org/10.1080/01972243.2013.777300

Buckley, Liam. 2000–2001. "Self and Accessory in Gambian Studio Photography." *Visual Anthropology Review* 16, no. 2: 71–91.

Buckley, Liam. 2003. "Studio Photography and the Aesthetics of Postcolonialism in the Gambia, West Africa." PhD dissertation, University of Virginia.

Buckley, Liam. 2006. "Studio Photography and the Aesthetics of Citizenship in the Gambia." In *Sensible Objects: Colonialism, Museum, and Material Culture*, edited by Elizabeth Edwards, Chris Gosden, and Ruth B. Philips, 61–85. Oxford: Berg.

Buggenhagen, Beth. 2014. "A Snapshot of Happiness: Photo Albums, Respectability, and Economic Uncertainty in Dakar." *Africa* 84, no. 1: 5–24.

Buggenhagen, Beth. 2023. *The Future Is in Your Hands: Portrait Photography from Senegal*. Bloomington: Indiana University Press.

Burns, Stanley B. 1990. *Sleeping Beauty: Memorial Photography in America*. 2nd ed. Altadena, CA: Twelvetrees Press.

Burns, Stanley B. 1995. *Forgotten Marriage: The Painted Tintype & the Decorative Frame, 1860–1910: A Lost Chapter in American Portraiture*. New York: Burns Press.

Burrows, R. 2009. "Afterword: Urban Informatics and Social Ontology." In *Handbook of Research on Urban Informatics*, edited by M. Foth, 450–454. Hershey, PA: Information Science Reference.

Campt, Tina. 2017. *Listening to Images*. Durham, NC: Duke University Press.

Carroll, B., and K. Landry. 2010. "Logging On and Letting Out: Using Online Social Networks to Grieve and Mourn." *Bulletin of Science, Technology & Society* 30: 341–349. http://dx.doi.org/10.1177/0270467610380006

Casilli, Antonio A. 2010. *Les liaisons numériques: Vers une nouvelle sociabilité*. Paris: Seuil.

Caswell, Michelle. 2014. *Archiving the Unspeakable: Silence, Memory, and the Photographic Record in Cambodia*. Madison: University of Wisconsin Press.

Cherry, Kendra. 2023. "The Psychology of Heroism: Are Heroes Born or Made?" *Verywell Mind*. https://www.verywellmind.com/the-psychology-of-heroism-2795905. Visited June 2025.

Chukwuma, Helen O. 1974. "The Oral Tradition of the Ibos." PhD dissertation, University of Birmingham.

Church, Scott. 2013. "Digital Gravescapes: Digital Memorializing on Facebook." *Information Society* 29: 184–189.

Coker, I. H. E. 1968. *Landmarks of the Nigerian Press: An Outline of the Origins and Development of the Newspaper Press in Nigeria, 1859–1965*. Apapa: Nigerian National Press.

Cole, Patrick. 1975. *Modern and Traditional Elites in the Politics of Lagos*. Cambridge: Cambridge University Press.

Coleman, James. 1965. *Nigeria: Background to Nationalism*. 4th ed. Berkeley: University of California Press.

Comaroff, Jean, and John L. Comaroff. 2001. "Naturing the Nation: Aliens, Apocalypse and the Postcolonial State." *Journal of Southern African Studies* 27, no. 3: 627–651.

Cooper, Frederick. 2018. *Citizenship Between Empire and Nation*. Princeton, NY: Princeton University Press.

De Perthuis, Karen. 2008. "Beyond Perfection: The Fashion Model in the Age of Digital Manipulation." In *Fashion as Photography: Viewing and Reviewing Images of Fashion*, edited by Eugenie Shinkle, 168–181. New York: I.B. Tauris.

de Witte, Marleen. 2001. *Long Live the Dead: Changing Funeral Celebrations in Asante, Ghana*. Amsterdam: Het Spinhuis.

de Witte, Marleen. 2003. "Money and Death: Funeral Business in Asante, Ghana." *Africa* 73: 531–559.

de Witte, Marleen. 2005. "The Spectacular and the Spirits: Charismatics and Neo-Traditionalists on Ghanaian Television." *Material Religion* 1, no. 3: 314–335.

de Witte, Marleen. 2010. "Religious Media, Mobile Spirits: Publicity and Secrecy in African Pentecostalism and Traditional Religion." In *Travelling Spirits: Migrants, Markets, and Mobilities*, edited by Gertrud Hüwelmeier and Kristine Krause, 83–100. New York: Routledge.

de Witte, Marleen. 2011. "Of Corpses, Clay, and Photographs: Body Imagery and Changing Technologies of Remembrance in Asante Funeral Culture." In *Funerals in Africa: Explorations of a Social Phenomenon*, edited by Michael Jindra and Joël Noret, 177–206. New York: Berghahn Books.

Degroot, J. 2012. "Maintaining Relational Continuity with the Deceased on Facebook." *Omega: Journal of Death and Dying* 65: 195–212. http://dx.doi.org/10.2190/OM.65.3.c

Dejung, Christof, David Motadel, and Jürgen Osterhammel, eds. 2018. *The Global Bourgeoisie: The Rise of the Middle Classes in the Age of Empire*. Princeton, NJ: Princeton University Press.

Delaplace, Grégory. 2008. *L'invention des morts: Sépultures, fantômes et photographie en Mongolie contemporaine*. Paris: Centre d'Études Mongoles et Sibériennes.

Deleuze, Gilles. 1992. "Postscript on the Societies of Control." *October* 59: 3–7.

Derrida, Jacques. 1995. "Archive Fever: A Freudian Impression." Translated by Eric Prenowitz. *Diacritics* 25, no. 2: 9–63.

Derrida, Jacques, and Bernard Stiegler. 2002. *Echographies of Television: Filmed Interviews*. Translated by Jennifer Bajorek. Cambridge: Polity Press.

Dilmac, Julie Alev. 2018. "The New Forms of Mourning: Loss and Exhibition of the Death on the Internet." *Omega: Journal of Death and Dying* 77, no. 3: 280–295.

Dodge, M., and R. Kitchin. 2008. "Software, Objects and Home Space." NIRSA Working Paper No. 35. NUI Maynooth. Visited February 2025. http://www.nuim.ie/nirsa/research/documents/NIRSAWP35Software_objects_and_home_spaceDodge.pdf

Duyile, Dayo. 1987. *Makers of Nigerian Press: An Historical Analysis of Newspaper Development, the Pioneer Heroes, the Modern Press Barons and the New Publishers from 1859–1987*. Lagos: Gong Communications.

Ebere, Charles, and Constance L. Shehan. 2016. "Veneration of the Dead Among the Igbo." In *The Wiley Blackwell Encyclopedia of Family Studies*, edited by Constance L. Shehan, Chichester: John Wiley & Sons. https://doi.org/10.1002/9781119085621.wbefs335

Eck, D. 1998. *Darsan: Seeing the Divine Image in India*. New York: Columbia University Press.

Eco, Umberto. 1989. *The Open Work*. Cambridge, MA: Harvard University Press.

Edwards, Elizabeth. 2001. "Photography and the Performance of History." *Kronos: Journal of South African History* 27: 15–29.

Edwards, Elizabeth. 2005. "Photographs and the Sound of History." *Visual Anthropology Review* 21, nos. 1–2: 27–46.

Edwards, Elizabeth. 2009. "Photography and the Material Performance of the Past." *History and Theory*, Theme Issue 48: 130–150.

Edwards, Elizabeth. 2021. *Raw Histories: Photographs, Anthropology and Museums*. Oxford: Berg.

Edwards, Elizabeth, Chris Gosden, and Ruth B. Phillips, eds. 2006. *Sensible Objects: Colonialism, Museums and Material Culture*. Oxford: Berg.

Edwards, Elizabeth, and Janice Hart. 2004. "Mixed Box: The Cultural Biography of a Box of 'Ethnographic' Photographs." In *Photographs Objects Histories: On the Materiality of Images*, edited by Elizabeth Edwards and Janice Hart, 47–61. London: Routledge.

Enwezor, Okwui, and Octavio Zaya. 1996. *In/Sight: African Photographers 1940 to the Present*. New York: Solomon R. Guggenheim Museum.

Evans, Caroline, and Minna Thornton. 1989. *Women & Fashion: A New Look*. London: Quartet Books.

Ezeokafor, Paulinus. 2017. "Significance of Anambra Bill on Control of Funeral Ceremonies." Public presentation by His Lordship Most Rev. Paulinus C. Ezeokafor, the Catholic Bishop of Awka Diocese, at the Public Hearing on the Bill for a Law to Control Burial/Funeral Ceremonial Activities in Anambra State, at the Conference Room, Anambra State House of Assembly Legislative Complex, Awka, April 5.

Fahd, Cherine. 2023. "Destigmatising Infant Loss with Photography and Hashtags on Instagram." *Photographies* 16, no. 2: 109–132. https://doi.org/10.1080/17540763.2022.2150877

Falase, Olugbenga Samuel. 2019. "The Context of Children in Yoruba Popular Culture." *Global Studies of Childhood* 9, no. 1: 18–28.

Favero, Paolo S. H. 2017. *The Present Image: Visible Stories in a Digital Habitat*. New York: Palgrave Macmillan.

Favero, Paolo S. H. 2022. "It Begins and Ends with an Image: Reflections on Life/Death Across Autobiography and Visual Culture." *Anthropological Journal of European Cultures* 31, no. 1: 72–87.

Fernandez, Ingrid. 2011. "The Lives of Corpses: Narratives of the Image in American Memorial Photography." *Mortality* 16, no. 4: 343–364.

Fiefer, J. 2013. "Obama's Funeral Selfie Is a Fitting End to My Tumblr—Selfies at Funerals." *The Guardian*, December 11. https://www.theguardian.com/commentisfree/2013/dec/11/obama-funeral-selfie-tumblr-mandela-teens

Fiske, Susan T., and Shelley E. Taylor. 2008. *Social Cognition: From Brains to Culture*. New York: McGraw-Hill Education.

Foucault, Michel. 1976. *The Birth of the Clinic: An Archaeology of Medical Perception*. Translated by A. M. Sheridan Smith. London: Tavistock Publications.

Fraser, Nancy. 1990. "Rethinking the Public Sphere: A Contribution to the Critique of Actually Existing Democracy." *Social Text* 25–26: 56–80.

Geary, Christraud M. 2013. "The Past in the Present: Photographic Portraiture and the Evocation of Multiple Histories in the Bamum Kingdom of Cameroon." In *Portrai-*

ture and Photography in Africa, edited by John Peffer and Elisabeth L. Cameron, 213–252. Bloomington: Indiana University Press.

Gell, Alfred. 1998. *Art and Agency: An Anthropological Theory*. Oxford: Clarendon.

Gerlitz, Carolin, and Anne Helmond. 2013. "The Like Economy: Social Buttons and the Data Intensive Web." *New Media & Society* 15, no. 8: 1348–1365.

Giaxoglou, K. 2014. "'R.I.P. Man . . . U Are Missed and Loved by Many': Entextualising Moments of Mourning on a Facebook Rest in Peace Group Site." *Thanatos* 3, no. 1: 10–28.

Gibbs, James. 2005. "'Give Sorrow Words': An Examination of Ghanaian Funeral Brochures and Their Place in Contemporary Local Publishing." Paper presented at the "Postcolonial Lives of the Book" conference, University of London, Institute of English Studies, November 3–5.

Gibbs, Martin, Marcus Carter, Bjorn Nansen, and Tamara Kohn. 2014. "Selfies at Funerals: Remediating Rituals of Mourning." *Selected Papers of Internet Research* 15.0, Daegu, Korea, October, 21–24.

Gibbs, Martin, James Meese, Michael Arnold, and Marcus Carter. 2014. "Funerals and Instagram: Death, Social Media and Platform Vernacular." *Information, Communication & Society* 17, no. 3: 407–419. https://doi.org/10.1080/1369118X.2014.987152

Giddens, Anthony. 1991. *Modernity and Self-Identity: Self and Society in the Late Modern Age*. Cambridge: Polity Press.

Glaser, Greta. 2017. "Platinum Enlargements." In *Platinum and Palladium Photographs: Technical History, Connoisseurship, and Preservation*, edited by Constance McCabe, 192–203. Washington, DC: American Institute for Conservation of Historic and Artistic Works.

Gomez Cruz, Edgar, and Eric T. Meyer. 2012. "Creation and Control in the Photographic` Process: iPhones and the Emerging Fifth Moment of Photography." *Photographies* 5, no. 2: 203–221.

Gore, Charles D. 2001. "Commemoration, Memory, and Ownership: Some Social Contexts of Contemporary Photography in Benin City, Nigeria." *Visual Anthropology* 14, no. 3: 321–342.

Gozlan, A., and C. Masson. 2013. "The Theater Facebook: Reflection on Psychological Issues for the Adolescents." *Adolescence* 2, no. 84: 471–481.

Gunner, Liz, ed. 2001. *Politics and Performance: Theatre, Poetry and Song in South Africa*. Bloomington: Indiana University Press.

Guyer, Jane. 1995. "Wealth in People, Wealth in Things." *Journal of African History* 36: 83–90.

Habermas, Jürgen. 1974. "The Public Sphere: An Encyclopedia Article." Translated by Sara Lennox and Frank Lennox. *New German Critique*, no. 3: 49–55.

Habermas, Jürgen. 1991. *The Structural Transformation of the Public Sphere: An Inquiry into a Category of Bourgeois Society*. Translated by Thomas Burger. Cambridge, MA: MIT Press.

Habermas, Jürgen. 2022. "Reflections and hypotheses on a further structural transformation of the political public sphere." *Theory, Culture & Society* 39, no. 4: 145–171.

Hafsteinsson, Sigurjón Baldur. 1999. "Post-Mortem and Funeral Photography in Iceland." *History of Photography* 23, no. 1: 49–54.

Hajek, Andrea. 2012. "'Mmmmm quanti, ma quanti ricordi mi evocano queste foto . . .': Facebook and the 1977 Family Album. The Digital (R)evolution of a Protest Generation." *Italian Studies* 67, no. 3: 375–396.

Hallam, Elizabeth, and Jenny Hockey. 2001. "Remembering as Cultural Process." In Hallam and Hockey, *Death, Memory and Material Culture*, 1–21. New York: Berg.

Hallam, Elizabeth, Jenny Hockey, and Glennys Howarth. 1999. *Beyond the Body: Death and Social Identity*. New York: Routledge.

Haney, Erin. 2010a. *Photography and Africa*. Chicago: University of Chicago Press.

Haney, Erin. 2010b. "Film, Charcoal, Time: Contemporaneities in Gold Coast Photographs," *History of Photography* 34, no. 2, 119–133. https://doi.org/10.1080/03087290903361464

Haroche, Claudine. 2011. "L'invisibilité interdite." In *Les tyrannies de la* visibilité*: Être visible pour exister*, edited by Nicolas Aubert and Claudine Haroche, 77–102. Toulouse: Érés.

Harris, Clare. 2004. "The Photograph Reincarnate: The Dynamics of Tibetan Relationships with Photography." In *Photographs Objects Histories: On the Materiality of Images*, edited by Elizabeth Edwards and Janice Hart, 139–155. London: Routledge.

Hartmann, Wolfram. 1998. "Funeral Photographs: The Funeral of a Chief." In *The Colonising Camera: Photographs in the Making of Namibian History*, edited by Wolfram Hartmann, Jeremy Silvester, and Patricia Hayes, 125–131. Cape Town: Out of Africa, University of Cape Town Press; Athens: Ohio University Press.

Haskins, Ekaterina. 2007. "Between Archive and Participation: Public Memory in a Digital Age." *Rhetoric Society Quarterly* 37, no. 4: 401–422. https://doi.org/10.1080/02773940601086794

Hayes, Patricia. 1998. "Northern Exposures: The Photography of CHL Hahn, Native Commissioner of Ovamboland, 1915–1946." In *The Colonising Camera: Photographs in the Making of Namibian History*, edited by Jeremy Silvester, Patricia Hayes, and Wolfram Hartmann, 191–215. Cape Town: UCT Press.

Hayes, Patricia, and Gary Minkley. 2019. *Ambivalent: Photography and Visibility in African History*. Athens: Ohio University Press.

Heidemann, Frank. 2022. "How Does an Image Relate to What It Shows? The Uses of Photography Among the Badagas of South India." *Visual Anthropology* 35: 80–92.

Henisch, Heinz K., and Bridget A. Henisch. 1996. *The Painted Photograph, 1839–1914: Origins, Techniques, Aspirations*. University Park: Pennsylvania State University Press.

Hockey, Jenny, Trish Green, Andy Clayden, and Mark Powell. 2012. "Landscapes of the Dead? Natural Burial and the Materialization of Absence." *Journal of Material Culture* 17, no. 2: 115–132.

Hoskins, Janet. 1998. *Biographical Objects: How Things Tell the Stories of Peoples' Lives.* New York: Routledge.

Howells, Richard. 2011. "Heroes, Saints and Celebrities: The Photograph as Holy Relic." *Celebrity Studies* 2, no. 2: 112–130.

Hunter, Emma. 2018. "Modernity, Print Media, and the Middle Class in Colonial East Africa." In *The Global Bourgeoisie: The Rise of the Middle Classes in the Age of Empire*, edited by Christof Dejung, David Motadel, and Jürgen Osterhammel, 105–122. Princeton, NJ: Princeton University Press.

Hunter, Emma, and Leslie James. 2020. "Introduction: Colonial Public Spheres and the Worlds of Print." *Itinerario* 44, no. 2: 227–242.

Ihde, Don. 1999. *Expanding Hermeneutics: Visualism in Science.* Evanston, IL: Northwestern University Press.

Ikwuemesi, Chukwuezugo Krydz. 2023. "Celebrating Tragedy: Dying, Death and Mortuary Arts Among the Igbo." *Mortality* 28, no. 1: 126–153.

Ingold, Tim. 2011. *Being Alive: Chapters on Movement, Knowledge and Description.* London: Routledge.

Jindra, Michael, and Joël Noret, eds. 2011. *Funerals in Africa: Explorations of a Social Phenomenon.* New York: Berghahn Books.

Jurgenson, Nathan. 2019. *The Social Photo: On Photography and Social Media.* London: Verso.

Kalugin, Dmitri. 2015. "Soviet Theories of Biography and the Aesthetics of Personality." *Biography* 38, no. 3: 343–362.

Kalusa, Wilima T., and Megan Vaughan. 2013. *Death, Belief and Politics in Central African History.* Lusaka: Lembani Trust.

Kasfir, Sidney Littlefield. 1992. "African Art and Authenticity: A Text with a Shadow." *African Arts* 25, no. 2: 40–53.

Kasket, E. 2012. "Continuing Bonds in the Age of Social Networking: Facebook as a Modern Day Medium." *Bereavement Care* 31, no. 2: 62–69.

Keane, Webb. 2002. "Sincerity, 'Modernity,' and the Protestants." *Cultural Anthropology* 17, no. 1: 65–92.

Keightley, Emily, and Michael Pickering. 2014. "Technologies of Memory: Practices of Remembering in Analogue and Digital Photography." *New Media & Society* 16, no. 4: 576–593. https://doi.org/10.1177/1461444814532062

Keller, Candace M. 2008. "Visual Griots: Social, Political, and Cultural Histories in Mali Through the Photographer's Lens." PhD dissertation, Indiana University.

Keller, Candace M. 2013. "Visual Griots: Identity, Aesthetics, and the Social Roles of Portrait Photographers in Mali." In *Portraiture and Photography in Africa*, edited by John Peffer and Elisabeth L. Cameron, 363–405. Bloomington: Indiana University Press.

Kern, Rebecca, Abbe E. Forman, and Gisela Gil-Egui. 2013. "R.I.P.: Remain in Perpetuity. Facebook Memorial Pages." *Telematics and Informatics* 30: 2–10.

Ketelaar, Eric. 2001. "Tacit Narratives: The Meaning of Archives." *Archival Science* 1, no. 2: 138.

Knappett, Carl. 2016. *Thinking Through Material Culture: An Interdisciplinary Perspective*. Philadelphia: University of Pennsylvania Press.

Kopytoff, I. 1986. "The Cultural Biography of Things: Commoditization as Process." In *The Social Life of Things: Commodities in Cultural Perspective*, edited by Arjun Appadurai. Cambridge: Cambridge University Press.

Kratz, C. A. 2012. "Ceremonies, Sitting Rooms and Albums: How Okiek Displayed Photographs in the 1990s." In *Photography in Africa: Ethnographic Perspectives*, edited by Richard Vokes. Woodbridge: James Currey.

Krautwald, Fabian. 2021. "The Bearers of News: Print and Power in German East Africa." *Journal of African History* 62, no. 1: 5–28.

Kuhn, Annette. 1991. "Remembrance." In *Family Snaps: The Meanings of Domestic Photography*, edited by Jo Spence and Patricia Holland, 7–25. London: Virago.

Kunstmann, Rouven. 2014. "The Politics of Portrait Photographs in Southern Nigerian Newspapers, 1945–1954." *Social Dynamics* 40, no. 3: 514–537.

Kunstmann, Rouven, and Cassandra Mark-Thiesen. 2022. "The Memory Process in the Commemorations of the Dead in West African Newspapers." In *The Politics of Historical Memory and Commemoration in Africa: Essays in Honour of Jan-Georg Deutsch*, edited by Cassandra Mark-Thiesen, Moritz A. Mihatsch, and Michelle M. Sikes, 143–168. Boston: de Gruyter.

Kuper, Adam. 1988. *The Invention of Primitive Society*. London: Routledge.

La Gamma, Alicia. 2011. "Heroic Africans: Legendary Leaders, Iconic Sculptures." In *Heroic Africans: Legendary Leaders, Iconic Sculptures*, edited by Alicia La Gamma. New York: Metropolitan Museum of Art.

Laderman, Gary. 2003. *Rest in Peace: A Cultural History of Death and the Funeral Home in Twentieth-Century America*. New York: Oxford University Press.

Langford, Martha. 2001. *Suspended Conversations: The Afterlife of Memory in Photographic Albums*. Montreal: McGill Queens University Press.

Lapper, Ellen. 2017. "How Has Social Media Changed the Way We Grieve?" In *Digital Environments: Ethnographic Perspectives Across Global Online and Offline Spaces*, edited by Urte Undine Frömming, Steffen Köhn, Samantha Fox, and Mike Terry, 127–141. Bielefeld: Transcript Verlag.

Lash, Scott. 2006. "Dialectic of Information? A Response to Taylor." *Information, Communication & Society* 9, no. 5: 572–581.

Lash, Scott. 2007. "Power After Hegemony: Cultural Studies in Mutation." *Theory, Culture & Society* 24, no. 3: 55–78.

Lawal, Babatunde. 1977. "The Living Dead: Art and Immortality Among the Yoruba of Nigeria." *Africa* 47, no. 1: 50–61.

Lawuyi, Olatunde Bayo. 1991a. "The Dialogue with the Living: Biography in the Order of a Christian's Funeral Service in Yoruba Society." *Journal of Religion in Africa* 21, no. 3: 227–240.

Lawuyi, Olatunde Bayo. 1991b. "The Social Marketing of Elites: The Advertised Self in Obituaries and Congratulations in Some Nigerian Dailies." *Africa* 61, no. 2: 247–263.

Lee, Rebekah, and Megan Vaughan. 2008. "Death and Dying in the History of Africa Since 1800." *Journal of African History* 49, no. 3: 341–359.

Lenta, Margaret. 2007. "De-Authorising a Biography: Suresh Roberts Versus Gordimer." *Current Writing: Text and Reception in Southern Africa* 19, no. 1: 87–102.

Lentz, Carola. 2009. "Constructing Ethnicity: Elite Biographies and Funerals in Ghana." In *Ethnicity, Belonging and Biography: Ethnographical and Biographical Perspectives*, edited by Gabriele Rosenthal and Artur Bogner, 181–202. Berlin: Lit Verlag.

Lesy, M. 1973. *Wisconsin Death Trip*. New York: Pantheon.

Lingel, J. 2013. "The Digital Remains: Social Media and Practices of Online Grief." *Information Society* 29, no. 3: 190–195.

Linkman, Audrey. 2011 [2001]. *Photography and Death*. London: Reaktion Books.

Little, Kenneth. 1965. *West African Urbanization: A Study of Voluntary Associations in Social Change*. Cambridge: Cambridge University Press.

Lofland, L. H. 1985. "The Social Shaping of Emotion: The Case of Grief." *Symbolic Interaction* 8, no. 2: 171–190.

Lutz, C., and J. Collins. 1991. "The Photograph as an Intersection of Gazes: The Example of National Geographic." *Visual Anthropology Review* 7, no. 1: 134–149.

Mack, John. 2019. *The Artfulness of Death in Africa*. London: Reaktion Books.

Mann, Kristen. 1985. *Marrying Well: Marriage, Status and Social Change Among the Educated Elite in Colonial Lagos*. Cambridge: Cambridge University Press.

Marwick, A., and N. B. Ellison. 2012. "'There Isn't WiFi in Heaven!' Negotiating Visibility on Facebook Memorial Pages." *Journal of Broadcasting & Electronic Media* 56, no. 3: 378–400.

Mbembe, Achille. 2002. "The Power of the Archive and Its Limits." In *Refiguring the Archive*, edited by C. Hamilton, V. Harris, J. Taylor, M. Pickover, et al., 19–26 Dordrecht: Springer.

Mbiti, John. 1990. *African Religions and Philosophy*. 2nd ed. London: Heinemann.

McCaskie, C. Thomas. 2006. "Writing, Reading, and Printing Death: Obituaries and Commemoration in Asante." In *Africa's Hidden Histories: Everyday Literacy and Making the Self*, edited by Karin Barber, 341–384. Bloomington: Indiana University Press.

McGrath, Roberta. 2020. "Reviewing the Gaze." In *A Companion to Photography*, edited by Stephen Bull. Hoboken, 189–207. NJ: John Wiley & Sons.

Meese, James, Marten Gibbs, Marcus Carter, Michael Arnold, Bjorn Nansen, and Tamara Kohn. 2015. "Selfies at Funerals: Mourning and Presencing on Social Media Platforms." *International Journal of Communication* 9: 1818–1831.

Meese, James, Bjorn Nansen, Tamar Kohn, Michael Arnold, and Martin Gibbs. 2015. "Posthumous Personhood and the Affordances of Digital Media." *Mortality* 20, no. 4: 408–420. https://doi.org/10.1080/13576275.2015.1083724

Mellor, P., and C. Shilling. 1993. "Modernity, Self-Identity, and the Sequestration of Death." *Sociology* 27: 411–432.

Meyer, Birgit. 2006. "Impossible Representations: Pentecostalism, Vision, and Video

Technology in Ghana." In *Religion, Media and the Public Sphere*, edited by Birgit Meyer and Annelies Moors, 290–312. Bloomington: Indiana University Press.

Miller, A. D., and W. K. Edwards. 2007. "Give and Take: A Study of Consumer Photo-Sharing Culture and Practice." In *Proceedings of the SIGCHI Conference on Human Factors in Computing Systems*, 347–356. New York: ACM Press.

Miller, Daniel. 1995. "Introduction: Anthropology, Modernity and Consumption." In *Worlds Apart: Modernity through the Prism of the Local*, edited by Daniel Miller, 1–12. New York: Routledge.

Miller, Daniel. 1998. *Material Cultures: Why Some Things Matter*. London: UCL Press.

Miller, Daniel, ed. 2005. *Materiality*. Durham, NC: Duke University Press.

Miller, Daniel, and Fiona Parrott. 2009. "Loss and Material Culture in South London." *Journal of the Royal Anthropological Institute* 15: 502–519.

Miller, Daniel, and Jolynna Sinanan. 2017. *Visualising Facebook: A Comparative Perspective*. London: UCL Press.

Miller, Daniel, and C. Tilley. 1996. "Editorial Introduction." *Journal of Material Culture* 1, no. 1: 5–14.

Moss, M. 2004. "Grief on the Web." *Omega: Journal of Death and Dying* 49, no. 1: 77–81.

Murray, Susan. 2008. "Digital Images, Photo-Sharing, and Our Shifting Notions of Everyday Aesthetics." *Journal of Visual Culture* 7,no. 2: 147–163. https://doi.org/10.1177/1470412908091935

Mustafa, H. N. 2002. "Portraits of Modernity: Fashioning Selves in Dakarois Popular Photography." In *Images and Empires: Visuality in Colonial and Postcolonial Africa*, edited by D. D. Kaspin and P. S. Landau, 172–192. Berkeley: University of California Press.

Mustafa, H. N. 2005. "Portraits of Modernity: Fashioning Selves in Dakarois Popular Photography." *Politique africaine* 100, no. 4: 229–247.

Navon, Sarit, and Chaim Noy. 2021. "Conceptualizing Social Media Sub-Platforms: The Case of Mourning and Memorialization Practices on Facebook." *New Media & Society* 25, no. 11: 2898–2917. https://doi.org/10.1177/14614448211035769

Nesmith, Tom. 2005. "Reopening Archives: Bringing New Contextualities into Archival Theory and Practice." *Archivaria* 60: 259–274.

Newell, Stephanie. 2011. "Articulating Empire: Newspaper Readerships in Colonial West Africa." *New Formations* 73: 26–42.

Newell, Stephanie. 2013. *The Power to Name: A History of Anonymity in Colonial West Africa*. Athens: Ohio University Press.

Newell, Stephanie. 2016. "From Corpse to Corpus: The Printing of Death in Colonial West Africa." In *African Print Cultures: Newspapers and Their Publics in the Twentieth Century*, edited by Derek R. Peterson, Emma Hunter, and Stephanie Newell, 389–424. Ann Arbor: University of Michigan Press.

Newell, Stephanie. 2020. *Histories of Dirt: Media and Urban Life in Colonial and Postcolonial Lagos*. Durham, NC: Duke University Press.

Newell, Stephanie. 2022. "From Corpse to Corpus." In *The Politics of Historical Memory and Commemoration in Africa: Essays in Honour of Jan-Georg Deutsch*, edited by Cassandra Mark-Thiesen, Moritz A. Mihatsch, and Michelle M. Sikes, 143–168. Boston: de Gruyter.

Nwabueze, E. 1984. "Igbo Masquerade Performance and the Problem of Alien Intervention: Transition from Cult to Theatre." *Ufahamu: A Journal of African Studies* 14, no. 1: 74–92.

Nwafor, C. E. 2014. *Leopards of the Magical Dawn: Science and the Cosmological Foundations of Igbo Culture*. Pittsburgh, PA: Dorrance.

Nwafor, Okechukwu. 2021. *Aso Ebi: Dress, Fashion, Visual Culture and Urban Cosmopolitanism in West Africa*. Ann Arbor: University of Michigan Press.

Nwafor, Okechukwu. 2024. "New Online Histories from Memorial Portrait Photographs of Nigerian Nationalists Posted on Social Media." *Cahiers d'études africaines* 64, no. 1, 253: 61–91.

Nwalo, K. 1983. "Sociolinguistic Analysis of Obituary and In Memoriam Advertisements in Nigerian Newspapers." MA thesis, University of Lagos, Nigeria.

Nwoye, Onuigbo G. 1993. "The Informational Load of Nigerian Death Notices." *Archiv Orientali* 61: 195–205.

Ogbuagu, Stella C. 1989. "The Changing Perception of Death and Burial: A Look at the Nigerian Obituaries." *Anthropologica* 31, no. 1: 85–101.

Oke, Katharina. 2013. "The Colonial Public Sphere in Nigeria, 1920–1943." *Stichproben: Wiener Zeitschrift für kritische Afrikastudien* 13, no. 25: 29–56.

Okediji, F., and O. Okediji, eds. 2012. *The Sociology of the Yoruba / N.A. Fadipẹ*. Ibadan: Ibadan University Press.

Okigbo, Charles. 1987. "Death and Funeral Ads in the Nigerian Press." *Journalism Quarterly* 64: 629–633.

Okolie, M. A. E. 1992. "The Village Square in Igbo Cosmology." *Nigerian Heritage: Journal of the National Commission for Museums and Monuments* 1: 11–19.

Olusanya, Gabriel Olakunle. 1968. "The Lagos Branch of the National Congress of British West Africa." *Journal of the Historical Society of Nigeria* 4, no. 2: 321–333.

Omobowale, Ayokunle Olumuyiwa, Mofeyisara Oluwatoyin Omobowale, and Olugbenga Samuel Falase. 2019. "The Context of Children in Yoruba Popular Culture." *Global Studies of Childhood* 9, no. 1: 18–28.

Omoruyi, Joan. 1988. "Nigerian Funeral Programmes: An Unexplored Source of Information." *Africa: Journal of the International African Institute* 58, no. 4: 466–469.

Omu, F. I. A. 1978. *Press and Politics in Nigeria, 1880–1937*. Atlantic Highlands, NJ: Humanities Press.

Onwuejeogwu, Angulu. 1979. "The Genesis, Diffusion, Structure and Significance of Ọzọ Title in Igbo Land." *Paideuma: Mitteilungen zur Kulturkunde* 25: 117–143.

Onyeozili, E. C., and O. N. Ebbe. 2012. "Social Control in Precolonial Igboland of Nigeria." *African Journal of Criminology and Justice Studies* 6, nos. 1–2: 29–43.

Onyibor, Marcel I. S. 2012. "Death in Igbo Cosmology: A Hermeneutical Investigation." PhD dissertation, Department of Philosophy, Faculty of Arts, Nnamdi Azikiwe University Awka, Anambra State, Nigeria.

Onyibor, Marcel I. S. 2019. "A Critique of the Changing Trends in Igbo Traditional Conceptualisation of Death and Funeral Rites." *Nnamdi Azikiwe Journal of Philosophy* 11, no. 2.

Paoletti, Giulia. 2024. *Portrait and Place: Photography in Senegal, 1840–1960*. Princeton, NJ: Princeton University Press.

Parker, John. 2021. *In My Time of Dying: A History of Death and the Dead in West Africa*. Princeton, NJ: Princeton University Press.

Pauwels, Luc. 2008. "A Private Visual Practice Going Public? Social Functions and Sociological Research Opportunities of Web-Based Family Photography." *Visual Studies* 23, no. 1: 34–49.

Peffer, John. 2015. "Vernacular Recollections and Popular Photography in South Africa." In *The African Photographic Archive: Research and Curatorial Strategies*, edited by Christopher Morton and Darren Newbury, 123–145. London: Routledge.

Peffer, John, and Elisabeth L. Cameron, eds. 2013. *Portraiture and Photography in Africa*. Bloomington: Indiana University Press.

Péne, S. 2011. "Facebook Immovable: Intimate Grief and Common Causes." *Questions de communication* 1, no. 19: 91–112.

Perry, Adele. 2017. "Beyond Biography, Beyond Canada." *Canadian Historical Review* 98, no. 2: 321–337.

Peterson, Derek R., and Emma Hunter. 2016. "Print Culture in Colonial Africa." In *African Print Cultures: Newspapers and Their Publics in the Twentieth Century*, edited by Derek R. Peterson, Emma Hunter, and Stephanie Newell, 1–45. Ann Arbor: University of Michigan Press.

Pinney, Christopher. 1997. *Camera Indica: The Social Life of Indian Photographs*. Chicago: University of Chicago Press.

Pinney, Christopher. 2004. *Photos of the Gods: The Printed Image and Political Struggle in India*. New York: Oxford University Press.

Pinney, Christopher. 2011. *Photography and Anthropology*. London: Reaktion Books.

Pinney, Christopher, and Nicolas Peterson. 2003. *Photography's Other Histories*. Durham, NC: Duke University Press.

Poole, Deborah. 1997. *Vision, Race, and Modernity: A Visual Economy of the Andean Image World*. Princeton, NJ: Princeton University Press.

Recuber, Timothy. 2023. *The Digital Departed: How We Face Death, Commemorate Life, and Chase Virtual Immortality*. New York: New York University Press.

Reed, Bess, and Benjamin Hufbauer. 2005. "Ancestors and Commemoration in Igbo Odo Masquerades." *RES: Journal of Anthropology and Aesthetics* 47: 135–152.

Rigney, Ann. 2005. "Plenitude, Scarcity and the Circulation of Cultural Memory." *Journal of European Studies* 35, no. 1: 11–28.

Rinhart, Floyd, and Marion Rinhart. 1967. "Rediscovery: An American Way of Death." *Art in America* 55, no. 5: 78–81.

Robben, Antonius C. G. M. 2017. "Death and Anthropology: An Introduction." In *Death, Mourning, and Burial: A Cross-Cultural Reader*, edited by Antonius C. G. M. Robben. Hoboken, 1–16. NJ: Wiley Blackwell.

Roberts, P. 2004. "The Living and the Dead: Community in the Virtual Cemetery." *Omega: Journal of Death and Dying* 49: 57–76.

Rose, Gillian. 2014. "How Digital Technologies Do Family Snaps, Only Better." In *Digital Snaps: The New Face of Photography*, edited by Jonas Larsen and Mette Sandbye, 67–86. New York: Routledge.

Rose, Gillian. 2016. *Doing Family Photography: The Domestic, The Public and The Politics of Sentiment*. New York: Routledge.

Rosenbaum, A. 1998. "The Duty of Gaze." *Communication and Languages* 117: 28–34.

Røssaak, Eivind. 2010. "The Archive in Motion: An Introduction." In *The Archive in Motion: New Conceptions of the Archive in Contemporary Thought and New Media Practice*, edited by Eivind Røssaak, 11–28. Oslo: National Library of Norway.

Rotberg, Robert I. 2010. "Biography and Historiography: Mutual Evidentiary and Interdisciplinary Considerations." *Journal of Interdisciplinary History* 40, no. 3: 305–324.

Ruby, Jay. 1984. "Post-Mortem Portraiture in America." *History of Photography* 8, no. 3: 201–222.

Ryan, James. 1997. *Picturing Empire: Photography and the Visualization of the British Empire*. London: Reaktion Books.

Ryzova, Lucie. 2015. "Unstable Icons, Contested Histories: Vintage Photographs and Neoliberal Memory in Contemporary Egypt." *Middle East Journal of Culture and Communication* 8: 37–68.

Salmons, Jill. 1980. "Funerary Shrine Cloths of the Annang Ibibio, South-East Nigeria." In *Textiles of Africa*, edited by Dale Idiens and K. G. Ponting, 119–141. Bath: Maney Publishing.

Sandbye, Mette. 2014. "Looking at the Family Photo Album: A Resumed Theoretical Discussion of Why and How." *Journal of Aesthetics & Culture* 6, no. 1: 25419. https://doi.org/10.3402/jac.v6.25419

Sassoon, Joanna. "Photographic Materiality in the Age of Digital Reproduction." In *Photographs Objects Histories: On the Materiality of Images*, edited by Elizabeth Edwards and Janice Hart, 186–202. London: Routledge, 2004.

Sawada, Nozomi. 2016. "Selecting Those 'Worthy' of Remembering: Memorialization in Early Lagos Newspapers." *Journal of West African History* 2, no. 2:79–108.

Schneider, Jurg. 2013. "Portrait Photography: A Visual Currency in the Atlantic Visualscape." In *Portrait Photography in African Worlds*, edited by John Peffer and Elizabeth Cameron, 35–65. Bloomington: Indiana University Press.

Schneider, Jürg. 2018. "African Photography in the Atlantic Visualscape: Moving Photographers—Circulating Images." In *Global Photographies: Memory—History—Archives*, edited by Sissy Helff and Stefanie Michels, 19–38. Bielefeld: Transcript Verlag.

Sekula, Allan. 1982. "On the Invention of Photographic Meaning." In *Thinking Photography*, edited by Victor Burgin, 84–109. London: Macmillan.

Shelton, A. J. 1971. *The Igbo-Igala Borderland*. New York: State University of New York Press.

Shusterman, Richard. 2012. "Photography as Performative Process." *Journal of Aesthetics and Art Criticism* 70, no. 1: 67–77.

Silvester, Jeremy, Patricia Hayes, and Wolfram Hartmann. 1998. "'This Ideal Conquest': Photography and Colonialism in Namibian History." In *The Colonising Camera: Photographs in the Making of Namibian History*, edited by Wolfram Hartmann, Jeremy Silvester, and Patricia Hayes, 10–19. Cape Town: Out of Africa, University of Cape Town Press; Athens: Ohio University Press.

Sinha, Mrinalini. 2001. "Britishness, Clubbability, and the Colonial Public Sphere: The Genealogy of an Imperial Institution in Colonial India." *Journal of British Studies* 40, no. 4: 489–521.

Smith, Benjamin R., and Richard Vokes. 2008. "Introduction: Haunting Images." *Visual Anthropology* 21: 283–291. https://doi.org/10.1080/08949460802156292

Smith, Daniel Jordan. 2004. "Burials and Belonging in Nigeria: Rural-Urban Relations and Social Inequality in a Contemporary African Ritual." *American Anthropologist* 106, no. 3: 569–579.

Smith, Daniel Jordan 2018. "Migration, Death, and Conspicuous Redistribution in Southeastern Nigeria." In *A Companion to the Anthropology of Death*, edited by Antonius C. G. M. Robben. Hoboken, 7–83. NJ: John Wiley & Sons.

Smith, Daniel Jordan. 2024. "Conspicuous Redistribution: Money, Morality, and Masculinity in Nigeria." *Journal of Contemporary African Studies* 42, no. 2: 230–244. https://doi.org/10.1080/02589001.2023.2193367

Sontag, Susan. 1977. *On Photography*. London: Penguin Books.

Sorin, Gerald. 2012. "Writing Biography: The Historian's Challenge, Part 1." Jewish Book Council, November 6. Viewed May 28, 2017. http://www.jewishbookcouncil.org/_blog/The_ProsenPeople/post/Writing_Biography_The_Historian%E2%80%99s_Challenge,_Part_1/

Sprague, Stephen F. 1978. "How I See the Yoruba See Themselves." *Studies in the Anthropology of Visual Communication* 5, no. 1: 9–29.

Sprague, Stephen F. 2003. "Yoruba Photography: How the Yoruba See Themselves." In *Photography's Other Histories*, edited by Christopher Pinney and Nicolas Peterson, 240–264. Durham, NC: Duke University Press.

Spyer, Patricia, and Mary Margaret Steedly. 2013. *Images That Move*. Santa Fe, NM: SAR Press.

Stevenson, I. 1985. "The Belief in Reincarnation Among the Igbo of Nigeria." *Journal of Asian and African Studies* 20, nos. 1–2: 13–30.

Stokes, P. 2012. "Ghosts in the Machine: Do the Dead Live on Facebook?" *Philosophy & Technology* 25, no. 3: 363–379.

Stoller, Paul. 1989. *The Taste of Ethnographic Things*. Philadelphia: University of Pennsylvania Press.

Strother, Z. S. 1995. "Display of the Body Hottentot." In *Africa and the Aesthetics of the Vulgar*, edited by S. Vogel, 1–61. New York: Prestel.

Strother, Z. S. 2013. "A Photograph Steals the Soul: The History of an Idea." In *Portraiture and Photography in Africa*, edited by John Peffer and Elizabeth Cameron, 177–212. Bloomington: Indiana University Press.

Strother, Z. S. 2016. *Humor and Violence: Seeing Europeans in Central African Art, 1850–1997*. Bloomington: Indiana University Press.

Stylianou-Lambert, Theopisti, and Lorenz Widmaier. 2023. "Everyday Photography and Mourning in the 21st Century." *Photographies* 16, no. 1: 3–18. https://doi.org/10.1080/17540763.2022.2158917

Tagg, John. 1988. *The Burden of Representation: Essays on Photographies and History*. Minneapolis: University of Minnesota Press.

Talbot, P. A. 1926. *The Peoples of Southern Nigeria*. 4 vols. London: Oxford University Press.

Tambiah, Stanley J. 1984. *The Buddhist Saints of the Forest and the Cult of Amulets*. Cambridge: Cambridge University Press.

Thimm, Caja, and Patrick Nehls. 2017. "Sharing Grief and Mourning on Instagram: Digital Patterns of Family Memories." *Communications* 42, no. 3: 327–349.

Thrift, Nigel. 2005. *Knowing Capitalism*. London: Sage.

Togonu-Bickersteth, Funmi. 1986. "Obituaries: Conception of Death in the Nigerian Newspapers." *IFE Social Science Review* (Journal of the Faculty of Social Sciences, University of Ife-Ife, Nigeria) 9, nos. 1–2: 83–93.

Uchendu, V. C. 1964. "The Status Implications of Igbo Religious Beliefs." *Nigerian Field* 29, no. 1: 27–37.

Uchendu, V. C. 1965. *The Igbos of Southern Nigeria*. New York: Holt, Rinehart and Winston.

Ugwuanyi, John Kelechi, and John Schofield. 2018. "Permanence, Temporality and the Rhythms of Life: Exploring Significance of the Village Arena in Igbo Culture." *World Archaeology* 50, no. 1: 7–22.

Ujumadu, Vincent. 2023. "Soludo Bans Use of Posters, Billboards, Brochures for Burials in Anambra." *Vanguard Newspapers*, October 22, 2023. https://www.vanguardngr.com/2023/10/soludo-bans-use-of-posters-billboards-brochures-for-burials-in-anambra/. Accessed June 25, 2025.

van der Geest, S. 1995. "Old People and Funerals in a Rural Ghanaian Community: Ambiguities in Family Care." *Southern African Journal of Gerontology* 4, no. 2: 33–40.

Van Dijck, José. 2007. *Mediated Memories in the Digital Age*. Stanford, CA: Stanford University Press.

Van Dijck, José. 2008. "Digital Photography: Communication, Identity, Memory." *Visual Communication* 7, no. 1: 57–76.

Van House, N., M. Davis, M. Ames, et al. 2005. "The Uses of Personal Networked Digital Imaging: An Empirical Study of Cameraphone Photos and Sharing." In *CHI'05 Extended Abstracts on Human Factors in Computing Systems*, edited by C. Gale, 1853–1856. New York: ACM Press.

Vansina, Jan. 1972. "Ndop: Royal Statues Among the Kuba." In *African Art and Leadership*, edited by Douglas Fraser and Herbert M. Cole, 41–55. Madison: University of Wisconsin Press.

Veale, K. 2004. "Online Memorialisation: The Web as a Collective Memorial Landscape for Remembering the Dead." *Fibreculture* 3. http://three.fibreculturejournal.org/fcj-014-online-memorialisation-the-web-as-a-collective-memorial-landscape-for-remembering-the-dead/

Vigliotti, Jeanette. 2016. "The Currency of Visibility: Visual Subjectivity and Memory on Instagram." *Comunicazioni sociali* 1: 64–68.

Vogel, Susan M. 1977. "Baule Art as the Expression of a World View." PhD dissertation, Institute of Fine Arts, New York University.

Vokes, Richard. 2008. "On Ancestral Self-Fashioning: Photography in the Time of AIDS." In "Haunting Images: The Affective Power of Photography," edited by Benjamin R. Smith and Richard Vokes, 345–363. Special issue, *Visual Anthropology* 21, no. 4.

Vokes, Richard. 2012. "Introduction." In *Photography in Africa: Ethnographic Perspectives*, edited by Richard Vokes, 1–29, Woodbridge: James Currey.

Vokes, Richard. 2019a. "Photographies in Africa in the Digital Age." *Africa* 89, no. 2: 207–224.

Vokes, Richard. 2019b. "Signs of Development: Photographic Futurism and the Politics of Affect in Uganda." *Africa* 89, no. 2: 303–322.

Vokes, Richard, and Darren Newbury. 2018. "Photography and African Futures." *Visual Studies* 33, no. 1: 1–10.

Welling, T., R. Hourizi, W. Moncur, and S. Pitsillides. 2011. "Does the Internet Change How We Die and Mourn? Overview and Analysis." *Omega: Journal of Death and Dying* 64: 275–302.

Welling, William B. 1978. *Photography in America: The Formative Years, 1839–1900*. New York: Crowell.

Wendl, Tobias. 2001. "Entangled Traditions: Photography and the History of Media in Southern Ghana." *RES: Journal of Anthropology and Aesthetics* 39: 78–101.

Wendl, Tobias, and Nancy du Plessis. 1998. *Future Remembrance: Photography and Image Arts in Ghana*. Göttingen: Institut für den Wissenschaftlichen Film.

Werbner, Richard. 1991. *Tears of the Dead: The Social Biography of an African Family*. Washington, DC: Smithsonian Institution Press.

Werbner, Richard. 1998. *Memory and the Postcolony*. London: Zed Books.

Werbner, Richard, ed. 2002. *Postcolonial Subjectivities in Africa*. London: Zed Books.

Werner, Jean-François. 2001. "Photography and Individualization in Contemporary Africa: An Ivoirian Case-Study." *Visual Anthropology* 14, no. 3: 251–268.

White, Richard. 2017. "Walter Benjamin: 'The Storyteller' and the Possibility of Wisdom." *Journal of Aesthetic Education* 51, no. 1: 1–14.

Williams, A. L., and M. J. Merten. 2009. "Adolescents Online: Social Networking Following the Death of a Peer." *Journal of Adolescent Research* 24: 67–90.

Wolf, Arthur P. 1974. "Gods, Ghosts, and Ancestors." In *Religion and Ritual in Chinese Society*, edited by Arthur P. Wolf, 141–176. Stanford, CA: Stanford University Press.

Woolf, Virginia. 1939. "The Art of Biography." *The Atlantic*, April.

Wright, Nicola. 2014. "Death and the Internet: The Implications of the Digital Afterlife." *First Monday* 19, no. 6 (June 2). http://dx.doi.org/10.5210/fm.v19i6.4998

Yékú, James. 2022. *Cultural Netizenship: Social Media, Popular Culture, and Performance in Nigeria*. Bloomington: Indiana University Press.

Yékú, James, and Ayobami Ojebode. 2021. "From Google Doodles to Facebook: Nostalgia and Visual Reconstructions of the Past in Nigeria." *African Studies Review* 64, no. 3: 498–522.

Zachernuk, Philip Serge. 1991. "The Lagos Intelligentsia and the Idea of Progress, ca. 1860–1960." In *Yoruba Historiography*, edited by T. Falola, 147–165. Madison: University of Wisconsin–Madison.

INDEX